China on the Eve of
Communist Takeover

China on the Eve of Communist Takeover

A. DOAK BARNETT

FREDERICK A. PRAEGER, *Publisher*
New York • London

FREDERICK A. PRAEGER, PUBLISHER
64 UNIVERSITY PLACE, NEW YORK 3, N.Y., U.S.A.
49 GREAT ORMOND STREET, LONDON W.C. 1, ENGLAND

Published in the United States of America in 1963 by
Frederick A. Praeger, Inc., *Publisher*

Library of Congress Catalog Card Number: 63-10824

This book is Number 130 in the series of
Praeger Publications in Russian History and World Communism.

Printed in the United States of America

PREFACE

The tragic period of Nationalist collapse and Communist takeover on the China mainland, in the years 1946–49, is still so recent that few thorough or systematic studies of it have been attempted. It may not be possible to write an adequate history of the period for some years to come. It will take time for historians to assemble the required data, and to acquire greater perspective and detachment, before valid historical judgments can be made.

Yet this period, in which China's non-Communist regime and society crumbled, providing the Communists with their opportunity to seize power, is a crucial one which urgently demands increased understanding. Even though the massive domestic crisis that China suffered at that time had numerous unique characteristics, it involved many problems relevant to other societies in revolution that are currently attempting to cope with both the difficult transition from traditionalism to modernism and the serious threat of Communism. Much that we should know about the general process of revolution in today's pre-modern societies can be learned from the failures of the non-Communist regime in China just before 1949.

In studying international Communism today, some observers concentrate almost solely, in their analysis, on the nature of Communist strategy and tactics. But it should never be forgotten that the threat of internal Communist takeover rarely becomes serious except in situations of great domestic crisis, when the existing non-Communist regimes prove unable to solve their most pressing problems. The Communists would not have been able to achieve victory in China if the old regime and society had not virtually disintegrated in the late 1940's.

Greater knowledge of this period is also necessary for an understanding of subsequent events in China itself. The conditions that existed just prior to 1949 provided the immediate starting point, the base line, from which the Chinese Communists, once in power, embarked upon their tremendous political, economic, and social transformation of Chinese society. Without some knowledge of conditions prior to 1949, therefore, it is difficult to have any sound basis for understanding either the problems that the Chinese Communists initially faced or the revolutionary changes that they have subsequently engineered in the years since they achieved control of the most populous—and one of the most complex—nations in the world.

This book attempts to illuminate some of the trends and conditions in China just prior to, and at the time of, Communist takeover. It is not, and does not purport to be, either a history or an exhaustive analysis of those years. It is composed, in fact, of reports I wrote in China during that period, and, like all current reporting in times of rapid change, these reports have certain unavoidable limitations; they inevitably tend to be fragmentary and lack the kind of perspective only time can provide. Nevertheless, I believe that they do contain information unavailable elsewhere, and that they may convey a "feel" for many of the complex problems involved in the revolutionary upheaval in China which could not be obtained except from on-the-spot observation and study.

During 1947–49, I had an unusual opportunity to observe developments in many parts of China. As a Fellow of the Institute of Current World Affairs, and correspondent for the *Chicago Daily News* Foreign service, I traveled the length and breadth of the country. Most Western observers who were in China during that period were preoccupied, inevitably, with the dramatic events taking place on the national scene—with the latest military clashes in the bitter civil war between the Chinese Nationalists and the Communists, or with political developments taking place in the centers of Nationalist power, especially in China's political capital, Nanking, and its dominant economic center, Shanghai. I chose, however, to spend much of that period studying local situations in widely scattered regions and investigating a variety of problems in these areas.

In roughly two years, from the fall of 1947 to the fall of 1949, I visited almost all parts of Nationalist-held China, and spent over half a year in one area under Communist rule. My travels took me to many remote interior and borderland regions. In all these areas, I studied problems of local government and politics, as well as existing economic and social conditions, from the local vantage point.

Travel was difficult in many instances. On some of the longer trips, it was possible to find modern forms of transportation; for example, I went by air to Sinkiang (Chinese Turkestan) and to Chungking and Kunming in the southwest, by train to Inner Mongolia and from Shanghai to Canton, by river boat down the Yangtze and by steamer along the China coast from Hong Kong to Hainan and to Shanghai. But in much of the interior of China, travel was extremely primitive. Mail trucks, when available, were frequently the best transport, and often one had to travel by foot, donkey cart, sedan chair, or horseback. Altogether, I spent almost a full week during the year 1949 on horseback, making a number of short trips in Sinkiang, Ninghsia, Chinghai, and Sikang; and one journey I made, to the capital of Sikang Province in Inner Tibet, required nine days of walking.

On many of these trips, I stayed in local Chinese inns. Sometimes, however, official Chinese government hostels were available, and occasionally Western missionaries or consuls were willing to put up visitors from afar. At each major stopping point, I tried to stay long enough—sometimes weeks, occasionally months —to interview systematically the key local officials, identify and talk with leading private citizens, obtain and study whatever documentary material was readily available on the local situation, contact and converse with "ordinary people" of many different sorts, and discuss the local situation with any "outside observers" (either Chinese or Western) who might be there, as well as to observe local conditions myself.

During these two years, in addition to news reporting, I wrote approximately forty reports for the Institute of Current World Affairs, covering a wide variety of subjects, and the Institute distributed them within the United States to a small group of interested specialists on China. But the circulation of these reports was relatively limited, and subsequently it was suggested that they might be put together in book form.

This volume is the result. It contains a selection of twenty-three of the reports I wrote during 1947–49. They have been arranged by major categories, rather than simply in chronological order, so as to highlight some of the major problems and trends in China during that period. In all essentials, the reports are presented as originally written, and a dateline on each indicates the time and place at which it was written. In putting them into one volume, though, I have found it necessary to do a considerable amount of cutting, as well as some stylistic polishing. However, I have steered clear of doing anything that might change the original character of the reports and have carefully avoided rewriting their substance with the benefit of hindsight.

Most of the contents of these reports describe and analyze current situations as I observed them during 1947–49. In several instances, however, I included a certain amount of historical data providing general background to the current situation. It should be noted that this historical information could not, under the circumstances, be based upon extensive library research; essentially, it drew upon information locally available, and it may in certain instances, therefore, be useful primarily as an indication of local views on events prior to 1947–49. Most of the reports, though, deal with things as they were when I studied them, and they are therefore based upon data that could only be obtained through interviews and observation on the spot.

I am deeply indebted to the Institute of Current World Affairs, which made it possible for me to study and write in China during that period, and which has granted me permission to publish these reports in book form. Above all, I am indebted to the former Director of the Institute, Walter S. Rogers, whose profound insights into the problems of studying and understanding contemporary affairs have had an enormous impact upon all those who have been privileged to be Institute Fellows under him.

There is also a very large number of other persons whose knowledge, judgment, and friendship were of incalculable value to me when I was in China writing these reports. Unfortunately, it is not possible to mention them all here. I particularly regret that I cannot acknowledge my debt to many Chinese friends and acquaintances, a large number of whom now live under Communist rule; mention of their names would hardly be a favor to them. I will, however, mention a few Americans—scholars, reporters, and diplomats—who, like myself, were in China during the late 1940's attempting to analyze and write about the revolutionary course of events then in progress. All of them shared their knowledge or insights with me, and some shared certain of the trips and conversations upon which my reports were based. They included, to mention just a few: Henry Lieberman, Frank Robertson, Christopher Rand, Albert Ravenholt, Gerald Stryker, Peggy and Tillman Durdin, Howard Boorman, LaRue Lutkins, Frederic Schultheis, Philip Valdes, Harriet Mills, Archibald Steele, James Burke, Ian Morrison, and Jean Lyon.

I am also extremely grateful to a number of scholars in the United States who have read portions of this manuscript. They include K. C. Hsiao, T. K. Tong, S. H. Chou, Edmund Clubb, Robert Ekvall, John Hangin, and Donald Gillin. They have all helped me to avoid some errors, especially in the historical material in the reports. Needless to say, however, they are in no way responsible for whatever errors may remain.

Mrs. Mary Schoch deserves sincere thanks for assisting at every stage in the preparation of the manuscript for press.

I should like also to express my gratitude to Frederick A. Praeger, who urged me to put these reports in book form, as well as to Arnold Dolin, who has ably edited the manuscript.

And, as usual, my wife, Jeanne, has given me invaluable and essential assistance, without which this book would not have been possible.

Finally, a word is necessary on the system of Romanization used in the reports. Any author who writes material containing numerous Chinese personal and place names faces a dilemma in deciding how to Romanize them. The problem arises largely from the fact that, although there is a standard system of Romanization—the Wade-Giles system—that is widely accepted by scholars in the West, many Chinese place names, and some Chinese personal names, are familiar to Western readers in forms based on other Romanization systems. Consequently, consistency is virtually impossible, unless one is writing for a very limited audience of specialists. In the hope that the readership of this volume will include others than China specialists, I have compromised, as most authors do. In general, I have used the Wade-Giles system, with diacritical marks, for Chinese personal names and administrative titles; however, personal names that are widely used in the West in some other form are reproduced in the form popularly used. For well-known Chinese place names and nonadministrative institutional titles (e.g., names of universities), I have generally used the most widely accepted Western forms (usually not based on the Wade-Giles system); however, for Chinese place names not widely familiar in the West, I have used a modified Wade-Giles system, without diacritical marks. Like all compromises, this one is not wholly satisfactory, but it seemed to be the best under the circumstances.

—A. D. B.

Dedicated to

Walter S. Rogers

CONTENTS

China on the Eve of
Communist Takeover

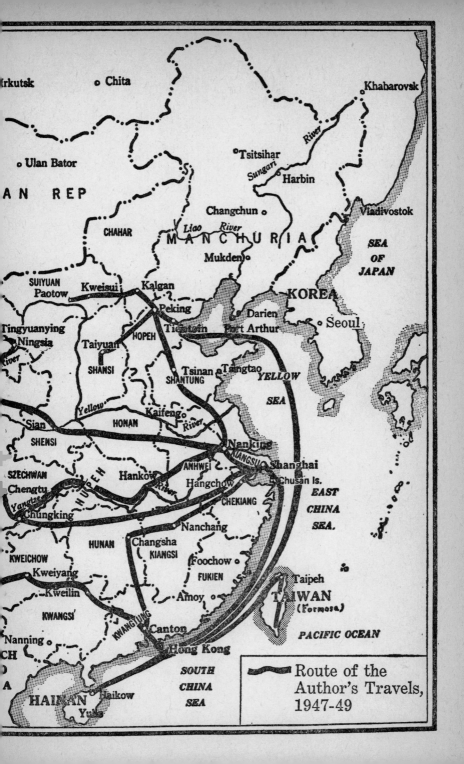

Route of the
Author's Travels,
1947-49

INTRODUCTION

For decades, one of the most extensive revolutions in history has been taking place in China. Like all great political and social upheavals, it has involved both the emergence of powerful new forces and the collapse of an old order, and it has gone through several distinctive stages.

This book deals primarily with elements in the Chinese situation that contributed to the final collapse of the Nationalist regime on the China mainland during the late 1940's. These elements of political and social breakdown, comparable to those that are present in many other revolutionary situations, must be grasped if one is to understand the essential character of the revolutionary process in China. Yet, they are often overlooked or underplayed.

Whenever a new revolutionary group moves to the center of the stage, it inevitably dominates the scene, and the past tends to fade into obscurity. Subsequently, the new revolutionary leaders propagate the myth that their successes have been due solely to their own omniscience and omnipotence, rather than to the failures and weaknesses of their predecessors. Generally, however, a collapse of the old order is an essential prerequisite to the success of any major revolutionary movement. In China, this collapse was so thorough that by 1949 the Communists were able to take over the country with ease. In a sense, they simply moved into a vacuum.

Although the political disintegration and social chaos that enabled the Communists to seize power in China reached their climax in the years just prior to 1949, one must bear in mind that the Chinese revolution had gone through many different stages before that time—and will doubtless go through others in the future.

Throughout the modern period, China has been engaged in an intense and painful revolutionary process. In fact, the decay of its traditional society and political structure can be dated to the middle of the nineteenth century, when it first encountered a combination of disruptive foreign influences and serious domestic crises. In the half-century that followed, the old order was slowly undermined, and the Chinese people groped toward new values and institutions.

During the early years of this century, a movement led by Sun Yat-sen—one that was eventually to become the Chinese Nationalist Party, or Kuomintang—emerged as the most important revolutionary force in the country, but the collapse of the old Manchu Dynasty proceeded even more rapidly than the growth of this new movement. When the old regime toppled in 1911, therefore, there was really nothing to move into the vacuum. As a result, China literally fell apart, and for almost two decades the Central Government in Peking controlled only small portions of the country, while great areas were ruled by local warlords.

The Nationalists continued to develop their political movement, however, and by the 1920's they had become the primary focus of hope for those who yearned for national reunification, political modernization, and economic development. As their strength grew, they slowly acquired the basis for attempting another political revolution. Under the leadership first of Sun Yat-sen and subsequently of Chiang K'ai-shek, and with the support of the small Chinese Communist Party (founded in 1921), they proceeded in the late 1920's to overthrow China's weak Central Government and were able to bring some of the local warlords under control and to establish a new national government in Nanking in 1927–28.

Following the Nationalists' takeover, the first decade of their rule—up until the outbreak of the Sino-Japanese War—was a period of considerable progress and hope. The new regime started to modernize the country. It introduced some moderate social reforms. And it took initial steps toward fostering economic development.

Even in this period, however, the Nationalists encountered serious problems, and they were not able to go very far either in implementing reforms or in solving the most basic and urgent problems confronting the country.

One of their problems was created by the nature of the Nationalist movement itself. From the start, it was composed of heterogeneous, conflicting interests and was hampered by internal divisions that made it difficult either to adopt clear-cut policies or to implement them vigorously. Moreover, it lacked the strength to overcome the remnants of political and military regionalism in China or to impose its will on traditional vested interests in either the countryside or cities. In many local areas of the country, regimes of a warlord sort persisted, blocking genuine national reunification. In the countryside, conservative landlords obstructed the implementation of reforms that were urgently needed to cope with China's fundamental economic problems—problems created by a rapidly growing population and a serious shortage of agricultural land. Within the Nationalist Party itself, factionalism and old-fashioned clique politics sapped the vitality and discipline that the Party's leaders were attempting to create.

Another challenge that faced the Nationalists from the start was posed by domestic Communist revolt. In 1927, the Nationalist-Communist alliance (which had been formed in 1923) split apart. The Nationalists thereupon attempted to crush the Communist movement, but they were unsuccessful, and the Communists went into open insurrection. Even though the strength of the Chinese Communist Party was still small at that time, the Party was able to establish a geographical base for revolution in east-central China (as the Nationalists themselves had done in the south in the early 1920's), to mobilize peasants within this rural area to form a revolutionary guerrilla army, and to start its protracted armed struggle for power. In the early 1930's, the Nationalists mounted several major military campaigns in an attempt to defeat the Communists—campaigns that constituted a significant drain on their resources and energies—but they were never able to destroy the Communist forces completely or to prevent them from retaining a foothold in the countryside.

In the mid-1930's, after they had been forced to retreat to an isolated area in northwest China, the Communists were not, it is true, yet a very formidable immediate threat; but they continued to hold together a revolutionary movement possessing a guerrilla army and a definite geographical base of operations, they had been greatly toughened by their difficult struggle, and they had gained valuable experience in revolutionary techniques. Whether, if China had enjoyed relative stability for several years, the Communists would ever have been able to put this experience to such use that they could present a major threat to the Nationalists is difficult to guess. The tragic fact, however, is that China's brief period of relative stability under the Nationalists was destroyed by Japanese aggression in the 1930's, and the resulting Sino-Japanese War not only struck at the foundations of the Nationalist regime, but also presented unprecedented opportunities for the Communists to pursue their evolving strategy of protracted guerrilla warfare.

Actually, the threat of Japanese aggression was the greatest single problem facing the Nationalists almost from the day they assumed power. Since 1894, the Japanese had made one encroachment after another on China's territory and sovereign rights, and, as they saw China beginning to make some progress toward reunification and modernization, they stepped up the pressure. In 1931–32, they seized Manchuria, one of China's richest regions, and established a Japanese-controlled regime there. Subsequently, they steadily extended their interference and penetration throughout north China. Finally, in 1937, they initiated a major undeclared war against the Nationalist regime, one which soon developed into a full-scale military conflict that was ultimately to merge with World War II.

The prolonged Sino-Japanese conflict, which lasted altogether for eight years, had a shattering effect upon China. It was during this period that the process of social disintegration which was to lead ultimately to the collapse of the Nationalist regime began. Much of China, including the major urban areas which had been the main sources of the Nationalists' strength, fell into Japanese hands, and the military struggle imposed an intolerable strain on the restricted areas that the Nationalists were able to retain. Forced into backward, isolated, interior regions, the Chinese government had to struggle hard, under the most difficult conditions, simply to survive. Conservative and reactionary forces reasserted their power and influence. Instead of pushing forward with needed reforms, the Nationalists postponed them indefinitely, and resorted increasingly to repressive controls. The economy, subjected to excessive burdens, began to weaken. Inflation reached dangerous proportions, threatening the very foundations of stability. China's intellectuals and students—its modernized and educated elite—became increasingly disillusioned and bitter. Morale and discipline within the Nationalist bureaucracy itself—within the Party, government, and army—were steadily undermined. Cynicism, corruption, and mismanagement grew to serious proportions. Somehow, things held together, and many people clung to the hope that the end of the war would bring not only peace but revitalization. But even before the war had ended, the Nationalists had been gravely weakened by internal decay, and victory in 1945 had a hollow ring.

By contrast, the Sino-Japanese conflict presented the Chinese Communists with unprecedented opportunities to increase their revolutionary strength, and they exploited the wartime situation to the full to enhance their power and influence. In the name of nationalism and patriotism, they formed a second short-lived alliance (or perhaps it should be called a temporary truce) with the Nationalists. By developing successful guerrilla warfare against the Japanese, they were able both to build up their military forces and to exert a considerable appeal to Chinese patriotism. Departing from many of the more extreme revolutionary policies that they had pursued earlier—and were to pursue again later— they implemented in the rural areas under their control a relatively mild land-reform program which created in the minds of many Chinese the image of Communism as a moderate reform movement—an image that was not entirely dispelled until some time after the Communists had achieved power and had begun to put into effect new and drastic revolutionary programs. During the war, as many Chinese intellectuals became progressively disillusioned with the Nationalists, more than a few were attracted by the Communists' general program, innocuously labeled "new democracy" during that period. Most important of all, the Communist movement itself rapidly increased in size and strength. By the end of the war, the Communists controlled and governed most of rural north China—apart from the cities and railways held by the Japanese—and had built up a party of over a million and a revolutionary army of comparable size. They were immeasurably better prepared, in short, than they had been eight years earlier to pursue their struggle for power.

Although the internal balance of power in China between the Nationalists and the Communists had shifted substantially during the war, in purely military terms the Nationalists still had a great preponderance of power—i.e., of men and matériel—in 1945. Both sides were, not surprisingly, highly suspicious of the intentions of the other, and, even before the war had ended, they had begun to jockey for position, preparing for possible civil war. This jockeying continued immediately after the war. With American assistance, Nationalist troops moved rapidly to take over the major cities and rail lines that had been held by the Japanese. The Communists quickly moved some of their best troops into Manchuria, which had been occupied by the Russians during the last few days of the war, and there, with the help of the Russians, they were able to seize substantial stocks of Japanese military equipment.

Yet, despite the intense hostility existing between the Nationalists and Communists, both sides—with American encouragement—were at least willing to talk peace and compromise. There was great war-weariness in China, and a widespread recognition that full-scale civil war would be a major tragedy for the country.

The Nationalists were not unaware, in view of their earlier failures to defeat the Communists' guerrilla forces, that full-scale civil war would be a prolonged and difficult struggle and that, if it occurred, China, already seriously weakened by almost a decade of warfare, would encounter enormous difficulties in achieving the hoped-for postwar recovery. The Communists seemed to believe that outright civil war would involve undesirable costs and risks for them, and that they could continue their struggle, and make gains, by other means. Also, the Russians apparently underestimated the seriousness of Nationalist weaknesses and did not believe the Communists could easily achieve military success in China at that time; although the Chinese Communists had greater confidence in themselves, they, too, may well have believed that a full-scale military conflict with the Nationalists could not be won quickly or easily—as it was, in fact, not long thereafter.

This was the context in which the United States Government made a major effort, soon after the war, to mediate the Nationalist-Communist conflict and to prevent the outbreak of civil war. Actually, such efforts had started during the latter stages of the war, the aim then being to bolster China's position in the fighting against Japan. After the war, the American aim was to prevent the outbreak of major civil war in China and to encourage the reunification of the country by peaceful means.

However, the mediation mission of General George C. Marshall proved to be a failure. Whether it ever had any real chance of success is a question that will doubtless be debated for many years to come, as will the question of whether the Nationalist regime might have been able to survive on the mainland if it had obtained a significant breathing spell after the war in which to try to revitalize itself and cope with some of China's most urgent problems. But no peace or breathing spell was possible. The hostility and suspicion between the Nationalists and Communists were so great that even the temporary truce arranged by Marshall broke down in mid-1946, and open civil war erupted between the two antagonists. The conflict rapidly reached its climax, and by the end of 1949, the Communists had won the struggle on the China mainland, while the Nationalists had taken refuge on Formosa.

Clearly, many of the most important causes of the Nationalists' defeat during this decisive period were military ones. The Nationalists pursued a self-defeating strategy; instead of undertaking offensives aimed at seeking out and destroying the main mobile and guerrilla units of the Communists, they holed up for the most part in isolated, vulnerable, defensive positions, allowing the Communists to concentrate their forces, to besiege, attack, and overwhelm such positions one by one. Moreover, the Nationalists made many disastrous errors in specific military operations. For example, Generalissimo Chiang decided, against the best military advice available, to commit some of the Nationalists' most modern forces and equipment to Manchuria at a time when Communist forces there controlled much of the countryside and supply and communication lines linking Manchuria to the rest of the country were highly vulnerable. Perhaps most important of all, however, was the deterioration of morale among the Nationalists' troops. Many crucial battles during 1947–49 were lost without a fight, as hundreds of thousands of Nationalist troops simply defected or surrendered.

This volume will not describe the course of the military struggle. Suffice it to say that, although the Nationalist forces clearly had the upper hand in mid-1946—possessing much greater supplies of modern military equipment and, according to American official estimates, outnumbering the Communists' forces by roughly three million to one million—the Communists seized the strategic initiative during 1947, carrying the struggle from Manchuria into north China; during 1948, the military balance shifted decisively in favor of the Communists; and by 1949, the Communists had achieved basic military control over the China mainland. Communist victories, in rapid succession, at Tsinan, Mukden, and Hsuchow in late 1948, and at Tientsin and Peking in early 1949, followed by the crossing of the Yangtze and the capture of Nanking and Shanghai in the spring, sealed the Nationalists' fate on the China mainland. Everything thereafter—in the northwest, southwest, and south—proved to be simple mopping-up operations for the Communists.

The underlying causes of the Nationalists' collapse can hardly be sought by analyzing these military events alone, however. Actually, the demoralization and defeat of the Nationalist forces were merely a reflection of the much broader and more basic process of political, economic, and social disintegration that took place in Nationalist-held China during 1946–49 at a headlong pace. It is this process of disintegration that is described in this volume. Not all the factors involved are dealt with, by any means; but those that were most visible and striking to one observer on the scene are described in some detail.

As mentioned earlier, most of these forces of disintegration had first begun to be felt some years previously, during the Sino-Japanese War. After they had appeared, it was clear that the Nationalist regime would need to undergo a heroic political regeneration in order to survive. But once full-scale civil war had broken out, instead of the situation improving, the Nationalist regime collapsed with calamitous speed.

It is difficult to assess the relative importance of the varied factors causing this disintegration. The political disunity existing within Nationalist China was certainly one of the most fundamental. Many areas of so-called Nationalist territory—some of them ruled by old-style warlords—became increasingly alienated from the Central Government; eventually, several of these areas came to terms separately with the Communists, and even those that tried to resist could not do so on their own with any success. Within the Nationalist Party itself, clique politics and factionalism reached a point where unified, vigorous action—either to solve the problems in Nationalist-held territory or to fight against the Communists—was virtually impossible. Runaway inflation reached incredible proportions, creating great instability and insecurity, ensuring corruption, crippling government finance, and causing general demoralization. China's intellectuals, who have played an extremely important role in modern Chinese history and have affected the political climate far more than their real political power would seem to warrant, became almost universally disaffected, drifting steadily toward the Left. They were not alone in their disaffection. Other key groups were almost equally estranged. Many of China's businessmen, for example, lost all faith in the government, and reached the point where they, too, actively hoped for a change of regime—even a Communist takeover. Organized labor, while playing almost no significant insurrectionary role of the sort once expected by orthodox Marxists, nevertheless became increasingly dissident when the deterioration of economic conditions resulted in general hardship. In the countryside, conditions stagnated, and the peasants were subjected to an enormous and growing economic burden. There was no general uprising of the peasants in Nationalist-held territory, but neither was there any significant positive support of the existing regime. Even the most politically passive peasants were predisposed to react favorably when the Communists, backed by their revolutionary armies, suddenly appeared and promised them "liberation" and land. In short, public morale throughout Nationalist China reached such a low point that the basis for any effective resistance to the Communists completely disappeared.

The actual pattern of Communist takeover in China hardly fitted into traditional Marxist concepts, however. It was not an urban insurrection, a *coup d'état*, or even, for that matter, a general peasant revolt. Instead, the pattern was one of systematic military conquest—or, in the latter stages, of negotiated surrenders imposed by the Communists, who by then had achieved clear military predominance. True, the Communists had built their revolutionary armies in certain areas of rural China by arousing and organizing peasant revolt, but then these armies moved rapidly and efficiently to seize and occupy the rest of the country during the climactic civil-war years of 1946–49.

The relative ease of the final Communist takeover was a result in part, of course, of the strength of the Chinese Communist revolutionary movement forged during the previous two decades of armed struggle, but the speed of the takeover was also the result of the completeness of the demoralization, disintegration, and collapse of the Nationalist regime on the mainland.

There are some who would argue that there is little or no value in examining this process now. A few would even argue, in fact, that by doing so one can only harm the Nationalist regime, which has survived, with American support, on the island of Taiwan (Formosa) in the years since 1949. But such arguments are not convincing. Certainly, nothing can be gained—either by the United States, by the Nationalist regime itself, or by other non-Communist nations that face a Communist threat—by obscuring the past or by refusing to learn the lessons of previous failures and defeats in China. Clearly, the Nationalist regime that survives on Taiwan today should not be judged on the basis of its past mistakes. Even though it has by no means entirely escaped from its past and is still suffering from some of its previous political weaknesses, it has nevertheless shown some evidence of new vitality and effectiveness. It should be judged now and in the years immediately ahead, therefore, on its record in a new situation and under new circumstances. There is little doubt, however, that this record will reflect, to no small extent, the degree to which the Nationalists themselves are willing and able to learn from the past in order to improve their capacity not only to survive, but also to govern effectively and to solve the many serious problems they will continue to face in the future. In recent years, some significant progress has been made toward this end. That, however, is another story. This book concerns the tragic story of failure and collapse on the China mainland as I observed it during 1947–49.

PART I

DISINTEGRATION:
NATIONALIST CHINA'S URBAN BASE

RIDING HIGH FOR A FALL

Shanghai
November, 1947

Shanghai today is bursting its seams. Between 10:44 and 10:45 A.M. on November 3, seventy-seven vehicles streamed along Szechwan Road, past its junction with Hankow Road, in downtown Shanghai. Szechwan Road is approximately as wide as 46th Street in New York City. Trucks, cars, rickshaws, pedicabs (bicycle-drawn rickshaws), motorcycles, bicycles, and pushcarts made up the solid mass of moving vehicles. This traffic is duplicated on almost every street in the downtown sections of the city during working hours every day. Virtually all transport is filled beyond capacity. On a bus with seats for twenty-five, one may find as many as seventy-six passengers. On a trolley (called a "tram" here), one may ride four stops before the conductor can collect the fare.

Descriptive adjectives alone can hardly convey a true impression of how crowded and hectic Shanghai is today. It is like nothing I have ever seen. It is far different from both the Shanghai that I knew and lived in eleven years ago and the one that I visited again briefly two years ago. Between 4 and 5 million people are now crowded into roughly the same area in which 3 million lived, worked, and played just a few years ago. Everywhere there are people, people, and more people, many of them newcomers who have pushed into a city already greatly overcrowded. And because, in a time of inflation, business must be done today rather than tomorrow, Shanghai's millions seem to be constantly on the move.

One might expect to see evidence of widespread poverty in Shanghai under existing conditions. Instead, surprisingly, people in the streets appear to be better clothed and fed than they used to be. Beggars are less common than in the past. Both Chinese and foreign-style clothes of substantial fabrics are no longer restricted to a wealthy few. Leather shoes are common, while straw sandals, formerly so widely used, are now conspicuous because of their rarity. Many street stalls sell wheatbread and coffee to coolies and laborers; in the past, rice products and weak tea were the standard fare. Watches, fountain pens, and other manufactured articles seem to be owned by a great many people of modest means who would hardly have known how to use them a decade ago. Shops, stores, and markets are filled with all sorts of manufactured consumer goods and foodstuffs.

In terms of real income and consumption, the average standard of living of Shanghai's masses appears to be higher than ever before. This does not mean that everyone is well off, nor does it mean that the city has eliminated poverty. It does mean, however, that the average Shanghai citizen now seems to consume more and live a more comfortable life than he did before the war. This fact can be directly observed on the city's streets and in its homes; it is confirmed by economists, businessmen, and bankers. The existence of this relative prosperity is mystifying, in many respects. The mystery might be summarized as follows:

1) Shanghai's trade is hampered and disrupted by runaway inflation, lack of foreign exchange, official corruption and inefficiency, restrictive government policies, and civil war in the hinterland.

2) Its industry, recovering from occupation and war, is hampered by these same factors.

3) The city has a greatly increased population.

4) Yet, the general level of prosperity and the standard of living appear to be higher than in the past.

How? It is difficult to obtain a completely satisfactory answer to this question, but many clues can be found if one examines the present situation closely.

First of all, Shanghai's current balance of trade shows a large surplus of imports over exports, made possible by the use of accumulated reserves of foreign exchange. (These reserves are steadily dwindling, however.) More than a little UNRRA material, sent to China for relief purposes, has reached Shanghai and gone no farther (although obviously some has reached other destinations). One sees "relief" goods sold everywhere on the streets. A larger percentage of Shanghai's industrial products is consumed within the city itself than in years past. China's large inland market has been partially cut off, while the local Shanghai market has grown.

The concentration of money, capital, and wealth in Shanghai is greater than ever before. Large sums of money are sent from Manchuria, north China, Hupeh, Anhwei, and elsewhere. In August of this year, for example, the amount remitted to Shanghai from other parts of China through private banks (mainly non-government remittances) reportedly was CNC $1,468,073,411,000 (U.S. $15–20 million, roughly) in excess of the amount remitted from Shanghai. The excess for September is believed to have been over $2 trillion (CNC). Also, a very large share of the Chinese government's expenditures is made in Shanghai. It is estimated that of all national government expenditures, which currently total approximately CNC $5 trillion per month, one-third is spent in Shanghai. In August, deposits in private banks in Shanghai were estimated to be 56 per cent of total national deposits in such banks. The figure is believed to be even higher now.

There has been a drastic redistribution of wealth and income in Shanghai since the end of the war. Part of this has been the "natural result" of inflation, but government policy has aided in the process. The result: A small upper stratum has accumulated great wealth, the working class has improved its economic position tremendously, and the middle class has been "virtually wiped out as an economic class." The key groups that have profited most are cotton-mill owners, stockbrokers, a few corrupt officials and army officers, and some real-estate dealers. Most people agree that many officials and officers are honest and long-suffering, but there are also many who are not.

The working class has done well because wages have been set at a high level and pegged to a monthly commodity price index. Many people assert that this has been dictated by fear on the part of the government of disaffection and Leftist sentiment among the working class. In any case, the present prosperity of the masses has resulted from this policy. Although the commodity price index has reportedly been manipulated to a certain extent in recent months, wages are still high.

As is usually the case during inflation, the salaried groups have suffered most, and the prosperity of the average working man is due, at least partially, to a transfer of wealth from the middle class. A college professor in Shanghai earns about the same amount as a rickshaw coolie does in a good month, and many organizations are embarrassed by the fact that their professional workers are paid at about the same level as their manual laborers. Government employees are terribly underpaid, and a good deal of the existing corruption is attributable to this fact. A recent government decision increasing salaries by 125 per cent helps, but, despite this raise, civil servants are still poorly paid.

Many of the factors underlying the present economic situation in Shanghai are highly artificial, and therefore temporary, and not a few people feel, as one person said to me, that the city may be "riding high for a fall." It is clear, also, that Shanghai's relative prosperity is due, in part, to the fact that income and wealth are being channeled into the city from other parts of the country; in this sense, it is at the expense of the rest of the country.

One cannot escape the inflation in Shanghai, any more than one can elsewhere in China. It is ever-present and all-important. A dollar is worth more today than it will be tomorrow; consequently, all money is "hot money." As a general rule, people spend money as soon as they get it, if they can. Printed notes are converted into more substantial commodities, such as silver dollars, foreign currencies, gold, cloth, fuel, land, or—in the case of the average person—more consumer goods. Despite the astronomical figures for bank deposits, savings in currency are now much lower in real value than before the war. The manager of one of Shanghai's large private banks reports that the U.S. dollar value of savings deposits in his bank has been reduced from $20 million to $100,000. Insurance savings have been wiped out completely. A Chinese friend of mine, whose insurance policy was worth roughly U.S. $1,000 before the war, estimates that it is now worth U.S. $00.0064, less than a penny!

Prices continue to skyrocket. In the first three weeks of October, the wholesale commodity price index in Shanghai rose from 74,367 to 108,357 (1931 = 1). The current interest rate for loans from the bank mentioned above is 16 per cent per month, and the bank does not make loans for periods longer than a month. The free market exchange rate for U.S. dollars is now over 80,000:1, and the trend is steadily upward. The most important single cause of this inflationary situation is not difficult to define. With a civil war on its hands, the Chinese Nationalist Government is spending much more than it receives in revenue. The difference is being made up by the issuance of paper money. The current rate of note issue, although not made public (for obvious reasons), is "reliably estimated" to be around CNC $40 billion per day.

This is the economic setting of life today in Shanghai. The political setting is not so chaotic, perhaps, but in many respects it is no less complicated. There are undercurrents of political ac-

tivities and machinations of many sorts. Although Shanghai is
a Kuomintang-controlled city, numerous opposition groups function in various ways. Much, if not most, political activity is secret
or underground, however, and it is difficult to obtain more than
hints of what is really going on. Some people say that Shanghai
rather than Nanking is the real center of organized political activity in Nationalist China; others assert that major policy decisions are made here rather than in the capital. But how much all
the political activity in Shanghai affects China's millions, scattered throughout the country, is difficult to estimate.

The most notable recent development affecting the local political atmosphere has been the Nationalists' clampdown on the
groups that call themselves China's "liberals." About two weeks
ago, on October 28, the Ministry of Interior announced that the
Democratic League has been declared illegal because of new evidence revealing collaboration with the Communists. The League,
a loose combination of non-Communist and non-Kuomintang
groups, has been the focal point for organized non-Communist
opposition to the Kuomintang, and around it have clustered
many different sorts of individuals and organizations dissatis-
fied with the present regime. Recently, I participated in a discussion that included a few of the top leaders of these so-called liberal elements in Shanghai which have grouped themselves around
the League and have looked to it for direction. Some of what these
men had to say may be worth quoting:

"What should America do about the present situation in
China? It should give moral, and purely moral, support on the
side of peace, unity, and democracy. It should otherwise follow a
hands-off policy, because the present government isn't worthy of
its support: (a) because it doesn't represent the people; (b) because it is so rotten and corrupt that it cannot be helped; and (c)
because even if it could be propped up for a little while, it would
mean misery for the people and continued civil war, and ultimately it would collapse."

"We see no evidence of Soviet help to the Communists. Not
even the United States and Chinese governments can present any
such evidence."

"The loss of Outer Mongolia and Dairen is regrettable, but it is
due to: (a) international complications such as the Yalta Agreement, and (b) Kuomintang misrule. If Mongolia hadn't been
misruled, it wouldn't have gone over to Russia."

"If the United States and other countries will give China moral support, but keep their hands off, then the Chinese will be able to solve their own problems. If the United States interferes, even with good intentions, it will, in effect, impose its will on the Chinese people. If the Chinese are left alone, they can work out their own salvation."

"The present regime is so utterly corrupt that it is beyond redemption. It is beyond the possibility of any help. It is not worthy of any help."

"We may have reason to have some fear of the Communists, but at least they are going in the right direction. They are for the people and are going in the direction of justice and democracy."

"The present regime must go. Something will come next. It couldn't be as bad as the present regime. Even if it has faults, the people will be able to cope with the situation."

"We are against the Kuomintang, but not all of us will go all the way with the Communists. Lo Lung-chi [spokesman for the Democratic League], for example, says he goes 70 per cent of the way with the Communist program, and that's probably about right."

"Ideally, our middle group would like to see a third party or group of parties in power. Unfortunately, there is no hope for that under the present regime. You would say that there probably wouldn't be any more chance for it under the Communists. We don't believe that is so, because the Communists are at least going in the right direction. We believe we would fare better under the Communists."

The men whose opinions are quoted above are among the top leaders of the group vaguely called "China's liberal leaders," a group often singled out by the press in America as China's hope. Although they appear to be idealistic and sincere intellectuals, however, they are extremely disappointing on several counts. None of them seems to have a positive, constructive program to propose, and even their dislike of the Kuomintang is expressed in highly emotional criticism, rather than in the form of well-reasoned criticism. Their political thinking is fuzzy and, in many respects, naïve. Their entire position is based on assumptions and convictions that evidently have not been carefully thought out. Their general approach is uncritically favorable toward Russia and the Chinese Communists (none of these particular men, it should be noted, has been in Communist territory), damning in regard to the Kuomintang, and suspicious toward the United States.

These men themselves claim to represent "the people." Others assert that while they have no political power, they do represent an emotional point of view, and attitudes, shared by many people in Shanghai today—people who are so fed up with the present regime that they want almost any kind of change. Most qualified observers, whatever they feel about these "liberals," believe that it was a serious blunder for the government to outlaw the Democratic League, since this step eliminated China's last important, vocal, non-Communist opposition group.

Not many people are willing to attribute any important role in the current situation to the other small non-Communist parties, such as the Democratic Socialist Party or the Young China Party. The opinions of their leaders are of some interest, nevertheless; they are quite different from those of the League's leaders. Carsun Chang, head of the Democratic Socialist Party, summed up his general point of view a few days ago in the following statement to me: "I believe that more can be accomplished by trying to reform the present government from within than by working from the outside." How much Chang himself is accomplishing in this respect is a moot point, but in contrast with the League leaders he does, at least, have some concrete and specific criticisms of the present political and administrative system, and is able to outline specific constitutional and political changes that, in his opinion, would improve the situation.

One finds a wide spectrum of political views, actually, among non-Communist intellectuals who oppose the Nationalists, but do not go along fully with the Democratic League. The comments made to me recently on the subject of American policy by a leading editorial writer of one of Shanghai's largest Chinese "independent dailies" were of particular interest. This man is one of the most intelligent, analytical, and well-informed persons in Shanghai today. He is a nonparty independent ("I have vowed not to join a party and not to get personally involved in politics"), but he is extremely critical of the present Nationalist regime. This was his advice:

"I think America should aid China, but only under certain conditions. America should oversee the way in which the aid is used, and should ensure that the aid is not wasted and that it is used in ways that benefit the Chinese people. Of course, America will be accused of interference and imperialism, but it is in a position where it will be subject to such accusations in any case, and a policy of supervised aid would prove that the United States is interested in the welfare of the Chinese people, and not solely in its security position vis à vis the Russians. It is true, also, that the present government in China would probably resent supervision, but the United States has to choose between keeping the friendship of the Chinese government or the Chinese people. If it gives aid that is unsupervised, and which merely serves to prolong the civil war, the government leaders will remain its friends, but it will lose the friendship of the Chinese people. If it insists on supervising aid in a way which improves conditions in China, it may antagonize many Chinese government leaders, but it will gain the real friendship of the Chinese people."

2

UNEASY ISOLATION

Peiping
January, 1948

Peiping, in this winter of 1947–48, is a Nationalist island in north China. Except for railway links to a few other similar islands, it is surrounded by Communist territory and has almost no hinterland. To date, however, the shifting tides of China's civil war have merely lapped the island's shores without causing serious damage, and, although the city is uneasy, it remains peaceful and quiet.

Somehow, Peiping retains its traditional serenity, beauty, and charm. One can still find here a rare combination of intellectual and aesthetic satisfactions. The city's cultural heritage is strong and has a widespread influence that seeps far below the social level of those directly concerned with its numerous libraries, universities, museums, and theaters. In an indefinable way, this heritage seems to affect the man in the street and to create an atmosphere that fully justifies Peiping's reputation as the traditional cultural capital of China.

The architectural setting remains much as it was before World War II, and it continues to captivate visitors and to inspire quiet pride in the city's permanent residents. The fading red walls and golden roofs of the Forbidden City dominate the center of Peiping. From Coal Hill, one sees on all sides the colored tile roofs of both ancient temples and palaces and modern buildings, sometimes reflecting the brilliant winter sun, at other times enshrouded in delicate evening mists. Beyond Coal Hill, the Bell Tower and Drum Tower rise majestically above the city. South of the City Wall are the Temple and Altar of Heaven, and toward the Western Hills is the Summer Palace, each beautiful and inspiring in its own unique way. These and other architectural wonders of Peiping remain essentially unchanged by war, foreign occupation, or time.

It is not imperial architecture alone, however, that creates the unique atmosphere in Peiping. At Pienyifang, a restaurant just south of the City Wall, long rows of fatted ducks line the dingy corridor. After critically eying all of them, the customer chooses one; half an hour later, he is rewarded, in a small upstairs room, with the succulent creation called "Peking duck." If he is still hungry, he can order "chicken velvet," and marvel at the consistency of its smooth white meat. Warm, yellow rice wine or fiery, clear *pai kar* accompanies the meal. And, if it is a special occasion, the customer may decide to top it all off with "Peking dust," a mixture of crushed chestnuts enclosed by a wall of glazed fruit.

At the Tengshihkou Theater, a group of earnest young actors produces excellent modern Chinese plays. The gate receipts— even when supplemented by government subsidies—are not sufficient to provide luxuries, so the spectators sit huddled in their overcoats, and the actors' breaths vaporize as they speak, but the performances are first-rate. One play produced recently, *Under Shanghai Roofs*, was a realistic portrayal of life in a Shanghai tenement-apartment, in a style reminiscent of Clifford Odets. It provided two hours of stimulating entertainment—for about U.S. $0.15. Chinese opera is also still very much alive in Peiping. It is performed nightly in several different theaters, where one can chew watermelon seeds and sip tea while actors in traditional costumes gesticulate, tumble, fight, and sing.

At the Tungan Market, a seemingly endless maze of interconnected alleys is covered to form an arcade that is a shopper's paradise. Innumerable stores and stands display almost everything under the sun in bewildering profusion and confusion: food, books, clothes, luggage, hardware, art work, curios, trinkets, and so on, ad infinitum. Buying and selling are refined skills, and a sale is usually preceded by long bargaining. The laws of supply and demand operate without disguise, and each transaction is a battle of wits and a process of compromise. The Tungan Market is only one of many fascinating market places in the city. The Lungfoszu Temple is another, and the fair held there three times a month is justly famous. Perhaps the most interesting place of all, however, is Chienmenwai—Outside Chien (or Front) Gate— where each street specializes in a different product.

At Peihai, hundreds of young men and girls skate on the ice, to the accompaniment of lilting, modern Chinese music. Bundled in their warm clothes, they brace themselves against the cold winter wind that sweeps down the lake and lifts the snow into flurries.

Peiping's atmosphere is hard to define. All these things contribute to it. And one could add many more: wide imperial thoroughfares, with high archways; dirty little *hutungs,* or alleys, shadowy and intimate; old houses with quiet courtyards, beautiful moongates, and crimson, brass-fitted doors. Most important of all are the people who live in this setting, who help to create the atmosphere and also absorb something from it. However one wishes to define it, Peiping's atmosphere is a thing of unusual charm. The impact of war and politics on the city is severe, but it is superimposed upon this background.

Despite its calmness, however, Peiping is in many respects an anxious city. Small military engagements take place within a few miles of the city wall. There is constant fear of Communist infiltration on the part of the authorities, and, periodically, local citizens are stopped in the streets and searched for hidden arms. A tight curfew is imposed from midnight until early morning, and the streets are dead during those hours. Occasionally, disquieting false rumors sweep the city, such as the recent one that the Nationalist Government was already giving up all of Manchuria. For the most part, however, panic is confined to a small minority. The majority of the population appears to be confused, uncertain of the future, and inclined to be skeptical of reports and claims from both sides of the civil war, but people go about their business with a high degree of normalcy, considering the existing circumstances.

There are some, however, who are convinced of the inevitability of Communist victory and who prophesy doom or salvation, depending on their particular predilections. Most of these are intellectuals, many of whom are completely embittered by the present chaos in China. A few people every month decide to join the Communists and slip quietly out of the city into the limbo of Red territory. According to one reliable source, from "a few to a hundred" (it varies) Peiping students leave monthly to join a Communist university called Lienta—North China Associated University—which occupies nine villages some distance south of Peiping. This exodus is more than counterbalanced, however, by an even larger influx of refugees seeking sanctuary in Peiping after leaving battle zones or Communist-held areas. Some of these are cared for by government agencies or private philanthropy, but many are simply absorbed into the households of families, friends, and acquaintances.

A general uneasiness in Peiping is not surprising, for irruptions and explosions in China's civil war constantly take place on all sides, and people do not know what to expect next. The fighting in north China has become increasingly intense this winter.

Moreover, it is common knowledge that the Communists have been winning most of the battles and that the government is fighting with its back to the wall, trying simply to hold is remaining islands—the major cities—against increasing Communist pressure. Peiping is in the middle of this war. To the south, the Peiping-Hankow Railway goes only as far as the Hopeh provincial capital of Paoting, where it runs into a fighting zone. To the east and northeast, the Peiping-Mukden Railway skirts dangerously close to battle zones near Tientsin and around Mukden, and at intervening points as well. To the northwest, the Peiping-Suiyuan Railway leads to the only region in north China that is relatively quiet at present. All these railways have been periodically disrupted, and for one brief period recently the Communists cut all three main railway arteries simultaneously, at points near Peiping. Except for the railways, and the few cities that they link, most of north China is now in Communist hands.

The critical state of military affairs has increased the importance of Peiping as the government's headquarters in north China. Not long ago, General Fu Tso-yi was appointed Commander of a new North China Communist Suppression Headquarters, with its center here, to direct and control all military operations in the provinces of Jehol, Chahar, Suiyuan, Hopeh, and part of Shansi. (There is another Communist Suppression Headquarters in Manchuria, and similar military headquarters, under different names, are located elsewhere.) Soon thereafter, Nanking announced that Peiping had been designated an "Auxiliary Capital" of China—two others being Chungking and Sian. Among political observers, there are different interpretations of the significance of these moves. Some believe they reveal the government's determination to hold north China and to embark on offensive operations, directed from Peiping, with the objective of "cleaning up" north China. Others believe these moves indicate that the government realizes it is losing north China, fears that the region will be cut off from Nanking, and therefore is attempting to prepare Peiping to carry on, as best it can, on its own. Some of the latter assert that General Fu, who is not close to the "inner circles" in Nanking, will be a scapegoat for the government's ultimate defeat and withdrawal.

Whichever of these interpretations is correct, recent developments have made Peiping increasingly important in a military sense. It is now the key government headquarters between Mukden and Nanking, and General Fu Tso-yi holds the limelight in this part of the country. Fu is a popular leader and has a good reputation, based on his past leadership in Suiyuan Province. I have yet to hear anyone—official, businessman, professor, or rickshaw coolie—question his honesty or deprecate his military ability. Many people feel that if anyone can put the government on the offensive again militarily in north China, Fu can do it. Yet the attitude encountered most frequently is that, while General Fu is a good man who can mobilize considerable support, it is doubtful that he has the strength to clean the Communists out of north China.

General Fu has primary responsibility for all government military operations in north China, but Peiping is also the seat of a bewildering complex of civil and military organizations that, when lumped together, can be considered "the government" in a broad sense of the term. Fu is naturally very senior in the chain of command, and he can give orders to all civil and military bodies in Peiping—with one exception. That exception is the Personal Representative in Peiping of the President of China. Fu is "almost on a par," in the words of a member of his staff, with this representative, and in theory the two men's responsibilities are not supposed to overlap (the one being military, the other political and economic), but in actual practice the President's Personal Representative is *the* senior authority.

These representatives, in charge of the various field headquarters of the President of the Republic of China, are universally recognized as the ultimate local authority in all the areas to which they are assigned. There are representatives of this sort in several different parts of China: Ch'en Ch'eng in Mukden, Ch'eng Ch'ien in Hankow, T. V. Soong in Canton, and Chang Chihchung in Tihwa. In Peiping, the man holding this important post is General Li Tsung-jen, who has been prominent in national affairs since the early days of the Chinese revolution, and is well-known both for his leadership in Kwangsi Province (together with Pai Ch'ung-hsi) and for his victory against the Japanese at Taierchuang in 1938. Li is the final arbitrator in any conflicts or disputes between any governmental or quasi-governmental bodies in Peiping; he can and occasionally does give direct orders to the numerous governing agencies in the city. As a general rule, however, he stays in the background and exercises his authority sparingly.

Below the President's Personal Representative, there are actually three separate channels of authority that must be considered a part of "the government" in Peiping: the Kuomintang, the Peiping Garrison, and the Peiping Municipal Government. In political influence and power, they are generally recognized to be approximately on a par, but they function in different areas and in different ways. Some might dispute the validity of classifying all three groups as part of "the government," but there are good reasons for doing so. For example, all three exercise the power of arrest under certain circumstances.

The director of the Peiping Kuomintang organization is a man named Wu Chu-jen, who was formerly a member of the Central Executive Committee of the Party. He was appointed by and is responsible to the Board of Organization of the Kuomintang in Nanking. The direct political influence of his Party apparatus in Peiping is very great. Party branches extend to each *Ch'ü*, or District, in the city. The Party maintains its own secret police organization. Virtually all prominent men in the municipal administration are Party members. The Party exerts a continuing influence on, and sometimes exercises direct control over, the major nongovernmental organizations in the city, such as the Chamber of Commerce. And there are times when the city Mayor must turn to the Party if he wishes to accomplish his objectives. There are, as yet, no parties other than the Kuomintang with any real influence or control in Peiping. The Democratic Socialist Party is virtually the only other one that even occasionally comes before the public eye.

Lieutenant General Ch'en Chi-ch'eng commands the Peiping Garrison. Primarily responsible to the Ministry of National Defense in Nanking, he is charged with the local defense of Peiping, and commands a special garrison force for this purpose. General Ch'en also commands the gendarmerie in Peiping, a special group of military police that has a semipolitical character, and which in some cities is under a separate commander. Normally, Ch'en, like Li, appears to stay in the background in political affairs, but his reserve powers and authority are substantial, and his role can be important not only when there are external threats to the city, but also when any internal disorders—such as student strikes—occur. When martial law is declared, his military courts take precedence over the civil judicial system. At times, even when martial law has not been formally put into effect, his subordinates tend to usurp the functions of the civil courts in certain types of cases. At present, for example, there is a long-standing dispute over several students who were arrested many months ago and have yet to be released by the Garrison Commander for civil trial.

Then, of course, there is the Peiping Municipal Government.

Peiping is a "Special Municipality," a classification given to a number of major cities in China—including Nanking, Shanghai, Tientsin, Mukden, Canton, and Chungking—and as such it is administered directly by the Central Government, or, more specifically, by the Executive Yüan. As a Special Municipality, Peiping has the same status as a province, for purposes of representation in national bodies. It is not responsible to the Hopeh Provincial Government, even though it is centrally located in the province, and relations between the province and the city seem to focus mainly on differences of opinion about the geographical definition of the municipality's authority. Peiping, in short, is a political as well as a military island.

The organizational structure of the Municipal Government is an administrator's nightmare. It is a top-heavy structure, hanging from above rather than growing from below. Almost all of its components serve more than one master; they are not only responsible to, but actually receive orders from, several different sources. In many respects, it is not a "local" government at all, but is simply a cluster of branches of various Central Government agencies.

The Mayor—French-educated Ho Szu-yüan, who previously was Governor of Shantung Province—was appointed by, and is responsible to, the Executive Yüan. Under him are nine bureaus whose directors are also appointed by the Executive Yüan and are directly responsible to it and to one or more national ministries, as well as to the Mayor. In addition, there are several municipal offices that are responsible to ministries and to either the Examination Yüan or the Control Yüan, as well as to the Mayor. Coordination of these units involves tremendous problems, but the Mayor attempts to cope with the situation by holding regular meetings of bureau chiefs each Tuesday and alternate Fridays and short sessions every Monday and Thursday. In practice, however, a bureau director may receive direct orders from the Executive Yüan, the President's Personal Representative, and the North China Communist Suppression Headquarters Commander, or he may find himself at loggerheads with the Garrison Commander or the Director of the Peiping Kuomintang. The picture is further complicated by the fact that certain governmental functions in the city are carried out by organizations that are purely and simply branches of the Central Government, without any direct connection with the Municipal Government. Centralism is carried to such an extreme that instructions from Generalissimo Chiang K'ai-shek himself may be injected into the picture at any one of these levels. Occasionally, there are direct contacts between Chiang and the mayors of Special Municipalities that bypass all intervening levels of authority. Obviously, operating such a system involves great skill, compromise, and a delicate balancing of all organizations and personalities involved.

Appointments within the Municipal Government are fully controlled by Nanking. There are three main categories of personnel. The first may be recommended by the Mayor, but must be approved by the national ministry involved and then appointed by the Executive Yüan or, in a few cases, by the Examination or Control Yüan. The second may be recommended by bureau heads and confirmed by the Mayor, but these too must be appointed by Nanking. Only the third, or lowest, grade may be appointed solely by the Mayor, and even these are provisional until reviewed and approved by the Central Government.

In a similar way, the Municipal Government is financially dependent on Nanking. It is allowed to handle only those taxes that are of relatively minor importance. Altogether, these meet only about one-fourth of its budgetary needs. Taxes that produce the most revenue—in Peiping, the income, inheritance, and commodity taxes—are levied by the Central Government's Direct Tax Bureau in Peiping, and the revenue from them is forwarded to Nanking. The Central Government then appropriates the necessary amount of money to keep the Municipal Government running. The city is always, therefore, in the position of a beggar; it rarely has enough money to carry out projects it would like to initiate, and with its budget it can do little more than pay the salaries of its employees, who totaled 22,653 (8,643 civilians and 14,010 police) early this year.

Under the Municipal Government, Peiping is divided into 20 *Ch'ü*, 336 *Pao*, and 6,982 *Chia*, which correspond roughly to districts, neighborhoods, and streets. The *"Pao-Chia* system," as it is usually called, may not necessarily be a bad one, in theory—it has a long history in China, but had not been utilized for many years until it was reintroduced by the Kuomintang in the 1930's —but in practice it is inefficient and often corrupt. One old Chinese gentleman in Peiping, who refused the job as head of his *Pao*, recently summed up his feelings about it as follows: "As it works now, it is worse than anything we have seen since the Revolution of 1911." This may be somewhat of an exaggeration, but it is a view shared by many. There is little doubt that the system at present is neither democratic nor efficient.

The heads of *Pao* and *Chia* in Peiping are elected, theoretically, every three and two years, respectively. Some people claim that there are really no elections at all. Others assert that, although elections take place, they are completely manipulated. Neither of these claims is entirely correct, but both are partially true. Virtually everyone agrees that most of the *Pao* and *Chia* heads have poor qualifications, do not really "represent" their constituencies, and, as a rule, accept the posts for personal gain rather than public service. Furthermore, the *Pao* Meetings (open sessions of all citizens in a *Pao*, scheduled to be held every two months) and the *Ch'ü* Assemblies (composed of two representatives from each *Pao*, and scheduled to convene every three months) appear to meet only irregularly, to accomplish very little, and to be of almost no practical importance in the governing of the city.

At least part of the explanation for the ineffectiveness of popular government at this level in Peiping is the prevailing lack of public interest and responsibility. A general political demoralization must also bear some of the responsibility. But it is true that the possible democratic nature of the *Pao-Chia* system is perverted by manipulation from above that tends to turn it into a system of bureaucratic control rather than one of popular representation.

Every *Pao* and *Chia* chief is provided with various assistants, paid by the Bureau of Civil Affairs, and at least one of these, the census representative, is generally recognized as the man who supervises, checks, and reports on what goes on in each local area. Many people label these census representatives "secret agents," but this title, with all its sinister implications, is a popular one applied to many persons in China today by those discouraged about the general situation and eager to assign blame for all their troubles to identifiable scapegoats. In any case, the system of popular representation, such as it is, goes only as high as the *Pao*. Each *Ch'ü* head is appointed by the Mayor, on the basis of recommendations by the Director of the Bureau of Civil Affairs, and is responsible to the latter.

All of this adds up to a very confusing and cumbersome system of government. It is often confusing to employees within the government, as well as to outside observers. One cannot avoid suspecting that parts of the system "just grew." How the system works is a separate question. It is obvious that personal relationships are extremely important. These involve national as well as local personalities, for, under the existing system, national politics—which today means, above all, Kuomintang intraparty politics—is projected strongly into the local scene.

The wonder of it is that the system works at all, and it does manage to function reasonably well under the circumstances. Streets are cleaned, garbage is collected, refugees and destitute persons are cared for, order is maintained, utilities are operated; in short, the routine municipal functions are carried out, with relative smoothness and dependability. But this is true in spite of the system rather than because of it. At best, the city administration can do little more than "go along" under the circumstances. Ambitious planning for development, or change of any sort, is practically impossible. Recently, the Mayor described to me in a rather wistful manner a number of projects that he would like to carry out, and then after describing them admitted that they were really just "dreams."

Actually, although government and politics directly or indirectly affect everyone in the city, they are generally in the background in people's minds and in their everyday life. The same can be said even about the current civil war with the Communists. In the foreground are the economic situation, the problem of making a living, and the ever-present inflation.

Two factors make Peiping's economic position today particularly precarious. One is the city's isolation, its island characteristics; there is very little hinterland from which it can draw food and other supplies. The other is the fact that Peiping itself produces very few basic necessities. Economically, it is merely limping along, therefore, and it is dependent upon one all-important lifeline—the Peiping-Tientsin Railway—for imports of such necessities as food and cloth.

Approximately one-fourth of the food consumed by people in Peiping now comes from central and south China via Tientsin. Only three-fourths of the city's needs can be met by north China sources of supply. Part of the latter comes from the 47,000 acres under cultivation within the municipality, part comes from the limited rural hinterland under government control, and part is smuggled in from Communist territory. To date, there has been no starvation, or even imminent threat of starvation, but food prices are higher than in any major city south of Manchuria, there are no safe food reserves, and people are eating less than before the war.

In contrast to prewar conditions, the city is stagnant economically. One of Peiping's main "industries," the tourist trade, is virtually dead. The coal mines at nearby Mentoukou are producing more than enough coal for the city, but in no other necessity is Peiping's own production sufficient to meet its needs. The city's only big industrial enterprise, an iron mill west of the city wall, is operating far below capacity. A number of small flour mills are working, but they do not come close to meeting the city's needs. Peiping has never manufactured much cloth, and even so-called "patriotic cloth," manufactured in small shops, is being produced at only one-fourth the prewar rate. Normally, Peiping's main manufactured products are luxury articles—fine rugs, cloisonné, brasswork, enamelware, embroideries, and other handicraft items —produced in small guild-controlled shops, but today production of these things is crippled by a lack of markets; some of the skills are said to be dying out gradually.

The existing situation naturally produces hardship. There are large numbers of unemployed persons in the city, and more than a few destitute people. The Municipal Government feeds about 40,000 a day, at present, and provides shelter for a sizable number. In some respects, however, it is surprising that there is not more evidence of poverty. Most of the people one sees on the streets look reasonably well fed and well clothed. The explanation undoubtedly is that "the people are living off their fat," as the Mayor recently expressed it to me, and are skillful at patching old clothes.

However, a feeling of economic insecurity is universal, even among those who are not too badly off. In Peiping, the inflation is worse, and the prices even higher, than in less isolated cities, and the spiral keeps going up. There is no confidence in money, and people try to invest what little savings or profit they can make in commodities such as wool yarn, gold, or American dollars. There are many national laws and regulations aimed at controlling the inflation, but they are completely ineffective. Illegal business is commonplace, and it is condoned by average people on the grounds of necessity.

Uncertainty about the future is perhaps the keynote in Peiping today. There is a widespread feeling that maybe something big and important will happen this coming spring—perhaps a Communist move against Peiping or a concerted government drive. But few people are willing to plan for or predict the future. They live from day to day, harassed by the inflation and discouraged by a civil war with no end in sight. But despite all their troubles, most of them still manage to derive some pleasure and enjoyment from their environment—from the serenity, beauty, and charm of Peiping.

3

"WAR" IN THE SUBURBS

Peiping
February, 1948

Pachiatsun, or Eight Families Village, lies on the outskirts of Peiping. The highest point in the village is a small building that is a part of the local Buddhist temple. Standing on the balcony of this building, one can view much of the surrounding countryside. Other villages—including another Pachiatsun, because many years ago the village was split into "front" and "rear" sections that are now separate divisions—are marked by a few scattered trees which dot the landscape and break the monotonous yellow-brown aspect of the flat land. The hazy purple of the Western Hills borders the plain a few miles away, and the hills are clearly visible. Visible, too, is the central building of the Summer Palace, the magnificent folly of the Empress Dowager Tz'u Hsi, who built it with funds appropriated for the Chinese Navy. It looks remote and unreal, which it is for the villagers of Pachiatsun. Peiping, which lies a few miles to the east, is not visible. To the north, a tall smoke-stack rises from the plain about half a mile from Pachiatsun. It is a part of the textile factory, now manufacturing military supplies, in the town of Chingho. Chingho is the market town where the villagers of Pachiatsun buy and sell, and it is the economic focal point of the locality.

It was an unseasonably warm, spring-like day when I stood on the temple balcony in Pachiatsun last week. The brown fields around the village were unplowed and devoid of activity, since spring plowing and planting will not begin for about a month. The scene was one of complete calm and serenity. A young sociologist on the faculty of Yenching University was standing next to me. He raised his arm and pointed to the north. "Do you see that smokestack there?" he asked. "A half-mile beyond that is Communist territory."

I had known that villages near to Peiping were in Communist hands, but the way in which he casually pointed to a place about a mile away and said, "There they are," gave me somewhat of a shock. It would probably be correct to call the placid countryside north of Pachiatsun a "front" in China's civil war. Yet there were no signs of battle, no moving troops, no fortifications, in fact nothing to indicate even preparations for a military struggle.

From a different front in China's civil war, newpaper dispatches sent on the same day I visited Pachiatsun described the situation as follows:

> Fall of another "outpost" of Mukden was imminent today as thousands of Communist troops stormed into the coal-mining center of Penki, 40 miles southeast of Mukden, after a week-long siege. . . . At the same time, elaborate Communist preparations for an early attack on Sinmin, 30 miles west of Mukden, and Tiehling, 40 miles to the north, are reported. . . . A sizable Red Army is at present marching on Yingkow from the recently captured steel city of Anshan. . . . Considerable uneasiness is said to prevail in Mukden as the Communist stranglehold on the metropolis tightens, with prices of commodities and vital necessities standing at dizzy heights.

The present civil war in China is bitter and violent. In Manchuria, it is now a war of mass battles, artillery attacks, and heavy casualties. Current reports indicate that the military situation there is not only explosive, but is actually exploding, and the fate of the remaining Nationalist troops in that region is highly uncertain. But civil war in a country as large as China means different things at different times and in different places. For the present, at least, the environs of Peiping enjoy an uneasy stability. There is little offensive action initiated by either side, and both the Communists and the Nationalists are, for the most part, "sitting it out." Attrition is gradually undermining the government position, however, and Nationalist leaders in Peiping have their eyes fixed anxiously on the northeast, where the outcome of the fighting in Manchuria will inevitably affect Peiping's position. But the villagers of Pachiatsun have their eyes fixed primarily on their fields, for in about a month their real work will begin. They are not unaware of the civil war. It is affecting them in many ways. But their attention is still directed mainly toward their major and immediate problem, the problem of extracting the necessities of life from the brown north China soil.

Pachiatsun has a population of about 350 persons. Perhaps as many as one-third of these are refugees, virtually all of them relatives or friends of local villagers, who have fled from active war areas. It is difficult to see where this many people live, for one can walk the circumference of the village in a few minutes.

The village is a relatively prosperous one. Each family—many of them include three or more generations—has a compound containing all the buildings and equipment necessary for a self-sustaining farm unit. Most of the buildings are substantial, and some compare favorably with city houses in Peiping. Although a large percentage of the land tilled by the local villagers belongs to absentee owners in Peiping, those who farm it seem to have fared reasonably well in the past. But in many ways, the villagers are hard hit by existing economic conditions. The prices of manufactured products have risen more than the prices of agricultural goods, and consequently purchasing power has slowly dwindled.

Many of the village's economic activities have steadily declined. The principal nonagricultural industry in the area is a family-owned weaving establishment, equipped with simple human-operated machinery, which makes cloth from yarn purchased in the city. At one time, the owners hired a number of laborers, and operated on a scale unusually large for a village the size of Pachiatsun. Now, the industry is operated entirely by family members, and usually only one small loom is used. One respected old farmer in the village, a man with a wonderful face that looks as if someone had accidentally applied the plow to it, formerly raised ducks in large numbers, to supply the discriminating palate of Peiping. He is still known locally as the "Duck King," but at present he has only twelve fowl. Even though they are bringing excellent prices in Peiping, the cost of grain to feed them is more than he can afford.

Part of the quietness that I encountered in Pachiatsun was, of course, merely a seasonal phenomenon. Some villagers go every day to work in the textile factory at Chingho, but for most of them this is still the slack season. Virtually the only work in progress during my visit was being done by women and children. A small boy was operating the village's loom. Two healthy young women were supervising a blindfolded donkey as he made his circuit around a grindstone, converting corn into flour. And other women were busying themselves with various small jobs. Children were much in evidence in the "streets," since the village school, which normally gathers them into the Pachiatsun temple, was still closed for the protracted Chinese New Year holiday. They interrupted their games and kite-flying to troop along with the visiting strangers, and obligingly preceded us to silence the mongrels that serve as watchdogs in every household. The men seemed to be enjoying an afternoon of leisure, and they had plenty of time for a cup of tea and polite conversation.

At the home of a village "doctor," I met the local census representative of the Peiping Municipal Government—which has jurisdiction over Pachiatsun—a well-dressed and polite young soldier who was making his daily rounds. Every day, this young man visits the half a dozen or so villages in his territory to check on new arrivals and departures, and to observe the general situation. And every night, according to the villagers, Communists from "across the way" also come into the village, to observe the situation. Apart from the visiting census representative, there was not a single person in uniform, nor any other evidence of war, in the village. There was, in fact, a curious air of unconcern and relaxation.

Whether the existing peace and calm in Pachiatsun continue will be determined by factors that the local villagers cannot control and probably will not be able fully to understand. At present, however, they are simply waiting, quietly and peacefully, for spring.

4

STUDENT DISAFFECTION

Peiping
March, 1948

On February 7 of this year, a mass student meeting was held on "Democratic Ground," a large square centrally located in the Hsiatan area of Peita (Peking or Peiping National University). Students from all the colleges and universities in Peiping and Tientsin represented in the North China Student Union assembled to demonstrate and protest against the government. The incidents inspiring this "accusation meeting" were both national and local. Several days previously, a demonstration at Tungchi University in Shanghai had resulted in injuries to a number of students and the arrest of many more. In Peiping, five university and college students had just been arrested by the Garrison Commander on charges of Communist conspiracy and were being held incommunicado. The February 7 meeting was convened to express sympathy for the Tungchi students and to protest the Peiping arrests.

About 2,000 students assembled in front of an improvised stage at one end of the square. The majority sat closely packed on the ground. They were ringed by a line of standing students whose hands were joined to prevent arrivals and departures from disturbing the main body. There were numerous placards identifying various groups, while others bore slogans. Nearby walls were plastered with handwritten newspapers carrying accounts of the recent events, as well as political slogans and exhortations to the students. Cartoons on the walls depicted oppression by Kuomintang authorities; more than one showed a sinister Uncle Sam as an "ally of reaction."

While the mass of students sat listening, quietly, a succession of student leaders and sympathetic professors rose and spoke from the platform. They talked with emotion, and often their voices rose to a shrill pitch. Decrying the recent events, they strongly condemned both the Kuomintang and the Central Government, and called for student unity:

"The sacred word 'constitution' has been stained by the government."

"Students should not only go to the library for books, but should do something to protect themselves."

"Students must organize against the antidemocratic government."

"The present government officials cannot reconstruct China. Only the students, when organized, can do it. Reconstruction of China is impossible unless the whole of China is awakened to the incapabilities of the government, and the whole of China can only be awakened by the students."

The audience listened intently and periodically broke into applause and cheers.

At the close of the speeches, several short plays were presented. Each was a variation of the theme of government oppression, and the victims must have used several bottles of ketchup, or a suitable "bloody" equivalent. The audience was responsive and approving. In the intervals between the plays, the students joined in singing stirring songs, some directed, others spontaneous.

The climax came as the students rose in a body and, with upraised arms, repeated an oath:

"We students of the National Peking University, Tsinghua University, Yenching University, National Normal College, Franco-Chinese University, Nankai University, and Peiyang University—all with an iron will and determination—take this oath and determine to protect our basic divine rights, safeguard our democratic student self-governing associations, and oppose the regulations for the organization of student self-governing associations newly promulgated by the Ministry of Education. From today on, we will unite and fight together for our existence. If one school self-governing association suffers oppression, all schools will concertedly arise and with determination resist until our divine rights are restored. We take this oath with deliberation."

The students then formed a long procession and marched around "Democratic Ground," singing songs and shouting slogans: "Oppose oppression," "Protect the student self-governing association," "Stop illegal arrests and cruel acts." Finally, the demonstration broke up, and the students returned to their respective schools.

This demonstration never left the Peita campus; in previous ones, clashes with police and gendarmes had taken place on the city streets, and the students were now ordered to stay within the confines of the university. During the meeting, clusters of uniformed, but unarmed, policemen filled the streets surrounding the campus—just in case—but no disorders or conflicts took place. Within the inner sanctum of the campus, the students were unmolested.

At about the same time that this particular demonstration took place, student delegations visited key officials in the city. By the end of the month, three of the arrested students had been released, and the other two had been turned over to the jurisdiction of the local civil courts by the Garrison Commander. It is difficult to say whether this was the result of student pressure, but it may well have been.

The February 7 student demonstration was merely the most recent of many that have taken place in Peiping, and elsewhere in China, during past months. In fact, to see it in perspective, one must relate it to the entire background of the Chinese Student Movement. The development of the Chinese Student Movement—a title the students themselves constantly use—has involved a long history of collective action by students against the existing government authorities in China. At times, this action has been fairly well organized. At other times, it has been spontaneous and rather uncoordinated. Nevertheless, it has been a real force and influence, sometimes in the foreground and sometimes in the background, in Chinese history ever since the movement first began in 1919. In perhaps the majority of instances, Peiping has been the city where student action has been initiated, with Peita, Yenching, and Tsinghua universities taking leading parts, and demonstrations have spread from Peiping to other parts of the country. Certain important dates are milestones in the movement's history, and Chinese university students know these dates as well as an American schoolboy knows 1776, 1789, and 1812. They constantly refer to them in abbreviated form, such as "five-four"—fifth month, fourth day—for May 4, 1919.

May 4, 1919, was the day on which the Chinese Student Movement was started, at least in a formal sense. On that date, students in Peiping rose in indignation against the Versailles agreement regarding Shantung Province, and protested against the Chinese Government's unwillingness, or inability, to protect China's national interests. Demonstrations subsequently swept the country.

Many other dates are almost equally well remembered. On May 30, 1925, students protested loudly against the killing of a number of Chinese civilians in Shanghai by foreign police and troops. On December 9, 1935, they demonstrated against the Nationalist

Government and demanded that it resist Japanese aggression and stop the civil war. On December 1, 1945, students in Kunming protested against the government because of the murder of two prominent liberal professors. The case of a United States Marine who allegedly raped a Chinese girl set off demonstrations in Peiping on December 30, 1946, against the Nanking Government and American intervention in China.

In the past year, demonstrations have become increasingly numerous. In Peiping, these have included protests against the widespread arrests that took place in February, 1947; a demonstration with varied causes that developed, after a widely publicized student arrest in Hangchow, into an "anti-civil war," "anti-hunger," and "anti-oppression" campaign in May-June, 1947; a "protect civil rights" movement in November, 1947; and the recent "accusation" demonstration.

Throughout its history, the Chinese Student Movement has been an active, vocal, and significant force through which students have been able to exert pressure upon the existing political authorities. Even though armies have been a fundamental factor in Chinese politics since the Revolution of 1911, and the students have had no armies, the Student Movement has been, and still is, able to exert considerable influence through the power of "public opinion." It is difficult to evaluate its influence with any accuracy at present, but there is no doubt that student opinion still evokes a certain amount of deference on the part of the government, and exerts considerable influence among literate Chinese. It is probably true to say, in fact, that the students are the most vocal opposition group within Nationalist China today.

A kind of equilibrium now exists between the government—with its political authority and instruments of rule and coercion—and the students—with their sensitivity to all government control, their aggressive idealism, and their willingness to speak up in no uncertain terms when they feel the occasion demands it. There is no doubt that students are subjected to illegal and arbitrary arrests, oppressive regulations and restrictions, and occasional mistreatment. There is also no doubt, however, that students are allowed more privileges and freedom than other groups in China. In fact, inflammatory statements and agitational activities of the kind now characteristic of Chinese students might well provoke harsher and more stringent government suppression in other countries engaged in civil war. In China, students clearly have acquired a special position on the national scene.

At present, there are certain trends in student activities, opinions, and relations with the government that may be of consider-able significance for the future. One is the increasing organiza-tional unity of the Student Movement. "We are stronger than we have ever been before," a prominent Peiping student said to me recently, "and we have more self-confidence. We are begin-ning to get well organized."

Much of the past action of Chinese students has been very loosely organized, based simply on informal liaison between in-dividuals in different parts of the country. It now appears that informal relations are crystallizing into stronger, more concrete organizational links. This process has been taking place ever since the end of World War II. Student self-governing associations have sprung up in virtually all Chinese colleges and middle schools, city-wide federations have been formed in the major cities, and some regional federations have appeared. Of particular im-portance are the federations that have taken shape in north China and in the Shanghai-Nanking-Soochow-Hangchow region. In June of last year, students met in Shanghai and attempted to form a national federation, but government opposition prevented its establishment.

The Peita Student Self-Governing Association is a good ex-ample of existing student bodies, although it may be stronger than most. It has now become an established university institu-tion, elected annually by universal student suffrage, and it con-trols almost all student activities. It also provides liaison between the students and the university administration, and mobilizes student opinion on political or other issues of general student interest.

Because Peita as an institution is geographically split, its stu-dent association has five branches. The largest and most im-portant of these is the Hsiatan Branch, which includes the Col-leges of Public Affairs, Liberal Arts, and Science. Each branch has an Assembly, and, for the university as a whole, there is an over-all Representative Assembly composed of delegates from each class in each department; it meets regularly at least once each semester and may have special sessions. In addition, there is a twenty-five–member Board of Directors, elected by the branch boards. This Board, which holds regular meetings every two weeks, is the active executive body of the association, and it elects, as chief executive, a triumvirate of directors. The Board also is organized into a secretariat and sections for general administra-tion, academic activity, public service, entertainment, and com-munications, which are its main functioning bodies.

Recently, an additional body, the Civil Rights Protection Committee, has been formed, and it is now regarded by Peita students as one of the most important student organs. Composed of seven members elected by the Board of Directors, it goes into action and becomes the main focus of student interest whenever students are arrested or their civil rights are impinged upon. Naturally enough, law students are prominent in this committee. These various bodies are generally recognized to be the representative agencies and spokesmen for the students in Peita.

Above the Peita association, there is a North China Student Union. With the exception of a few academic institutions, which Peita students claim are filled with "reactionaries" and are under the thumb of the Kuomintang Party, each of the major universities, colleges, and middle schools in Nationalist north China —which now, for all practical purposes, means the cities of Peiping and Tientsin—elects three representatives to the Union. These representatives, in turn, elect a Standing Committee, which meets regularly about every two weeks and may have informal meetings more often. Although this body is not officially recognized by the government, it has received *de facto* recognition when its delegates and petitions have been received by the authorities, and consequently it is the organ that coordinates the entire student movement in the Peiping-Tientsin area.

All these organizations play a very important role in student life, and they make possible a high degree of concerted action on issues that arouse student opinion. It is interesting to note that at Peita all the major extracurricular groups serve as valuable auxiliaries to the Student Self-Governing Association, especially when student political action is initiated. The two glee clubs handle mass singing. The two dramatic clubs produce political plays at demonstration meetings. And wall newspapers serve up a mixture of news and propaganda to the students. The wall newspapers are a particularly interesting phenomenon. There are more than twenty of them in the university, all with dramatic names, such as *The Storm, The Torch, The Torrent, The Yellow River.* In a strict sense, they are not really newspapers at all, for they are simply handwritten single sheets pasted on the university walls for all to see, but they are nevertheless regarded as such. About ten are published weekly, and the others irregularly. Each is put out by a newspaper society (the largest has more than sixty members, but the average size is between ten and twenty), and to each publishing society there is attached a reading society that organizes "collective reading." Some of the reading societies own small libraries containing magazines and books not carried in the university library. Except for three or four papers published by pro-Kuomintang students, the rest of the societies are organized into a Wall-Newspaper Union, which strongly supports the Student Self-Governing Association in all of its many activities.

At a recent luncheon I attended, a group of professors from several leading Peiping universities all agreed that "almost all students are antigovernment." Of course, the majority of professors are themselves estranged from the government, but this particular group was not strongly antigovernment; one even holds a semiofficial post in addition to his professorship. Some of their comments on student attitudes bear quoting:

"There is a Leftist trend among students, but it is not well thought out or coherent. But the most brilliant students are Leftist, and they are the most popular ones also."

"Students are extremely disillusioned. Almost no one has a solution any more. They don't think a coalition [government] is possible. They don't think division of the country is a solution. They don't know what to think. They just want peace."

"Student opinion is subdivided into innumerable factions of all political shades, but the over-all organization functions in a unified way during times of crisis."

"Students don't accomplish much, but they do act as a sort of 'national conscience,' and about 70 per cent of the time they are right in their emotional reactions and stands."

Not long ago, when I was in Nanking, American Ambassador Leighton Stuart, who has unusually close contacts with Chinese academic circles, said to me that good friends of his in Peiping estimated that "90 to 95 per cent of the students are opposed to Communism in China, and 90 per cent are opposed to the present government."

Recently, when talking with a highly intelligent senior at Peita, a student who himself is both antigovernment and anti-Communist, I asked what his opinion was of the Communists' strength among Peita students. "There are very few actual Communists," he answered, "but I would say that at least 50 per cent are sympathetic to Communism—or at least the Chinese Communists. At least 50 per cent!"

"What does 'sympathetic' mean?" I asked.

"Well, it means that they think the Chinese Communists are a better group than the present government."

"Do any students think a coalition is still possible?" I inquired.

"None that I know of," he replied. "That used to be the students' hope, but no more."

"Do the students think either side can win the civil war?"

"Until recently, they didn't, but a great many students now think the Communists will win."

"From what you have said, do you mean that many or most students now feel that a Communist regime would be better than a Kuomintang regime, that the Communists are winning anyway, and that they deserve the students' sympathy?"

"Yes, a great many, if not most, students feel that way, but they don't arrive at that position on any ideological basis."

I have not polled student opinion in Peiping, but if one uses Ambassador Stuart's statement as an indication of student opinion only a short while ago, more recent evidence points toward an increasing alienation of students from the Central Government and a definite shift to the Left, in the sense that more and more students are showing sympathy toward the Chinese Communist Party, and now regard Communist takeover as the only alternative to what they consider to be an intolerable situation.

The political interests of students in Peiping center almost entirely on the one basic issue of the civil war and its outcome. They show little concern about more immediate problems or possible solutions. Their lack of interest in Peiping local affairs can be explained, at least partially, by the fact that they come from many parts of the country, and consequently are not concerned with local politics in what is merely a temporary residence; but even the practical problems of national politics are apparently of only minor interest to them. Undoubtedly this is natural, because of their lack of political power, responsibility, and experience, but it is a characteristic that disturbs some who would like to see them act as a more constructive force.

Ambassador Stuart recently made an unusual public statement in which he appealed to "the patriotic educated people to organize and study what the national problems are and arouse and instruct the people so that they may realize a democratic government. In so doing, the patriotic intellectuals can correct whatever distrust they have with the present government and in that way support it in its effort to bring peace to China."

Ambassador Stuart's statement prompted a reply from Dr. Hollington Tong, head of the Government Information Service, in which he said:

China is glad that it has . . . intellectual critics. . . . But to assume from this that there is any mass opposition of the intelligent [sic] in China to the government is farfetched. . . . It is as inaccurate to assume that China is drifting toward the Left because many university students are repeating the familiar process of the young everywhere in criticizing the present as to assume that the United States is going Marxist because there is a strong socialist club at Harvard. . . . Actually, the great body of China's intellectuals are now working devotedly and faithfully within the national government . . . they are the backbone of the government.

Tong's statement revealed the tendency of the Nationalist Government to underestimate both the extent and the possible significance of present student dissatisfaction, as well as the degree to which intellectuals and students are inclined, consciously or unconsciously, to boycott current politics, and ignore immediate political problems, in Nationalist China today.

It is significant that most Chinese students at present think of China's civil war in purely domestic terms. They tend, in short, to ignore any possible connection with, or orientation toward, Russia on the part of the Chinese Communist Party. They like to think that China's present problems are nobody else's business. They resent all foreign interference or intervention and constantly assert that the Chinese people can solve their own problems. This sensitivity to any foreign action that appears in any way to compromise China's national sovereignty dates to the beginning of the Student Movement. Today, most students oppose any United States aid to China and, during the past two years, they have protested several times against actions that they have labeled American intervention in China's domestic affairs. There is absolutely no personal animosity toward individual Americans, but one constantly encounters suspicion of the motives underlying United States policy toward China.

Even though there is a high degree of solidarity among students in the leading universities in Peiping, not all students conform to majority opinions. For one thing, there are undoubtedly a few outright Communists. Most students assert that they do not personally know any, however, "You can never identify any students who are Communists," one boy said to me. "If they are [Communists], they can't expose themselves or they would be arrested." But there is a constant trickle of students who decide for various reasons, to leave school and join the Communists in their so-called "Liberated Areas." This is a step that is very difficult to make, emotionally and psychologically, for it involves a decision to burn all one's bridges. However, once made, it is easy enough to accomplish; a person merely has to walk to certain villages a few miles from Peiping and "join up."

Another small minority group among the students is made up of pro-Kuomintang students. Such students receive official support in various minor, indirect ways, but they are extremely unpopular among the other students, partly because some are employed by the local Kuomintang Party headquarters as informers, to report on student activities and opinions. Last year, this group had enough influence and strength to attempt to break up an antigovernment student demonstration, but the other students say they "wouldn't dare" now. It is worth noting that the most unpopular man in Peiping among most students is the local Kuomintang chief, Wu. The Garrison Commander, General Ch'en, runs a close second. By contrast, the President's Personal Representative, Li Tsung-jen, is generally given some credit as being "not too bad," which is really high praise indeed for a government official from the disillusioned students of China today.

What has caused the present acute disaffection of so many Chinese students? According to the students themselves, it is government oppression, and that is all. One cannot help but believe, however, that other factors are also involved. A sense of disillusionment after ten years of war, and a feeling of hopelessness because the future seems so dark, are probably contributing factors. The economic status of the students doubtless also contributes to their present mood. Government universities in Peiping are overcrowded and uncomfortable. Most students are barely making ends meet financially, and a majority depends on government subsidies. Part of the students receive only a one-half subsidy, but even the full subsidy is very small. Last month, it was thirty-two catties of flour (one catty is a little over a pound) and CNC $1.5 million in cash (a little over U.S. $5.00 at the prevailing black-market exchange rate); this is a pittance, even though room and tuition are free and the students' requirements are not great. Living on the brink of pauperism undoubtedly intensifies the students' feeling of dissatisfaction.

Government oppression, or repression, of students is clearly a major factor in the situation, however. In addition to imposing certain types of controls and regulations that might seem justifiable in view of the existing civil-war situation, the government has been responsible for a steady succession of arbitrary and illegal arrests, plus numerous cases of violent treatment and a few killings of students. The circumstances of many incidents indicate that they were consciously intended to intimidate the students and to discourage them from expressing opposition to the government. It does not take many such incidents to inflame student opinion.

Current government policies toward students reflect the Kuomintang's over-all thinking on how to deal with the complex problem of loyalty. Ch'en Li-fu, Minister of Organization of the Kuomintang Party and one of the most powerful men in China, expressed his thinking on the problem succinctly during an interview I had with him last November in Nanking: "Communists everywhere are like small nerve cells that are controlled and connected to a foreign brain," he said. "If you don't uncover the real Communists, you have disloyal people in your midst. . . . It is extremely difficult to define who is a Communist. There are different degrees of Communism. There is a small inner circle of real Communists. Around them is a group that they consider 70 per cent reliable. Around them is another considered about 50 per cent reliable, then another that is 30 per cent, and another that is 10 per cent, and so on. Only the inner circle knows who is what. To know who are the real Communist leaders, you have to get people into the inner circle, and that is extremely difficult. This presents real problems. . . . The problem is to uncover and deal with real Communists without making mistakes about people who are not. . . . It is a great problem in student groups."

Unfortunately, however, the Nationalist Government seems to have attacked the problem of rooting out Communists without really having solved the problem of discriminating between the 10 per cent "Pinks" and the 100 per cent Reds, and expressions of dissatisfaction have been confused with professions of Marxism. It is fair to say that the results have been negative. Pressure from the outside has pushed the outer circles Ch'en Li-fu talked about closer to the center, and the orientation of many students has turned in the direction of the Chinese Communist Party more out of desperation than conviction.

What do students in Peiping hope for in the future? The slogans they use are the slogans of liberal, parliamentary democracy. Such slogans undoubtedly mean different things to different persons, but this is what they mean to one student friend of mine in Peiping. "The first thing we want and need is peace and effective constitutional government: the protection of civil rights under a rule of law. When that is achieved, we can bring about the necessary economic revolution, and attack the problems of agrarian reform and industrialization on the basis of a sort of socialist economy." This, in a rather small nutshell, sums up the hopes of most students in Peiping. Without being able either to explain or defend all of their beliefs and assumptions, they now tend to believe that there would be more chance of achieving these goals under the Communists than under the Kuomintang.

However, when it comes to constructive proposals about what can and should be done in China now, most students today are blank. They simply throw up their hands and shrug their shoulders.

5

BUSINESS DEPRESSION

Tientsin
April, 1948

Tientsin is a great, sprawling commercial and industrial city lying a few miles inland from the Gulf of Pohai in north China. A small river, the Haiho, twists its way from the city to sea outlets at Taku Bar and Tangku. Hugging the banks of this stream are wharves and docks capable of accommodating small ships, and back from the banks stretch the Westernized downtown sections of the various prewar concessions that constitute the heart of the city. Like Shanghai, and other major coastal cities in China, Tientsin owes its modern economic development primarily to the stimulus of foreign capital, and the city is a cosmopolitan mixture of Western and Chinese elements. Prewar maps of Tientsin show a colorful checkerboard: British, French, Japanese, and Italian concessions, together with "special areas" converted from the relinquished concessions of other countries—including Russia, Germany, and Austria—made up the central portions of the city. To the north was the old Chinese City, a symmetrical square surrounded by broad streets that had replaced the original city wall; around it were the other areas under Chinese administration. Today, this anachronistic checkerboard has disappeared from the maps, erased by the administrative unification that took place under the Japanese, the relinquishment of special rights by the Western nations, and the postwar administrative reorganization under the Chinese. Tientsin is now one city, a Special Municipality under the Executive Yüan, and ten administrative districts have taken the place of the prewar municipal divisions.

The port facilities available to Tientsin at Taku Bar and Tangku are poor, to say the least—even though work on the Tangku New Harbor, started by the Japanese, is continuing—but since north China is singularly lacking in good harbors, Tientsin was and is the natural sea outlet for all of the north and northwest. Somewhat to the south, Tsingtao serves the Shantung peninsula, and, to the north, Chinwangtao provides port facilities for a limited hinterland. But practically speaking, Tientsin serves all of the tremendous hinterland of China between the Yangtze's outlet, Shanghai, and the Manchurian ports of Dairen, Port Arthur, Yingkow, Hulutao, and Antung. This huge area includes not only north China and Inner Mongolia, but, to a lesser extent, far western regions and even fringes of Manchuria. Such a commanding position makes the city a natural trade center. In normal times, China's major trunk railway lines in north China converge at Tientsin and link it with its extensive hinterland. The Tientsin-Pukow Railway connects the city with central China, and the Peiping-Mukden Railway passes through Tientsin, linking it with Manchuria. Another major line leads into Inner Mongolia. Secondary routes tap all the important areas of north China. Tientsin's location and transportation facilities have made it one of China's foremost centers of trade and industry in modern times.

Today, the railways still converge at Tientsin, barges and small boats still go up and down the Haiho, steamers still call at Taku Bar and Tangku, and some trade continues, but present trade activity is small compared with prewar years. Tientsin is one of the many indirect casualties of the civil war in China.

The import trade at Tientsin, as elsewhere in China, is rigidly limited by the Central Government's Revised Foreign Trade Regulations of November 17, 1946, which provide for strict regulation of all of China's foreign trade. These regulations divide import commodities into various categories, and the amounts that can be imported by any one region are centrally determined and strictly regulated by a system of import licenses. The allotment of regional quotas of this sort has cut the imports of the Tientsin region—including nearby Chinwangtao—to a figure considerably below its prewar share of China's total imports. Last year, for example, imports via Tientsin were limited to about 15 per cent of China's total imports, by value, whereas before the war they were between 18 and 20 per cent. The quotas announced this February for certain categories of imports, including industrial raw materials, limited Tientsin to 7.8 per cent of the national total, which is roughly one-half of its share before the war. Many Tientsin businessmen feel that the Central Government is consciously discriminating against the city, and against north China as a whole. The head of the Tientsin Regional Office of the Central Government Export-Import Board admits privately that the system does, in fact, result in discrimination, but he denies that there is any malicious intent behind it. However, private businessmen attribute the discrimination to the Central Government's desire to favor the business interests of government officials in Shanghai and other areas, and to its fear that the situation in north China is so precarious that a minimum should be risked in the area at present. The resentment of certain Tientsin businessmen is increased by the fact that they believe the volume of imports to any region should be linked to the volume of its exports. Tientsin in the past has always had an export surplus in foreign trade, and it is considered "unfair" that the city is not now allowed to use all of the foreign exchange earned by its exports. Tientsin still maintains an export surplus, but the total volume of both its exports and imports is gradually dwindling.

The most important reason for the continuing decline of Tientsin's export trade is, of course, the constant widening of civil-war zones in north China. The fighting has cut off Manchuria, and it has reduced the north China hinterland to one thin ribbon of territory bordering the railway to Peiping and another paralleling the Tientsin-Pukow Railway as far as Tangkuantun, about 40 miles south of Tientsin. Within the past two weeks, a flare-up of fighting in Chahar, northern Shansi, and Suiyuan has cut off Inner Mongolia. Steadily, the hinterland continues to shrink, and, as a result, Tientsin's export trade continues to dwindle.

Egg products for export formerly came to Tientsin from north Honan and south Hopeh; the railways to these areas are now cut. Casings for sausages used to come from Kansu and Sinkiang; this trade dropped to a low level some time ago and then was completely cut off by the recent disruption of the railway line to Paotow, the collection center for trade in the west. Shelled walnuts are a major export product that used to come from the Fen River valley in Shansi; much of that region is now in Communist hands, and the rest is surrounded by the Communists. Straw-braid was an important exportable handicraft product manufactured in the coastal towns in Shantung and Hopeh; most of these are now Communist-ruled towns. One by one, the sources of Tientsin's export products have been cut off from the port.

In some cases, factors other than the disruption of transportation have also seriously hindered trade. For example, for a variety of complicated reasons, the price of raw wool in early 1947 was actually lower in Tientsin than in Paotow, the collection point for wool in Inner Mongolia. As a result, large amounts—estimated by informed sources in Tientsin to be between 20 and 40 million pounds—accumulated in the northwest and now remain there, still unused, while the value of wool exports from Tientsin to the United States in 1947 dropped to less than 5 per cent of the level of a prewar year such as 1935. The price of furs and skins in New York has declined to the point where it is now unprofitable to export them from Tientsin on a large scale. Tientsin wool rugs likewise have been almost eliminated from world markets as a result of price trends. In 1947, only 61,787 square feet of woven wool carpets were exported to the United States, as compared with over 5 million square feet in the heyday of the trade, in the late 1920's. The decline of rug manufacturing has been a particularly severe blow to the city's economy, because it is estimated by some that at one time the industry, directly or indirectly, supported almost a quarter of a million people.

Today, Tientsin is still exporting a variety of goods: pig bristles, beans (including soya beans), furs, skins, sausage casings, some rugs and carpets, nuts, and negligible amounts of straw-braid, wool, horsehair, vermicelli, and Chinese medicines. But last year, pig bristles alone made up 60 per cent of the value of its total exports. In fact, the exportation of bristles, on a scale almost as large as in the 1935-40 period, is virtually the only thing that makes Tientsin an important exporting city today.

The gradual extension of Communist control over north China, the steady spread of fighting, and the disruption of transportation have been the most obvious, and undoubtedly the most important, causes of Tientsin's trade decline, but many people in Tientsin strongly feel that the Central Government's economic policies, its constant interference, and its numerous regulations have crippled trade and made it smaller than might have been expected even under existing conditions.

The large and unrealistic gap between the official and the black-market rates for foreign exchange provides the main cause of complaint. On the black market, a constant process of currency devaluation goes on: As the government printing presses keep working at capacity, the black-market value of foreign exchange keeps going up. It is true that the official rate of exchange is now adjusted periodically, and these adjustments have been more frequent since the establishment of an "official open market" rate last August, but the gap between the official and black-market rates is never reduced to realistic proportions. In effect, the gap imposes an indirect tax of 50 to 60 per cent on exports, and provides an indirect subsidy of a similar amount to those granted import licenses—and one constantly hears accusations of discrimination and favoritism in the allocation of import licenses. The prices of Chinese export products, therefore, are kept at an extremely high level. Traders claim that, without this artificial price handicap, the export record of products such as wool, furs, skins, and rugs might have been quite different during the past year or so. Businessmen claim that the government's regulations, which may have been sincerely designed to conserve foreign exchange for much-needed uses, actually result in an ever-decreasing volume of exports, a shrinking supply of foreign exchange, and, consequently, a lower volume of even the most essential imports.

Industry in Tientsin is affected by many of the same factors that cripple trade, and industrial rehabilitation since the end of the war has been extremely slow. Prior to World War II, Tientsin had a sizable industrial plant, and the Japanese, during their occupation, invested large sums of capital in further industrial development. Although a number of the major industries that operated under the Japanese have continued operation, and a few have even expanded output, most of the intermediate and smaller plants built by the Japanese have been dismantled or remain idle, and the prospects for their effective utilization become poorer each month. In many cases, former Japanese-owned factories sold by the Chinese Government to private entrepreneurs have been dismantled for scrap, or sent to locations farther south.

Among the many factors that have retarded the industries that have tried to keep operating are: raw material shortages; the rising costs of labor, power, fuel, raw materials, equipment, and financing; the increasing disruption of inland transport, which adds to the inaccessibility of raw materials and inland markets; and the general inflationary spiral. Raw materials from the interior are extremely difficult to obtain. For example, Tientsin's cotton textile industry—the city's major modern manufacturing industry—normally relies almost completely on Hopeh cotton, but recently it has been forced to obtain 80 per cent of its requirements from abroad. Many other raw materials have been difficult to obtain either at home or abroad. The existing import quota and licensing system is supposed to give priority to capital goods and essential raw materials, but in practice the complicated mechanics of the system often hamper deliveries.

The most important industry operating in Tientsin at present is still cotton textile manufacturing; it is almost entirely government-owned. Of the nine mills in and around the city, the seven major ones were taken over by the government from the Japanese and are now a part of China Textile Industries, Inc., which is managed by the Ministry of Economics. Many other local industries are owned and managed by the National Resources Commission.

Private enterprise is hanging on, however, in some other important industries—chemicals (including soda ash, caustic soda, ammonium sulphate, and salt), rugs, and cement—but it is subject to continuous government pressure, regulation, and intervention. Even though there is talk of the government selling its textile plants to private business during the coming year, there are indications that perhaps government participation in business may increase rather than decrease. A top official in the biggest chemical company in Tientsin told me that the government has repeatedly tried to force its way into control of the company— and is still trying to do so. The omnipresence of the Central Government in the economy has made things extremely difficult for private enterprise since the end of the war.

The largest production increases in Tientsin during the past year have been in the cotton mills, which produced about 200,-000 bales of yarn and well over 4 million bolts of cloth in 1947. The government-owned mills increased production by 100 per cent over the previous year. But many of Tientsin's private industries have received serious setbacks. For example, in January of this year, twenty-one out of fifty-four soap factories temporarily suspended operations (ten of these subsequently closed down completely), while all thirty-six vegetable oil refineries in the city were forced to close their doors.

The failure of local industry to recover since the end of World War II has been particularly disappointing to Tientsin businessmen because the prospects for private business in the city seemed good immediately after the war. Businessmen believed that the industrial expansion resulting from Japanese investments offered new opportunities to Chinese business when the Japanese assets were taken over. The general opinion now, however, seems to be that much of what the Japanese built up has already been destroyed, to a large extent as a result of dismantling and disuse. One major example of this is the steel and metals industry built by the Japanese; it is now completely inoperative.

The present economic depression in Tientsin causes a good deal of hardship, but there are not many signs of unrest. It is particularly surprising that the labor scene is normally quiet. One reason for this is that the government is following a conscious policy of keeping wages high to placate labor. Another, as the Tientsin Garrison Commander frankly stated to me, is the fact that a constant and strict vigil is kept by both the military and police authorities for any indications of unrest or disloyalty among the working class; prompt action is taken when any such indications occur. Nevertheless, it is somewhat surprising that, even though Tientsin is almost surrounded by the Communists—they are 30 miles west of the city, 40 miles south, and 30 miles northeast—and contains one of the largest concentrations of industrial proletariat in China, its labor force seems to be almost free from Communist infiltration and influence. It is a striking example of at least one of the differences distinguishing the Chinese Communist Party from its counterparts in most Western countries, where the urban proletariat is often the basis of Communism's strength.

Although the working industrial labor force in Tientsin receives preferential treatment, there are large numbers of unemployed persons in the city. The population is constantly growing, from the influx of refugees, and has increased from 1.68 million to 1.8 million in the past year. Tientsin is now the most thickly populated city in China, according to Ministry of Interior figures, with a density of more than 23,000 per square mile. Everyone in the city suffers from the chronic inflationary spiral, which is ubiquitous in China today. Last month alone, the price of cotton cloth rose 89 per cent, and food prices increased 30 per cent. During the same one-month period, the black-market exchange rate for American dollars jumped 114 per cent, to over 500,000:1.

Unquestionably the most serious problem affecting the man in the street has been the food shortage. Not only is Tientsin cut off from most of its food-producing hinterland, but last year the local spring harvests in areas immediately around the city were 20 to 25 per cent below the previous year; good summer crops did not completely offset these losses. The main cause of the food shortage, however, has been the loss of agricultural areas to the Communists. Recent reports indicate that the current crop prospects in nearby Communist areas are extremely good.

During the past year, Tientsin's food shortage has become steadily more serious, and the local authorities have become increasingly alarmed. In March of last year, the Central Government suspended direct commercial purchases of wheat and flour from foreign markets, to conserve foreign exchange, and although it guaranteed that north China would be supplied with grain from the Yangtze Valley, shipments were not delivered during the latter part of the year. In June, the Communist capture of Tsanghsien, an important grain-collecting center south of Tientsin, cut off a major nearby source of supply. Grain supplies from

Inner Mongolia then began to fall off because of the local require-ments of the military forces there. By January of this year, the food situation was becoming dangerously critical.

Now, the *deus ex machina* that promises to save the situation is a four-month food-rationing plan, soon to be introduced, which is supported by the United States China Relief Mission. Al-though, according to the North China Regional Director of the Mission, the rationing is intended primarily to be a price-stabiliza-tion device rather than a direct relief measure, its effect will be to supplement the over-all food supplies in Tientsin and to pre-vent what otherwise might become a real food crisis. If the food problem is successfully met, Tientsin can probably expect, in the immediate future at least, continued internal stability and calm —which would be a marked contrast to the recent disorders re-ported from Shanghai.

A great many people, including Chinese Nationalist military officers in Tientsin with whom I have talked, believe that the Communists could take Tientsin if they were to concentrate their efforts on the job. But at the moment there is no important mili-tary activity around the city; the Communists are busy elsewhere. As in the other areas that I have visited in recent weeks, however, there is not much evidence that the Nationalists are thinking seriously in terms of offensives or counteroffensives. Last year, a 15-mile defense moat was dug around Tientsin, at an estimated cost of CNC $24 billion—raised by "voluntary" contributions from the Chinese Chamber of Commerce, local industries, and others—and about 300 brick and concrete pillboxes were built around the city's perimeter. These symbolize the prevailing de-fense mentality. The Tientsin Garrison Commander, General Ma Fa-wu, recently told me that he believes the Communists will leave Tientsin alone for some time to come because, as he put it, they are not qualified or ready to take over the city and administer it. This is the current belief, or at least the hope, of many others with whom I talked in Tientsin.

6

CLIQUE POLITICS

Nanking
May, 1948

"China's First National Assembly" opened in Nanking on March 29, and its sessions continued throughout the month of April. It provided a good many surprises for those who expected it to be nothing more than a colorless and meaningless "Kuomintang show," put on to impress naïve observers at home and abroad. But it was disappointing to those who believed, or hoped, that it might be able to make a thoroughly democratic beginning toward constitutional government in China.

The Chinese National Assembly is probably one of the largest representative bodies ever to meet in any country. Its theoretical membership is more than 3,000, and the actual number of delegates elected since last fall is somewhat more than 2,700. This huge group is a heterogeneous cross section of many elements in Chinese society. Although it is representative primarily of upper- and middle-class groups, many occupations, vocations, and professions, as well as cultural minority groups, are included.

When the first session convened on March 29, the Assembly Hall, crowded with delegates from all parts of China, presented a colorful spectacle. Twelve big klieg lights focused on the auditorium stage. At the rear was an enormous oil portrait of Sun Yat-sen, framed by an even larger national flag. A portrait of Chiang K'ai-shek hung on the edge of the auditorium balcony, and colorful flags of various sorts were draped throughout the hall. Surrounded by these ubiquitous symbols of Republican China, the delegates were equally colorful. They included Uighurs from Sinkiang wearing embroidered Muslim skull caps and high leather boots, Mongols in long native gowns with sash belts, and Tibetans in orange Lamaist robes. Many of these border-region representatives could not understand the official *kuo yü*, or Mandarin, the national language used in all the meetings, and they constantly had to ask companions for whispered translations.

Some of the "Han" Chinese had difficulty understanding the heavy provincial or local accents of a few delegates.

The language problem was not the major one, however; *kuo yü* is now almost universally known among literate Chinese. But in view of their varying backgrounds, the delegates certainly did not all "speak the same language" in other respects. Scholarly old men with magnificent white beards, modern businessmen in well-cut foreign clothes, beautiful young women, political bosses, party hacks, well-known modern intellectuals, earnest young men in "Sun Yat-sen uniforms," plump old women—all were jammed together in this strange social conglomeration. The roster included some of China's best-known leaders, including cabinet ministers, semi-independent warlords, and famous generals. One illiterate farmer-delegate looked as if he had come directly from spring plowing. The oldest delegate was eighty-six, the youngest twenty-three. Two were blind. The glamour girl of the Assembly was a beautiful Manchu descendant of the Imperial family, who was given the unofficial title of Miss Assembly and was greeted with whistling and cheering whenever she appeared on the stage.

The convocation of this colorful and impressive group did not arouse much nationwide enthusiasm or interest, however. During the course of the Assembly meetings, I passed through Peiping, Tientsin, and Chungking, and visited Nanking, and in none of these cities was there more than casual interest in the sessions in progress in the nation's capital. This lack of interest did not extend to the Assembly Hall itself, however. A great many of the delegates took themselves, their responsibilities, and their opportunities very seriously. The sessions were lively, and often tense. But the earnestness and good intentions of the majority of the delegates were constantly confronted with the double obstacle of apathy outside the Assembly and intervention by the well-organized Kuomintang machine within the Assembly.

For a group of such unwieldy size, the Assembly was extremely well run. Preparations for its meetings began in the fall of last year, even before the election of delegates. On November 21, the government appointed a Preparatory Committee, with Sun Fo as Chairman, to handle the problems of drawing up procedures and arranging for housing, food, and transportation for the multitude of delegates. When the opening date of the Assembly was postponed from December 25 to March 29, this committee was given ample time to prepare for the meetings. As a result, the delegates were well taken care of when they reached Nanking, and the Assembly was run with an organizational efficiency that was impressive. A fleet of shiny buses was assigned to delegates, hotels and public buildings were procured as Assembly hostels, and arrangements were made with local restaurants to serve delegates on a meal ticket basis. At the Assembly Hall itself, seating and other requirements were carefully prearranged; special gendarmes were assigned to the task of controlling traffic and guarding the auditorium; information services were established; provisions were made to print and distribute copies of all Assembly proceedings; tearooms and rest rooms were set up, and special facilities of all sorts made the hall an efficient, modern establishment.

The meetings themselves were run with scrupulous fairness and diligent regard for accepted parliamentary procedures. Delegates who wanted to speak had their say. Voting facilities were arranged so that complete secrecy of balloting was possible and the stuffing of ballot boxes was inconceivable. The Presidium, or Steering Committee, elected by the Assembly, rotated the chairman's position among its members, and no favoritism was shown to any person or group in Assembly proceedings.

Freedom of speech was exercised with gusto. This was one of the most interesting and encouraging aspects of the sessions. It surprised many people, and distressed others, when the self-assertiveness and independence of the delegates gathered momentum during the course of meetings. Before it was over, the Assembly had become an open forum on national affairs and a sounding board for public opinion. Once inhibitions had been destroyed, all kinds of discontent were publicly aired, and criticism of the government was quite open. Occasionally, the give and take within the Assembly almost led to pandemonium. The lack of dignity at such times would have been discouraging in a long-established representative body with firm traditions of democratic action, but in these meetings it was an encouraging sign, in a sense, of the eagerness with which many delegates insisted upon exercising freedom of speech, even at the expense of decorum. The near-riots, when groups of delegates arose and shouted heatedly at each other across the Assembly Hall, brought smoldering discontent and differences of opinion into the open. The dominant position of the Nationalist Party and Central Government leaders was never directly attacked, but many current problems and issues were raised and debated.

The free expression of opinion within the Assembly did not mean, however, that this was basically a democratic body, representative of its constituency of several hundred million people or free from outside interference and control. For such was far from the actual case. First of all, the election of delegates last winter encountered innumerable difficulties and obstacles—many of them inherent in the present general state of affairs in China—that prevented it from being a complete expression of popular will, in the sense that democratic elections theoretically should be. Under existing conditions in China, however, that was inevitable, even when good intentions were present. The Assembly was overwhelmingly Kuomintang in its composition, and minority groups were admitted on sufferance as a matter of Kuomintang policy—perhaps on the basis of a sincere desire to broaden the base of the government, perhaps to impress Chinese and foreign observers, or perhaps as a result of mixed motives. The inevitable one-party character of the Assembly was no more than could be expected.

An unexpected development took place before and during the Assembly sessions, however. A serious dispute developed over Assembly seats, and its "solution" cast a shadow over the meetings and threatened to make them a travesty on "the beginning of constitutional democracy in China." The origin of this dispute was a pre-election political deal made between the top Kuomintang executives and the leaders of the Young China and the Democratic Socialist parties, the two minority groups that had agreed to support the new constitution. The Kuomintang, anxious to have these small parties cooperate, to give the government at least the semblance of having a multiparty character under the new constitution, agreed to allot a certain number of seats to them by not proposing or backing Kuomintang candidates in certain districts. In this way, it was believed, a coalition government of sorts could be ensured. But the plan backfired. In the districts involved, many Kuomintang members ran for election without Party sanction and, on the basis of their own personal political resources, were successful in defeating minor-party candidates. The number of minor-party members elected, as a result, was far below the number promised in the pre-election agreement, and serious interparty and intraparty rifts developed. The minor parties complained bitterly, asserting that they had been double-crossed. They declared that the whole thing had been "purposely engineered," and they threatened to boycott the Assembly. This presented the Kuomintang leaders with a dilemma. They could either support the election results, and see their "coalition" crumble, or attempt to oust their own Party members who had been legitimately elected to the seats in question. They chose the latter alternative. More than 400 Kuomintang "independents" were involved.

At first, the Party asked these men to withdraw voluntarily and allow minor-party candidates to take over their seats. A few complied, but the majority adamantly refused. Then, all the power available to the Kuomintang was directed against the "rebels" to make them withdraw. They were threatened with expulsion from the Party, and Party leaders from Chiang down alternately pleaded with and thundered at them. A few more withdrew, but many were still firm in refusing to give up their "mandate from the people." Ten of the group went on a hunger strike. Finally, there was a sit-down strike in the Assembly Hall, on the night of March 28, which threatened to disrupt the opening session, until the "rebels" were forcibly removed a few hours before the meeting. When all these methods of pressure had failed to force the holdouts "voluntarily" to give up their seats, top Kuomintang officials saw to it that a group of "rebels" was refused certification as members of the Assembly. In this way, the "coalition" was preserved, and the Assembly opened as scheduled.

The dispute was significant as an indication that the Kuomintang machine today is not the omnipotent, monolithic political organization it is sometimes assumed to be. Although the top Party leaders finally did "solve" the dispute, by illegal fiat, this did not take place until after the dispute had highlighted divisions within the Party and indicated that the Party did not have absolute control over either the elections or the Party's membership. The fissures existing within the Party were to be dramatically highlighted again toward the end of the Assembly sessions, during the election of the Vice-President of China.

The initial Assembly meetings were devoted to organizational matters. Things moved rather slowly at first. There was considerable wrangling over procedural and organizational questions of minor importance. However, after a major dispute over the size of the Assembly Presidium was resolved by increasing the Presidium's membership from twenty-five to eighty-five, so that all important groups could be represented, the Presidium and Assembly officers were finally elected, and the first regular plenary session got under way on April 6.

The functions of the Assembly as outlined in the new Chinese constitution are very limited. It is not a legislative body; all legislative functions are assigned to the Legislative Yüan. The constitution states that the Assembly is to meet once every six years —except for extraordinary sessions—and has the right and duty to carry out four specific powers: (1) election of the President and the Vice-President of China, (2) recall of these two executive officers, (3) amendment of the constitution, and (4) ratification of constitutional amendments proposed by the Legislative Yüan. In short, according to the constitution, the Assembly is normally expected to act as an electoral college and do little else.

It soon became apparent, however, that the delegates to this first Assembly session did not think their functions should be so rigidly limited. From April 6 to April 8, during discussion of rules of procedure, there was heated debate finally resulting in the deletion of Article Seventeen of the rules, which stated that the scope of discussions had to be limited to the four powers enumerated in Article Twenty-seven of the constitution. A new article was adopted permitting the Assembly to request and hear administrative reports from government officials, make interpolations, formulate proposals, and discuss all important national affairs—before electing the nation's top executives. During the next few days there was feverish activity in the various government ministries in Nanking, by men who foresaw the possibility of being called to make a public accounting of their activities.

Chiang K'ai-shek made the first major report to the Assembly, on April 9. He expressed complete faith in the government's ability to defeat the Communists. "Nationalist China will not collapse in six months, in six years, or even sixty years," he said, and he blamed the fear of collapse on Communist propaganda and the predictions of foreign newspapermen and observers. But his account of the state of the nation was amazing. The gist of it was that "everything's fine and dandy." It contained more than a little sophistry. He claimed that China's currency, which continues to lose value at a rapid rate, still possesses better backing than before the war. His list of assets included all bullion in the Central Bank's vaults, foreign exchange held abroad, and industrial and commercial assets owned by the government. He failed to point out that none of these assets is available to provide convertible backing for the new paper money coming off of the printing presses every day. Chiang also claimed that the military situation is not serious. In explaining recent government withdrawals from several key points, he announced a strategy of concentrating military forces, instead of spreading them thinly, and he predicted that the Communists would be cleared from all areas south of the Yellow River within the next six months.

When a Honan delegate on the following day criticized Chiang's report as "inadequate," there was an uproar in the Assembly. After it had calmed down, the delegates decided it was time to call in important ministers to make further reports. General Pai Ch'ung-hsi, Minister of National Defense, was first. He was followed during the next few days by O. K. Yui, Minister of Finance; Ch'en Chi-t'ien, Minister of Economic Affairs; Yü Ta-wei, Minister of Communications, and Yü Fei-p'eng, Minister of Food. The ministers were questioned from the floor, and many economic and military questions were debated by the Assembly delegates.

The most serious discussions were not on the floor, however, but in committee rooms. Seven committees were established to consider problems and make proposals in the following areas: (1) constitutional amendments, (2) national defense, (3) foreign affairs, (4) education and culture, (5) economics, (6) social security, and (7) border regions. The organization of these committees was somewhat unusual, for each Assembly delegate could choose the one in which he wished to participate. The Committee on Constitutional Amendments was the largest (587 members) because the question of possible amendments aroused a great deal of interest. The Committee on Foreign Affairs was the smallest (45 members), but it was one of the most vocal. All committee meetings were open.

The issue of constitutional amendment was thoroughly debated. Although some delegates felt that the constitution should be given a chance to work before any changes were considered, there was considerable sentiment in favor of making a few changes immediately. Article Twenty-seven on the powers of the National Assembly, Article Fifty-seven on the relationship between the Executive and Legislative Yüan, and Article Sixty-three on the powers of the Legislative Yüan might have been amended if strong pressure from above had not discouraged it. Chiang and others appealed vigorously to the delegates to let the constitution stand. As a result, the question of constitutional amendment was temporarily dropped.

The net result of the committee work was a mass of hundreds of resolutions and recommendations. Because of the rush of time, these were passed by the plenary Assembly in a perfunctory manner, in some cases without a complete reading of the text; even after being passed, they had no binding force on the government. Nevertheless, they had some significance as expressions of popular sentiment. One called for the immediate liquidation of "wealthy families," and instructed the government to draw up specific measures toward this end within three months. Another called for an appeal to the United Nations if Russia continues to refuse to fulfill her obligations under the Sino-Soviet Treaty of 1945. The government was prodded on a number of sore points.

In one of its most significant actions, the Assembly on April 18 voted to grant the President extraordinary emergency powers for the duration of the "Communist suppression campaign." The validity of these "temporary constitutional provisions" is not altogether clear, but they were accepted without question, and in a sense they were natural and logical, in view of the seriousness of the civil-war situation. The measures passed give the President the power to act independently in emergency situations, but such acts may be modified or abrogated later by the Legislative Yüan, and either the Legislative Yüan or the President himself may terminate the period of these emergency powers. Then, on April 19, Chiang K'ai-shek was elected President of China.

Soon after the Assembly opened, Chiang without forewarning had shocked both the Assembly and the Kuomintang by announcing to an extraordinary session of the Central Executive Committee of the Kuomintang—which had met especially to select a candidate for the presidency—that he would not run for the job. The effect of his declaration was to mobilize universal support for him among all groups in the Assembly and virtually to eliminate any possibility of opposition. This may have been his deliberate intention. In any case, the way in which he was elected makes his position that of an "indispensable man" who was "drafted" for the job. Chü Cheng, a Kuomintang veteran who is President of the Judicial Yüan, also ran—to make it a race. His showing amounted to nothing more than token opposition, however, and the 2,430-to-269 vote was generally interpreted as a clear confirmation of Chiang's paramount position of personal leadership and prestige in Nationalist China. There is no one else at present who can compete for the number-one position.

The results of the presidential election were really a foregone conclusion, but the vice-presidential election was a genuine political struggle that was both tense and exciting, and it brought the Assembly to a dramatic climax. All the important national political cliques and groups mobilized their forces and threw them into the fray. Because the struggle was concentrated, in time and space, and because its progress was shown in recorded votes, it was an unusual opportunity to see the internal factions in the Kuomintang at work with, or against, each other.

After debate both in and out of the Assembly, the Kuomintang decided not to make an official party nomination for the vice-presidency. As a result, several members of the Kuomintang ran. Altogether, six candidates were nominated, by petition. The line-up was as follows:

1. Sun Fo—a Kuomintang member from Kwangtung—enjoys considerable prestige as the son of the founder of the Chinese Republic, Sun Yat-sen. Since 1933, he has been President of the Legislative Yüan. Normally, he is one of the lone wolves in Kuomintang politics and operates on the basis of his own friends, connections, and prestige. Formerly, he was considered to be a liberal, but at present he is regarded as a political opportunist by many. His original support in the Assembly came from Kwangtung delegates and Overseas Chinese, but then he received the backing of the powerful Kuomintang machine controlled by the so-called "CC Clique," under Ch'en Li-fu, Party Minister of Organization. Reportedly, this was because of the desire of the "CC Clique" to capture the presidency of the Legislative Yüan, which required giving Sun Fo another job in exchange. Sun Fo was the pre-election "best guess" of most informed observers, because of his backing by the machine.

2. Yü Yu-jen—a venerable Kuomintang member from Shensi —is a white-bearded scholar and noted calligrapher who is President of the Control Yüan. He also was reported to have the backing of the "CC Clique." This was said to be a maneuver by which the clique hoped to take away northern votes from General Li Tsung-jen.

3. General Li Tsung-jen—a Kuomintang member from Kwangsi—is well-known for his excellent military record, which included the 1938 Taierchuang victory over the Japanese, and a notable political career as joint leader, with General Pai Ch'ung-hsi (now Minister of National Defense), in a progressive, semiautonomous regime in Kwangsi. He has been the head of the President's Peiping Headquarters for the past two years. His backing in the Assembly included Kwangsi delegates, the Chinese Muslims of the northwest, and some other minority groups, largely because his friend and supporter Pai Ch'ung-hsi is the outstanding Muslim in the Central Government and a spokesman of sorts for minority groups. Support also came from many northerners whose backing he acquired during his tour of duty in Peiping. Despite his military background, Li is now considered to be a liberal and progressive leader—relatively speaking, at least—and in the weeks just before the Assembly he became a rallying point for liberal

elements within the Kuomintang, including an important group of Peiping professors. His relations with Chiang, although good in recent years, are somewhat uncertain in view of the fact that Li, together with Pai, was in open revolt against Nanking in the late 1920's and the mid-1930's. His election was actively opposed by the Kuomintang machine.

4. Hsü Fu-lin—a Democratic Socialist Party member, serving as party leader during the absence of Carson Chang—was prominent in the old Peking Government and for some years has been a State Counselor. A native of Kwangtung, he received the support of some southern delegates in the Assembly, in addition to the solid support of his own small party.

5. Ch'eng Ch'ien—a military man and Kuomintang member with a long but not too well-known history of work in the Party—is head of the President's Hankow Headquarters. His backing included Kuomintang and military friends, as well as many delegates from central China.

6. Mo Teh-hui—a "non-partisan" from Manchuria—at one time served as a sort of go-between, or liaison, between the semiautonomous Manchurian leader Chang Hsüeh-liang and the Central Government. His support in the Assembly consisted mainly of northeasterners.

The campaigning of these candidates was extensive and included dinners, teas, campaign speeches, posters, pictures, leaflets, sound trucks, and back-room deals. Sun Fo was most lavish in entertaining. Yü Yu-jen concentrated his efforts on inscribing personal scrolls and distributing them to delegates. Li Tsung-jen, aided by his vivacious wife and conscientious supporters, talked with hundreds of people, and, on the morning of the first balloting, he appeared on the steps of the Assembly Hall and shook the hands of almost all the delegates as they entered the building.

The voting and tabulation of results, which began on April 23, were slow and laborious, but they were dramatic. After the ballot boxes were opened, under the glare of spotlights, the name on each ballot was announced, and it was held up for all to see. The results were surprising right from the beginning. Li led the field, Yü Yu-jen made a poor showing, and Ch'eng Ch'ien obtained more votes than outside observers could explain. Li received 754 votes. Next were Sun Fo with 559 and Ch'eng Ch'ien with 552. The others—Yü Yu-jen (493), Mo Teh-hui (218), and Hsü Fu-lin (214)—were eliminated, according to the election procedure. The rules stated that if no candidate received an absolute ma-

jority of the total theoretical vote of the Assembly, only the top
three would be included on the next balloting. If no candidate received an absolute majority by the end of the third balloting,
only the top two would be included on the fourth balloting, and
then the person receiving the most votes would be elected.

Tension mounted as the election progressed, particularly after
the Kwangtung delegation, on the morning of April 23, left the
Assembly Hall immediately after voting and proceeded *en
masse* to smash the office and printing shop of the *National Salvation Daily*, which had printed attacks on Sun Fo. The second
balloting showed no change, however, in the position of the
leaders. Li received 1,163 votes, Sun 945, and Ch'eng 616. Fran-
tic last-minute political maneuvering took place.

Then, on April 25, an electrifying thing happened, throwing
the whole Assembly into confusion. Ch'eng Ch'ien withdrew
from the race, conceding defeat. Li then withdrew, asserting that
unfair methods were being used to intimidate delegates and prevent them from voting for him. Just to make things complete,
Sun Fo also withdrew. It was only after pleading by top Kuomintang officials, the Presidium of the Assembly, and many public
leaders, that Li Tsung-jen and the other candidates consented to
re-enter the race. When balloting was resumed on April 28, Li received 1,156 votes, Sun 1,040, and Ch'eng 515. Finally, on April
29th, Li Tsung-jen was elected Vice-President by a vote of 1,438
to Sun Fo's 1,295.

The election of the Vice-President assumed an importance all
out of proportion to the intrinsic significance of the job, which
is relatively minor unless the President dies. It became a major
political struggle in which rivalries within the Kuomintang came
into the open to an unusual degree and were fought out in a battle of ballots. The election of General Li Tsung-jen was a defeat
for the Party machine—and a victory for opposition forces within
the Party.

The grouping of relatively liberal elements around Li may be
significant for the future. Li is reported willing to listen to the
advice of the professors and others who have assisted him. When
the government administration is reorganized in the near future,
he may be able, therefore, to act as spokesman for certain opposition elements. However, the relations between Vice-President
Li and President Chiang are likely to be strained; it was reliably
reported that, during the election, Chiang personally ordered Li
not to run, and that he did so in defiance of his chief. In any
case, Li will be a man to watch in the future.

7

PRESSURES ON LABOR

Shanghai
October, 1948

Economic pressures on laboring groups in Shanghai are rapidly creating a situation of serious tension in this confused, hectic city. If these pressures are not relieved, labor unrest will grow, and the situation may soon become explosive.

"The present economic crisis in Shanghai is the worst I have seen in my forty years here," a local manufacturer said to me this week. His opinion is not an extreme one. Many people at all economic levels believe that the existing economic chaos is the worst within memory, and they look forward to the future with increasing apprehension.

The position of Shanghai's laboring force in this crisis becomes more unfavorable daily. All wages are now frozen at the level of August 15 of this year. Theoretically, all prices are also frozen, at the August 19 level, but actually, despite energetic attempts at control, black markets have reappeared and the prices of commodities are gradually climbing. Furthermore, many goods have disappeared from shop counters and cannot be found by the average purchaser. The flow of food and raw materials into the city from the interior has dropped to a fraction of normal. Farmers and other producers are either holding their goods, in anticipation of the collapse of price control, or selling them in places outside of Shanghai where official controls are less rigid. Existing stocks of commodities have been almost completely cleaned from the counters by panic-stricken buyers, for the recent conversion of gold, silver, and foreign currencies to the new monetary unit, the Gold Yüan (GY), flooded the market with idle capital which had few outlets. As confidence in the Gold Yüan evaporated, the average citizen frantically converted his money into commodities. Some of the remaining goods have gone underground, despite a vigorous crack-down against hoarders, because merchants are reluctant to sell all of their stocks at prices for which they cannot be replaced. Wages, however, have remained more rigidly frozen than most prices, because they are more easily controlled. As a result, the average working man not only finds it difficult to buy food and the other necessities that he requires, he also sees the real purchasing value of his wages dropping every day.

Unemployment and layoffs are increasing, mainly because manufacturers' stocks of raw materials are dwindling or have disappeared. Most factories continue some operations, but the future looks black because raw materials are becoming more scarce daily. Unemployment and idleness add to the laborers' difficulties. Last month, for example, roughly 10,000 of the estimated 85,000 textile workers in Shanghai lost over ten days of work due to curtailed production. There are no reliable estimates of the total number of unemployed in the city at present, but unofficial guesses vary from 100,000 to 300,000. If the inability of manufacturers to procure raw materials continues, the number of unemployed will increase rapidly in the near future, as shutdowns increase.

An additional element of instability is the enormous number of wretched refugees who have recently flooded the city. No one knows how many there are. Although a few have jammed into refugee camps, and large numbers are cared for by friends and relatives, the rest form a floating population of destitutes who sleep on doorsteps and in gutters. It is a mystery how they survive. In June of this year, it was estimated that the influx of these refugees into Shanghai amounted to 6,000 daily. Guesses concerning the total number now in the city vary from half a million to a million. Needless to say, they add to the prevailing confusion and uneasiness.

The process of accelerated economic deterioration which has led to the present situation began less than two months ago. Ironically, it was the result of the first major attempt at economic and financial reform carried out by the Chinese Government since the end of the war.

On August 19 of this year, the Central Government dramatically announced the issuance of its new currency. The Gold Yüan, the government said, was backed by a 100 per cent reserve made up of gold, silver, foreign exchange, bonds and securities, and government-owned properties. All gold, silver, and foreign currency in private hands was called in for conversion to the new notes. Definite conversion and exchange rates were established: CNC $3 million to GY $1 for the old Chinese currency, and U.S. $1 to GY $4 for American dollars. A legal limit for Central Bank note issuance was set at GY $2 billion. Immediate registration of all foreign exchange assets held abroad was ordered. A program of financial reform designed to balance China's national budget and international balance of payments was outlined. All prices and wages were frozen. Strikes, hoarding, speculation, and black marketeering were forbidden. And strict general economic controls were instituted.

The job of defending the Gold Yüan and enforcing the new controls in Shanghai fell to thirty-nine-year-old, Russian-educated Major General Chiang Ching-kuo, son of the Generalissimo. As head of the Shanghai Economic Supervisory Office (SESO), he immediately began cracking down on all violations of the new regulations. An expanded Economic Police Force started searching out black markets and combing Shanghai's warehouses for hoarded goods. Every effort was made to wipe out the "yellow ox gangs" engaged in speculative buying, and a "tiger hunt" was started against corrupt or illegal practices on the part of the "big shots." Numerous arrests were made; they included prominent and wealthy citizens—something almost unprecedented. A few executions were carried out with much publicity.

The methods used by Chiang have been described as "reform at pistol point." His energy, fearlessness, and honesty were admired by many, but it soon became apparent that his methods were antagonizing key groups whose cooperation was absolutely necessary for the success of such a program. Businessmen rebelled against his "stubbornness," and against the government's unwillingness to make much-needed adjustments in the regulations. Lack of discrimination on the part of the authorities meant that the crack-down hit legitimate as well as illegitimate business. It soon became apparent, also, that the program lacked the over-all planning that would have been necessary to ensure the success of such sweeping reforms. No provisions were made to establish adequate rationing of necessities, to ensure the continued flow of food and raw materials into the city, to absorb the idle capital created by the money conversion, or to carry out wage and price adjustments.

Initially, the public reacted enthusiastically to the reform measures, and the reforms actually worked for about a month. Then confidence cracked. In addition to the economic forces at work undermining the program, the Communist takeover of Tsinan— one of the major cities in north China—struck a telling blow at public confidence in the government's ability to survive. A downhill process then began, leading rapidly to the present situation where the entire economy of the city is on the verge of falling apart. Chiang Ching-kuo continues to hold the lid on the explosive situation—"at pistol point"—and discussions are in progress concerning the establishment of over-all rationing, the extension of economic controls to cover interior areas in a more effective way, steps to increase food and raw material supplies, and the adjustment of some price levels. But it is now difficult to say whether these steps, even if successfully carried out, can retrieve the situation. Some people believe that economic disintegration has already gone too far, and that now it is inevitable that the program of August 19 will collapse completely. There is not much optimism in any quarter that corrective measures can be completely successful at this stage.

In this situation, the leaders of organized labor in Shanghai still cling to the position that somehow labor's position must be improved without undermining the reform and control program as a whole. They are concentrating on pressing for immediate rationing of all necessities, and have refrained so far from demanding general wage adjustments or a return to the pre-August system of wages, which was based on a cost-of-living index. They fear that if the entire system of controls collapses, the result will be economic chaos; they are also alarmed that this might be the final blow to the Central Government, whose present position is shaky at best. Since many of the labor leaders in Shanghai have a semiofficial status, and almost all of them are unquestionably still pro–Central Government, these attitudes are understandable.

Shanghai's industrial labor force is the largest in China. According to H. Y. Shui, Chief Director of the Shanghai General Labor Union, it now totals about 800,000 men and women, of whom 547,000 are unionized. The organized union movement in the city includes 503 different unions, he says, and all of them are members of the officially sponsored organization that he heads.

Organized labor does not have a long history in China, but it undoubtedly is here to stay. It has become a force that cannot be, and is not, ignored. Chinese labor leaders themselves divide the history of the movement into several definite stages. The first halting steps toward organization were taken in the period just prior to 1922, when old-style mutual welfare societies and guilds were first converted into organizations resembling unions. Then a few real unions were set up, in modern industries. Slowly, as industrialism and nationalism developed between 1919 and 1922, the self-consciousness and urge to organize on the part of laborers increased also. Among the first to organize effectively were railway workers, miners, seamen, and mechanics.

The labor movement gained momentum in a spectacular way in 1922–23. The Communists, who spearheaded the organizing efforts at that time, established a China Labor Organization, the secretariat of which directed the widespread strike movement of 1922. Workers who returned from World War I Labor Corps experience in France and students who returned from a "work and study in France" project were prominent leaders. A wave of strikes took place. The most important were the Hong Kong seamen's strike and several railway strikes, the latter engineered for the most part by the Communist-led First Labor Congress, which met in May, 1922. Strikes also took place in Hankow, Changsha, Shanghai, and other industrial centers. Most of these—in fact, the whole labor movement at that time—were characterized by a strong antiforeignism.

From the repression of the Peking-Hankow railway strike, in early 1923, until the first part of 1925, the labor movement had to operate largely underground. Organizational activity continued, however, despite repeated attempts at suppression on the part of worried government officials, and on May 1, 1925, the Second Labor Congress met in Canton and formed an All-China Labor Federation. By this time the Kuomintang's interest in organizing and using labor groups had increased greatly, partly as a result of the Party's reorganization with Communist advice in 1924, and Kuomintang labor organizers soon became active alongside the Communists.

The following period was one of rapid development. A textile workers' strike in Shanghai in May, 1925, led to the May 30 incident, when mass demonstrations of workers and students against the British were accompanied by violence. This incident resulted in rising resentment and increased nationalism in many parts of the country; it also spurred further labor organizing activity. From then until 1927, the labor movement really merged with, and became an integral part of, the revolutionary tide that swept the Kuomintang into power in Nanking. In January, 1927, Hankow workers occupied the British Concession a day before the Nationalist armies took over. In March, 1927, a general strike was called in Shanghai, workers seized the police station, arsenal, and garrison, and a short-lived "people's government" was proclaimed. In effect, a worker's commune captured the city and turned it over to the approaching Nationalist troops.

The subsequent Kuomintang-Communist split, which took

place in April, 1927, again changed the labor picture radically. In the preceding period, both parties had been organizing labor, and they had used labor organizations for joint revolutionary purposes. After that date, the two parties competed for control of the labor movement. The Kuomintang held the better position, for it was in control of the major industrial cities where the urban proletariat was located. The Communists continued agitating among laborers, even though their influence and power among them declined. But after being forced into rural areas, they shifted their emphasis and concentrated upon agrarian reform and the mobilization of peasant support to a degree that has made them unique, in many respects, among Communist parties. They have never entirely given up underground activity among urban labor groups, however, and within their own territory they have pushed their own forms of organized labor wherever possible.

Since coming to power in 1927, the Kuomintang—apparently lacking confidence in the political reliability of labor groups and fearing Communist infiltration—has generally followed a policy of surveillance, supervision, and control of labor. During certain periods, it has suppressed some unions and concentrated on rooting out Communist elements. At other times, it has fostered the development of government-sponsored and government-supervised unionism. Often these two policies have been carried out simultaneously. The labor groups that have developed in Nationalist China during the past two decades cannot, therefore, be described as a completely "free" labor movement. Nevertheless, unionism and labor organizations have grown substantially in numerical importance and strength.

Today in Shanghai, it is difficult to make sweeping generalizations about existing labor unions and their leaders, because the unions are of many types, and they possess varying degrees of independence of action. On the one hand, there are groups —such as the postal and the telephone workers' unions—that have a fairly high degree of independence. Because their workers are both skilled and literate, and because their leaders are aware that they have a favorable bargaining position, unions such as these exercise a good deal of autonomy in making decisions and pursuing their own policies. The leaders of these unions, although all members of the Kuomintang, are actually elected by their union members and represent their interests. Other unions —such as the rickshaw pullers' and textile workers' unions—are led, in many plants, by men who are appointed directly by the Kuomintang headquarters and who often owe allegiance to the Party rather than to their union members. Between these extremes are unions that represent varying degrees of either independence or control. At the very bottom—particularly among the so-called "Pootung proletariat," made up of coolies, wharf workers, construction workers, and the like—the notorious secret society leader Tu Yüeh-sheng, who once was a dominant power among Shanghai labor, continues to wield considerable influence. Tu's power still extends into some other labor groups as well, but it does not seem to be the controlling force it once was.

The organizational structure of unions in Shanghai also varies. A few are branches of large national unions—railway workers, postmen, communications workers, seamen; the others are purely local organizations. Some are established on an "industrial," or vertical, basis and include all the workers in a large factory or industry. Others are organized on a craft basis; these craft unions are confined to single establishments and are not united into any over-all city-wide unions.

The rights and duties of labor unions in Nationalist China are defined by legislation such as the Labor Union Act of June 16, 1947. (The first Labor Union Act in Nationalist China was passed in 1929; it has been revised five times to date.) According to existing laws, the organization of unions in factories over a certain size is compulsory, and membership is also compulsory where such unions exist. In a city such as Shanghai, all unions must come under an officially sponsored General Labor Union. (The leadership of this union in Shanghai consists of fifty-one directors and twenty-five controllers elected by a general labor conference every two years. Seven standing directors, elected by the entire board of directors, meet every two weeks and conduct most of the union's important business.) This General Labor Union is "supervised" by the Shanghai Social Affairs Bureau (SAB), which in turn is supervised by the Ministry of Social Affairs in Nanking. Relations between the SAB and the General Labor Union are on "a close personal basis," according to both union and SAB leaders.

The system as it is set up is one in which the unions are susceptible to a large degree of control and interference by the government authorities. There are many features that make such unions seem strange to a person familiar with the labor movement in the United States or Western Europe. The leaders in many weaker unions, for example, are selected directly by the Kuomintang rather than by the rank and file of the union's membership. Actually, almost none of the union leaders is financially independent. According to existing laws and regulations, however, they continue to receive wages from their employers while engaged in union duties; when carrying out union activities, they are simply on "leave with pay" from their regular jobs. Union funds usually do not come from membership dues, but are obtained from a small "tax" that is levied on the basis of wages and salaries paid by the management of an enterprise and is then turned over to the unions. Legally, no strikes are allowed in labor disputes during a minimum cooling-off period, when conciliation methods of settlement are employed, and if the parties resort to mediation, then strikes are theoretically entirely forbidden. The SAB takes an active part in the negotiation of important agreements between labor and management, and it sits in on the settlement of major disputes.

However, not all labor unions are puppet organizations run by the SAB, by any means. A responsible local newspaper (city desk) editor states quite emphatically that in his opinion "nobody can really control the unions in Shanghai now." One Shanghai manufacturer asserts that the union in his factory "certainly isn't controlled by the government," and others agree with him. The situation actually seems to be one in which the degree of government control varies from nearly complete to almost none, in the cases of different unions.

The government seems to be extremely wary about the possibility of antagonizing labor, and this limits the extent to which control is attempted. A spokesman for the Shanghai SAB sums up present government policy toward labor as being aimed at "promoting labor-management cooperation." This is without doubt one of the SAB's objectives. But official policy also seems to include the following objectives as well: (a) to prevent the labor movement from getting too strong, by fractionalizing it and discouraging organization on a craft-wide or similar basis; (b) to exercise influence and, to the degree that is feasible, control over labor through officially sponsored general unions, such as the Shanghai General Labor Union; and (c) to pacify and satisfy labor by concessions and aid of various sorts.

Generally speaking, labor unions have been in a fairly good bargaining position in Shanghai. Vis-à-vis management, unions of skilled laborers have been in an excellent position because of the scarcity of skilled workers in China, and some of the other unions have been able to fall back on government support in dealing with their employers. In a vague but nevertheless real way, the influence of unions is also bolstered by the simple fact that tremendous numbers of people are directly or indirectly involved in them. One foreign observer estimates that union members, together with their families, dependents, and hangers-on, altogether include almost half of the total population in Shanghai. The sheer size of the labor movement makes some people in Shanghai apprehensive about it.

In recent years, labor has used its bargaining power to good advantage. Working conditions have improved considerably by comparison with before the war—at least until the start of the current trend toward economic deterioration. A survey made by the SAB indicates, for example, that average real wages among industrial laborers increased 3.15 times between 1936 and 1946. Some persons question the reliability of this particular figure, but all statistical studies indicate that a definite rise in real wages has taken place. Working hours are still long, but the above-mentioned SAB survey claims that the average number of hours worked per day declined from 10.57 to 9.94 between 1936 and 1946. Child labor has been virtually eliminated from modern factories, even though it persists, together with the apprentice system, in many handicraft industries. Female labor is almost as important as before the war, however, amounting at present to roughly one-half of the total industrial labor force. But women laborers do not generally work under the old "sweatshop" conditions, and wage discrimination against women has decreased, although it has not been eliminated. The contract system of hiring workers is much less common than previously; at present, it is found mainly where common, unskilled labor is required.

As mentioned already, until recently the government has tried to pacify and satisfy labor by granting concessions of various sorts. One of the most important of these has been in the field of wage policy—and it is the recent shift in wage policy that has hit labor hardest during the past two months.

For a short period after the war, it was touch-and-go whether control of Shanghai would be in the hands of the Communists or the Central Government. Communist military forces stood by outside the city while Communist leaders, including labor leaders, were working hard to expand their influence within. The allegiance of labor at that time was doubtful, since both the Communists and the Central Government had carried on underground work in Shanghai during the war. In that uncertain postwar atmosphere, the Central Government made a strong bid for labor support by pegging wages to a cost-of-living (COL) index and setting base wages at a high level. Using a prewar base year, the SAB established the basic wage of unskilled laborers at a level comparable to the prewar wage of skilled laborers and scaled other wages upward accordingly. Pegging wages to a COL index, furthermore, protected workers partially against the inflationary spiral. This was a bold step, in many respects, and it undoubtedly was an important factor in satisfying labor groups at that time and obtaining their cooperation. Since then, trouble has resulted whenever the government has modified this policy. When it attempted to freeze wages for a few months in early 1947, serious labor disturbances took place, and the COL formula had to be restored. The abandonment of the formula again in August of this year has created a parallel situation, but one that is much more critical because many other disintegrating factors are at work.

Despite government concessions, labor unions have not been entirely docile. At various periods since the end of the war, disputes and strikes have been numerous. Many of the strikes have been "wildcat." Most have apparently been economic rather than political in their motivation. In by far the majority of cases recorded by the SAB, the issues have concerned wages, bonuses, and discharge pay. In a minority, however, political instigation has undoubtedly been a factor. The SAB says that the labor disorders in January and February of this year were stirred up by political agitators, and they may well have been. In January, 6,000 cabaret dancers mobbed the SAB headquarters, and in February, there was a strike in Sung Sing Cotton Mill No. 9 that resulted in at least three fatalities and was quelled only after armored cars and tear gas had been used. Even since the strike ban of August, a few wildcat strikes have taken place, but all of them have been handled warily and with moderation by the authorities. There are other indications as well that labor is not entirely passive. For example, at the meeting in Nanking in April of this year which created a China Federation of Labor on a nationwide basis, labor leaders showed a considerable degree of initiative and independence in discussing labor problems and criticizing government policies.

Today, one of the largest and most important question marks about the labor situation in Shanghai is the strength of the Communist underground. There is no overt Communist activity, because it is strictly forbidden; agents who are discovered are disposed of without much to-do, as would be expected. Nevertheless, there is no doubt that an underground does exist and is of some importance. Few people venture to estimate its exact strength, but the prevailing opinion seems to be that, while it is not a very significant element in the labor picture at this particular moment, it might become important in the event of serious trouble and disorders. The Communists claim that their links with labor groups throughout China are still strong. Lu Ting-yi, a leading Chinese Communist labor leader, claimed, in an article published in the Russian magazine *New Times* in June of this year, that during 1947 the Communists in Shanghai, Tientsin, Canton, and Hankow induced 1 million workers to take part in more than 3,000 separate strikes. That figure is doubtful, but the claim is significant.

Recently, there have been indications that the Communists may be planning to put increased emphasis on activities among urban labor groups, perhaps in anticipation of the time when they hope to take over China's industrial cities. In June of this year, a well-publicized "Sixth Plenary Session of the All-China Labor Congress" was held in Communist-held territory, in Harbin, and it claimed to represent 2.66 million organized workers and employees in both Nationalist and Communist territory. At the meeting, it was asserted that the Congress was the direct lineal descendant of the China Association of Labor, a nationwide labor welfare society that became defunct for all practical purposes when its leader, after disagreeing with Central Government labor policies following the war, fled China and then eventually made his way back to Communist territory. These straws in the wind suggest that it is highly possible the Chinese Communists will begin to re-emphasize the importance of labor unions, and the urban proletariat in general, if and when they start to take over the large cities where industrial workers are concentrated.

Although, in the present economic crisis in Shanghai, the leaders of organized labor have given full cooperation to the government, it is certain that their cooperation cannot last indefinitely if economic conditions continue on the present dizzy downward plunge. These leaders, whether semi-independent or strong supporters of the Kuomintang, have many ties and commitments to the present Central Government, and they certainly are not revolutionists. But neither are they willing to go the whole way along the road to collapse. Rumblings are already being heard and are growing louder. During the past week, prominent Kuomintang leaders have been making many speeches to union representatives, but such speeches will not stop the rumblings unless conditions improve. The general demoralization that seems to have gripped almost everyone in Shanghai has not bypassed the union members or leaders, and, if no improvement in the situation takes place, pressure from below can be expected to force many union leaders to take action expressing popular feelings and demands. If they are slow to respond to such pressures from below, an explosion may take place without their leadership.

The most critical element in the present crisis in Shanghai is the shortage of food. Stocks have been allowed to drop to a dangerously low point. Some high-placed officials now express fears that, even if remedial steps are taken immediately, they may not be able to prevent disorders and violence, since it will take time to put such steps into effect. If violence does take place, it will probably begin with disorganized rice riots. If it develops into organized action—which is possible, since unionization has trained the workers in collective action—the political implications would be extremely serious for the government. It seems safe to predict that, if events reach this stage, a rapid and widespread alienation of laboring groups in Shanghai would be probable, and the government might be faced once again with the specter of 1927.

It should be noted that the economic aspects of the crisis now facing Shanghai—and its labor groups—are primarily man-made. In Nationalist-held rural areas not far from the city, there are ample food supplies gathered during the recent harvest. The shortage of food, and of other commodities, within Shanghai has resulted from a reform program, one of the government's last cards, misplayed because of bad planning and bumbling. This fact has helped to create the near-complete demoralization of people of all sorts and the prevailing feeling of cynicism and despair. More people than ever before feel that the present Central Government is approaching the point of complete bankruptcy.

8

MINOR PARTIES IN OPPOSITION

Hong Kong
December, 1948

On May 1 of this year, the Chinese Communist Party issued a sweeping appeal for a broad united front against the Nationalists:

Laboring people of the entire country, unite; ally with the intelligentsia, liberal bourgeoisie, all democratic parties and groups, social luminaries and other patriotic elements; consolidate and expand the united front against imperialist, feudal, and bureaucratic capitalist forces; fight together to destroy Kuomintang reactionaries and build a new China. All democratic parties and groups, people's organizations, and social luminaries, speedily convene a Political Consultative Conference, discuss and carry out the convoking of a People's Representative Assembly to establish a Democratic Coalition Government!

This appeal struck a responsive chord among a small group of Chinese political refugees in voluntary exile on the island of Hong Kong. To these dissidents, joined in opposition to Chiang K'ai-shek, the Communist May Day appeal offered an alliance, and they accepted the offer. Their telegram to Mao Tse-tung, Chairman of the Communist Party, on May 5 proclaimed: "We herein express our response and support to your call, and hope by its realization to meet our national renaissance." The telegram was signed by leaders of the Kuomintang Revolutionary Committee (KMTRC), Democratic League, Peasants' and Workers' Democratic Party (PWDP), National Salvation Society (NSS), China Democratic Promotion Society (CDPS), San Min Chu I Comrades Association, Kuomintang Democratic Promotion Society (KMTDPS), and Chih Kung Tang.

The alliance of these splinter groups in Hong Kong with the Communist Party lifted the names of their leaders from relative obscurity to prominence in the seething rumor markets of present-day China. There was even one rumor, for example, that the top KMTRC leaders, Li Chi-shen and Feng Yü-hsiang (before his death), were slated to become the political and military chiefs, respectively, of a new Chinese government set up under the Communists, with Communist leaders Mao Tse-tung and Chu Teh in the number two positions.

At the moment, representatives from these Hong Kong groups, meeting with the Communists in Harbin, are helping to plan the Communist-sponsored Political Consultative Conference (PCC) that is scheduled for early next year—"probably in Peiping, if the military situation permits," Li Chi-shen told me recently—to prepare for a "People's Representative Assembly to establish a Democratic Coalition Government." The most prominent of these representatives are General Ts'ai T'ing-k'ai (of the KMTRC), Shen Chün-ju, and Chang Po-chün (leaders, respectively, of the NSS and PWDP, but both representing the Democratic League in Harbin). Pro-Communist "luminaries" of many sorts, including Madame Feng Yü-hsiang, have converged on Harbin as these meetings proceed, and more representatives from Hong Kong groups are now en route, probably by ship via North Korea.

Already most of China north of the Yangtze River is in the hands of Communist armies, and military observers are virtually unanimous in predicting that their victories will continue. It is believed, therefore, that the Communists will proceed, as they have promised, to set up a government that will possess effective control at least over most of north China and will claim to be *the* government of China. Peiping is the most likely capital, according to the best sources in Hong Kong. This step will bring about an important change in the over-all China situation. It will mean that the Communists have definitely emerged from the mountains and the plains. It will mark the beginning of their final efforts to establish, consolidate, and legalize their control over the country.

To date, there has been no single government over all Communist territory; centralized control has rested with the Party and the army. This is true even today. Government in Communist territory is localized and provisional, and the "Liberated Areas" (Northeast, Northwest, Central, and East China) are admittedly temporary. The first attempt to set up something more definite was the establishment of a North China People's Government on August 19 of this year, but even this government is only regional (it includes two former Border Regions, Shansi-Chahar-Hopeh and Shansi-Hopeh-Shantung-Honan). The job of establishing a unified government over all Communist territory is the job of the forthcoming PCC and the assembly that it convokes. The Hong Kong political groups already listed have been given the role of junior partners in this job, and it is reasonable to assume they will be rewarded with political posts in the new government. No one will admit that definite promises have been made, but secrecy is endemic in Chinese high-level politics.

It is probable, therefore, that some time next year press dispatches and other reports of developments in China will contain the names of many political parties, groups, and leaders in China that heretofore have been virtually unknown, even to many people within their own country.

Before describing each of these groups now operating in Hong Kong, a few generalizations can be made about them, for they have many similarities. To begin with, none is really a political party at the present time, although several aspire to be. They are merely small political groups, each with a few hundred to a few thousand members. Not one of them has a mass following or a strong political organization. And they do not possess armies —a prerequisite for political power in China during recent decades. In short, they have none of the obvious qualifications for successful independent action in the rough and tumble of contemporary Chinese politics. In terms of tangible power, they cannot make a showing.

All the Hong Kong groups call themselves "liberals," and often they are labeled simply as "Chinese democratic groups." Without doubt, some of them can rightly claim to be liberals (although the word is a difficult one to define), but others are definitely political opportunists. As far as some of their top leaders are concerned, it is difficult to discover basic points of difference distinguishing them from Central Government leaders, except that they are now on the opposite side of the fence in the civil war.

Intellectuals and professional politicians make up almost the entire membership of these groups. The small Peasants' and Workers' Democratic Party asserts that 50 per cent of its members belong to the laboring class, but this claim, even if true, has little significance, because the party's total membership is pocket-size. The most important groups do not even claim a proletarian following at present.

One point of complete agreement between all the groups is their uncompromising opposition to Chiang K'ai-shek, and this really is their *raison d'être*. Their hatred of Chiang has probably been more important than their love of either Marx or Mao in drawing them into alliance with the Communists. A great many of these people once were respectable members of the Kuomintang, and many held high positions under it, but all of them are now dissidents for either personal or ideological reasons.

Their public statements frequently have a strong ideological flavor, but actually their platforms are vague, and, at present anyway, ideology seems to be of secondary importance to many of them. In a general way they are all Leftist, according to their own definition and admission, but practically speaking this has simply meant that, except for a few independents, they have strung along with the Communist line during recent months. They themselves admit that now there are few ideological differences among them, and they all accept the present Communist program of "New Democracy."

The personal element, so strong in all Chinese politics, is fundamental to an understanding of these groups. The nucleus of leaders within each group consists of a few men united by past friendship and association, and the major groups are linked by similar ties.

The main dissident elements in Hong Kong fall into two main categories: the KMTRC and its affiliates, and the Democratic League and its affiliates.

For many years the Kuomintang has been divided into numerous cliques, held together by their acknowledgment of Chiang K'ai-shek's leadership. The origins of the Kuomintang Revolutionary Committee can be traced to the clique politics of the war years, and, in many respects, it is simply a clique that now opposes Chiang K'ai-shek's leadership.

In 1940, one group of party dissidents, including General Feng Yü-hsiang and Marshal Li Chi-shen, began to hold regular secret meetings in Chungking to discuss the current political situation. These men formulated a program for "organizational democracy within the party and constitutional democracy throughout the country." Another group of Kuomintang "liberals"—this term is simply a label in many cases, not necessarily an accurate description of political beliefs—in Hong Kong, including Madame Sun Yat-sen, Liu Ya-tzu, and Madame Liao Chung-k'ai, established contact with them. Together they formed the Society of Kuomintang Democratic Comrades. Their activities in south China were placed under an executive board in Kweilin, which eventually included Marshal Li, Madame Liao, and Liu Ya-tzu. But soon thereafter, the Japanese drive southward and the fall of Kweilin disrupted the organization.

In the spring of 1945, Marshal Li and General Ts'ai T'ing-k'ai set up another group in south China to lead anti-Japanese guerrilla activities. Organization of this group had political as well as military implications. In Chungking, meanwhile, still another group of party "progressives"—simply one more label—including some of those already mentioned, began to hold secret sessions. Participants in this group included Sun Fo, Feng Yü-hsiang, Yü Yu-jen, and Shao Li-tzu.

These were the seeds that sprouted after the war into more clearly defined political organizations—organizations that included some, but not all, of those who had met together secretly during the war. In Canton, Marshal Li and General Ts'ai organized the Kuomintang Democratic Promotion Society. Its supporters were mainly natives of Kwangtung and Kwangsi, and many were former members of the Nineteenth Route Army under Ts'ai. When Marshal Li left Canton a few months later, Ts'ai took over as leader of the KMTDPS. His principal associates were Li Chang-ta (onetime chief of staff to Sun Yat-sen), Ch'en Ts'u-sheng (former dean of Kwangsi University), Mei Kung-p'in, (law professor at Sun Yat-sen University), Ch'u Yün-shen, and General Chang Wen.

In October, 1945, a general conference of so-called "party progressives" was called in Chungking under the joint sponsorship of Ch'en Ming-shu (onetime Minister of Communications, later an active leader of the short-lived Foochow People's Government), General Yang Chieh (former Ambassador to Russia and President of the Army College), Wang K'un-lun, Hsü Pao-chü, T'an P'ing-shan, and a few others. The group attending this conference set up the San Min Chu I Comrades Association. T'an and Hsü became its most active leaders.

Finally, last year, these two groups were joined in close alliance under the leadership of Li Chi-shen. Marshal Li is an old-timer in Chinese politics. Born sixty-three years ago in Kwangsi, he became a prominent member of the Kuomintang when the Party was still struggling for power. He was taken into the Kuomintang Central Committee in the mid-1920's, and on the Northern Expedition in 1926–27 he was Commander of the Fourth Army and Chief of Staff to Chiang K'ai-shek. Since that time, he has been alternately in and out of the government, continuing to hold high posts until recently, although most of them have been posts with prestige rather than power. On October 10 of last year, Li issued a declaration calling for a congress of "all Kuomintang democratic groups," and, a month later, on November 12, the KMTRC was formed, with the KMTDPS and Comrades Association as affiliates.

From the beginning, the KMTRC has been anti-Chiang, and it now claims to be the true inheritor of "the revolutionary spirit of the Kuomintang" and the only faithful adherent to Sun Yat-sen's Three People's Principles. Its program has demanded cessation of the civil war, establishment of a coalition government with the Communists, and termination of all foreign intervention in China. At present, the leaders of the KMTRC also place considerable emphasis upon what are called Sun Yat-sen's Three Great Policies: (1) cooperating with the Communist Party, (2) maintaining friendly relations with the U.S.S.R., and (3) laying the party's foundation on workers' and peasants' support.

The primary basis for the establishment of the KMTRC, as revealed by its history and composition, was the personal relationships between its members. More than anything else, it is a club of old friends who are political "outs." This fact is most clearly illustrated, perhaps, by the number of its members and leaders who participated in the 1933 Fukien revolt against Chiang, which established the ill-fated Foochow People's Government. Marshal Li and General Ts'ai were leaders of that revolt, and the Foochow People's Government included such men as Ch'en Ming-shu, Li Chang-ta, Mei Kung-p'in, and others who later tied their political careers to Li and his KMTRC—and indirectly to the Communist Party. It is interesting to recall also that the Foochow People's Government during its brief existence made a local truce with the Communists, whose base of operations in China at that time was in Kiangsi near the Fukien border.

The membership of the KMTRC and its affiliates is not revealed officially. Recently, however, one member of its Executive Committee told me unofficially that the Hong Kong membership is about 200—and most of its active membership is in Hong Kong. In short, the KMTRC is still primarily a political clique rather than a political party.

Despite its similarity to the KMTRC on some points, the Democratic League has a rather different character. It began as a union of several reformist, progressive groups, which met in Hong Kong on October 10, 1941, and formed the League of Democratic Political Organizations. From the start, liberal intellectuals have been predominant in the League's membership, and professors and scholars are more characteristic of the organization than militarists and politicians. The term "liberal" has more meaning when applied to the League, therefore, than when applied to the KMTRC.

In 1941, the main components of the League were the Third

Party, the National Socialist Party, the Youth Party, the Chih Chiao Group (Vocational Educationalists), the Hsiang Chien Group (Rural Reconstructionists), and a few leading nonpartisan individuals. At that time, as it has since, the League took a strong stand for civil liberties and democratization of the government.

Early in 1944, the present title was adopted because of the increasing number of persons who were joining the League as individuals. In October of that year, it held its first congress in Chungking, and a year later, in October, 1945, it adopted a program that is often described as similar to that of the British Labour Party. It participated in the postwar Political Consultative Conference in 1946, and its representatives played an important role in drawing up the conference's resolutions on political reform.

During the following year and a half, however, relations between the Democratic League and the Nationalist Government deteriorated badly. Several League leaders were murdered under circumstances that suggested Kuomintang instigation. After the breakdown of the postwar Kuomintang-Communist negotiations, when the resolutions of the PCC were shelved, the League placed the blame entirely on the Kuomintang. Suspicion and bitterness then increased on both sides, and the League gradually moved far into the anti-Kuomintang, pro-Communist camp. The final break was made by the government, which issued an order dissolving and banning the organization on October 28, 1947. The top League leaders—including Chang Lan, its chief, and Lo Lung-chi, its official spokesman—were placed under house arrest in Shanghai, where they remain today. Some lesser leaders slipped into Communist territory. Others moved to Hong Kong, and active leadership of the League passed to Chou Hsin-min, its general secretary, Shen Chün-ju, and Chang Po-chün.

Over the years since its founding in 1941, the Democratic League's component parts have changed. The Youth Party and the National Socialist Party (renamed Democratic Socialist Party) broke with it in late 1945 and 1946, respectively. Both joined the Kuomintang in the Central Government. The Chih Chiao and Hsiang Chien groups have faded into obscurity. The only organizations of any importance now associated with the League are the National Salvation Society, which joined in 1944–45, and the Peasants' and Workers' Democratic Party, formerly the Third Party. (In a formal sense, even these bodies no longer belong to the League, for in January of last year it was decided that membership would be limited to individuals rather than organizations.)

The Third Party is a group that was originally formed by Left-

Wing members of the Kuomintang soon after Chiang K'ai-shek's 1927 purge. Its principal founder, Teng Yen-ta, convened a congress of his supporters in Shanghai in September, 1930, which established the Provisional Action Committee of the Kuomintang. When Teng was executed about a year later, his group became active in instigating the 1933 Fukien revolt and creating the Foochow People's Government. One of the co-chairmen of the group, Ch'en Ming-shu, was a key leader in the Foochow Government. At a congress in Hankow in November, 1935, the title Kuomintang was dropped and a new name, Action Committee of China's National Liberation, was adopted. German-educated Chang Po-chün, who was a member of the Foochow Government and has headed the party since Teng's death, participated in the People's Political Council under the Central Government during the war, but soon thereafter the split between his party and the government became complete. The party finally changed its name to Peasants' and Workers' Democratic Party at a congress in Shanghai in January, 1946.

The present membership of the PWDP is estimated at approximately 6,000 persons, many of whom are sprinkled along the China coast from Kwangtung to Shanghai. The party's platform is vague, but is usually labeled "very Left," and its spokesmen use good Marxist jargon. The party leader, Chang Po-chün, has the reputation of being one of the most forceful personalities among the Hong Kong emigrés.

The National Salvation Society is even less of a political party, if possible, than most of the other Hong Kong groups. It came into existence before the Sino-Japanese War when about 300 intellectuals issued a patriotic appeal for resistance against Japan. In January, 1936, an organization advocating active anti-Japanese resistance was formed in Shanghai, and, in May of the same year, a national federation was organized. On November 22, 1936, the Nanking Government arrested seven members of the society—and created a *cause célèbre*. The trial of the seven attracted worldwide attention, but finally they were released just four days before the Marco Polo Bridge incident in 1937, which marked the start of major undeclared war between China and Japan. Once the fighting started, the society became inactive, and most of its leaders cooperated with the Central Government. It was revived late in the war, however, and under the leadership of Shen Chünju, a venerable political figure whose career started before the 1911 Revolution, it joined the Democratic League. Its present membership is insignificant and its politics vague, but the inclinations of its leaders, like those of the PWDP, are said to be "well to the Left"—whatever that may mean.

The most important segment of the Democratic League's membership cannot be classified into definite groups. They are individuals and consider themselves independents and nonpartisans. Many well-meaning liberals belong to this category, for, before it was banned, the Democratic League probably had a wider appeal among nonparty, liberal intellectuals than any other organization in China. It still has many sympathizers among mainland intellectuals under Nationalist rule, even though it is in exile as an organization. League spokesmen state that at its peak the total membership was "over 100,000." They no longer estimate total membership, but they do assert that they have approximately 8,000 members in Hong Kong and Southeast Asia, plus a large underground membership in China.

Most leaders of the League in Hong Kong have gone along with the other dissidents in echoing the Communist line since the May alliance. A few, however, have maintained their individuality and continue to stand for independent action, moderate socialism, and non-Communist methods. They are a minority, but some people believe that the pliability of the majority is temporary and tactical and that the Democratic League's liberal tradition will assert itself in the future. This is possible but not inevitable.

Two other Hong Kong groups should be mentioned briefly. One is the Chinese Democratic Promotion Society, under the leadership of Ma Hsü-lun. This society was formed in Shanghai soon after the end of the war to protest against government inefficiency. It consisted merely of a small group of scholars, but its influence was an important factor behind the formation of the Shanghai Federation of People's Organizations, a loose alliance of 68 organizations claiming a combined membership of 400,000. The CDPS was vociferous in its opposition to the civil war and the Central Government, and a handful of its leaders was compelled to flee to Hong Kong. Since then, Ma Hsü-lun, despite the nebulous character of his support, has been taken into the Communist bosom as an ally.

The other group deserving mention is the Chih Kung Tang, political offshoot of the Hung Men Chih Kung Tang, a Chinese secret society. The roots of the latter are said to go back almost 400 years, and the society was apparently actively involved in the Taiping Rebellion. Later, it helped to finance the revolutionary efforts of Sun Yat-sen. Before the Sino-Japanese War, the society claimed to have approximately 800,000 members, most of them overseas—a large percentage of them in the United States—and its leaders liked to call themselves "Chinese Masons." The present leader of the Chih Kung Tang in Hong Kong, Ch'en Ch'i-yu, is an old follower of Sun Yat-sen and a new follower of the Democratic League. Little is known of the political activities of the group, but the significance of its response to the Communist May Day appeal is probably financial. Contributions from Overseas Chinese have supported revolutionary groups in China in the past, and, although it would be difficult to prove it, the Chih Kung Tang may be the channel for such support at present.

These are the major Hong Kong groups that have joined the Communists in their united front. They are the midgets who are now partners of the practical, hard-bitten Communist Party, which has fought its way to power and now has an army of more than 2 million men and a party membership, according to recent claims, approaching 3 million.

After examining these groups as they exist today, one is apt to be rather bewildered and to ask: "What's all the noise about? In a civil war between mammoths like the Kuomintang and the Communist Party for control of China, how can this handful of men have any importance at all?" There are people who would answer that the noise is about nothing. "The importance of these political groups," one Chinese newspaperman in Hong Kong recently said to me, "is an invention of foreign correspondents."

There are reasons to believe, however, that these small groups —particularly the KMTRC and the Democratic League—may play a political role of considerable significance in the immediate future, a role created for them by the complex factors at work in the China situation. The period China is entering will be one of tremendous adjustment and change. Civil war, social and economic revolution, power rivalries, personal struggles, and international conflicts all enter into the confused picture. As the situation changes, many persons and groups will find it imperative to make adjustments, reach compromises, and find their places in a new political, social, and economic setting, and, for many, these adjustments and compromises will not be easy. The KMTRC and the Democratic League may be in an excellent position to play the roles of political middlemen and to facilitate the adjustments that many individuals and groups will find necessary, expedient, or desirable to make.

Alliance with the Hong Kong groups has obvious advantages from the Communists' point of view. The idea of a coalition government is popular in China. Since the end of the Sino-Japanese

War, in fact, coalition has been almost synonymous with internal peace in the minds of many people, and the term "coalition" has taken its place among the most respected catchwords in China's current political vocabulary. A coalition requires several parties, and the Hong Kong groups are ready-made for the purpose. They bear the popular tags of democracy and liberalism, and their names can be useful in dressing up a Communist government for both internal and international consumption.

There is evidence to show also that the Communists really do want an economic and social coalition, in the sense that they want the cooperation, under their leadership, of as many economic and social groups as possible. That is why they have broadened their united front. The Hong Kong groups may be the bait by which the Communists hope to lure certain key groups in the country—the "intelligentsia," "liberal bourgeoisie," and "social luminaries"—in order to obtain their cooperation, or at least acquiescence, under a new regime. Communist statements and action during the past year show that they consider this to be a major task.

With the expansion of their territory, the Communists have found it necessary to get along, temporarily at least, with many nonproletarians, and, as they have captured an increasing number of cities, they have become increasingly aware of the economic importance of industrial and commercial groups. Today, the pronouncements from Party headquarters place foremost emphasis upon production—especially industrial production—and this new policy has necessitated compromises to gain the support of key economic groups.

The KMTRC and the Democratic League are political organizations that may help to bridge the gap between the Communists and the bourgeoisie. Both the KMTRC and the League draw their members from this class, both have good contacts with industrial and commercial leaders, and both claim that in the future they will enlarge and become real political parties "defending and representing the interests of the industrial and commercial classes." Although it is doubtful whether many Chinese merchants and industrialists will embrace Communism in the near future, even under a Communist regime, it is probable that most of them will try to get along under any regime. If the League and the KMTRC can provide them with the cloak of political respectability, and perhaps with a political mouthpiece as well, many may find it worth while to join or support these organizations. And from the Communist point of view, the KMTRC and the

League will be performing a great service if they minimize the resistance and obtain the cooperation of important economic groups and their leaders.

Possibly the KMTRC and the Democratic League may play a similar role in bridging the gap between the Communists and two other important groups in China: the intellectuals and ex-civil servants.

Undoubtedly, a fairly large number of intellectuals—professors, scholars, students, some professional men—can be expected to join the Communist Party, in the territory under its control, and to accept its credo with enthusiasm—as some already have done. Marxist influences have figured strongly in the general atmosphere in which the Chinese intellectuals, particularly those connected with education, have lived and worked during the past twenty years. Even the most conservative intellectuals, in fact, believe that mild socialism of some sort is desirable for China. Nevertheless, many will not be willing to go the whole way with the Communists. The civil-rights issue may be an important point of difference between them and the Communists. The Democratic League will have a special appeal to these men (and women) and may gather them into its fold.

The second group is the large mass of government officials and civil servants, almost all of them Kuomintang members, who have not been involved in high-level politics. The Communists have promised "war crimes trials" after they set up a government, but have limited the definition of "criminals" so as to exclude the large mass of the Kuomintang's membership. It should be remembered that active participation in government administration has been limited to only a few in China. Political reasons are not the only explanation; there are only a few who possess the required skills. Until they have consolidated their position, therefore, the Communists can ill-afford to exclude from government the largest single group of people in China with administrative experience—namely, the membership of the Kuomintang. There are indications that the Communists will attempt to absorb these people into any regime they establish. For many, however, a direct jump from the Kuomintang to the Communists would be a violent transition. The KMTRC will have a special appeal to these men. The KMTRC, as already noted, claims to be the "true" Kuomintang, and if Kuomintang members find themselves under a Communist regime, many may suddenly decide that the KMTRC's claims are valid. This may apply not only to unimportant Party members, but to numerous well-known officials

and Party leaders who are not regarded as part of the so-called
"Right-Wing" of the Party. It is significant that, during the past
few months, many unofficial representatives of high Kuomintang
officials have surreptitiously visited Hong Kong for secret conversations with Marshal Li and others. At present, Marshal Li's
public stand regarding these people is that they must make some
sort of symbolic break with the Central Government, before it
falls, if they want to join the KMTRC, but he may not follow his
own dictum too rigidly.

It is possible, therefore, that the Democratic League and the
KMTRC may be in a position to play important roles as middlemen in the political situation in China in months to come. It is
difficult at this stage, however, to predict whether they will be
able to fill these roles successfully.

9

COLLAPSE OF PUBLIC MORALE

Hong Kong
December, 1948

As the battle for central China nears a climax in the Hsuchow-Pengpu area, hysterical rumors and speculation pour out of the national capital. Contradictions and official denials make the news almost incomprehensible to the average reader, and Chinese distant from the centers of military and political activity must rely on guesswork to piece together a picture of what is happening to their government and their country in this national crisis.

One persistent rumor, persistently denied, claims that the Central Government is preparing to evacuate Nanking. Canton, Taiwan, Chungking, and Hengyang are mentioned as possible places of refuge for various branches of the government.

This rumor, and the obvious military threat to Nanking, has stimulated widespread discussion of what will happen if and when—and most people now believe it is a question of when rather than if—Nanking falls to the Communists. Will the Central Government attempt to move south as an intact unit? Will it attempt to reorganize and continue resistance to the Communists from new geographical bases? If the answer to these questions is affirmative, what are its chances of success?

At present, it appears that if the Nationalists decide to shift their capital and continue fighting, the decision will be made at the last minute, and the move will be a disorganized scramble for safety. I was in Canton last week and saw no evidence that careful preparations had been made, or were under way, to receive a large influx of government personnel. Reports of such preparations in other possible evacuation centers are conspicuously lacking in press dispatches. In Nanking, furthermore, government spokesmen continue to deny that any move is under consideration. These facts do not necessarily indicate that the government will not attempt to move. They do suggest, however, that if a move is made, it may be disorderly and uncoordinated.

The possibility of continuing military action against the Communists from a new Nationalist capital will depend in part upon the success with which public support can be mobilized and a spirit of resistance revived. In short, the general morale of people south of the Yangtze River will become a vital element in the political situation in China, if Nanking falls.

Recently, I completed a trip by train and car through the provinces of Kiangsu, Chekiang, Kiangsi, Hunan, and Kwangtung. Political demoralization in these areas is almost universal, and morale is incredibly low. Almost no spirit of resistance against the Communists remains, and faith in the Central Government seems to have vanished. I talked with people of many sorts— businessmen, educators, rickshaw coolies, civil servants, technicians, merchants. All were psychologically prepared for a basic shift of political control and a change of regime.

This low morale stems from numerous factors: the difficulty of ordinary living, a longing for peace and stability, and a growing mistrust of the Central Government, as well as the ominous reports from fighting fronts. Remarks such as "This can't go on" or "Any change will be for the better" are accompanied by solemn head-shaking and dour expressions. The people with whom I talked face the future, and the prospect of a Communist-dominated government, with emotions that mix resignation, relief, and apprehension in varying degrees.

The "mood of the people" is an intangible thing that cannot be described in neat formulas or measurable terms. In China, the difficulty of defining the political mood is magnified by the scarcity of media of public expression. Whatever its validity elsewhere, the concept of "public opinion" is not generally applicable in China because the majority of the population is politically inarticulate. Furthermore, millions of people without access to reliable information have no clear-cut opinions about national political events. They react emotionally to such stimuli as grapevine rumors, incomplete news, distorted reports—and the local price of rice. They feel, rather than understand, political trends. The people I met between Shanghai and Canton feel that the time is ripe for a major political change in China. Even those who fear change seem to accept its inevitability with helpless resignation.

The literate, politically conscious minority in Nationalist China tries to obtain accurate information on current events, but can seldom find it in newspapers or elsewhere. The government's indirect censorship of news, whatever its motives, has discredited both the press and the government itself. "When Central News announces that a city has been 'saved,' " a railway engineer said to me, "we suspect that it has been lost or is about to fall." Cynicism, based on bitter past experience, is widespread. Lack of information is equally widespread. "What is going on in north China?" a group of Changsha professors and doctors asked when I was there. They were eager to hear a firsthand report from someone who might have access to reliable information. They knew nothing of the Communists' capture of Mukden, which had taken place nine days previously.

Many Chinese do not believe anything their government says now. When Generalissimo Chiang admits that it will take eight years to defeat the Communists, people remember irresponsible statements of a short while ago promising victory in six months. An increasing number of people feel that the Central Government has deceived and cheated them. The collapse of the recent economic reform program, more than anything else perhaps, has created public distrust of new government policies. Many people now regard the reforms as a clever fraud, a device whereby one kind of paper money was substituted for another as a means of gathering in the gold, silver, and foreign currency savings of the public. The number of people who are willing to make excuses for government mistakes and failures is decreasing.

Among government officials themselves, old patterns of thinking and acting persist, and as the general situation deteriorates, the public is less tolerant of them. Self-delusion, rationalization, and wishful thinking among officials and others closely allied to the Nationalist regime have often prevented them from attacking problems honestly and solving them efficiently. In the present gloomy political atmosphere, their wishful thinking is fast disappearing, but self-delusion and rationalization continue in the face of disaster. One of the most characteristic manifestations of these tendencies is the search for scapegoats and the refusal to accept blame for political failures or even to recognize failures.

"There are two main causes for the present economic chaos in China," a young government worker said to me in Nanchang, capital of Kiangsi Province. "One is President Truman's refusal to recognize the new Chinese currency. The other is manipulation of the black market in large cities by Russian agents and traitors hired by them." This young man refused to believe that the Central Government's economic reform measures might have been poorly conceived and implemented. He supported his "facts" with unquestionable "proof." In a speech two days previously, the most prominent Kuomintang leader in Kiangsi had explained the whole situation. Ordinary people who are not connected with the Nationalist Government are much less gullible, however, and they are openly showing their disapproval of the lack of honesty and frankness on the part of officials and politicos.

Facts such as these help to explain the loss of faith in the Central Government. They also help to explain the increasing credibility of claims and reports favorable to the Communists. "The Communists treated the people well after they took Tsinan [capital of Shantung]," a businessman said to me. "In fact, conditions improved remarkably after they took over." A weary pilot, on the train between Hankow and Canton, described the low morale of the unit he had just left in north China. He contrasted it with Communist morale. "The Communists," he said in partial explanation, "take care of the families of their military men so that they don't have any personal worries." Statements such as these are made today by people who would have called them absurd propaganda a year ago.

I met very few people south of Nanking who would welcome the Nationalist Government with enthusiasm if it packs up and moves. The government's rear is psychologically weak and vulnerable. If an evacuation southward is made, the government will find itself in a region where people have already lost faith in the fight. It will encounter distrust. It may even encounter intense resentment and active opposition. With public morale at such low ebb, the job of mobilizing support and reviving a spirit of resistance against the Communists will be colossal—if it is possible at all.

PART II

STAGNATION:
NATIONALIST CHINA'S RURAL
HINTERLAND

THE STATUS QUO IN THE COUNTRYSIDE

Hsiehmahsiang (*Szechwan*)
June, 1948

The province of Szechwan lies in southwest China, encircled by high mountain ranges that define it as a geographical region as well as a political unit. In area, it is about the size of Sweden; its population exceeds that of France.

No other province in China contains so many people. It is currently estimated that between 45 and 48 million people are crowded into Szechwan, most of them in the lush Red Basin. This regional title was first used many years ago by the geographer Von Richtofen, and it is appropriately descriptive of the dull red color of the fertile soil, a color caused by the layer of sandstone underlying most of the region. In a sense, the term "basin" is misleading, however. Except for the Chengtu Plain, the province is almost entirely covered by hills and mountains. The tops of the hills are normally about 3,000 to 4,000 feet high, and squeezed between them are innumerable valleys that twist and turn with the contours of the topography. The term "basin" is correct, nevertheless, for the outer boundaries are formed by barrier ranges that rise much higher and cut off Szechwan from the rest of China. Through these mountains, a few passes lead from and into adjacent areas, but the traditional approach into the basin is through the awesome gorges that the Yangtze River carves on its eastward descent to the province of Hupeh.

Szechwan means "four rivers" in Chinese. The Yangtze, fifth longest river in the world, is the main artery of the system of waterways that drains much of the province. It is fed by a complicated network of tributaries, the most important of which are the Min, Kialing, and Lu. These rivers are the principal means of long-distance transport in the province, and, together with the streams that feed them, they are important also in irrigation.

Land transportation in Szechwan is primitive and undeveloped. Reputedly, before 1927 there was not a single wheeled vehicle in Chungking, the largest city in the province and its economic center. Today, principally as a result of wartime developments, there are approximately 4,000 miles of motor roads, but these are mostly constructed of simple crushed rock, and they connect only the most important population centers. There are five short railways, used to transport coal and iron, but the first projected passenger line, from Chungking to Chengtu, is not yet completed. Even the use of pack animals is not practical in much of the region, and transportation is still predominantly a function of strong human backs. Narrow, stone-paved paths are the highways of trade and commerce in areas not served by waterways. Steam navigation on the Yangtze and Kialing and modern airlines touching at Chungking and Chengtu have revolutionized transportation in and out of the province, but the effects of this revolution have been felt only by a few.

Although level land is scarce in Szechwan, the soil is rich, and water is abundant. Rainfall varies from 35 inches in the north to 45 in the south, and the temperate, moist climate is excellent for agriculture. The province has a garden-like appearance. Trees are numerous, particularly on hilly ground, and the landscape everywhere is predominantly green. Agriculture has been adapted remarkably to the nature of the terrain. Terraces cover much of the land and creep up steep hills; only when slopes exceed 45 degrees are they completely devoid of cultivation. Much of the land is irrigated, and most of it is fertilized. In some areas, there are two or three crops a year.

The most important crop, which more than anything else determines the characteristics of economic life in the region, is rice. This fact immediately identifies Szechwan as one subregion in a much larger area. Although the province has many unique characteristics, its rice culture is similar, in essentials, to that throughout southwest China and in most of central and south China.

Agriculturally, Szechwan is distinctive for the great variety of its products: "Everything that can be grown anywhere in the country can be grown here." The province is self-sufficient in farm output except for cotton, which, although grown in the north, has to be imported from provinces such as Hopeh and Shensi. Even a partial list of Szechwan's agricultural products is impressive: rice, wheat, corn, potatoes, apples, oranges, tangerines, pomelos, cherries, peaches, pears, persimmons, grapes, ginger, tobacco, sorghum, millet, buckwheat, beans, sugar cane, peanuts, mustard, opium, indigo, camphor, hemp, sesame, rape, vegetables, pigs, pig bristles, tea, silk, tung oil. The list could be extended. Some of these products are valuable exports. Tung oil, pig bristles, and silk are particularly important.

Mineral resources in the province are abundant. Coal deposits are widely distributed, and Szechwan is estimated to have 4 per cent of the currently known reserves of China Proper, a more significant figure than it might seem, in view of the concentration of China's coal deposits in Shansi and Shensi. Some iron exists in scattered deposits. Salt is abundant and has been produced for hundreds of years in the famous Tzeliutsing wells. Other important resources include antimony, mica, lead, asbestos, limestone, mercury, gypsum, graphite, copper, gold, cinnabar, copperas, zinc, silver, sulphur, saltpeter, and some natural gas and petroleum. Forests are dense in the southwest part of the province. and Szechwan's potentialities for hydroelectric development are excellent.

This richly endowed region, called by one enthusiastic writer the "Eden of the Flowery Republic," is overcrowded with people, however, and its population density has almost reached the maximum limits under existing conditions. A majority of the people living in Szechwan are of the same Chinese stock that predominates in most of south and central China. They are short, energetic, and hardy. In the western part of the province, however, there are aboriginal groups—including the Lolo, Miao, Hsifan, and Mantzu—that are non-Chinese racially. These tribes —some of which practice slavery, live by illicit cultivation of opium, and make periodic raids on nearby Chinese settlements —are largely isolated from the rest of the province, and they are not significant numerically. The majority of the people in Szechwan share with other Chinese the common cultural heritage— with its deep philosophical, historical, and linguistic roots—that has kept China together as a nation despite regional differentiation. In addition, however, they have a regional consciousness, developed through centuries of relative isolation, which distinguishes them as Szechwanese. They think of themselves as being both Szechwanese and Chinese.

Szechwan was not incorporated into the political structure of China Proper until the fourth and third centuries B.C. Prior to that time, it was distinct and apart, and received strong cultural influences from India as well as from China. But once the states of Pa and Shu, in the area which is now Szechwan, were conquered by the rulers of what is now north China, they became an important source of raw materials and agricultural products, which helped them unite the whole country. Since that time, Szechwan has been one of the most important provinces in China.

Because of its remoteness and isolation, however, Szechwan has often enjoyed what in fact has amounted to local autonomy, and separatism has been a recurring theme in its history. It was a theme that recurred at the time of the Chinese Revolution of 1911. At approximately the time when the October revolt began in Wuchang, and the weakened Manchu Empire quietly collapsed, revolt occurred in Szechwan, and order and authority there disintegrated. For several years, the province was split into tiny private regions controlled by military leaders who collected their own taxes, maintained their own armies, and alternately fought and made shaky alliances among themselves. Taxes were collected decades in advance. Personal fortunes rose and fell. And a general state of near-chaos and anarchy existed.

Finally, one of these military leaders, Liu Hsiang, emerged as the strongest of the group and set up a local state of his own. Prominent since the early 1920's, by the early 1930's Liu had firmly established his power and had defeated, made deals with, or adopted the most important of his competitors. Although he was no reformer, his military rule did at least reduce the confusion and chaos.

Then came the Sino-Japanese War, and modern history began to catch up with Szechwan. The fighting gradually forced the Nationalist Government back into China's interior. The first move was from Nanking to Hankow. Then, when the Japanese threatened central China, the government packed up and moved almost as far as it could go—to Szechwan. Prior to that time, although the forces and ideas of the West, which had been infiltrating China for many years, had affected the major cities of the southwest, they had barely penetrated into the mountain-surrounded rural areas of the region. But when the capital was moved to Chungking, a horde of technicians, bureaucrats, businessmen, and intelligentsia came with the government. They were catalytic agents who initiated a process of fermentation and change. Industries were set up; mines were sunk into unexploited resources; roads were constructed. Every effort was made to turn Szechwan into an arsenal and a base to support the war against Japan. For seven long years, the government of China held out in its Szechwan stronghold. The stay there began with high hope and deteriorated into cynical pessimism, but the government held out nevertheless.

Important political changes took place in Szechwan during that period. Some years previously, the Central Government had recognized the legitimacy of Liu Hsiang's regime, because it could do little else at the time. Now, however, the old-time localism could not be tolerated. When the Central Government was formulating its plans to move westward, Liu Hsiang died—conveniently. A new provincial regime that was little more than a branch of the Central Government was established, and Chang Ch'ün was made Governor. During these war years, Szechwan—for the first time since the Revolution of 1911—was really integrated into the political and administrative structure of Nationalist China.

Then the war ended. The migration that had brought millions of Chinese from all over the country to the west was reversed. Most of the migrants went home. The center of political and economic power shifted back to the lower Yangtze valley. Industries packed up and left. Szechwan again became a backwater; it slipped back into "the interior." People began to forget about the "tremendous potentialities of west China," and about the comparisons some had drawn between China's wartime migrations and the opening of the West in the United States. But the war had left a mark that could not be completely erased. Szechwan was now more definitely a part of China politically and administratively than it had been for many years. Also, some industries stayed on, particularly around Chungking, and formed a nucleus of arsenals, coal mines, flour mills, and cotton and wool factories that looked as if it might be permanent.

But, despite the integration of Szechwan into the administrative fabric of Nationalist China as a whole, some of the old political forces soon began to reappear in the province. The old names cropped up again. Three generals who had ranked just below Liu Hsiang in local politics were still going strong. Teng Hsi-hou became Governor of Szechwan. Liu Wen-hui was Governor of neighboring Sikang. P'an Wen-hua was the military commander of the important strategic area overlapping the border of Szechwan and Hupeh. Even though these were all Central Government appointments, they tended to restore the political *status quo ante*. In the provincial capital, Chengtu—which is the second largest city in the province and is often called "Little Peking" because it is the cultural center of the southwest—unsavory machinations began to take place, and rumblings of trouble were heard. Madame Liu Hsiang cornered the rice market. Teng Hsi-hou began to show favoritism to his relatives and the "old gang." The Central Government was not getting the taxes

it expected. Student demonstrations and rice riots took place
and were mishandled.

As China's civil war dragged on, however, the Central Government
began to remember Szechwan; it was still a major arsenal
and an important source of food supplies. The Nanking authorities
did not like some of the things going on in Chengtu. In
May of this year, they suddenly appointed a new Governor, Wang
Ling-chi. Wang also had been a Szechwan general in the
Liu Hsiang period, but he was considered more reliable than Teng
and more capable of stabilizing what was felt to be a deteriorating
situation. His job was to calm what looked like the beginning
of unrest and to keep the rice coming and the arsenals going.
Teng Hsi-hou retired temporarily to Shanghai "to rest," and Madame
Liu decided to sell some of her rice.

But despite these changes, Szechwan still seems remote and
isolated. Last month, a long Communist thrust from north Shensi
almost touched the border of the province, frightening some people,
but the Communists were defeated by the Nationalist troops
of Hu Tsung-nan and Ma Hung-k'uei. Captured Communist maps
indicate Party cells throughout the province, but even though
there are a few irregular units in the mountains that may be Communist,
no Communist activity of real importance has occurred
in Szechwan since the Long March swept through the province
in the middle 1930's. All in all, Szechwan is still one of the quietest
areas in China, despite a growing apprehension that the civil
war will eventually engulf the southwest.

This, then, is the general setting today for local government
and politics in China's most populous province. In structure,
Szechwan's governmental apparatus—organized according to
Central Government laws and regulations—can be considered
representative of local government throughout Nationalist China.
As might be expected, however, the content of local politics, as
distinguished from the formal framework of administration, is
greatly influenced by local conditions and traditions. But this is
true, to some degree, of local government everywhere in Nationalist
China. The rules are laid down by the Central Government,
but there are many local variations in the way the game is played.

Most analyses of government and politics in China start at
the top and concentrate on the Central Government. A more
realistic picture can be obtained, however, if one starts at the bottom
and examines how government and politics operate at the
level where they touch the vast masses of China's rural popula-

tion. What is the impact today, for example, of Nationalist rule on a farmer, a village, and a rural district in Szechwan?*

Lin Hsiu-ch'ing is one of the millions of farmers in Szechwan. He is a member of the First *Chia* of the Twentieth *Pao* of Hsiehmahsiang, which is a part of the Fourth *Ch'ü* of Pahsien, which belongs to the Third Administrative District of Szechwan Province. In short, he is the lowest common denominator in Chinese political life. There are millions like him throughout China. They are the *lao pai hsing*, the "old hundred names," the common people. Collectively, they form the base of China's agricultural society. Although the government authorities sometimes forget it, they are the base of China's government as well.

In the Chinese political hierarchy, Lin has a legal status distinct from his status as an individual. He is the head of his family, a fact that gives him a political title: Head of a *Hu*, or household. Until recently, the other members of his family were not expected —and, in fact, had no right—to participate in political activity as individuals. The family head spoke and acted for the entire family. The head of a family was largely responsible for the actions of his wife and children. As modern Chinese legal and political thought has developed in recent decades, under the influence of Western theory and practice, collective responsibility for the acts of family members has been discredited, but not actually eliminated; the hold of tradition is strong.

---

* For readers unfamiliar with the political and administrative hierarchy in rural China during the late 1940's, the following glossary of terms may be useful:

Hu—a household.

Chia—an administrative unit of approximately 10 *Hu*.

Pao—an administrative unit of approximately 10 *Chia*.

Hsiang—an administrative and "self-governing" village, containing several *Pao*.

Chen—an administrative unit, at the same level as the *Hsiang*, with an unusually large market village—containing 6 or more *Pao*—within its territory.

Ch'ü—an intermediary administrative unit, mainly for liaison purposes, between the *Hsiang* (and *Chen*) and the *Hsien*.

Hsien—an administrative district at the base of the centralized bureaucracy of China, under a magistrate appointed by the Provincial Government and approved by the Central Government. (China had approximately 2,000 *Hsien* in 1948.)

Chuan Yüan Ch'ü—an intermediary administrative unit between the *Hsien* and the provinces.

Province—the major administrative division of China. (In 1948, China had 35 provinces.)

The Western conception that the individual, rather than the family, is the basic political unit has already altered Lin's position somewhat in theory. In voting for representatives to the National Assembly and the Legislative Yüan, for example, all the adult members of his family can vote individually. The practical importance of this change is not great, however. For one thing, these two bodies are so remote that they are beyond the comprehension or understanding of Lin himself, to say nothing of his wife and family. They have no knowledge of the issues or the personalities involved at that level of government, and, unless prodded from above, they would prefer not to bother with the whole business of national elections. Even if this were not true, and if the members of Lin's family were intensely interested in casting their vote for the highest representative bodies in China, it is almost certain that the family would vote as a unit. By custom and tradition—which are more real, more immediate, and more important to Lin and his family than legislation and laws passed in faraway Nanking—Lin is the unquestioned head of his family.

The position of the family as the basic political unit has not even been challenged, moreover, in the organization of local government, and national laws recognize the family head as representative of the family in local affairs. The head of every household, including Lin, has the right and responsibility to elect the head of his *Chia* and to serve as a member of his *Pao* People's Assembly. The other members of his family do not participate, even if they are adults.

Lin's direct participation in local government goes no further than the *Pao* People's Assembly, however. Each higher level of government is chosen by the level immediately below it and has no direct connection with the electorate.

As head of his household, though, Lin is an important member of another organization, which in some respects is just as important in his life as the government. That organization is the family clan, an extended kinship group that includes all the families of the same name in the vicinity. The clan is more than a loose grouping based on kinship, which it tends to be, if it exists at all, in Western countries. It meets for joint worship of the clan's ancestors. It maintains ancestral graves, temples, and shrines. Sometimes it owns joint clan land. It is both a social-security group and a credit and borrowing organization. In addition, it maintains an informal system of intrafamily law and justice; the clan's leaders mediate disputes and use their prestige to keep members of the clan in line, to ensure their good behavior so that the family name will not be injured. The clan has no recognized status in the structure of organized government under existing national laws, but its influence upon clan members is considerable. This influence is especially strong among the "gentry," but it is also significant among some peasants, including those in Lin's area.

Perhaps Lin's most important role in Chinese society, however, is in the economic sphere. He is the head of one of the closely knit, well-integrated, basic production units that go to make up China's agricultural economy. Division of labor and specialization of function have not progressed very far in China, but they exist to a certain extent within Lin's family. Each member of the family has his or her functions, and together they form a cooperative, self-supporting production unit, with Lin as its director. They work as a definite unit, and the product of their labor goes to the head of the family and is distributed by him. Even if one of Lin's sons left the farm and went to work in the city, he probably would find it difficult to break away completely from this concept of collective economic effort on the part of the family; undoubtedly, part of his income, if he accumulated any surplus at all over and above subsistence requirements, would be remitted to the family on the farm.

Lin's family has been in the Hsiehmahsiang region continuously since it moved to Szechwan from central China about 300 years ago, at the end of the Ming Dynasty. According to local people, they were part of a large migration that came to take over land that had been almost depopulated by a notorious Szechwan bandit, Chang Hsien-chung. Lin himself was born fifty-seven years ago in the farmhouse where he now lives. Life has never been easy for him. He has had twelve children, seven of whom have died. Always a tenant farmer, he has never owned the house in which he was born. There has been very little change or improvement in his status during the past half-century, and he has very little to show materially for his years of labor. But he is quite proud of the fact that two of his children can read and write, for he himself never had any education and is completely illiterate. He is also proud of the fact that one of his sons is a member of the Ko Lao Hui, the Brothers' Society, which is very influential locally.

The land that Lin farms consists of several tiny, scattered slices of land squeezed between the plots that his neighbors farm. Altogether, he rents 26 tan of rice land. It is extremely difficult to translate local measures such as "tan." The complications one encounters are numerous. For example, in the region where Lin lives, the tan is not only a measure for grain, but is also a variable measure for land area, expressed in terms of the productivity of the land. In the case of Lin's farm, it represents the amount of land that, theoretically, will produce one "old tan" of unhusked rice. (Less frequently, it is used to indicate an amount of land that, theoretically, will produce a crop that, when divided according to the terms existing between landlord and tenant, will give the landlord one "old tan" of unhusked rice.) The "old tan," the measure commonly used in much of Szechwan, is three times a "new tan," or picul, (approximately 133 pounds), which is now an official measure prescribed by national law. As a rough estimate, however, the average tan of land in Lin's area is said to be about the same as a mou, or approximately one-sixth of an acre.

Although Lin's land is supposed to be capable of producing 26 tan of unhusked rice in a year, whether it does or not depends on many factors in addition to Lin's own labor and skill. Rice pests are common, particularly when there has been no snow or heavy frost the previous winter. Water is uncertain. Rainfall is abundant, but for rice cultivation it must come at the right time or there can be disastrous results. There are no adequate irrigation canals in Lin's region, so he depends on the rain. His fields must be flooded by the time his rice seedlings are ready for transplantation from their small plot into the main fields in early May, yet if there is too much rain immediately after transplantation, the crop may be injured. Depending as he does upon natural rather than on controlled irrigation, Lin produces only one major crop a year. He cannot take the risk of draining the water from his fields, and using them for other crops during the winter, as farmers with an assured water supply can. He must let the rice fields stand wet and idle through the winter, so that he will have the moisture he will need in the spring if the rains fail him.

Whether or not Lin's 26 tan of land actually produce 26 tan of rice, the terms of his tenancy require that he give over 15 tan to his landlord as rent sometime during the eighth month of the lunar calendar, after the harvesting: His rent is fixed at 60 per cent in kind of the theoretical productivity of his rice land. (The secondary crops that he grows on the rough ground adjacent to his rice fields are entirely his own, however.) Lin's rent is just about average for his vicinity. Three standards for sharing the crop are prevalent: 70–30, 60–40, and 50–50. The most that any tenant farmer in the region gets is 50 per cent of the crop, and in areas not far away some get as little as 20 per cent.

The fact is that Lin's land recently has produced about 24 tan of unhusked rice a year. This means that after paying his rent he usually has had 9 tan of unhusked rice, or perhaps 4.5 tan of edible rice, for himself and his family—in addition to the secondary crops he grows. This is far less than he needs. One person with a good appetite can eat almost a tan of rice in the course of a year, and there are seven in Lin's household. Consequently, even though he is a rice producer, he is also a rice buyer. But since rice is the main cash crop as well as the principal subsistence crop in the region, to be reasonably well off a farmer should have a rice surplus to sell for money to buy needed supplies of salt, sugar, vegetable oils, meat, tobacco, coal, fertilizers, and cloth. He also needs money to hire temporary labor during the busiest planting and harvesting periods—which almost all farmers, including tenants, in the area find it necessary to do. A combination of too little land and too high rent places a heavy burden, therefore, on Lin and his fellow tenants. Livelihood is marginal, and the problem of getting enough to eat is real and immediate.

Because his basic product, rice, is primarily a rent crop, Lin must rely heavily on the secondary crops grown on the high ground adjacent to the rice fields, the narrow ridges between the fields, and any scraps of land that cannot be used for rice cultivation. These crops, in his case, include small amounts of kaoliang (sorghum), corn, wheat, barley, soybeans, peppers, and miscellaneous vegetables. All that he can produce of these crops is consumed by his family.

The major source of the small amount of cash income that trickles into the family coffers every year is straw-hat weaving. Lin's wife and daughter, and the wives and daughters of virtually every other farmer in the region, make such hats. They are woven laboriously by hand from carefully cut and prepared wheat stalks, and are sold at the nearby market village, whence they go to other local markets all over the province. The hat-weaving home-industry is based on a well-developed local skill that is found in only a relatively small region. Special handicrafts such as this characterize the production of the various rural districts within the broader region to which Hsiehmahsiang belongs.

Lin's money income is not sufficient, however, to meet the minimum needs of his family, and currently he is in debt for CNC $10 million (U.S. $10–20 at present). Even though he borrowed this money from members of his clan, the interest rate now is 20 per cent a month.

Farming is backbreaking work for Lin and his sons. As many observers of Chinese rice cultivation have remarked, it is more like gardening than farming. There is an unexpressive but accurate term for it in economic phraseology—"labor-intensive." Land is scarce, and capital goods are prohibitively expensive—as well as difficult to utilize in rice cultivation—while labor is relatively plentiful and cheap. As a result, although land productivity is reasonably good, labor productivity is low. In human terms, all this means that Lin and his sons must work long and hard with very little mechanical help to extract a living from the soil. It means that they must spend hours and days sloshing knee-deep through the mud, plowing their fields; that they must carefully plant each rice stalk individually; that they must tread endlessly upon wooden water wheels to distribute water between their terraced fields, and that they must pick each weed and finally cut each ripe stalk by hand. Their capital equipment is primitive: a wooden grinding machine, a husking "wind cart," a plow, a few simple tools, a buffalo. They are particularly fortunate to have a buffalo; many tenants must rent theirs. In addition to his work, the buffalo contributes his share to the family's supply of organic manure.

The Lin family lives in a rambling house that belongs to their landlord and is located right next to his mansion. Their house is quite a big place, but they share it with another tenant family. In the central part of the house is a courtyard where most of the family works and relaxes when the weather is fair, and a ceremonial hall, containing a plaque dedicated to their ancestors. The animals—two pigs and several chickens, as well as the buffalo—live under the same roof, in a barnlike annex adjoining the kitchen. Except for the open court and the half-open ceremonial hall, the house is dark and gloomy. There are no exterior windows; the house is completely self-enclosed for protection against robbers. Several dogs, well trained to make plenty of noise when any stranger approaches, act as the family's burglar alarm. The main walls of the house are made of thick mud blocks, and the others are of simple bamboo laths covered with mud plaster. The roof is tiled—only the very poorest houses in the region have thatched roofs—and by local standards, the house is a good one. Although it is dark, dirty, and smelly, it is quite spacious and is well constructed.

Life for all the members of the Lin family involves hard work, and there is little to relieve its monotony. There is almost no organized recreation, and diversions are few. But the family members do get pleasure and enjoyment from little things. They enjoy the feathery bamboo trees clustered about their house and the mountains that surround their green valley. They enjoy their family life. They particularly enjoy going to the village on market days. Although they work hard, they are not downtrodden, and there is an impressive dignity about these people who live on and from the soil—even if they are tenant farmers.

The horizons of the Lin family are extremely limited, however, almost as limited as their topographical horizons which are defined by the mountains surrounding their valley. "One world" does not include the Lin family as informed and participating members. Lin himself made a trip to Chungking once, but that was a long way for him to go. He has never heard of Truman or Stalin. Although he is vaguely aware of the fact that a civil war is in progress in China, he has no clear idea of what it is all about; it seems a long way off. He says he has never heard of Mao Tse-tung, and Chiang K'ai-shek is just a name to him. He knows of the Kuomintang, but has never had any sort of contact with it himself. His knowledge and his interests are confined to his immediate surroundings, to the people he knows and to the problems he himself faces.

Although life is far from easy for him, he accepts it. There is a certain equilibrium between him and his environment, both physical and social, which apparently is quite stable. He is not agitating against tenancy, although he would like to own a plot of land. He is not indignant against the high rent he has to pay, although he would like to pay less, because that is just the way things are. He is conservative and accepts things as they are.

There is very little collective life to be shared with his neighbors—less than in north China, for in Lin's region farmers do not live in villages of the kind found in the north. Probably owing in part to the nature of the terrain and the type of agriculture that is prevalent, farmers' households are scattered throughout the farming region, rather than concentrated in villages. Usually, in the case of tenant farmers, two families live in one house, and occasionally half a dozen houses are clustered together in a group, but there are no real farming villages. The only villages are market villages, which serve as economic focal points for the scattered farmers.

Farmer Lin's house is one of a cluster of seven houses perched in a slow-curving arc around the base of a small, wooded hill.

These seven houses together form the First *Chia* of the Twentieth *Pao* in Hsiehmahsiang.

The *Pao-Chia* system of governmental administration has a long history in China. The practice of organizing rural households into small groups developed in local areas during the first millennium A.D. During the Han Dynasty, an empire-wide system was used in which ten *Li* formed one *T'ing*, and ten *T'ing* one *Hsiang*. Then, in the eleventh century, the *Pao-Chia* system was originated as a national system—with purely military functions— by the celebrated Chinese reformer Wang An-shih. At that time, administrative units were made up of 10, 50, and 500 families. Changes were made from time to time: During the Ch'ing, or Manchu, Dynasty, the units—now both administrative and military in function—were 10, 100, and 1,000 families, called *P'ai*, *Chia*, and *Pao*. The system does not have a continuous history, however. Under the Republic, it lapsed at first. Then, in 1932, Chiang K'ai-shek and his government revived it in certain areas, principally, it is said, because it was believed to be an efficient system for mobilizing the people militarily. At that time, however, all *Pao* and *Chia* officials, down to and including the lowest levels, were appointed from above. During the Sino-Japanese War, in 1939, steps were taken to convert the system into one of partial self-government. In that year, innovations were introduced that made all local government, up to and including the *Hsiang*, elective and representative. It took several years to put these changes into operation, but they are now in effect, in Hsiehmahsiang at least. The new Chinese constitution provides for extending self-government to the *Hsien* and Province, but practical steps toward that end will undoubtedly be slow and difficult.

Even though today the *Chia*, *Pao*, and *Hsiang* in the Hsiehmahsiang region are self-governing units in some respects, their form of organization, their functions, and their responsibilities are rigidly regulated from above, by national statutes supplemented by provincial regulations. Local practice does not always conform in detail to these laws and regulations, however, and what is most important is not how these units are defined by the statutes, but how they are organized and function in the local situation.

The First *Chia* of the Twentieth *Pao* of Hsiehmahsiang, to which farmer Lin belongs, is a representative *Chia* in this one area. It contains a total of fourteen *Hu*, or households, crowded into a small cluster of seven houses. Although it is more physically compact and concentrated than some other *Chia* in the region, it is fairly typical, nevertheless.

Two of the fourteen householders in the First *Chia* are land-lords; the other twelve are their tenants. This *Chia* is a micro-cosm, therefore, of the landlord-tenant relationships typical of the whole region. There is a sharp distinction between landlords and tenants in their manner of living. The tenants are the pro-ducers. The landlords do not produce; they live on rent and live a more leisurely and sophisticated life. A few bare facts about the people in the First *Chia* may help to clarify the great differences between landlords and tenants, and the relationships between these two groups.

One of the two landlords in the First *Chia* is a seventy-year-old gentleman who owns several hundred tan of land, some of it in the immediate vicinity of his house and some in other regions. He lives with his family and servants in a tremendous three-story brick mansion, known by local people simply as the "foreign house" because of its style of construction. (Some other landlords in the area have similar houses.) The mansion is large but not comfortable, and he uses only a part of it; it is, in fact, an excel-lent example of "conspicuous consumption." This old gentleman rents all of his land to tenants, and he lives on the rice income from rent. Being a landowner, he has to pay the land tax, which according to his figures amounts to a little over 20 per cent of the rice that he receives as rent. He inherited most of his land and has never been in debt or had financial trouble. When he was a boy, he was tutored in a "family school" for ten years and consequently is literate. He has traveled some, and, although he has never been out of Szechwan Province, he is considerably better informed about national affairs, in a general way, than are his tenants. His life is quiet. He reads, relaxes, and visits with his friends. He is a member of the local Brothers' Society, but he is not a member of the Kuomintang. Unlike some of his landlord friends, he does not participate actively in politics.

The other landlord in the *Chia* is a man of fifty-five who has less land and lives more modestly. He, too, inherited his land and does no farm work himself. He is educated, also having been tu-tored in a "family school," and has traveled a good deal in and out of Szechwan Province. Like the other landlord in the *Chia*, he belongs to the Brothers' Society, but not to the Kuomintang. However, he is active in politics and is now the *Pao* Representa-tive of the Twentieth *Pao* in the *Hsiang* People's Representative Assembly.

The twelve tenants in the *Chia* all rent their land from one of these two landlords. The amount of land they rent varies considerably, however. The largest amount is 28 tan, the smallest less than a tan. Actually, of the twelve tenants, only six rely primarily on farming for their livelihood. The other six, although farmers, have so little land that they depend principally on secondary occupations. One buys pig bristles, processes them, and resells them. One raises ducks. One makes kaoliang wine. One makes mosquito punk. The others depend primarily on wages for labor performed in nearby areas. All the families rely heavily on income from hat weaving.

The average household of these twelve tenants contains 5.5 persons, and they vary from three to twelve. None of the tenants has ever owned, bought, or sold any land. All but three of the twelve are in debt. Only four own their own buffaloes. One measure of their struggle for existence is the fact that the twelve families altogether have lost thirty-two children who died during childhood.

About half of the twelve family heads have had two or three years of schooling, but not all of these can be called literate. Only three can really read and write. One is a middle-school graduate, but he does almost no farming. His wife makes mosquito punk, and he works for wages; at one time, he even tried his hand at managing a restaurant in the village. None of the tenants has ever been out of Szechwan.

Although both of their landlords are members of the Brothers' Society, only four of the twelve tenants are members, and none of the tenants has ever held any political position above the level of the *Pao*. No one in the *Chia* belongs to or is interested in the Kuomintang.

These fourteen families, landlords and tenants, together form a political unit, a *Chia*, and occasionally they sit together in informal sessions called *Chia* Affairs Meetings. They elect a *Chia* Chief every two years, and he serves without salary. At present, this Chief is one of the tenant farmers, a man who is literate and belongs to the Brothers' Society, but who economically is one of the most hard-pressed men in the *Chia*. He is heavily in debt, and it is only by making kaoliang wine, in addition to farming, that he can keep the twelve members of his household fed.

The functions of the *Chia* Chief and the *Chia* Affairs Meetings are simple. They are to carry out orders that come from above, from their *Pao* Chief. Whenever instructions are passed down the line, the *Chia* Chief calls all the family heads together and explains what he has been told and what must be done. The *Chia* is organized to see that instructions reach the end of the line. All fourteen household heads are also, however, members of the *Pao* People's Assembly.

In the Twentieth *Pao* of Hsiehmahsiang, there are altogether 10 *Chia* containing a population of 854 persons. Hsiehmahsiang has 31 *Pao* of approximately the same size.

The Twentieth *Pao* is roughly a mile square, and it is a picturesque country spot. The tiny valleys are a bright yellow-green by the end of May, after the rice has been transplanted to the terraced fields, and low, rolling hills break the landscape into an irregular pattern. There are numerous clumps of trees and bamboos on the hillsides and along narrow streams that meander peacefully toward distant rivers. Narrow stone paths, just wide enough for a single person, wind through the paddy fields, connecting the scattered farmhouses and leading off to the market village not far away. By the side of these paths are small stone shrines containing carved figures of the earth gods painted in brilliant colors. Farmers in wide straw hats work in the fields, and there are a few slow, lumbering water buffaloes. It is quiet and peaceful.

Altogether, there are 149 households in the *Pao*. Two of these are small establishments that are the equivalent of an American general store, but the rest are the households of farmers or landlords. Most of the cultivable land is owned by the landlords, sixteen of whom live within the *Pao* and nineteen of whom (not included in the total) are absentee. Some of the latter live in nearby Chungking. The big landlords in Szechwan gravitate to two places, Chungking and Chengtu. In Chungking, some of them enter business and trade. In Chengtu, they exert a strong influence on the Provincial Government. They almost always keep on investing and reinvesting in land, not only because traditionally it is the most secure form of investment in China, but also because other outlets for investment are limited. The constant depreciation of money discourages any accumulation of fluid savings or capital. Within the past few months, this pattern has been shaken slightly, even though it has not yet basically changed. Apprehension about possible Communist takeover and ultimate expropriation of the land has forced land values down considerably. It is reported that some landlords in the Chengtu region are selling their land. But this is not taking place yet in Hsiehmahsiang.

Of the nonlandlord households in the Twentieth *Pao*, 92 are tenants, 36 are owners who cultivate their own land, 2 are owner-cultivators who rent some land out, and 1 is part owner and part tenant. In the whole *Pao*, there are 1,535 tan of rice land. Of this, 1,137 tan, or roughly 75 per cent, are farmed by full tenants. Only 398 tan are farmed by men who own all or part of their land. The total agricultural produce of all the cultivable land in the *Pao* amounted, in 1947, to 1,163 tan of rice, 80 tan of other grains, and some sweet potatoes, beans, and other minor crops. The farmers in the *Pao* also raised 203 pigs and wove 10,000 straw hats.

This region, organized politically as a *Pao*, is not a community in the real sense of that word. Its members do not form an integrated group. Lin's family is a closely knit organization; the First *Chia* (already described) is tied together by proximity and by the relations between the landlords and tenants living there (although this is not true of all *Chia*); and Hsiehmahsiang is a natural economic region centering on a market village. The Twentieth *Pao*, however, is merely an arbitrary administrative district demarcated on the basis of size and population. It is, nevertheless, a convenient intermediary between *Hsiang* and *Chia* that facilitates administration.

The characteristics of organized government begin to appear faintly at the *Pao* level. There is a *Pao* People's Assembly which is supposed to meet once every month, although sometimes the meetings are postponed during the busiest farming periods. Every household head is a voting member of this body. The most important function of the People's Assembly is the election of a *Pao* Chief and an Assistant Chief, both of whom serve two-year terms. The Chief is given a nominal salary (not enough to live on), but the Assistant Chief does not receive any remuneration.

The incumbent Chief of the Twentieth *Pao* is a relatively young man who was formerly a merchant but now owns 20 tan of land in the *Pao*. He is a graduate of primary school and is, therefore, literate. Normally, he works his own land, but his duties as *Pao* Chief now keep him so busy that he cannot farm himself, and he finds it necessary to hire laborers to do it for him. He is a very energetic young man, interested in his work and his responsibilities. He is a joiner. He belongs to both the Brothers' Society and the Red Gang, and he is one of the few members of the Kuomintang in Hsiehmahsiang.

The *Pao* Office in the Twentieth *Pao* is located in the Chief's home, but the Chief himself spends a good deal of his time making the rounds of the households in the *Pao*, going to and from the *Hsiang* Office, and chatting over a cup of tea in Hsiehmachang, the market village of Hsiehmahsiang. His job is to see that orders and instructions from the *Hsiang* Office are carried out. Sometimes this involves nothing more than calling his *Chia* chiefs together and passing the word along. Sometimes it involves more than that, and then decisions must be made on how orders from above are to be implemented. In these cases, the problem is usually presented to the *Pao* People's Assembly where a democratic decision is made by voting.

Two other officers work under the *Pao* Chief. They are nominated by him and appointed by the *Hsiang* Chief. Both are full-time jobs, and both officers receive a small salary. One is the Population Officer. His job is to keep track of all births, deaths, arrivals, and departures, and to submit regular population reports to the *Hsiang* Office. The other is the *Pao* Troop Commander, who is responsible for handling all orders and instructions on conscription and organizing self-defense units. In addition, the *Pao* is supposed to have an Economic Officer whose job is to assist in tax collection, but this post is unfilled in the Twentieth *Pao*.

The Troop Commander in the Twentieth *Pao* is in charge of a loosely organized squad of about ten men, which he sometimes calls his "Self-Defense Troops" and sometimes his "Volunteer Policemen." They are simply men within the *Pao* who possess their own guns. They receive no training and are inactive almost all the time, but theoretically they can provide local defense if it is required. Occasionally, they are called together to perform guard duties at the end of the year, when robbery increases because of the Chinese custom of paying off all debts at that time.

The financial expenses of the *Pao* are nominal. They consist only of the money necessary to buy paper, pens, ink, and incidental supplies necessary for the *Pao* officers to write reports and carry out their duties. The money required for these expenses is decided upon by the *Pao* People's Assembly, and is then collected from the Assembly's members. The salaries of the *Pao* officers, however, come from the *Hsiang* Office.

Another duty of the *Pao* People's Assembly is to assist the Troop Commander when a call for conscriptees arrives from higher authority. This comes in the form of an order that simply says that the *Pao* must provide a stated number of men between certain age limits. An order of this sort originates from the Central Government, but it is passed on down the line, quotas being constantly redivided on the basis of the population in lower administrative areas. When it reaches the *Pao*, however, it has reached rock bottom, and the men must be found somewhere.

Theoretically, the *Pao* Troop Commander handles a drawing of lots from the names of all the eligible men in the *Pao*. In practice, however, this is seldom done. The people in the *Pao*, through the Assembly, get together and "buy" conscriptees. This means that they pay men to go into the army to fill the *Pao* quota. Such men are usually "bought" in neighboring regions; the current price is CNC $10 million. The soldiers procured in this manner are usually the flotsam of society who cannot make a living and who go into the army out of desperation. This procedure is illegal, but the national laws regarding it are not enforced, and locally it is the accepted system of filling conscription quotas. Occasionally, the *Hsiang* will "buy" enough conscriptees to fill the whole *Hsiang* quota, thereby relieving its several *Pao* of the responsibility, but, whether it is done by the *Hsiang* or by the *Pao*, this system gives a clue to the type of raw material that is often provided for the Chinese Nationalist Army.

Apart from its functions of deciding how conscription quotas will be filled, how the *Pao* Office's expenses should be met, and how various orders and instructions from the *Hsiang* Office will be carried out, the *Pao* People's Assembly does not do very much. Its members can, of course, discuss common problems and occasionally do. But the Assembly is not expected to formulate and enforce policies of its own; in fact, it has no authority to do so.

The *Pao* Assembly has one link connecting it with higher authority and giving it a voice in *Hsiang* affairs. It elects a *Pao* Representative to the *Hsiang* People's Representative Assembly. The Representative for the Twentieth *Pao* is one of the landlords in the First *Chia*.

There are seventy-one *Hsiang* and *Chen* (one of which is a "Special District," but is no different from the others in essentials) in Pahsien. Each of these is an integrated economic region, the center of which is a market village. Occasionally a *Hsiang* or *Chen* contains two market villages, and in rare cases they have none, but these are exceptions. If the population of the market village itself is large enough to be organized into six or more *Pao*, the region is called a *Chen*. If the market village is not that large, the region is called a *Hsiang*. There are also distinctions drawn among various *Hsiang*, and they are classified in three grades on the basis of size and population. None of these distinctions is very important, however. All *Hsiang* and *Chen* are essentially similar, and have the same sort of governmental structure.

The *Hsiang* (or *Chen*) is labeled the highest level of local self-government in China today. This means that it is the highest level that selects its own local executive officers. In Hsiehmah-siang, for example, as in all other *Hsiang*, the *Hsiang* People's Representative Assembly, composed of representatives chosen by the *Pao* Assemblies, elects its own *Hsiang* Chief and Assistant Chief. Calling the *Hsiang* a self-governing body, however, should not obscure the fact that it is far from being completely independent. Although the *Hsiang* Chief and the Assembly manage some local affairs, they also receive orders from the *Hsien* Government, over which the local people have almost no control. The *Hsiang*, therefore, is really both a self-governing unit and an administrative subdivision of the *Hsien*.

Hsiehmahsiang is a *Hsiang* of the highest grade. This means that its market village, which contains slightly over 1,200 people organized into two *Pao*, is not large enough to be classified as a *Chen*, but nevertheless is considered to be one of the more important markets in the region. The village itself is called Hsieh-machang, which means "the market where the horse was rested." Local tradition, or perhaps myth, maintains that over 2,000 years ago, during the Three Kingdoms period, a famous general of the Kingdom of Shu, Chang Fei, rested his horse at the spot where the village temple now stands.

It may be justifiable to call Hsiehmachang a market town, but village really seems more appropriate in view of its size and layout. It is nothing more than one street, 5 or 6 yards wide. A few side alleys branch off from it, and some buildings have mushroomed around it in a confused and irregular pattern, but the life of the village centers on the one thoroughfare. Local people, as a matter of fact, do not go "to the village" or "to market"; they go "to the street."

This street stretches for a distance of between one-half and three-quarters of a mile. It is straight for the most part, but follows the gentle undulation of the terrain. The central part is covered over with a high roof, which makes it a dark and gloomy sort of arcade. Open shops line both sides of the street in this section. Stretching out from the center in both directions are shops which line only one side of the street. The width narrows as one goes away from the center, and at both ends the street—which is never much wider than an alley at its best—tapers imperceptibly into country paths and disappears into the rice fields.

This street and its immediate environs form the economic heart of the surrounding agricultural region. It is a heart that beats with a regular pulse. Each lunar month is divided into three ten-day periods, and every first, fourth, and seventh day is a market day.

Early in the morning on market days, the network of transportation arteries in the *Hsiang*—the serpentine stone-paved pathways —is filled with farmers and their families threading their way toward "the street." For a few hours, the temperature in the village rises. The street is a milling mass of people, jostling each other good-naturedly, passing on the latest gossip, catching up on the news, and buying and selling. Then, in the afternoon, they drift back to their homes, and the street is "cold" until the next market day. On "cold" days, shopkeepers and artisans work hard in preparation for the next market day, but the street itself is almost deserted. A few mangy dogs grub for scraps of food, scattered chickens and a pig or two wander aimlessly about, and the shopkeepers' wives nurse their babies on their doorsteps, but they do not disturb the dark, gloomy, dead atmosphere of the street.

The markets where farmers sell their produce are not actually on the main street itself, but are located in its immediate vicinity. There is a separate market place for each product. Pigs are sold under a huge tree at one edge of the village. Rice and other grains are sold on a small hill near one end of the main street. Straw hats are sold on the bank of a stream at the other end of the village. There are market places for poultry, for sugar cane, and in fact for almost everything that the local farmers produce, and buyers come from near and far to buy these products.

The street itself, however, is the place where farmers and their families buy. Many wandering salesmen come to the village to hawk their trinkets and gadgets. Market days in adjacent towns are held either on the second, fifth, and eighth, or on the third, sixth, and ninth days of each cycle. This synchronization is for the benefit of itinerant peddlers, city buyers, and the like. The main needs of the farmers, however, are met by the village shops whose sole purpose is to serve the population of the surrounding agricultural countryside. There is really no internal market for goods in the village; the village is an inseparable part of the agricultural countryside.

The village performs numerous functions. It is a market where farmers sell their surplus produce, a workshop where artisans make necessities required by the farmers, a place where merchants sell manufactured goods brought in from nearby cities, a gathering point for social intercourse, and the seat of local government.

There are 181 shops in Hsiehmachang. Among them are shops that make or sell food, wine, stationery, vegetable oils, candles, chinaware, herb medicines, salt, incense and other funeral supplies, coffins, pottery, metalware and tools, sauces, shoes, clothing, candy, gift scrolls, name seals, cigarettes and tobacco, tin kettles, bamboo utensils, trunks and boxes, rope, and wooden tools. There are small inns, blacksmith shops, butcher shops, pharmacies, and general stores.

Except for the few general stores, each shop specializes in one or two products. The degree of this specialization can be illustrated by the food and drink shops, which, incidentally, are more numerous than any other type of establishment. There are seventeen wine shops, seventeen tea houses, sixteen combined wine shop–restaurants, fifteen wineries, three noodle shops, two candy shops, two combined teahouse–general stores, two combined restaurant-inns, one sweet-drink shop, one combined wine-medicine shop, one combined restaurant–sweet-drink shop, one combined teahouse–soy-sauce shop, one combined teahouse–medicine shop, one combined teahouse-candlemaker, and one combined wine-tobacco shop.

Hsiehmahsiang is not entirely self-sufficient in basic necessities. Many supplies not provided either by the farmers themselves or by the handicraft shops in the village come from the mountains nearby. Coal, some iron, bamboo, plaster, coarse paper, and other materials are produced by workmen and artisans in the mountains. Other necessities must be brought in from outside the *Hsiang*, however. Although a limited amount of cloth is made in farmers' houses, it cannot really compete with machine-made cloth, which is bought in Chungking and elsewhere. Some building materials, such as wood, and some foodstuffs, such as tea, salt, sugar, and vegetable oils, also are imported from nearby regions. In addition, chinaware, "foreign goods," and miscellaneous manufactured products are imported from places both in and out of the province. The "foreign goods"—which are foreign-style goods, not imports from abroad—may come from such faraway places as Shanghai and Tientsin. The immediate source of most of these imports for Hsiehmachang is the nearby town of Peipei, located on the Kialing River. Peipei buys in Chungking, which is the commercial and industrial center of the whole region. Although a road connects Hsiehmachang with Chungking, not much trade travels this route. It is 40 miles by road to Chungking, and the water route, although longer and slower, is still cheaper.

There are two establishments in Hsiehmachang that might be called factories. Both are shops producing tung oil. These small, dingy workshops have a strangely medieval atmosphere. Almost no light relieves the gloom within the shops. On one side of a large room, the tung nuts are ground into a pulp by plodding, blindfolded oxen. On the other side, the oil is pressed out in primitive presses that operate on the wedge principle. A huge, metal-tipped hammer, perhaps 10 feet long, is suspended from the ceiling and is swung like a pendulum to batter metal wedges into the horizontal, box-like presses. Each blow of the hammer, accompanied by weird, musical cries on the part of the operator, strikes a wedge a fraction of an inch into the press and forces a few precious drops of oil to trickle into a vat below.

Hsiehmachang also has a post office, and last month, the first bank (a small one-room shop) in the village's history was opened by several wealthy men in the *Hsiang.* Not far away from the village street, there is also a health station, run by the *Hsien* Government but partially supported by the *Hsiang.*

The village is a social center as well as an economic one. There is a recreation club that meets every day to sing and play ancient Chinese operatic tunes, taught by an old-time teacher hired from a nearby village. The club members meet in a teahouse and take turns clanging the cymbals, beating the drums, and singing in falsetto voices. Participation in the club is limited, however, to the few who have the necessary leisure time and money. The principal recreation for the average farmer and his family takes place on market days. On these days, jugglers, storytellers, magicians, soothsayers, and fortunetellers stop at Hsiehmachang and perform for enraptured clusters of children and adults. There is an open-air opera stage, crumbling with age, in the center of the village, but it is idle most of the time. Once or twice a year, however, itinerant opera troupes perform there, and these are gala occasions.

The village of Hsiehmachang is within walking distance of all parts of the *Hsiang.* It is located approximately in the center, and the distance to the farthest point in any direction is about 10 li (or between 3 and 4 miles). It serves a population of more than 22,000 people, who belong to slightly more than 4,100 households. Of these, roughly 1,700 are tenant farmers, 200 are part-tenants, 400 are laborers, over 800 are owner-cultivators, 400 are landlords, and 600 are merchants, artisans, professional people, public servants, and so on.

The seat of the local government for this region is in the market village. Located on a hill, which is the highest point in the village and overlooks rice fields stretching in all directions, is the *Hsiang* Office. It is the most imposing building in the village and consists of an open central room, containing a conference table under the eye of the ubiquitous portrait of Sun Yat-sen, and side rooms that serve as offices. There is also a guardhouse at the gateway of a small courtyard in front of the building.

This is the official government house. Unofficially, however, much business is transacted in the teahouses on the village street. Two teahouses run by the Brothers' Society are the most important ones. There the leaders of the community spend endless hours discussing problems and chatting about everything in general and nothing in particular. The comfortable reclining chairs lining both walls of the teahouses are almost always filled. These teahouses are indispensable in the life of the *Hsiang*, and the "important people" can usually be found there, reclining in their bamboo chairs, teacup in hand.

In the social setting within which the Hsiehmahsiang Office functions, there are two groups of men who are extremely important. One of these groups is the organization called the Brothers' Society. The other is a loose conglomeration of wealthy, prominent citizens, the "gentlemen," or gentry.

The Brothers' Society (sometimes translated as either Elder Brothers' Society or Brothers' and Elders' Society) is a "secret society." There is nothing secret about it in Hsiehmahsiang, however. Everybody who is anybody belongs to it, and it operates quite openly. The fact that it is outlawed by the Central Government does not seem to bother anyone concerned, or, it might be added, deter anyone from becoming a member if he is invited. The origins of the society are rather obscure, but according to one theory it arose as an underground movement of anti-Manchu intellectuals at about the beginning of the Ch'ing Dynasty. It is said to have originated in east China and spread westward, but today it is probably more extensive and stronger in Szechwan than in any other part of the country. It was outlawed by the Manchus because it was an underground opposition group, and the Nationalist Government has also declared it illegal. It is not an active opposition group now, but it is a powerful organization which, the Kuomintang fears, could become a focus for opposition. However, in practice, men can belong to both the Brothers' Society and the Kuomintang simultaneously, and some do.

Ostensibly, the purpose of the Brothers' Society is to promote eight fundamental Confucian virtues: filial piety, love for one's brothers and sisters, loyalty to one's superiors, faithfulness, courtesy, shame, probity, and righteous self-sacrifice. Actually, it inevitably is an organization of considerable political significance. In the Chengtu Plain, for example, it is said that the society constantly interferes in high-level politics, and it is known more for its criminal activities than for its development of virtue. Bad elements have mixed with the good in many places and have given the society a reputation for gangsterism. The opium trade with the Lolos in west Szechwan, for example, is said to be a monopoly of the Brothers' Society.

In Hsiehmahsiang, however, the society does not operate directly in politics, and it is not labeled as an organization carrying on criminal activities. But it does have great political power. Almost all the people of wealth and education in the *Hsiang* are members, and the society has considerable control over its membership. Membership in the Brothers' Society is virtually the *sine qua non*, in fact, for participation in local government. At present, every officer in the *Hsiang* Office is a member, and probably the majority of *Pao* Chiefs are members as well. The few lone wolves in *Hsiang* politics who are not members of the society are exceptional, and even they must be on good terms with the society. The membership in Hsiehmahsiang includes some representatives of all economic classes, but it is heavily weighted in favor of upper-class and educated groups.

There are four different branches of the Brothers' Society in Hsiehmahsiang. Although they have different names, they subscribe to the same principles and cooperate closely. They are differentiated mainly on the basis of the type of persons accepted for membership. One concentrates on educational and political leaders, another on merchants, and so on. The most important politically is the Jen, or Benevolence, Society to which the majority of politically minded community leaders belong.

The territorial sphere of all the society's branches is the *Hsiang*. They have no organizational connection with the innumerable branches in other parts of the province, but they are informally connected, and members from other regions are welcomed and taken care of if they come to Hsiehmahsiang.

In Hsiehmahsiang, the Director of the local Benevolence Society is a landlord who possesses 200 tan of land. He is a man who has been prominent in governmental affairs in the past, but at present holds no official post. He and the other officers are chosen by the members of the society for an indefinite term. Although all members of the society are considered to be brothers, there are various ranks or grades that are conferred by the Director at the society's annual meetings. Two regular meetings are held every year, and all members are expected to attend. One, which is the principal business meeting, takes place on the thirteenth day of the fifth moon. The other, which is a social gathering, takes place at the Chinese New Year. Membership in the society theoretically is based only on the character of the applicant, but a person must be introduced by four members to be considered. The Benevolence Society in Hsiehmahsiang is estimated to have about 1,100 members.

In many respects, societies of this sort function as extralegal government. They settle disputes and sometimes try to discipline members. They provide mutual defense and social security. And they exert strong pressures on persons and groups outside of the society.

Although it is ostensibly a social rather than a political organization, the Brothers' Society is, in many respects, as important as the recognized government of the *Hsiang* in its control and management of local affairs, and it exerts strong influence on the recognized government.

There are also branches of two other secret societies of a similar character in Hsiehmahsiang: the Red Gang and the Green Gang. Although some members of the *Hsiang* Office belong to these organizations (a person may theoretically belong to the Brothers' Society, the Red Gang, and the Green Gang simultaneously, and a few persons do), they are comparatively small and relatively unimportant. The main strength of these societies is in the lower Yangtze valley region, not in Szechwan.

The other important group in Hsiehmahsiang is composed of local "gentlemen." These men, the current Chinese version of gentry, are not organized and do not form a completely cohesive group, but they are united by common interests and by friendship. Their prominence is due primarily to wealth; they are all landlords. Also, all of them are educated, mostly in old-style "family schools," but a few in modern middle schools and universities. They are all recognized leaders of the community.

One cannot define this group in Hsiehmahsiang exactly, because some men are on the fringes and may or may not be included, but there are at least twenty-one men who would indisputably be included by the local people. The land owned by these twenty-one men averages 135 tan; the largest holder in the group owns 500 tan and the smallest 30 tan. These gentlemen are persons of wealth, education, ability, culture, and leisure. Their opinions are consulted on all important problems. Apparently, in the final analysis, they are the ones who decide which men will be elected to posts in the local government. Their influence seems to be exercised primarily on the basis of leadership and prestige, however, rather than by open pressures or dictation, even though they are the ones in whose hands economic power is concentrated. Their opinions carry such weight that, if the word is passed around that they are in favor of this person or that action, most people go along with them. Quite naturally, they play leading roles in the various branches of the Brothers' Society. Often they participate directly in the local government, and only one of the twenty-one has never held a political post. Eight of them have, at some time, held the post of *Hsiang* Chief or Assistant Chief. Eleven are currently active in political positions. One is now *Hsiang* Chief; another is Assistant Chief. One is Chairman of the *Hsiang* People's Representative Assembly, and three others are members of the Assembly. One is *Hsiang* Representative in the *Hsien* Council. One is Chairman of the *Hsiang* Mediation Committee, and three others are members of that committee. In other words, either through direct participation or indirect influence, the few men play the leading roles in local government.

Trade and craft guilds, which play such important parts in urban centers in China, are almost completely absent in Hsiehmahsiang. There is one guild, to which the local pig butchers belong, but it is politically inactive.

The only political party in the *Hsiang* is the Kuomintang. It might be saying too much, however, even to call it moribund, for it is doubtful whether it ever had any life of influence in Hsiehmahsiang. Although there are about a hundred men in the *Hsiang*, including three who hold positions in the *Hsiang* Office, who have joined the party, the local branch of the Kuomintang exists on paper only. There have been no meetings, no collection of dues, in fact no activities of any sort in recent months (perhaps years), and the Secretary, who is titular head of the local branch, is a merchant who spends only a fraction of his time in the area.

Hsiehmahsiang, as previously mentioned, is considered to be a self-governing unit, and in some respects it is. Its representative body is called the *Hsiang* People's Representative Assembly and has a membership of thirty-one unsalaried representatives who serve a two-year term. These men are elected by the *Pao* Assemblies. Since the latter contain all the household heads in the *Hsiang*, one can say that, in a sense, the *Hsiang* Assembly is popularly elected. It meets regularly in the *Hsiang* Office, every three months, and it may hold extraordinary sessions.

The principal function of the Assembly members is to choose the important *Hsiang* officers. They elect the *Hsiang* Chief and an Assistant Chief, a representative to the *Hsien* Council, a Mediation Committee, and Property Custodian Committee. They can also recall these officers for corruption or incompetence. In addition, the Assembly draws up the *Hsiang* budget, but this document must be sent to the *Hsien* Government for approval before it can go into effect. The Assembly also hears reports from the officers it has elected and may, although it seldom does, make suggestions to them. If the Assembly formulates anything resembling a policy, it must obtain the *Hsien* Government's approval. If a dispute between the Assembly and the *Hsiang* officers whom it has elected results in a deadlock, the *Hsien* Government is requested to solve it, but this is a rare occurrence. The *Hsiang* Chief does not have to follow the Assembly's recommendations when they are "impractical," but if differences of opinion cannot be resolved by compromise, the *Hsien* is the ultimate arbiter. In practice, the Assembly does very little besides electing the officers already mentioned.

The Mediation Committee in the *Hsiang* Government is a five-man board (according to the regulations, there should be seven) responsible for administering justice. There is no court of law in the *Hsiang*. All disputes that can be handled locally are settled by this committee on the basis of equity. For example, if a man is accused of robbery, his neighbors escort him to the Mediation Committee, which hears both sides of the case, decides whether or not the man is guilty, and then proposes some sort of settlement that is accepted by all concerned. Crime is not a serious local problem, however. In the rare cases where a serious crime is committed, the man is sent to the Chungking Local Court for trial. Normally, he would be sent to the *Hsien* Local Court, but Pahsien has no court of its own and uses the one nearby in Chungking.

The Mediation Committee holds its sessions on market days, and at each session a minimum of three committee members must meet to handle the cases brought before them (they average two to six cases each market day). Decisions must have the concurrence of at least two committee members and the committee's chairman. If the disputes are trivial and informal, the meeting is held in a teahouse. If they are more serious and a formal written report is presented, then the session is held in the *Hsiang* Office. All the current committee members are old men who have the respect, and command the deference, of the entire community. Four of the five belong to the group of twenty-one gentlemen already mentioned. None of them receives any salary for serving on the committee.

The cases brought before the Mediation Committee in Hsieh-mahsiang include petty criminal cases such as stealing, commercial disputes, personal arguments, debt trouble, and landlord-tenant disputes. The disputes between landlords and tenants are particularly numerous and important. A local person who should know estimates that about 80 per cent of these disputes are decided in favor of the landlords. This does not necessarily mean, however, that there is gross discrimination against tenants; it may simply mean that the tenants are most often the ones who are forced by circumstances into the position of being unable to fulfill their contract obligations.

The Property Custodian Committee of the *Hsiang* Government is a seven-man, unsalaried board that is responsible for supervising the finances of the *Hsiang* Office and protecting the *Hsiang's* resources of money and grain. Taxes collected by the *Hsiang*, money and rice subsidies given by the *Hsien* Government, and rice left with the *Hsiang* for safekeeping by the *Hsien* Government are its responsibility. In short, it handles a sort of *Hsiang* treasury. The grain and money under its supervision are kept in a special room in the *Hsiang* Office, and the committee hires two special officers to guard it. No money or rice can be withdrawn without a special request form that bears the signature of the Chairman of the Property Custodian Committee as well as that of the *Hsiang* Chief. No withdrawals can be made legally, moreover, unless they are in accordance with general authorizations already made by the *Hsiang* Assembly.

The actual administration of the *Hsiang* is carried out by the *Hsiang* Chief and by a number of administrative officers who are nominated by him and formally appointed by the *Hsien* Government. All these administrative appointees are salaried officers on an indefinite term. Excluding the Chief and Assistant Chief, there are eight officers in the *Hsiang* Office. There are secretaries for civil affairs, population, economic affairs, and cultural affairs, and there is also a troop commander. In addition there are: an accountant, who keeps all financial records; a buyer, who acts as a sort of purchasing agent and also as a secretary for incoming and outgoing reports; and an assistant secretary, who is a general handy man, clerk, recording secretary, and assistant to the Chief. In Hsiehmahsiang, all these officers are graduates of middle school or the equivalent, but none is a college graduate. Some have made government service a profession, but others are landowners or merchants.

The Civil Affairs Secretary's primary responsibility is that of carrying out national or provincial laws and regulations concerning administrative organization and procedures. For example, he must see that the *Hsiang* Office and the *Pao* and *Chia* under it are organized as prescribed, and that personnel qualifications, salaries, and so on, are in accordance with the laws governing them. He handles elections, and sees that they are carried out at the proper time and in the proper manner. He is also general coordinator of all the work done by the various officers in the *Hsiang* Office. He is responsible, for example, for land administration—recording ownership of land, registering transfers, and so on—although the actual work is done by the Assistant Secretary. He is responsible for opium suppression (there is still some opium-smoking in Hsiehmahsiang, although much less than there used to be, and it is now secret and underground), although the Troop Commander carries out any suppressing which must be done. He is also responsible for administering "voluntary labor service."

"Voluntary labor service" refers euphemistically to a national system of compulsory labor service. According to the law, as explained by members of the *Hsien* Government, every able-bodied man must perform twenty days of "voluntary," unpaid labor for the government every year. Decisions on when and where such labor will be employed are usually made by the *Hsien* Government, although occasionally they are made at a higher level. Then, as in the case of military conscription, quotas are assigned to each *Hsiang* and passed on down the line to the *Pao* and *Chia*. As in the case of conscription, also, substitute workers are hired by those who can afford to do so. The average farmer, however, cannot afford to hire a substitute, and since the requirement is for a period of limited service, usually during slack periods in the farming calendar, he is not too unwilling to do the work. The laborers collected under this system may be used anywhere in the *Hsien*, and occasionally even in other *Hsien*. They travel on foot, carrying their own work tools, to the place where they have been instructed to go. They receive no pay. Theoretically, they must provide their own food, but in Pahsien food is provided for the workers, either by the *Hsien* Government or by contributions on the part of the other members of the *Chia* or *Pao* from which the workers come. Not everyone is required, in practice, to work or hire a substitute every year, even though everyone is theoretically liable. In slack years, the assigned quotas for laborers are well below those authorized by law.

The Civil Affairs Secretary is considered to be the topranking appointed officer in the *Hsiang* Office. Early this year, in fact, the

Szechwan Provincial Government ordered a reorganization of the *Hsiang* Offices, as a result of which the other secretaries would be clearly subordinate and responsible to the Civil Affairs Secretary, who would then have a new title—General Secretary—but this reorganization has not yet been carried out in Hsiehmahsiang.

The responsibility of the Population Secretary is simply to keep complete statistics on the population of the *Hsiang*. He makes regular reports to the *Hsien* Government.

The Cultural Affairs Secretary is in charge of *Hsiang* educational matters, and he must make regular reports to the *Hsien* Bureau of Education. His actual responsibility is limited by the fact that the principals of all public schools are appointed directly by the Bureau, and the principals themselves select their teachers. However, he does control a portion of their salaries; they receive their cash payments from the *Hsiang* and their rice ration from the *Hsien*. There are sixteen public schools in Hsiehmahsiang, all of them primary schools. Thirteen are *Pao* People's Schools, with a four-year curriculum, and three are so-called Central Schools, with a six-year curriculum. In theory, there is supposed to be a *Pao* People's School in each *Pao*, but it will probably be many years before that goal is reached. Nevertheless, Hsiehmahsiang is better off educationally than many nearby *Hsiang*; about 40 per cent of its population are literate.

The Troop Commander in the *Hsiang* is in charge of all military and police affairs, actual suppression of opium-smoking and gambling, and maintenance of law and order. He must make a yearly survey of all able-bodied men between the ages of eighteen and forty-five and report the results to the *Hsien* Government. He handles the details of conscription. He also distributes the rice ration given to families of soldiers on active duty. As police chief, he has a force of twenty armed policemen who live in the guardhouse at the *Hsiang* Office. These may be supplemented by Voluntary Police from each *Pao* if necessary. If any serious criminal offense is committed in the *Hsiang*, his policemen make the arrest and detain the criminal in the *Hsiang* Office until he can be sent to Chungking for trial.

The Troop Commander is also in charge of organizing self-defense units in the *Hsiang*. According to law, all *Chia*, *Pao*, and *Hsiang* are supposed to have well-organized and well-trained units with the *Chia* Chiefs, *Pao* Chiefs, and *Hsiang* Chiefs as titular heads, and the *Pao* and *Hsiang* Troop Commanders as active commanders. To date, no such self-defense organization has been set up in Hsiehmahsiang, but the Troop Commander says that he received instructions from the *Hsien* last month to do something about it, and that he is proceeding with plans to organize self-defense units that will be trained by local men who have had military experience. He thinks the force will total about 2,300 men.

The *Hsiang* Economic Affairs Secretary handles taxation for the *Hsiang* Office, and administratively he is in charge of all financial and budgetary matters. The *Hsiang* Office is far from being self-supporting financially, however, and the most important taxes levied in the *Hsiang* are collected by agencies operating at the level of the *Hsien* Government. A few taxes, though, are collected by the *Hsiang* Office for its own use. Among them are weights and measures taxes; every article that is weighed or measured in the village market places is subject to a 2 per cent tax. The sale of straw hats is likewise subject to a 2 per cent tax. These taxes are collected on market days by representatives of the *Hsiang* Office, who are on hand to observe all transactions and to collect from the buyers. There is also a 2 per cent tax on the purchase of any land. The *Hsien* authorities collect a similar tax, but their tax rate is much higher. There is a tax on feasts that is theoretically quite high, but in practice rarely exceeds 2 per cent, if it is collected at all. In addition, there are several other taxes on the books that are not actually collected. The most important local tax, however, is the self-government tax. This is a variable levy imposed on all the people in the *Hsiang,* and the rate depends on the amount of income required by the *Hsiang* Office. The *Hsiang* Assembly decides how much is needed, and then the total is divided up among the *Pao,* according to the amount of cultivated land in each *Pao,* and is collected from both landowners and tenants.

The total tax income of the *Hsiang* Office, including that from the self-government tax, is a small sum, however, and the *Hsien* Government must subsidize the *Hsiang* Offices to keep them going. In 1947, the Pahsien subsidy to Hsiehmahsiang was larger than the *Hsiang's* income from all of its taxes, and the total income of the *Hsiang* Office—even including the subsidy—was still extremely small. Consequently, the budget was allotted almost entirely for salaries and administrative purposes. The salaries of government officers and teachers accounted, in fact, for over 70 per cent of the total. Office and administrative expenses required the use of over 12 per cent, while routine building repair required about 8 per cent. Everything else—health, education (other than salaries), social welfare, and relief—together amounted to roughly 6 per cent of what was a very small budget to begin with.

The financial position of the *Hsiang* Office is one factor that makes it incapable of doing much beyond maintaining an office, keeping law and order, conducting the routine of administration, providing conscriptees and workmen to the higher authorities, and carrying out various orders passed down to it. This sort of role is, as a matter of fact, the only one that the officers of the *Hsiang* accept as their responsibility. They do not conceive of themselves as being active leaders of local reform, economic development, or welfare improvement. In their own minds, their primary responsibility is to keep things going, and to carry out or pass along orders from above. For this reason, the *Hsiang* Affairs Meetings, at which the *Hsiang* Chief meets with all the *Pao* Chiefs, is in many respects more important than the *Hsiang* Assembly sessions, for it is through the *Pao* Chiefs that instructions from above are sent on their way toward their ultimate destination—Lin Hsiu-ch'ing and his neighbors.

In what respects, then, are Hsiehmahsiang and its 31 *Pao* and 321 *Chia* self-governing units? They do have "representative" bodies and they do elect their own executives. The election of these representative bodies and their meetings are thoroughly democratic in a procedural sense, even though their social composition is much less so. That is about as far as self-government goes, however. These bodies and the executives whom they elect can be overruled on almost any question by higher authorities, upon whom they are financially dependent, and, practically speaking, their main job is to carry out orders received from above. This does not mean, however, that no progress has been made toward self-government in recent years. On the contrary, the introduction of elections, representative assemblies, and other procedural aspects of democracy is a step of considerable importance, and local people say that there is now a good deal more self-government than there was before these things were started. One must remember, also, that organized government does not intrude itself into all aspects of people's lives and that "higher authorities" are a long way off. Practically speaking, in a rural area such as Hsiehmahsiang, many local affairs are out of the realm of government, and are regulated by tradition and by nongovernmental groups such as families, clans, and secret societies.

Hsiehmahsiang is, as stated earlier, one of seventy-one *Hsiang* and *Chen* in Pahsien, whose governmental seat is about 50 miles away from Hsiehmachang, on the opposite side of the Yangtze River. It is fairly inaccessible, therefore, and not much intercourse, other than in written form, takes place between the *Hsiang* and the *Hsien*. Twice a year, the Hsiehmahsiang Chief attends special administrative meetings that all *Hsiang* Chiefs must attend, at the *Hsien* Magistrate's office. This year, he also attended a training class run by the *Hsien* Government. Four times a year, the elected *Hsiang* Representative attends the regular sessions of the *Hsien* Council. And once or twice a year, the Magistrate of Pahsien finds time to visit Hsiehmahsiang. The most continuous link between the *Hsien* and the *Hsiang*, however, is provided by a special District Officer, who is appointed by the *Hsien* Government and confirmed by the Provincial Government. Pahsien is divided into ten *Ch'ü*, or Districts. The Fourth District contains seven *Hsiang* including Hsiehmahsiang. The Director of the Fourth District, one man without office or assistants, visits Hsiehmahsiang at least once a month to check on the general state of local affairs, and to see whether or not orders and instructions from the *Hsien* Government are being carried out. He reports on these visits to the *Hsien* Government. His function is simply to improve the links between the *Hsiang* and the *Hsien*. Such links are essential, because it is at the *Hsien* level that complex, centrally directed governmental administration begins—or perhaps one would say ends, if one were viewing government from the national capital.

Most *Hsien* capitals are walled towns which not only serve as political centers, but are usually also the economic centers of the agricultural regions surrounding them. Originally, although the precise layout of these towns was often determined in accordance with the requirements of Chinese geomancy—"the wind and the water"—the general location was determined by the productivity of the agricultural land in the area, the location of transportation facilities, and strategic considerations. These towns, consequently, are normally centers of transport, communications, and economic life in the *Hsien* districts, and each depends on the agricultural surplus of its hinterland. The functions of such towns are varied. They serve as the seat of government and administration, a defense position for local garrison troops, and a refuge for the agricultural population in time of danger. They are living places for the wealthier gentry who leave the countryside to enjoy a more urban and sophisticated life. And they are focal points of transport, trade, and commerce, as well as centers of handicraft production, which serve the market towns within their spheres of economic influence.

The capital of Pahsien does not fit this pattern, however, and therefore it is by no means typical. In fact, it is not really a town at all, but simply a cluster of government buildings, in a mixed rural-urban setting, which serves only as a center of administration. This is because it is a new and artificial creation. Before the Sino-Japanese War, the capital of Pahsien was the great, sprawling, commercial metropolis of Chungking, which is piled up in a confused jumble on the banks of Yangtze and Kialing rivers. During the war, however, Chungking was made a Special Municipality governed directly by the Executive Yüan of the Central Government, and the Pahsien Government had to move out, in 1941. It moved to a spot on the south bank of the Yangtze, about 12 miles upstream from Chungking, and began building its headquarters on a hill between two small villages and a factory district. Today, it possesses the buildings necessary to carry out its administrative functions, but in all other respects it is merely an appendage of Chungking.

Pahsien is one of 142 *Hsien* in Szechwan Province—which also contains one Special District and two provisional units that will be made into *Hsien*—and it is one of approximately 2,000 *Hsien* in all of China. It is, therefore, one of the key units at the bottom level in the chain of command that begins with the Central Government and passes through the Provincial Governments. All levels of government in China, down to and including the *Hsien*, are part of a system of administrative centralism in which authority is concentrated at the top and is merely delegated to those below. It is a pyramidal structure of authority with the Central Government at the peak, Provincial Governments at the halfway mark, and the *Hsien* Governments at the base. (Between Pahsien and the Szechwan Government, there is a *Chuan Yüan* with a small staff of thirty-two civilian and six military officials; he supervises ten *Hsien* and one Special District, a population of about 5 million.) As noted already, the authority and influence of "higher authorities" in this system of centralized government administration certainly extends below the *Hsien*, but, as far down as the *Hsien*, the executive officers are all appointed from above.

In some respects, the *Hsien* is the most important level of government administration in China; even though all important policy decisions are made at higher levels, it is the *Hsien* that does most of the actual work of administration and government that is felt directly by the mass of the people. The Central Government and the Provincial Governments are geographically and psychologically rather remote from the people and the facts of life in rural areas.

There are six different ranks of *Hsien* in China. Pahsien belongs to the highest rank because its population of over 800,000 is considerably larger than that of the average *Hsien*, which has a population of less than 300,000. As a *Hsien* of the first grade, its organization is slightly more complicated and larger than some others, but, in essentials, the structure of government in all *Hsien* is the same.

The chief executive of Pahsien, the Magistrate, is appointed by the Szechwan Government, but his appointment is provisional until confirmed by the Central Government. The present Magistrate is an able, efficient, well-educated man, a university graduate and native of Szechwan. He nominates all his important subordinates, such as department heads, and they are appointed by the Provincial Government. All minor officers and employees of the *Hsien* Government are appointed by the Magistrate himself and do not need the approval of higher authorities.

The division of responsibilities and functions at the *Hsien* level is somewhat confused, in an administrative sense, by the fact that the *Hsien* Government consists of several departments directly under the Magistrate, and a galaxy of independent bureaus and offices that are supervised and coordinated by the Magistrate but, strictly speaking, are responsible directly to the Provincial Government. These independent bodies are, in fact, only semi-independent, because the Magistrate has a certain amount of control over them, but they are located in separate buildings and operate on their own, under normal circumstances. The establishment of such independent bodies makes it possible, however, for higher authorities to have more direct control over certain governmental functions, especially tax collecting, than would be the case if these functions were handled by departments within the *Hsien* Government itself.

Directly under the Magistrate in the *Hsien* Government are several important officials and units: the *Hsien* Secretary, the Departments of Civil Affairs, Finance, Reconstruction, Social Affairs, and Military Affairs, the Offices of Accounting, Statistics, and Population, and the Land Administration Special Officer. However, the Magistrate has final authority and responsibility for all that goes on in the *Hsien*, and the key officers under him act, in a sense, as his local cabinet and do the detailed work for him, in his name.

The *Hsien* Secretary is the Magistrate's principal administrative assistant, and coordinates internal affairs within the *Hsien* Government. He deals with personnel problems, checks documents coming into and going out of the office, and acts as intermediary between the Magistrate and department heads. He is also a sort of Vice-Magistrate, and takes over executive responsibilities when the Magistrate is absent.

The Department of Civil Affairs is responsible for general administration, personnel, elections, and training, in the *Hsien* as a whole. For example, the appointment of all *Hsiang* secretaries must receive his approval. According to law, there are definite requirements or qualifications laid down for various political positions, even those which belong to the self-governing levels, and it is the responsibility of the Department of Civil Affairs to see that the laws are followed—although in practice they cannot be universally enforced. The main requirements are always educational. For example, a man is theoretically required to be a middle-school graduate before he can be elected Chief of a *Hsiang* (in Pahsien, the educational level of local leaders is unusually high; about one-third of the *Hsiang* Chiefs are college graduates), and at least a primary-school graduate before he can be elected a *Pao* Chief. This is in keeping with the Chinese tradition of the scholar-official. The law also provides for the training of all officials in executive positions right down to and including the *Hsiang*. Each *Hsien* is supposed to have an Office for the Training of Local Administrative Officers, but in Pahsien the training of *Hsiang* Chiefs is carried out by the Magistrate, with the assistance of the Department of Civil Affairs. It is also the function of this department to see that the elections and meetings of *Pao* and *Hsiang* Assemblies and the *Hsien* Council are carried out at the proper time, in the proper way. In a vague sort of way, the Department is also responsible for the maintenance of public order, but the practical duties involved are carried out by two independent bodies, the Police Bureau and the Self-Defense Organization.

The Department of Finance coordinates financial matters for the entire *Hsien*. The *Hsien* budget is drawn up by this department and submitted to the *Hsien* Council, which has the final say locally—although it must be approved by the Provincial Government before it is finally accepted. Accounts are kept by the Accounting Office, which makes regular reports in duplicate to the Magistrate and the Provincial Government. Custody of *Hsien* funds is vested in the *Hsien* Treasury, which is a part of the *Hsien* Bank, an institution owned partially (60 per cent) by private citizens and partially (40 per cent) by the *Hsien* Government. Collection of taxes is done by independent bureaus, which will be described later. It is the job of the Head of the Department of Finance to coordinate all of these varied activities. He also keeps an eye on *Hsiang* finances, and every *Hsiang* budget goes to him for perusal and approval. In regard to *Hsien* funds, every withdrawal must receive written approval from him, as well as from the Magistrate and the Head of the Accounting Office.

All development and public works projects in the *Hsien* are managed by the Department of Reconstruction. This is a department that should be extremely important, but, for financial reasons, its activities are very limited. There are some scholars of Chinese history who assert that one of the most important, if not the most important, factor in the historical rise and growth of the Chinese state was the successful mobilization by the state of collective efforts to construct public works, particularly irrigation projects which are so essential for the kind of agriculture that exists in China. The basis and justification for a highly centralized administration in a country with a decentralized agrarian economy is not unrelated, even today, to the effectiveness with which the administration can mobilize collective labor and resources to accomplish numerous tasks, especially the construction of public works, which are difficult to accomplish locally. This is particularly true in respect to the Central Government, but it is important even at the *Hsien* level. The agency in the *Hsien* Government for doing this sort of thing is the Department of Reconstruction.

The main projects currently planned by the Pahsien Department of Reconstruction fall into four categories: development of the *Hsien* capital, irrigation, roads, and communications. Plans for developing the *Hsien* capital call for building a number of new office buildings, repairing local roads, installing a running-water system, and encouraging the growth of a commercial area. To accomplish the last objective, a decree has been issued stating that all merchants owning land within a certain area must build commercial establishments on the land within a stated period or it will be subject to expropriation by the *Hsien* Government. Plans for irrigation development include two types of projects: reservoir pools and canals. Proposals for building reservoir pools originate from special committees formed for that purpose in local areas.

These are submitted to the Department of Reconstruction, which, if it approves, then assists the local committees in getting the necessary loans from the Farmers' Bank of China, which will provide low-interest loans amounting to 80 per cent of the amount needed—the other 20 per cent must come from local funds—if they also approve of the project. Construction of irrigation canals is done by the *Hsien* itself, in cooperation with the Provincial Government. Canals are badly needed in Pahsien and, if extensively constructed, would raise the agricultural productivity of the region tremendously. One canal over 20 miles long is currently being dug, and a section 17 miles long will be completed by the end of 1948. The Department of Reconstruction has also drawn up plans recently for three new roads with a total mileage of about 40 miles. The budget for these roads was approved somewhat reluctantly by the *Hsien* Council; it insisted upon stretching out the period of construction from two to four years. Roads are badly needed in Pahsien; at present, a great many *Hsiang* have no motor road connection at all. Another project of the Department of Reconstruction is the extension of telephone service. Currently, there are about eighty phones in forty-five *Hsiang*, most of them in *Hsiang* Offices. They are managed by the Telephone Management Office, which is an independent body but is supervised by the Department of Reconstruction. The immediate objective of the department is to have telephones installed in every *Hsiang* Office. Another independent body supervised by the Department of Reconstruction is the Agricultural Development Office. In an agrarian region, one would expect a body such as this to be of major importance, but the only real project it is able to carry out at present is one involving the distribution of tung tree seedlings to farmers in various parts of the *Hsien*. It also sends regular reports on local agricultural conditions, the weather, crops, pests, and so on, to the Provincial Government, but lack of personnel and funds make it little more than a shadow organization.

In constructing canals, roads, and the like, the Department of Reconstruction works closely with the *Hsien* Voluntary Labor Organization. This organization handles the system of compulsory labor already described. It assigns labor quotas to each *Hsiang*, assembles the laborers to work on projects for the Department of Reconstruction or the military authorities, and supervises the management of labor on such projects.

The Department of Reconstruction's projects and plans, described above, are indicative of some of the needs of Pahsien, but its accomplishments do not begin to meet these needs. In the categories of canals and roads alone, it will be many years before the government completes a fraction of what is needed. The main reason the department cannot do more, however, is a financial one. As in the case of Hsiehmahsiang, so much of the Pahsien budget is consumed by the expenses of simply keeping the machinery of government administration operating that not much is left over for public welfare or development projects. The *Hsien*, in contrast to the *Hsiang*, is self-supporting, and it balances its budget, but it does so only by restricting activities other than routine administration to a minimum.

In its 1947 budget, Pahsien used between 80 and 90 per cent of its cash income, and almost all of its rice income, for one purpose: salaries of administrative officers. Health, relief, social welfare, reconstruction, education, and development projects altogether accounted for only 6.39 per cent of the budget. This situation is, of course, intimately related to the prevalent low level of productivity of China's agrarian economy. Under the existing economic and social system, there is not a large enough surplus to support much more in the way of government than bare administrative machinery. This is not the whole explanation, however. In many cases, private accumulations of wealth are not heavily taxed, despite the fact that the sources from which the government can obtain funds with which to carry out projects of general benefit are limited. Furthermore, the surplus currently available—i.e., that amount now collected in taxes—undoubtedly could be used more wisely. If a larger percentage was invested by government agencies in policies and programs that gradually helped to raise the level of agricultural productivity (such as irrigation canals), not only would the cost of government be proportionately less of a burden on the populace than it is now, but the government itself would find it possible to expand its field of operation.

In addition to the departments already described, the *Hsien* Government has two other important units of similar status: the Department of Social Affairs and the Department of Military Affairs.

The Department of Social Affairs has various responsibilities. On the one hand, it is responsible for social welfare, which includes relief and care of the aged, the blind, the infirm, and so on. At present, it does very little along this line; again the reason is lack of funds. Another of its responsibilities is the registration of every association and organization in the *Hsien*. All organizations must register their constitutions, their membership, and their officers, and must make regular reports on their activities. The Department of Social Welfare has the authority to suppress or dissolve any organization considered to be subversive. "Subversive" is a term, it should be noted, that includes not only any activity connected with Communism or the Communist Party, but which tends to be stretched to include any activity or group of actual or potential political significance, other than long-established conservative groups.

Secret societies, such as the Brothers' Society, are officially ignored at the *Hsien* level. Suppression of such societies is one of the duties of the Department of Social Affairs, but it follows the easiest, most practical course and overlooks them. It is most interesting that, without exception, every officer of the rank of department or bureau head in the *Hsien* Government disclaims any connection with the Brothers' Society, but, in view of the influence of the society throughout the region, it is difficult to believe such claims. Some probably do belong, but they apparently believe that it is wise to conceal their membership, or at least not to reveal it officially.

A number of nongovernmental organizations are officially sponsored by the Department of Social Affairs in Pahsien, as in other parts of the country. These include a Pahsien Chamber of Commerce and a number of labor unions and farmers' unions. If Hsiehmahsiang is typical, however, the farmers' unions exist on paper only. Theoretically, they are supposed to be cooperative welfare organizations through which farmers can improve their conditions, but in Hsiehmahsiang, there is one man appointed to be leader of the organization, and there are no other members.

Probably the most active and important organizations that come under the surveillance of the Department of Social Affairs are the numerous trade and craft guilds in the *Hsien*. These are restrictive, monopolistic, economic organizations, which prescribe rules for the members of particular trades or professions, and they wield considerable economic power. In Hsiehmahsiang, as has been mentioned already, they are unimportant because it is an area almost completely agrarian in its character. Guilds are more important in urban, or semiurbanized, areas where trade and handicrafts, as well as industrial production, are more highly developed. Pahsien is basically a territorial unit composed of *Hsiang* similar to Hsiehmahsiang, but there are a few areas that are considerably more urban, commercial, and industrial (particularly in the immediate environs of Chungking). Guilds, therefore, are important in the economic life of the *Hsien* as a whole, even though they are almost nonexistent in Hsiehmahsiang. There are, in fact, approximately fifty guilds in Pahsien organized on a *Hsien*-wide basis. Many of them have teahouse headquarters near the *Hsien* Government. Because of their economic power, they have considerable political significance and are a force with which the *Hsien* Government must deal and get along.

In addition to registering all private organizations, the Department of Social Affairs is expected to sponsor certain public movements. These all originate as ideas passed down from the Central Government, and they seem to have lost all force and vitality by the time they reach the *Hsien*. The department apparently has no desire to do very much about them. In Hsiehmahsiang, as a consequence, most people have no inkling what they are all about, although occasionally a few publicity posters are hung in the village. These movements include the New Life Movement —which disapproves, among other things, of gambling, smoking, drinking, spitting, and the use of cosmetics—and the People's Health Movement, which approves of exercise. There are occasional athletic meets sponsored by the government, however.

The *Hsien* Department of Military Affairs is responsible for keeping an up-to-date survey of all able-bodied men, for seeing that soldiers' families and retired soldiers receive their rice allowances, and for carrying out conscription orders. It coordinates the work of the Troop Commanders in the various *Hsiang* Offices. Conscription is its most important job. The department receives orders from a Conscription Area Office, which handles several *Hsien*, and must produce the quotas of men requested. Between 1937 and 1947, Pahsien produced more than 80,000 conscripts as grist for the Chinese military machine, first for the war against Japan and then for the civil war campaigns. Despite the prevalent system of buying substitutes, most of these men came from within the *Hsien*. Many of the 80,000 have never come back. As a result, the *Hsien* is now suffering from a shortage of agricultural labor. The character of China's labor-intensive agrarian economy is such that one sometimes encounters an anomalous situation in which an overpopulated region (in terms of the resources and volume of production that must support a given number of people) is suffering from a real labor shortage in terms of the number of able-bodied men required to keep up the current level of production with existing, technologically primitive methods of production.

The Department of Military Affairs is also theoretically responsible for the organization of so-called National People's Soldiers. This title is a vague generic term that includes all able-bodied men between the ages of eighteen and forty-five. In theory, all such men are organized into units in each *Chia, Pao,* and *Hsiang,* and receive a certain basic training, after which they are a reservoir not only for conscripts, but also for Volunteer Policemen and so on. In Pahsien, no real organization of this sort has been instituted, however.

Organization of self-defense is a separate matter. Self-Defense Troops are no longer under the Department of Military Affairs, but are the responsibility of the newly created People's Self-Defense Headquarters. This organization appears to be seriously approaching the job of organizing and training effective local defense units on a rational and selective basis, but its work is just getting under way. It plans to organize small but well-trained defense units in every local area; however, it does not know where the necessary military supplies, mainly rifles and ammunition, are coming from. They do not seem to be forthcoming from higher authorities. There are 9,800 privately owned rifles registered in the Pahsien, but these are mostly of ancient vintage. They belong to farmers who find them effective in scaring off robbers (in the old days, bandits), but they would not be good for much else. It is rather amazing that, to date, no real self-defense units have been organized in this region, despite the constant talk about such units during the past decade and despite the fact that the Nationalist Government spent long years with its back against the wall in this region. The explanation of local leaders in Pahsien, who strongly favor the idea of building effective local defense organizations and want to be prepared if the civil war spreads to Szechwan, is that the Central Government lacks confidence in decentralized militia and fears arming the common people, but they hope and believe that these attitudes are changing now that the national civil-war situation has become desperate.

Over-all military command of the region that includes Pahsien is in the hands of the Chungking Garrison Commander. He maintains a branch office adjacent to the Pahsien Government, just to keep an eye on things, but there are no regular troops in Pahsien, and the Commander does not interfere very much in *Hsien* affairs. Any criminal cases of a political nature, however, such as those involving persons accused of Communist activity, are turned over by the *Hsien* to the Garrison Command's military courts in Chungking. And if and when the civil war spreads to

Szechwan, the civil government of Pahsien will inevitably take a back seat. In times of crisis, the military takes over.

Until recently, there was a sixth department in the *Hsien* Government, the Department of Land Administration. In 1946, however, a Central Government order abolished this department and replaced it with a Land Administration Officer, who has only one assistant. (The personnel of a department varies from four to ten.) One duty of this officer is the administration of China's land laws.

Nationalist China's present basic land law is, on paper, an enlightened piece of legislation which deals with many of China's fundamental agrarian problems, including tenancy. It states that a Provincial Government "may . . . limit the acreage of private land owned by an individual or a body corporate." A Municipal or *Hsien* Government "may . . . decide on a minimum area unit, and prohibit the further subdivision of such a unit." And a Provincial Government "may limit the highest liability incurrable by farm land owned by a self-cultivating farmer." However, none of these optional steps has been taken in Szechwan, or in most other parts of China. The law also states that "a transfer of ownership of private agricultural land shall be made only to a transferee in a position to cultivate the land himself after the transfer." It declares that tenants of landlords who are absentee or who do not cultivate land themselves, "after having tilled [a given piece of land] for eight years continuously may apply to the competent district or municipal government to buy it over on his behalf." It also states that "governments of various grades, requiring land for the purpose of creating self-cultivating farms, may . . . expropriate" for that purpose. It further stipulates that "rental shall not exceed 8 per cent of the value of the land." Full implementation of these clauses of the basic land law would involve a fundamental revolution in existing economic and social relationships in a region such as Pahsien where tenancy is so prevalent. It would be a difficult and slow process to implement the law, even if the government went about the job energetically. Yet the Central Government in 1946 eliminated the department in the *Hsien* Government that was responsible for such matters and replaced it with a Special Officer who is virtually impotent to make even an attempt at implementation. In the Administrative District to which Pahsien belongs, there are some unusual men who are attempting to press a measure of land reform, and the local government authorities are giving them moral support, but a full-scale, direct governmental attack on the problem is not possible without administrative machinery for that purpose. The local authorities and leaders in Pahsien who are sympathetic toward land reform feel that the abolition of the Department of Land Administration is tangible proof that many men in the Central Government use land-reform slogans merely as shibboleths and that they are not really interested in implementation of the basic land law.

At the level of the *Hsien* Government, there are, in addition to the regular departments, many semi-independent bureaus and offices, a few of which have already been mentioned. The most important ones are larger than the departments within the *Hsien* Government itself, and are themselves broken down into three or four departments. Their personnel is appointed by the Provincial Government, and they all are responsible to some organization within the Provincial Government, even though they are supervised by the *Hsien* Magistrate. The most important of these are the Police Bureau, the Bureau of Education, the Tax Collection Bureau, and the Land Tax Bureau.

The Pahsien Police Bureau maintains one central police station at the *Hsien* capital and four branches in different parts of the *Hsien*. The central station has 154 officers and men, with 111 pistols and rifles. Each of the branch stations has 40 officers and men, with approximately 30 pistols and rifles. The Pahsien police force, therefore, totals slightly over 300 men, in addition to the aggregate of the small forces maintained at each *Hsiang* Office. This is not a very formidable group, but it seems to be adequate for maintaining normal law and order. The absence of any *Hsien* court, however, is felt to be unfortunate by local leaders who believe such a court would be closer to local problems, and would have a better understanding of local conditions, than the courts in Chungking.

The *Hsien* Bureau of Education is a recent creation, established in 1947 to place more emphasis on education than was the case when it was handled by a *Hsien* Department. The job of the bureau is not only that of maintaining existing educational institutions; it is a job of development as well. Although compulsory primary-school attendance is prescribed by law, it cannot be enforced when there are not sufficient schools. The head of the bureau estimates that in Pahsien at present, only 30 per cent of the children of school age attend school, and only about 20 per cent of the population is literate. There are, however, 600 *Pao* People's Schools and 102 Central Schools in the *Hsien*, with a total enrollment of approximately 50,000 children. The principals, who must be graduates of a normal school or the equivalent, are appointed and supervised by the bureau. Educational standards, textbooks, and curriculums are all prescribed by the Ministry of Education, but the bureau must see that standards are maintained and regulations followed. In addition to supervising these primary schools, the bureau itself maintains three middle schools —the only public middle schools in the *Hsien*—a normal school, and an agricultural school. There is no tuition in any of these schools, but there are fees for books and supplies.

A new body, called the People's Education Organization, has recently been established under the Bureau of Education to promote adult education, but all significant work in this field is actually being done by a private organization, the Mass Education Movement, which, however, has the backing of local governmental authorities.

The Pahsien Tax Collection Bureau is a large organization responsible for collecting all taxes in the *Hsien* except for the Land Tax, other national taxes collected by the Direct Tax Bureau or the Commodity Tax Bureau—which are Central Government organizations—and those assigned to the *Hsiang* Offices. The most important tax that the Tax Collection Bureau handles directly is the slaughtering tax, a 7 per cent levy on all pigs killed. It is important because pork is the staple meat in the local diet, and all the income from this tax is kept by the *Hsien* Government. Next in importance is the land deed tax, imposed on all land purchases. Every land buyer must pay a tax amounting to 18 per cent of the land's value. Six per cent, or one-third of the total income from this tax, is turned over to the Provincial Government, and the rest is kept by the *Hsien*. There is also a business tax, on profits (3 per cent) or income from interest (6 per cent), which is divided evenly between the Province and the *Hsien*. The bureau also collects rent on public lands that are owned by the *Hsien* and rented to tenants.

In terms of value, however, by far the most important tax, from the point of view of the *Hsien* Government, is the land tax, which is collected in kind by the Land Tax Bureau. Grain taxes of this sort have, in fact, been one of the main financial supports of the Chinese Government for hundreds of years. For a number of years, the Central Government abandoned traditional practice and levied the land tax in money instead of grain, but, during the Sino-Japanese War, it switched back to the old system—partially as a result of the rapid depreciation of money.

In Pahsien, the land tax is collected—by twenty-three collection offices—from all landowners in the *Hsien* in September, after the rice harvest, and it must be paid in unhusked rice. Computation of the tax is extremely complicated, but, since it plays such an important role in public finance in China, perhaps it is worth describing how it works in Pahsien.

The basis for imposing the tax is land value. All land is classified as belonging to one of nine grades, depending on its quality. Each mou (roughly one-sixth of an acre) is given a tax value depending on its grade. For example, a mou of the first grade is given a tax value of CNC $0.20, and a mou of the lowest grade CNC $0.01. A landowner's holdings are totaled up on this basis, and the tax rate is expressed in terms of a definite amount of grain per CNC $1.00 of land.

The present Land Tax in Pahsien is really a combination of four taxes and a forced loan. The basic tax is computed according to Central Government orders. The Central Government, depending on its needs, sets a figure that is divided among the provinces on the basis of cultivable land, and in turn is divided among the *Hsien.* The figure that the *Hsien* must contribute is considered to be 30 per cent of the basic tax. This means that the total basic tax collected is an amount that is finally divided so as to give the *Hsien* Government 50 per cent of the total, the Provincial Government 20 per cent, and the Central Government the required 30 per cent. Once the total figure for this basic tax is computed, the tax rate is determined by the total value of cultivable land on which it can be collected.

A second tax is added by the Provincial Government, and is divided among its *Hsien,* and all of the receipts from this tax go to the Province. The other two taxes are added by the *Hsien* Government, one to meet its current needs and the other to accumulate a grain reserve as insurance against years of bad harvest. The forced loan is a Central Government levy. Every landowner with over CNC $1.00 worth of land must loan a specified amount of rice per mou of land. The loan is supposed to be paid back by the Central Government, through the various Land Tax Bureaus, in yearly installments over a five-year period, with interest that is less than 1 per cent. The repayments are made not in rice, but in money on the basis of current rice prices at the time of repayment. All of these five elements, the four taxes and the forced loan, are lumped together and collected at the same time.

The Head of the Pahsien Land Tax Bureau asserts that these taxes together amount to between 15 and 20 per cent of the total value of rice production in the *Hsien* at the present time. That figure is difficult to check, but it seems to be roughly correct.

The Land Tax is one of the most important single taxes in China today, because Central, Provincial, and *Hsien* governments all rely heavily upon it. The Central Government has other important sources of income, including the customs, salt, commodity, income, and inheritance taxes, but these miss rural China for the most part, or at least they miss Pahsien. The Commodity Tax Bureau, which has representatives in the major modern factories in the *Hsien*, collects a certain amount, but it is not large enough even to warrant the establishment of a branch office in the *Hsien*. The Direct Tax Bureau does have an office in the *Hsien* capital, but its receipts are almost nothing. In fact, although the wealthier citizens in the *Hsien* are certainly covered by the Income Tax laws, the Head of the Direct Tax Bureau somewhat sheepishly admits that last year not a single person paid it, and evidently he could not do very much about it.

In addition to the organizations already described, there are a few other semi-independent bodies connected with the *Hsien* Government. The most important one not mentioned previously is the Health Office, which maintains ten branches and twenty-four health stations in the *Hsien*. Within the limits of its abilities, it is doing a much-needed job of providing medical service. It is badly handicapped, however, by the lack of funds, personnel, and equipment, and consequently, modern medical service is available to only a fraction of the population of Pahsien.

All the *Hsien* bodies described so far are administrative bodies, and all their personnel is appointed. What sort of men fill these posts? They vary, of course—good and bad, competent and incompetent. They are all fairly well educated; many are college or university graduates. Most of them have made a profession of civil service, and many have worked in several *Hsien* governments over a period of years. There is not much chance of promotion above the *Hsien* level for most of them, according to their own testimony, and, even within the *Hsien* Government, a Department Head has only a small chance of becoming a Magistrate. Apparently a man becomes a professional Department Head or a professional Magistrate, and may be shifted around between departments or transferred from *Hsien* to *Hsien*, but has only a slight chance of being promoted to a post of higher rank with greater responsibility. Almost all these men have some source of outside income (many own land), because present salaries—even though they form such a high percentage of *Hsien*'s expenses—are not really enough to live on.

All these men have one thing in common. All the executive officers, and all department, bureau, and office heads, without exception, are members of the Kuomintang. While membership in the Kuomintang is not important in the Hsiehmahsiang Office, it appears to be a prerequisite for appointment to any responsible *Hsien* position. In many respects, membership in the Kuomintang seems to be in the nature of a union card and not much more than that. There are men of all types who carry the cards. Some are dead weight in the *Hsien* Government, but many are capable and forward-looking men who are doing their best to provide good government for Pahsien. One has to distinguish between the party organization and the party membership, because the membership is all-inclusive and contains all kinds of people.

The Party itself in Pahsien, however, is an uninspired, listless, rootless organization that apparently is not interested in doing much of anything except maintain its monopoly position in politics and government service. The Secretary of the Executive Committee of the Pahsien Kuomintang Headquarters claims that there are 34 Area Party Headquarters and 236 Party Branches in Pahsien, with a total membership of about 6,000 (including both regular party members and Kuomintang Youth Corps members, the latter having been merged with the Party recently). These figures, although they do not agree exactly with statistics published by the *Hsien* Government, are probably substantially correct. The figure for total membership is small, however, for an area with a population of more than 800,000, and if Hsiehmahsiang is typical, many of those who hold party cards are inactive and only nominal members. The Kuomintang has never had real competition from any other organized political party in this region since it was first organized, and this fact may help to explain its loss of vitality and its degeneration into a political organization that has almost no roots, no mass following, and no program or activities, but which nevertheless maintains a monopoly of higher political posts.

Theoretically, there is a *Hsien*-wide Party Representative Assembly, elected every two years, which selects the thirteen-member Executive Committee that runs Party affairs; its head, the Party Secretary, is appointed by the Provincial Party Headquarters. There is also supposed to be an eight-member Examination Committee that checks on the Executive Committee. Actually, however, the last time there was even a nominal meeting of such an assembly was in 1944, and there are no plans for any meetings in the near future. The Party receives its mandate and instructions from the hierarchy above, rather than from below.

Financially, the Kuomintang in the past has depended upon subsidies from the government. Party and government were not clearly separated, but rather were joined in a legally defined form of political matrimony during what was called the "period of political tutelage." This year, with the beginning of constitutional government, the two were to have been divorced. This was to involve, among other things, the end of government subsidies to the Party. It is interesting to note, however, that in Pahsien the Party Headquarters, which is located in one wing of the *Hsien* Government building, is still subsidized by the *Hsien* treasury. The amount of this subsidy is not large, but it maintains an official link between the Party and the government. The Party Secretary denies that this subsidy continues, but his principal assistant and the *Hsien* Accountant both are more frank in revealing the facts. The subsidy may be discontinued in the near future, they claim, but at present it remains as one more example of the lag between the promulgation and implementation of law in China.

Fortunately, the character of the Party in Pahsien does not determine the basic character of the *Hsien* Government. The government contains a number of able and liberal officials who are attempting to improve conditions, and who are cooperating in a program of reform that is being pushed, with the cooperation of the Mass Education Movement, in the entire Third Administrative District of Szechwan to which Pahsien belongs. Reform is exceedingly difficult and discouragingly slow, however, and existing "democratic" bodies do not help very much.

The one elective and representative institution in Pahsien is the *Hsien* Council. This body, which meets every three months, has 101 unsalaried members, 71 of whom are elected by the *Hsiang* Assemblies, and 30 by various professional organizations and occupational groups. It concerns itself almost exclusively with financial and budgetary matters presented to it by the *Hsien* Government. Procedurally, it is thoroughly democratic. Questions referred to it by the *Hsien* Government are debated openly, in sessions which are notable for rhetoric as well as for serious discussion. All of its decisions must be approved by the Provincial Government before they become final, but the Council has some real power based on its share in controlling the purse strings. The *Hsien* Government must obtain the Council's approval for its budget and for all expenditures. The Council, therefore, in a negative way helps to determine policy through its veto in financial matters.

The complexity of the problem of achieving change and progress in China by peaceful, non-revolutionary means is illustrated, however, by the fact that this element of democracy in the *Hsien* Government is far from being an unqualified blessing in Pashien. The present impulse toward, and stimulus for, change and reform in the region come neither from the masses, who still remain politically passive for the most part, nor from the landowning gentlemen represented in the *Hsien* Council, but from a key group of idealistic men in the Administrative District Office, the *Hsien* Government, and the Mass Education Movement. The "democratic" *Hsien* Council tends to be an obstacle to, rather than an instrument of, change. The reasons for this should be obvious in view of what has already been said about social organization in the region. As one high-ranking member of the *Hsien* Government expressed it to me: "There isn't a single tenant in the whole Council. Many of the Council members are able men, but they are all men of wealth, education, and leisure. They are conservative and aren't interested in changing the *status quo*. The *status quo* is not bad at all from their own personal point of view, which is the only point of view most of them have."

PART III

FRAGMENTATION:
WARLORDS, BORDERLANDS, AND
POLITICAL DISUNITY

11

OLD-STYLE WARLORDISM

Taiyuan (Shansi)
March, 1948

Thirty-seven years ago, when the wave of revolt stirred by the Nationalist revolution in central China reached the city of Taiyuan, in Shansi Province, a young colonel named Yen Hsi-shan made an important decision. On October 29, 1911, he went over to the revolution, taking with him all the Imperial troops under his command. Since that day, the career of Yen Hsi-shan and the history of Shansi Province have been inseparable. Today, Yen is a living myth in China, and he still rules in Taiyuan, capital city of Shansi.

Shansi is a distinct geographical entity in the heart of north China. Although a part of the extensive highlands of China's north and northwest—an area distinguished by its thick covering of yellow, wind-deposited, loess soil—Shansi has natural boundaries that set it apart. Mountains such as the Taihang and Wutai ranges cover most of the province, except for the Tatung Plain in the north, the Fen River valley near Taiyuan, and the Chiehchow Plain in the south. Plateaus intersperse these ranges, but they are cut by deep gorges and valleys that lie between vertical walls of loess, and the plateaus are almost as rugged as the mountains. To the east, the mountains drop abruptly to the north China plain, and the Shansi border follows this terrain line. The province's western boundary is clearly defined by the north-south course of the Yellow River, and the river curves and forms most of the southern boundary as well. The inner loop of the Great Wall forms the northern limit of the province, and a special southern branch of the wall separates Shansi from Hopeh.

The mountainous terrain of Shansi tends to isolate the province, and this has resulted in distinct Shansi dialects and customs. Isolation is one of the major factors that has made it possible for a leader such as Yen Hsi-shan to establish a provincial regime that has long maintained a high degree of political independence. There have been extended periods during the past thirty-seven years when the inclusion of Shansi within China has been more nominal than real.

Present-day Shansi cannot be understood without some knowledge of the background of its dominating personality, Marshal Yen Hsi-shan. Born in the Wutai district of northern Shansi, in 1883, Yen completed his basic education in a military institution in Taiyuan, and from there went on to take infantry courses in the Military Cadets' Academy in Tokyo, from 1908 until 1910. While in Japan, he joined the T'ung Meng Hui, forerunner of the Kuomintang, and made his first contacts with Chinese revolutionary leaders. After returning to Taiyuan, he started to build up a model brigade in the province, and then, in 1911, the spark lit by the Nationalist revolution presented him with the opportunity to start his climb to power. He emerged almost immediately as a key military figure in the province, and was granted recognition by the Nationalist leaders. In March, 1912, he was appointed Military Governor of Shansi. In June, 1914, he was made a general, with the special title "Tung-Wu." In September, 1917, he was appointed acting Civil Governor. By this time, he had achieved undisputed control in Shansi. Over the years, more titles and honors were added. In the autumn of 1918, he was officially designated "Model Governor" of China by the Central Government in Peking. In January, 1920, he was awarded the "First Order of Merit." In February, 1923, he was made a full general, and in November of the same year, he became a Marshal. These titles and appointments, however, were merely ex post facto recognition, by successive national authorities, of Yen's unshakable position in his home province. National regimes rose and fell, and other local leaders came and went during this chaotic period of China's history, but Yen remained in control of Shansi.

Although Yen focused his attention at home, he did not refrain completely from participating in national politics. He was, in fact, extremely shrewd in making opportunistic political alliances with other Chinese leaders to strengthen his own position. From 1912 to 1915, he gave moral support to President Yüan Shih-k'ai, only to desert him when he was losing his power. During the next four years, until 1919, he supported Tuan Ch'i-jui's Anfu Clique. When that clique lost power, Yen played both sides of the fence in the struggle between the anti-Anfu warlord Wu P'ei-fu and General Feng Yü-hsiang. In 1925, Yen formed a new political alliance, this time with the Manchurian warlord Chang Tso-lin, who had defeated Wu P'ei-fu. Then, when the Kuomintang successfully fought its way northward and set up its capital in Nanking in 1927, Yen came to terms with Chiang K'ai-shek.

These complicated maneuvers enabled Yen to maintain his power and protect Shansi. As a result, Shansi experienced an unusual degree of peace and stability during a period when much of north China was engulfed by civil wars between numerous warlords. In Shansi, Yen carried out extensive reforms in the early years. He reorganized the provincial administration from the villages up, reformed the school system, built roads, launched campaigns against queue-wearing and foot-binding, and encouraged the development of irrigation and agricultural improvement. Accounts written by visitors to the province during those years indicate that much progress was made, and evidently Yen's popularity among Shansi people was real. Previously, Shansi had been considered an area of unusual backwardness—one explanation undoubtedly being its mountain isolation. According to one story, perhaps apocryphal, Confucius once traveled to a point a few miles west of Taiyuan and then turned back because of disgust at the ignorance of the people. In any case, Yen introduced many reforms into this backward area, particularly emphasizing the development of schools and roads.

During the years following 1927, when the Nanking Government was attempting to consolidate its power, Yen Hsi-shan was drawn more closely into its orbit. In the spring of 1928, he was appointed Commander-in-Chief of the Nationalist's Third Army Group in north China; in the summer, he was appointed Garrison Commander of the Peiping-Tientsin Area; in September, he was elected to membership in the Kuomintang Central Executive Committee and the Central Political Council, and in October, he was made a member of the State Council in Nanking.

Soon thereafter, however, Yen's independence reasserted itself. Although he was appointed Minister of Interior, he did not take up the post. Then, during the following two years, 1929–30, Yen became the leader of a revolt of northern generals against Chiang K'ai-shek. After a quarrel with Chiang in the summer of 1929, Feng Yü-hsiang, whom Yen had previously fought on two occasions, sought sanctuary in Shansi. Yen soon became involved in the quarrel, and open revolt broke out, with Yen, Feng, Wang Ching-wei, and others cooperating against the Central Government. Over ten provinces "elected" Yen as Commander-in-Chief of the "National Army, Navy, and Air Forces"; from May to September, 1930, these northern forces fought against Chiang.

Yen was even "elected" President of China by an "Enlarged Committee of the Kuomintang," which tried to establish a new government. All these machinations were fruitless, however. The northern forces were soon defeated, and Yen was forced to go into temporary exile in Dairen. But his retreat was short-lived. The very next year, 1931, he returned to Shansi.

During the early 1930's, Yen again concentrated his efforts on the internal development and reform of Shansi, emphasizing this time a policy of "building up industries for the salvation of China." An extensive industrial program was launched in 1932, under a provincial Ten-Year Plan.

However, when the Japanese reopened their undeclared war against China, in 1937, Shansi was not exempted from attack. Yen's troops reportedly fought well for a brief period, but then retreated to a mountain position near Chihsien in southwest Shansi, and there set up a headquarters called "Konanpo" ("Hillside of Conquering All Difficulties"), where Yen remained during most of the war. The facts of what happened in much of north China from 1938 to 1945 are difficult to establish, but it is claimed that, during the latter stages of the war, active opposition to the Japanese in Shansi was carried on mainly by the Communists, while Yen maintained a delicate buffer position between the forces of the Nationalists, Communists, and the Japanese, attempting to play each against the others. There is no doubt that, during this period, some of Yen's troops, in particular the so-called "New Army," left him and joined forces with the Communists' Eighth Route Army.

When V-J Day arrived, Yen bounced back and raced into Taiyuan with his remaining troops. But the Communists already held much of Shansi, especially rural areas that they had taken during the war, and Yen was able to re-establish control only over certain parts of the province. Since then, a bitter and continuous struggle has been going on between Yen and the Communists. This struggle is part of the general civil war now in progress in China, but, as one might expect from the historical background, there are many features about the situation in Shansi that are unique. One recent observer described Shansi as a "foreign country," and there is no doubt the contrasts between Yen's province and the rest of the country are numerous and striking.

At present, the territory in Shansi still held by the "Nationalists"—that is, by Yen—includes 36 *Hsien* out of a total of 105 in the province. Eight are in the Tatung area in northern Shansi, bordering the Suiyuan military region. That area is theoretically under General Yü Chen-ho, one of Yen's men, but, in reality, military authority appears to be divided in a rather vaguely defined way between Yen and General Fu Tso-yi, the Nationalist commander for all of north China. Two *Hsien* are in the immediate vicinity of Linfen, south of Taiyuan. Under the command of General Liang Pai-huang, this is a small, besieged pocket. Sixteen *Hsien* are in the immediate vicinity of Taiyuan, in central Shansi, and this area—Yen's principal remaining stronghold—is also completely surrounded by the Communists. Until recently, a fairly large section of southwest Shansi was occupied by non-Shansi Nationalist troops under the command of General Hu Tsung-nan, but recently this territory was almost completely abandoned by the Nationalists, when threats to the city of Sian forced Hu Tsung-nan to shift his troops so as to protect Shensi, his own military bailiwick.

Theoretically, there is no distinction between General Yen's Shansi troops and other Nationalist troops. His military forces are part of the National Army, and he is the Nationalist commander of what is called the Taiyuan Pacification Area, under the Ministry of National Defense. In reality, however, the distinction is real. Yen's soldiers make up what is essentially a personal, provincial army, one that at present is merged with the Central Government armies by virtue of the existing political alliance between Yen and the Central Government. Yen's troops are almost entirely recruited within Shansi, however, and they are kept within the province.

Theoretically, also, Yen is under the over-all command of General Fu Tso-yi's North China Communist Suppression Headquarters in Peiping. Actually, however, he follows his own independent course. As General Kuo Tsung-fen, Chief of Staff of the Taiyuan Pacification Area, carefully explains, Fu Tso-yi was formerly a subordinate of Yen Hsi-shan, and this creates a special relationship between the two men. This special relationship apparently means, in practice, that Yen has permission to go his own way, as he pleases. Although General Kuo claims that relations between Yen and Fu are all that could be desired, he goes on to explain that liaison is maintained entirely by wireless, and that there is no exchange of liaison officers by the two headquarters. In short, there is no effective military liaison at all. In the military sphere, as in others, a façade of normal good relations is maintained between Shansi authorities and Central Government authorities, but, in reality, the special and unique arrangements that exist mean that Shansi is exempted to a large extent from

Central Government regulation and control. Today, relations between Marshal Yen and the Central Government appear to be neither cordial nor antagonistic. The two are simply allied, loosely, in opposition to a common enemy, the Communists.

By far the largest part of Shansi Province is now under Communist control, as it has been for some years, and this Communist-controlled territory falls into several "Liberated Areas." Militarily, the territory comes under several well-known Communist commanders, Ho Lung in the northwest, Nieh Jung-chen in the northeast, Liu Po-ch'eng in the southeast, and Ch'en Keng in the south. The main Communist military command headquarters, however, is said to be Hsinghsien in the northwestern part of the province. This is the town to which top Communist leaders such as Mao Tse-tung and Chu Teh were reported to have moved not long ago, after the fall of Yenan; Yen's military lieutenants in Taiyuan claim that they are still there and that consequently Hsinghsien might be called the Communist capital in China at present.

The existing balance of military forces in Shansi is summarized as follows by Yen's Chief of Staff, who appears to be unusually frank and forthright. Yen has 200,000 regular troops in the Taiyuan area, 12,000 in the Tatung area, and 20,000 in the Linfen area. In addition, all able-bodied men not on active military duty are organized as militiamen in the Soldier-Farmer Unification program and belong to the so-called People's Self-Defense Army. Old men, young boys, and some women are organized into the People's Self-Defense Corps. The organizational intricacies of the entire military structure are too complicated to describe in detail, but the guiding principle is the aim of mobilizing all possible groups. The People's Self-Defense Army is claimed to have 300,000 members who are able to use a rifle. They are trained by about 5,000 regular troops; theoretically, they can elect their own officers. Some buy their own arms; others are loaned arms by the government; some do not possess any weapons. The Self-Defense Corps is much more loosely organized, its numerical strength is vague, and only a few of its members get training of any sort.

In addition to the regular army and the militia, there are also a number of other military organizations in the Taiyuan area. These include troops under the Taiyuan Garrison Commander, who is responsible for local order; the Peace Preservation Commander, whose duties involve military enforcement of political policies; the Military Control Headquarters Commander, who handles conscription; and so on. There is also a large regular police force, under joint military-civil control of the Garrison Commander and the Civil Affairs Commission. All of these, added together, form the active and reserve military potential available to Yen. On the Communist side, Kuo says, there are between 150,000 and 200,000 regular troops in Shansi—slightly fewer than Yen's. They, too, however, have organized and trained the people as militia, the numbers of which are probably considerably larger than Yen's, since they have a larger population to draw from. According to Kuo, out of a total Shansi population of 15 million, approximately 11 million are under Communist control and 4 million under Yen.

It is not easy to ascertain the quality and morale of troops simply by observing them, but one can make certain judgments on the basis of their general appearance and behavior. The troops that I have seen in Taiyuan and Taiku, in Yen's territory, do not make a good impression. The streets are filled with them, some marching or carrying out duties of various sorts, but most simply loafing. The majority look dirty and unkempt. They do not show much spirit. The impression they make is very different from that made, for example, by the clean, smart, spirited troops of Fu Tso-yi in Suiyuan. My own observations tended to confirm the opinion of a competent foreign military observer who recently reported that Yen's troops are about as poor as they come, even in China.

Yen's situation in regard to military supplies and material is more impressive, however. In the relatively small Taiyuan area, there is an amazing concentration of light and heavy industries that contains some of the largest and best now operating in north China. These are said to produce 80 per cent of Yen's military needs. The monthly output, it is claimed, includes 8 75mm. guns, 60 7.9mm. machine guns, 3,000 rifles, more than 300 light machine guns, 2,000 5cm. mortars, plus grenades, bayonets, swords, and ammunition. By contrast, the Communists merely have a few small military industries in local areas in southeast and northwest Shansi; they do not have any large-scale industry in the province. The food situation is reversed, however. In Yen's territory, the food situation is critical. First priority on existing stocks goes to the military, however, so it seems likely that the troops will be well fed, even at the expense of the civil population. The Communists, on the other hand, hold the best food-producing region in the lower valley of the Fen River.

This is the general military balance of power in Shansi. But at present, there is relatively little fighting going on. It is true that Yen's small pocket at Linfen is currently under severe Communist attack and siege. But military activity on the fringes of Yen's main stronghold, around Taiyuan, is confined for the most part to small-scale foraging or reconnaissance thrusts by both sides. Nearby cities such as Paoting in Hopeh, Loyang in Honan, and Sian in Shensi have recently become the objects of major Communist attacks or threats, but the situation around Taiyuan still remains relatively quiescent.

However, Taiyuan and its environs, surrounded by Communist territory, are under siege. The dramatic evidences of this fact create quite a spectacle. Military personnel and activities are visible everywhere. Thousands of concrete, stone, and brick pillboxes dot the landscape. One official states that there are 2,000 immediately around Taiyuan, and 7,000 in the surrounding countryside. These pillboxes are awkward, tall structures about 30 feet high. They appear to have been built with almost no regard for the "field of fire" requirements of the terrain, and they would be extremely vulnerable to artillery fire, but doubtless they have a certain effectiveness. In addition, there are many wide, moat-like ditches protecting railway stations and other key spots. Building and digging activities are under way in a great many places. Occasionally, one sees troops going through training exercises in the countryside. The final touch, though, is the armored train that makes daily runs around the city of Taiyuan on a special military railway encircling the city.

Within this besieged stronghold, Yen is now carrying out drastic economic and political policies, which are profoundly affecting the lives of the entire population. His motives and objectives are not simple to analyze. He proclaims the policies he has instituted in Shansi to be radical, progressive, and reformist, but these terms can have many meanings. Yen is familiar, in a vague and incomplete way, with the issues involved in the ideological struggle between capitalism and Communism as economic systems. His writings (he is prolific) are full of pseudo-intellectual discussion of these issues, but they actually show a remarkable lack of information and understanding of the issues. His inadequacies have not prevented him, however, from formulating a "new system" of his own. He outlined this system in a long conversation with me. He accepts, he says, the thesis that capitalism should be abolished because of its weaknesses and injustices. Furthermore, Communism is, in his opinion, the best substitute that has been developed to date. The principal trouble with Communism, he says, is that its methods are wrong. Therefore, he has worked out a program that has much in common with what he believes Communism to be, but which supposedly uses better methods. The manner in which Yen's policies are implemented, however, leads one to conclude that the ideological glamor in which he tries to clothe them is simply camouflage. But, in conversation, he places much emphasis on ideology. He will assert, in one breath, that his policies are designed specifically to meet current conditions in Shansi, and then in the next he will suggest, somewhat coyly, that possibly they would be the solution to China's, and even the world's, present problems. He is not a modest man.

In some respects, Yen's policies simply represent an effort to fight the Communists by using their own methods, slogans, and catch-phrases. He has borrowed freely from them, and frankly admits that he has done so. He is shrewd in recognizing and sizing up the popular appeal of a radical reform program such as that of the Chinese Communists, and unlike some Chinese, he does not underestimate its power and appeal. Like the Communists, also, Yen has appeared to be obsessed, since the 1930's, with the aim of mobilizing all resources for increased production, and especially for industrialization.

The two programs that embody the major elements of Yen's economic policies are labeled Soldier-Farmer Unification and the People's Economy. The former is the program for rural areas, and the latter is designed for, and applied to, Yen's one important urban center, Taiyuan.

The Soldier-Farmer Unification program was begun in 1943, admittedly as a method of increasing the number of men available for active military service. Today, this still seems to be one of its major objectives. The essence of the program, in theory, is as follows: All agricultural land is redistributed. The government neither buys nor expropriates it, however, and landowners keep title to their land, but they lose all right to till it, decide how it will be used, or fix rents. In short, land is indirectly nationalized —by a not very indirect method.

The basis for redistribution of the land is an arbitrary "land unit" that, theoretically, is large enough to support eight persons and would normally require two men to till. The average size of such a unit is said to be about 40 mou (6 to 7 acres). Six of these units are combined into one "large land unit," which is assigned to six (not twelve) able-bodied men between the ages of eighteen and forty-seven and physically fit to farm. These men form a mutual aid "small group." One of the six must go on active duty into the army. Another is classified as a reservist on call; since war is in progress, he, too, must now join the regular army. The remaining four, enrolled in the People's Self-Defense Army, are responsible for farming the "large land unit," in a semicollective manner, and must support all families. In this way, one-third of all able-bodied men are drafted, and the other two-thirds are made militiamen. The men on active duty must serve at least three, and in some cases, four years, after which they are replaced by two others from the group; cultivation of the land unit is thus rotated among the six. Since the large units are of a size that would require twelve men to farm them, and there are only four men assigned to farm, these men must rely on the assistance of their family members and on men above or below the eighteen to forty-seven age limits, who in theory are assigned among the land units as they are needed.

The distribution process is supposed to be accomplished as much as possible in accordance with the needs and decisions of local villagers. Provision is also made in the program, as officially outlined, for continued payment of government-fixed rents to the landowners. Land is divided into seven grades, and rents are supposed to be paid, in kind, on the basis of rates fixed for each grade—the highest being under one-tenth of the land's produce and the lowest about one-fortieth. Both rent and taxes are based theoretically on the estimated total produce of the land, minus the amount necessary to sustain eight persons. This is arbitrarily set. If a family assigned to one of the land units exceeds eight persons, it must rely on government relief to supplement farm income.

Special administrative bodies are required to implement the Soldier-Farmer Unification program. A mass meeting in each village is supposed to elect a nine-member Soldier-Farmer Committee responsible for carrying it out. These nine members all have defined responsibilities, as follows: head of the village, head of political organization of the people, head of mutual aid organizations, head of the local self-defense corps, representative of all families whose men are in the army, judge of land value, agricultural technician, educational advisor, and relief advisor. Provision is also made for one non-voting woman member.

The People's Economy program is a more recent innovation. It was put into effect last May, when the economic situation in Taiyuan became critical. It is as comprehensive a program for Taiyuan and its suburbs as the Soldier-Farmer Unification is for rural areas. It includes a system for rationing basic necessities, price control, establishment of cooperatives, regulation of consumption, limitation of profits and interest, prohibition of speculation, and control of housing and rents. A separate, special, organizational structure has been established for this program as well. At the base are "consultative conferences" composed of family heads in the basic territorial districts, assisted by representatives of higher authorities. They are supposed to meet weekly to discuss proposals sent to them, and to make suggestions to higher authorities. They also elect a People's Mobilization Committee to provide liaison with higher authorities. The main responsibility of this body, which has scheduled monthly meetings, is to help enforce the program. The top body is the People's Economics Executive Committee. Presided over by the Mayor of Taiyuan, it has eighteen members: four elected by administrative districts inside the city wall, two by districts outside the wall, and two each by various population groups—merchants, laborers, farmers, factory workers, self-defense bodies, and women. Under the Executive Committee, there are a Standing Committee of ten members, a Secretariat, and sub-committees or bureaus for investigation and control, cooperatives, price control, labor distribution, housing and building control, people's mobilization, and others. In theory, bureau heads are elected by a representative municipal body called the *Lü* People's Representative Assembly, and they are responsible for administering the numerous aspects of the program.

Under the People's Economics program, ninety-three consumers' cooperatives in the city sell food, cloth, salt, and coal; sixteen in the suburbs sell the same items except for food. In addition, there are eight Supply and Demand Stores in the city, which sell miscellaneous goods, such as soap, handkerchiefs, and the like. All the cooperatives buy their supplies from the government (except that, in the case of food, they occasionally buy directly from the farmers), and theoretically they sell at cost. Membership in the cooperatives is optional; at present, it costs about CNC $12 million a share (set in terms of *Yüan Fapi*, a special monetary unit invented by Yen). Any person over twelve years old can buy one share; children from six to twelve can buy half a share, and children under six can buy one fourth of a share. The amount of goods that can be purchased in these cooperatives is fixed for each category of member. One can belong to only a single cooperative, and furthermore, a person who joins a cooperative is, theoretically, not entitled to the cards issued to all other people entitling them to buy legally on the open market. The basic necessities handled by cooperatives are also supposed to be rationed, and only "reasonable" profits (now considered to be 10 per cent) are allowed. Open market prices theoretically are also controlled by the government, but officials privately admit that the open market is not controlled with complete strictness.

For rationing purposes, food is divided into two categories, for military and non-military personnel. Military personnel get the first-grade ration; all others get the second. The kinds and amounts of food allowed for each grade are prescribed on the basis of daily quotas.

A unique rent system has also been put into effect under the People's Economy program. All buildings are divided into two categories, residential and commercial, and these are subdivided into seven grades. Rents are fixed by the government, according to the grade, in terms of *Yüan Fapi* ("original legal tender"). This hypothetical, noncirculating, monetary unit was devised by Yen and was originally designed for wide application, but it has now been abandoned except for use in fixing rents, fees, and the like. It is based on the 1937 value of a bolt of No. 3 cotton cloth in Taiyuan. In 1937, such a bolt cost CNC $7.00, but it is now worth CNC $4 million, so the *Yüan Fapi* should be the equivalent of CNC $600,000 now. Actually, however, the government has departed arbitrarily from its own formula and has set it at CNC $200,000, thereby in a single stroke eliminating two-thirds of the rent received by the owners of buildings. All rents are collected by the government directly from the building occupants, and the government then keeps 80 per cent of the income from commercial rents and 40 per cent from residential rents. Theoretically, the government uses this money for constructing new mass housing projects—500 units of which are said to have been built so far. On the rent remaining after the government has taken its cut, a 5 per cent tax is imposed for the relief of poor landlords and houseowners! The balance is supposed to be paid to the owners. This means that a property owner is legally entitled to a maximum of 15 per cent (on commercial buildings) or 55 per cent (on residential buildings) of a government-fixed rent, and that he must accept payment at an exchange rate based on a fictitious monetary unit that reduces the value of what he receives by two-thirds.

Interest rates are also controlled in Taiyuan. At present, the maximum legal rate is 2 per cent a day.

This comprehensive economic program is unique in Shansi

and, needless to say, could only be carried out by a special body with unusual powers. The Shansi Economic Control Bureau is just such a body. Added to the usual provincial organs normally authorized by the Central Government, it has now been recognized and authorized by the Central Government, and this, in effect, adds to Shansi's economic autonomy. It is another example of the special relationships that exist between Yen and the Central Government, and of the Central Government's inclination to grant *de jure* recognition to *de facto* situations that it cannot do anything about.

Yen's individuality stamps his entire administration. For example, although the *Pao-Chia* system is the standard administrative structure adopted by the Central Government for the entire country, Yen has instituted another system, similar in many ways but different in details. Until recently, Shansi was given a special dispensation by the Central Government for its peculiarities in this regard. Then, last year, this was ended, and the province theoretically changed to conform to the general pattern. But Yen's own system is, in fact, still in effect.

The basis of administrative organization in rural areas of the province is Yen's *Ts'un-Lü* system, started in 1922. Under this system, the smallest units are the *Lin*, composed of five families. Next are the *Lü*, composed of five *Lin*, or twenty-five families. The *Ts'un* is the village. In the city of Taiyuan, the system is a little different. The smallest units are the *Yüan*, or courtyards. Above them are *Lin*, *Lü*, and then *Chieh* (literally, "street").

Many of the special bodies established by Yen to carry out his own programs are not officially recognized by Nanking, and this makes it necessary for Yen to engage in a certain amount of financial chicanery. He depends for his bank notes, and for considerable financial support, upon the Central Government. Because of this fact, he now allows a branch of the Central Bank of China to operate in Taiyuan; before the war, he did not. In many parts of China, this bank is looked upon as a stronghold of conservative, even reactionary, supporters of the government. In Taiyuan, however, because it is an important Central Government agency, it is eyed suspiciously and looked upon as being almost subversive. Its officials feel uncomfortable and unwanted, and their functions are extremely limited. Almost all they do, in fact, is to funnel bank notes into Yen's Shansi Provincial Bank, which handles all of the province's monetary affairs. Every month, the Central Bank brings in, by air, a large sum (recently about

CNC $400 to $500 billion a month) that is provided as a Central Government subsidy to pay the troops and salaries of officials and employees in provincial government bodies that are recognized by the Central Government. The current basis for computing the monthly total is a salary index of CNC $200,000 for civil officials and employees within the city of Taiyuan itself and CNC $85,000 for everyone else. Yen, however, pays everyone on the basis of the CNC $85,000 figure and uses the money saved to pay the employees of provincial bodies not recognized by the Central Government. The Central Bank of China does not siphon any money out of the province. The amount that the Central Government Direct Tax Bureau in Taiyuan is now able to collect each month in income and commodity taxes is so small that it is hardly worth bothering about. Shansi Province does not send the Central Government a share of its land tax receipts, as specified in the national statutes.

On paper, much of what Yen Hsi-shan is now doing in Shansi sounds fairly progressive, but there is a terrible chasm between theory and practice. Most of the major policies, such as the redistribution of land, have been put into effect, but in ways disastrous to average people. Yen's Shansi is, in practice, a police state, ruled with an iron hand, and a place of near-starvation, fear, and despair. The evidence for this is readily available, even to an outsider visiting the province, if one probes below the surface by talking with people of varied sorts—although talking with private citizens usually has to be done in a conspiratorial manner.

In practice, the Soldier-Farmer Unification program, and the type of taxation that accompanies it, have imposed a terrible burden on the farmers in Yen's territory. Farmers are reported to be in almost universal opposition to it. There are many reasons for this. In fact, as contrasted with theory, the assigned land units are often not capable of providing support for the number of people who must depend on them. Moreover, taxes tend to be based on overestimates of the probable production of land and/or underestimates of the probable food needs of those who depend on the land. As the system works, many persons not in the eighteen to forty-seven age group are deprived of their means of existence; often they are farmers still able to work the land, and in many cases, land is actually taken away from them. Furthermore, the farmers dislike being shifted, arbitrarily, from one piece of land to another. Local villagers often do not have any real voice in how the land is apportioned. And because of their natural conservativeness, most farmers disapprove, on principle, of a system that disorganizes their existing life, prevents them from acquiring land they can call their own, and forces them to move their place of residence every few years.

Despite these objections, the system might be bearable if the government's taxation policies were not so ruinous. Officially, it is claimed that land taxation is based on Central Government regulations. The tax that these regulations, as interpreted and described by Shansi officials, permit is not light in itself. For every 12 mou of "good land" (adjustments are made for different qualities of land), the provincial authorities may levy 7 tou of grain (one tou is about 16.5 pounds) in a direct tax, and 7 tou as a forced loan (on which interest payments and repayments are indefinitely deferred). In addition, the authorities may "purchase" 21 tou, paying for it with paper currency. (Payment may be temporarily deferred, also, and thereby made in depreciated currency.) The "real taxes" amount to 20 tou. This would not be too unreasonable. However, in practice, the entire system is ignored, and virtually everything except what is necessary for bare existence is taxed away. In many cases, even this limit is exceeded. The farmers have no recourse. If they cannot pay the tax demanded, they have to sell personal possessions and buy grain to turn over to the government. If a farmer has a surplus after payment of his regular taxes, various methods are used to deprive him of it. One is to make him pay the taxes of some neighboring farmer who cannot pay in full. Another is to force him to "sell" his grain and then to make payment in bolts of cloth, matches, or cigarettes. When this is done, the grain is usually undervalued and the commodities used for payment overvalued. Moreover, the farmers have difficulty converting these commodities into food, or even into money with which to buy food. Sometimes a farmer's grain surplus is simply requisitioned, without all these camouflaging niceties. As a result of these taxation policies, a considerable number of farmers have actually abandoned their land. Tracts of such abandoned land can be seen between Taiyuan and Taiku.

Partly as a result of all these factors, the food situation in the Taiyuan region is now extremely critical for civilians. There is a threat of famine. Even now, many farmers are known to be subsisting on such things as wheat chaff, sorghum husks, and ground-up corn cobs. The food shortage is not entirely the result of the government's taxation policies; last year, there was a severe drought in the province that reduced the output in some areas by 50 per cent. But the government's tax policies are largely responsible for the plight of the farmers.

Officials admit that military requirements come first and must be met, regardless of other considerations. Yen's Chief of Staff claims, moreover, that military food stocks will not last out the year without replenishment from the new harvest. Private citizens estimate, however, that the army still has large stocks; some say it is enough to last nine years, others say at least one year. Some people believe Yen is stripping the countryside to prevent the Communists from getting anything if and when they take over. Others think he is piling up food stocks for a long siege. A few believe he is cornering all grain to make a huge profit by selling it at a later date. It is impossible, however, to find out what his actual stocks are.

Although not many people in Shansi are yet starving to death, local doctors say that dangerous signs of widespread malnutrition are increasing. Whether people will starve will depend on the size of this spring's crops—and the government's future taxation policies. So far, the crop prospects look unusually good, but the farmers are very much afraid that the tax collectors will arrive at the moment the harvest does. General Yen made a radio address to the people on the day that I arrived in Taiyuan. He announced that no one in his territory needs to worry about starvation. Spring will soon arrive, he said, and there will at least be tree leaves and grass. This diet, however, does not seem to hold any great attraction for the farmers, who see their wheat, sorghum, millet, and corn beginning to come up in their fields. However, there are, already, known cases of people who have been reduced to eating this diet.

The People's Economy has not been such a complete failure as the Soldier-Farmer Unification, and its impact on ordinary people has been a mixture of good and bad. The cooperatives, for example, do sell at prices below the open market; this month, the prices of millet and kaoliang are exactly one-half of open market prices. However, the cooperative ration tickets for the month only provide for fifteen days' food supply, and cooperative members must somehow obtain the remainder of what they need elsewhere. Many people fear, moreover, that as soon as cooperatives achieve a complete retail sales monopoly, eliminating private competition, the government will then be able to manipulate prices at will—a fear that reveals the prevailing attitudes toward the government.

In any case, general price control has been completely unsuccessful in Taiyuan. Prices of most commodities are two to three times as high as in Peiping. They are probably, in fact, the highest in north China. And actual interest rates are far above the theoretical maximum. Currently, the average rate on loans is about 4 per cent a day. A black market of considerable proportions exists, and it tends, inevitably, to destroy the effectiveness of rationing.

One side effect of Yen's policies, however, has been the virtual wiping out of private monied classes in Shansi. In practice, owners of agricultural land receive no rent. Owners of city property sometimes do receive payments, but these amount to almost nothing by the time they receive them. Businessmen must compete unequally with government monopolies, and must contend with innumerable government controls and restrictions. Because it is the center of government-owned industry, Taiyuan still has considerable general economic activity, but outlying towns are stagnating. Taiku, the home of H. H. K'ung (Chiang K'ai-shek's brother-in-law and one of the leading financial as well as political figures in China), and formerly the banking center of Shansi (Shansi had the reputation of providing most of China with bankers), was once a rich city. Today, shuttered business establishments line its dead main streets. In both Taiku and Taiyuan, buildings, streets, and everything else look run-down and in need of repair. Actually, many businessmen are leaving the province, if and when they can.

These grim economic facts give only part of the picture of how people are affected by Yen's regime, however. Government controls and interference affect almost everything the people do, and the prevailing practices of a police state are accompanied by all the usual police-state trappings. Everywhere, one sees groups of men, women, and boys being publicly lectured, drilled, and given political indoctrination. Passes are required for almost any activity, and travel is difficult almost to the point of being impossible for most people. For example, to enter the city of Taiyuan, a person not only needs a special pass, but he must also have guarantors willing to attest to his political reliability. Once he enters the city, he must obtain an additional permit to buy foodstuffs. Every household must make detailed reports to the police about all visitors. Political slogans, many of which the people must memorize, have almost displaced commercial advertising on walls and buildings. Political meetings, at which attendance is compulsory, are held frequently. People are subject to many kinds of forced labor without recompense. Groups of forced laborers can be seen in many areas building pillboxes, digging trenches—or working on the new airfield that Yen is building closer to the city wall than the existing one. Sometimes, the entire population of a village or city must perform forced labor. When I visited Taiku, almost the only activity visible in or near the city, apart from trench-digging by gangs of labor near the railway station, was the feverish moving of bricks by everyone—men, women, and children. An order had just been issued that, within a ten-day period, each person in the city had to carry 200 bricks from certain brick dumps to specified sites where new pillboxes were to be built. This work was not to be counted as a part of the twenty days unpaid labor that everyone is legally required to perform for the government each year.

Arrests of people suspected of political disloyalty are frequent and arbitrary in Yen's territory. And a much-dreaded secret-police force reaches into the privacy of virtually every individual's life. Freedom of speech does not exist; any grumbling or criticism leads to suspicion of political disaffection. Thought control is the aim of the government's extensive propaganda. Teachers in schools are gradually being given special indoctrination. And Central Government textbooks have been replaced by provincial texts in which even language lessons are based on readings about the People's Economy and Soldier-Farmer Unification programs. Shansi University, theoretically a national institution, has a bad reputation even within the province. Its academic standards are said to be very low. And when student political demonstrations sweep the country, Shansi University students are conspicuously quiet.

The most recent innovation in Shansi, however, is the "Three Self" program, aimed at "self-purification, self-defense, and self-government." Self-purification is the core of the program. It is handled by Liang Hua-chih, one of the nine provincial commissioners, who has the reputation of being Yen's strong-arm, secret-police man. Every man, woman, and child over the age of thirteen within Yen's territory must go through the process. It consists of three stages and takes three to four hours every day for a period of thirty days. The first stage is one of political indoctrination. The second is one of confession, during which each individual must relate everything he or she has done—since the age of thirteen, or since the date when Communist activities in Shansi first began—that might have any conceivable political significance. The final stage is Tou Cheng ("Struggle"), in which the people accuse, sentence, and punish those guilty of collaboration with the Communists.

This "Three Self" program is carried out in small groups, by the members of a village or an administrative district, and the basic objective is to root out all Communist sympathizers or collaborators. A person who confesses and repents, however, is supposed to be forgiven. But he or she must go through a special training course. Unrepenting criminals are sentenced by general "agreement of the group." Often the sentence is slow death by beating, with sticks. Liang, and other government officials including Yen himself, blandly explained to me that this is the result of spontaneous enthusiasm on the part of the people; popular justice, even if it is somewhat crude, cannot be interfered with by the government, they say. Actually, it is clearly a fact that the meetings are planned, scheduled, directed, and manipulated by the government. Special authorities handle them. I myself was an uninvited spectator at one of the meetings and saw it managed by men, well identified by red-ribbon badges, who explained to me their managerial duties.

This form of "popular justice," including the term *Tou Cheng*, has been borrowed directly from the Communists, as have other aspects of Yen's "reforms." I do not know how it works in Communist territories, but in Yen's region it is primitive and medieval. In fact, it produces a reign of terror. In Shansi today, a person never knows who might accuse him of disloyalty, or on what grounds, or for what motive. Not a few suicides and suicide attempts have resulted simply from the strain of the process, evidence of which I saw in local hospitals. The actual number of people sentenced and executed is probably relatively small, considering the number of people involved, but it is large enough to make a very great impression on the population as a whole. On one particular day this year, for example, more than a hundred persons were beaten to death in the vicinity of Taiku.

Policies of this sort are doubtless due, in large part, to real fear of Communist underground activities and infiltration. Yen himself apparently has almost no confidence any more in the loyalty or support of his people. In a somewhat amazing way, he summarized for me his own estimate of the reliability of his support: In Communist territory, he said, about 70 per cent of the people (the poor) actively support the Communists because they are offered material rewards; the other 30 per cent (the well-to-do) support them because of coercion and fear. In his own territory, he said, the 70 per cent may be attracted by the Communists' bait, and the 30 per cent may be politically apathetic. If his estimate is correct—and it may not be far off the mark—it is difficult to see where it leaves Yen. He went on to say that this situation can only be changed by a reawakening of the people, which, presumably, his policies are designed to bring about.

It is true that many people in Yen's territory have had some contact with the Communists in the past. This is not surprising. During the war against Japan, much of Shansi was under Communist rule. In recent years, the population of Taiyuan, now estimated to be about 300,000, has grown to between two and three times its prewar size, and many of the newcomers were at one time in areas under Communist controls. Moreover, large numbers of refugees still come from Communist territory. In one Lü in Taiyuan, for example, of 160 persons involved in the "Three Self" program, 140 confessed some past connection with the Communists. In one refugee camp, of a total of 597 refugees, 57 had at one time been members of the Communist Party, and more than 200 others had held some sort of office under the Communists. This is the situation Yen confronts, and the "Three Self" program is his method of trying to cope with it.

It is not surprising that a regime such as Yen's does not evoke great popular support or enthusiasm. It is more surprising that there are few indications of active underground opposition or pro-Communist tendencies. Persons within close contact with ordinary people explain that people fear the Communists at least as much as they do Yen's regime, and possibly even more. One indication of this is the stream of refugees still coming into the area. A representative of a relief agency in Taiyuan states that there are now 37,000 refugees camped around the city wall of Taiyuan, and perhaps as many as 700,000 in the entire area under Yen. Stories emanating from refugee groups indicate that the Communist regime in Shansi does not present an attractive alternative to Yen's rule. The Communists' land policy, for example, as described to me by an ex-Communist Party member who is now a refugee, seems to offer little to the average farmer. This particular man reported that his land was reduced from 20 mou (small for Shansi) to 6, which is considerably less than that distributed under Yen's system. Probably, also, the anti-Communist propaganda put out by the Shansi government has some effect on the people. It is strong stuff, crudely pornographic in its representation of Communist tortures. The people in Shansi, in short, are caught between the devil and the deep blue sea. And the lack of any real opposition group seems to be due not only to the effectiveness of

Yen's police-state controls, but also to the absence of any rallying point for opposition.

Throughout this report, I have constantly referred to Yen's area and Yen's government. One reason has been the necessity to distinguish the area under his control from Communist-held areas in the province. Another, however, is the fact that both the government and the territory are very much Yen's personal domain. The structure of power is that of a hierarchical pyramid, with Yen at the apex. Decision-making power is highly centralized, and persons who know Yen well say that he has a finger in every pie. Despite his age, he is robust and active, and is said to make personal decisions on many matters of detail.

Yen relies considerably, however, on an important body of close supporters, most of whom depend completely upon him for their livelihood, position, and whatever power or influence they wield. Theoretically, the broad base of Yen's support is his own political party. This party, organized in the city of Linfen during the retreat from the Japanese in 1938, is called the People's Revolutionary Comrades' Party. Yen's top officials claim it has had as many as 800,000 members, and that 200,000 of them are in Yen's territory at present. They also say that the party is connected somehow with the Kuomintang, but the connection certainly appears to be tenuous, even though it is true that members of the Comrades' Party can be, and often are, members of the Kuomintang. The Kuomintang itself, although it has branch party units in Yen's area, has few members; it is really an orphan organization in Shansi, without any real power.

Members of the Shansi bureaucracy and army form a more closely knit and important core of group support for Yen; these men are dependents of Yen's in almost every way. The quality of this group of men is difficult to judge. A man close to government circles claims that the small circle of top officials around Yen probably is fairly free from corruption, because they are under Yen's own vigilant surveillance, but that Yen himself has accumulated, and is still accumulating, substantial personal wealth outside of the province, and that many minor officials and bureaucrats are profiting from corruption on a small scale. It is certainly of some significance that no complete provincial budget or accounting is made public.

The inner circle of Yen's closest supporters is a somewhat mysterious group referred to as the thirteen Kao Kan (which might be loosely translated as "top bosses"). This is an informal group that is said to advise Yen on all important policy matters.

Its existence is supposedly secret (although it is a rather open secret). People do not talk about the group; it is not mentioned even by government officials. Its members are known, nevertheless. Some of the thirteen are members of the group by virtue of their government positions, while others hold jobs that sound unimportant but exercise real power behind the scenes. A few of them have had affiliations of various sorts with the Communists in the past, which may be one explanation for Yen's eclecticism in regard to Communist methods. People in Shansi do not venture to name Yen's probable successor, but if he tried to groom an heir, the man would doubtless come from this group.

The future of Yen's regime is now a question mark, however. The regime is hard-pressed and seems to be built on sand, but it will probably not collapse by itself. Some military observers seem to feel that the Communists could take the Taiyuan area if they wanted to expend the necessary effort, but that the costs would be considerable, despite the low quality of Yen's troops. They also feel that it stands low on the Communists' list of priority objectives and will probably, therefore, be by-passed for some time to come. This is the belief of Yen himself, and of many of his top officers and officials. They frankly admit that they are not thinking in terms of offensive action against the Communists. What Yen wants is for the United States to declare war on Russia immediately, and he doesn't mind saying so. He and his supporters assert that a third world war is inevitable, and they wish it would come soon. They believe such a war would defeat world Communism—and Yen's enemies in Shansi.

If the Communists do decide to make a serious effort to take Taiyuan earlier than people expect, the lure will undoubtedly be Yen's "industrial empire" located in and around the city of Taiyuan. This is the most impressive accomplishment of Yen's regime. It is almost unbelievable, in an area surrounded by mountains and Communists, to see large factories going full blast and huge shops, containing hundreds of machine tools, turning out complicated metal products.

Almost all industry in Yen's territory is a part of the Northwest Industrial Company, a government monopoly controlled by Yen himself through a board of directors headed by a man named P'eng Shih-hung. This company, started in 1932, is supposed to be a "people's enterprise." The original capital of CH $30 million (prewar dollars) theoretically was subscribed to in the following manner: Stock quotas of 30,000 shares were assigned to each *Hsien* in the province, and the "people" collectively purchased the stock and elected representatives as stockholders. Even according to the company's charter and laws, however, no dividends were to be distributed on this stock for forty-two years! A man who should know says that the capital came directly from government funds and that there actually are no "stockholders" at all. In any case, all profits are reinvested in the company—or at least there has been no public distribution.

The company developed rapidly between 1932 and 1937, and at the end of that period it had fifty-one factories. Then, during the war, the Japanese who occupied Taiyuan operated only a few of the industries and ultimately removed 3,700 out of a total of 4,000 machines. Now, however, thirty-six plants have been restored and are operating, and they employ about 25,000 workers. Production is geared primarily to Yen's military requirements, but some consumer goods are produced. The company's products include iron, steel, cement, chemicals, leather goods, paper, matches, cigarettes, alcohol, woolen goods, cotton goods, and flour. Amazingly enough, a full-size locomotive has recently been completed. All of this industry is impressive, and the metals and heavy industries are astounding.

Shansi has the richest coal deposits in China Proper, and all the necessary raw materials for a steel industry (except specialized alloys) lie within a radius of less than 20 miles of Taiyuan. Yen's heavy industries utilize these local resources. At present, the daily production of coke, pig iron, and steel is 180 tons, 50 tons, and 50 tons, respectively. In addition, most of the machine tools now being used in the Taiyuan area have been produced there from Japanese, German and American models. The top technicians in the Northwest Industrial Company, incidentally, are Chinese, but there are six or seven fugitive Nazis serving as technical advisors, and a fairly large number of Japanese technicians and mechanics who stayed on after the end of the war.

Linked to the Northwest Industrial Company's activities, there is a fantastic import-export trade now going on, by air in commercial carriers, between Taiyuan and other Nationalist areas. Imports include raw materials, such as cotton, tobacco, oil, and specialized goods, such as steel alloys and dyes. Exports include chemicals, steel products, and cement—all shipped out by air.

This operating industrial center could be an extremely valuable arsenal for the Communists; conceivably, it might inspire them to turn their attention toward Taiyuan sooner than some people expect—particularly if they are successful in their current military campaigns in surrounding areas.

For the present, however, Yen Hsi-shan still rules in Taiyuan. There is no doubt that the character of this man is extremely complex. In some respects, he appears to be the most notable surviving relic of China's warlord era. In others, he shows surprising modernity, superficially at least. He professes to be a reformer; it is even possible that he has convinced himself that his reforms are progressive, despite the fact that he is certainly not unaware of the tragic results of some of his policies. Personally, he is witty, charming, and delightful. And, although some aspects of his character are confusing, one thing is absolutely clear: He is an extremely shrewd old man. Some people suggest that when the time is ripe he may come to terms with the Communists. This does not seem likely, but Yen's imagination does not seem to have disappeared yet, and he may still have a trick or two up his sleeve.

A man who knows Marshal Yen well, and for many years was closely associated with him, says that his egotism and his lust for personal power have, if anything, increased during the past few years, so it seems unlikely that he will disappear from the Shansi stage if he can possibly hang on. Even if the curtain does fall on his thirty-seven-year-long performance, he will not be soon forgotten, for the imprint and memory of his rule will be indelible for many years to come.

12

MUSLIM AUTHORITARIANISM

Lanchow (Kansu)
October, 1948

Lanchow, the largest (204,000 population) and most strategic city in northwest China, is the official capital of Kansu Province and the unofficial capital of the entire northwest. Here, Governor Kuo Ch'i-ch'iao runs a provincial administration governing 7.25 million people scattered along the weirdly shaped Kansu corridor from the border of Sinkiang to the border of Shensi. Here also, General Chang Chih-chung maintains his Northwest Headquarters—the Northwest Political and Military Authority—which is theoretically the ultimate authority in the four provinces of Kansu, Sinkiang, Chinghai, (Tsinghai), and Ninghsia (Ningsia). General Chang is an urbane, conciliatory, and intelligent (one might also say shrewd) leader who has a rare reputation in many quarters in China for his success at middle-of-the-road politics. He has done much of the Central Government's negotiating with the Chinese Communists, and, even though he now holds one of the highest political posts under the Central Government, he apparently still commands the Communists' respect—which may be one factor helping to explain why the four northwest provinces under his authority have to date rarely been molested by them.

Although General Chang Chih-chung is not currently plagued, as is much of China, by attacks or pressure from the Communists, he has his share of problems. The most critical of these are the unsettled Ili Revolt and Peitashan Incident in Sinkiang. ("No prospect of a solution is in sight," he told me.) In addition, he is also confronted with certain problems that are endemic to northwest China. One of these is the problem of relations between the Chinese Muslims and the Han Chinese. Officially, General Chang, who is a cautious man, asserts that there is "no problem," but relations between the Muslims and Han Chinese actually have been a serious problem for centuries and remain so today. Currently, relations are comparatively amiable, but the existence of a Chinese Muslim belt running through Ninghsia,

Kansu, and Chinghai is one of the most basic political facts of life in the region. It is a fact that definitely does present problems to both the Chinese Central Government and its local representatives in the area, for the Muslims are politically the most aggressive and militant group in the region, and they are dominant in two of the four provinces under General Chang's authority. The regimes that they maintain in these two provinces, Chinghai and Ninghsia, are, in fact, authoritarian, semiautonomous governments whose relations with the Central Government and Chang's Northwest Headquarters can be described more accurately as political alliance than political integration.

Ethnically, most Chinese Muslims are a racial mixture, combining Chinese blood with that of various Muslim groups that migrated to China centuries ago from the "West," from various parts of the region between Arabia and Afghanistan. Some of China's Muslims are scattered over east and southwest China; these are mainly descendants of Arab traders who reached China by sea. The major concentration, however, is in the Muslim belt in the northwest, and these people trace their blood ties to groups that migrated via Central Asiatic routes.

Religiously speaking, the majority of the Muslims in the northwest are "good Muslims." They are strict about following the religious taboos, such as the ban on pork; as a rule, they do not drink or smoke; and they always wear skull caps. Mosques are located wherever there are Muslim settlements, and festivals such as Ramadan are universally observed. Arabic is generally used in both religious services and ecclesiastical schools. Generally, although they may not be as sensitive or aggressive about their religion as Muslims in some parts of the world, the Muslims in northwest China have not allowed their religion to be appreciably diluted. In most secular matters, however, their cultural assimilation by the Chinese has been almost complete.

In appearance, these people are clearly distinguishable from other Chinese. The men's skull caps and women's hoods are identifying marks, but, in addition, their facial features are quite distinctive. Their noses are larger and their eyes rounder than those of typical Chinese, and the men wear luxuriant beards and bushy sideburns. Some have features and coloration so Occidental that they are startling in a remote Oriental setting.

Within the northwest Muslim belt, there are several different groups. The Salars are one. Reputed to have come originally—sometime about the twelfth century—from Samarkand in Central Asia, they settled in the region of the Yellow River bend near the present provincial border of Kansu and Chinghai. Another group is the Tunghsiang, or "East Country," Muslims, in Kansu. They are somewhat of an ethnological curiosity, for they speak a language that is clearly Mongolian and are probably, therefore, of Mongol stock. Most important, however, is the Muslim group in Hochow, a region in south Kansu that was once a single administrative unit, but is now divided into several *Hsien*.

Hochow is sometimes called (by Westerners) the "Mecca of Chinese Islam," for it is the home and homeland of Muslims who have spread throughout northwest China to become the most energetic, virile, and politically active group in the whole region. The Hochow Muslims trace their ancestry, at least partially, to Arab mercenaries who served under the Chinese T'ang Dynasty —and are said to have come overland to China sometime around the eighth century.

During recent decades, until just a few years ago, politics in Kansu itself were dominated by Hochow Muslims. At present, the leadership in the adjoining provinces of Chinghai and Ninghsia—both of which were formed from parts of Kansu Province that were joined with adjacent border territory—is still provided by Hochow Muslims who retain close ties with their home district.

Strictly speaking, there is no special Muslim center within China, and Chinese Muslim pilgrims are among those who make the long journey every year to Mecca. Organization of Chinese Muslims is largely on a regional basis. Generally, each mosque has autonomy under its own *ahung*—the equivalent of mullahs elsewhere. (In the Chinese Muslim belt of northwest China, "mullah" is the title applied to student priests.) But there are also several regional centers of religious importance— such as Sining in Chinghai, Chinchihsien in Ninghsia, and Hochow in Kansu—where ranking Muslim leaders are located.

Although not a religious capital, Hochow is nevertheless a center that many Muslims all over northwest China consider home, and which they periodically revisit. In a sense, it is a unifying element that holds the group together.

The history of political relations between the Chinese Muslims and the Han Chinese has, at times, been bitter and violent. This was particularly true during the latter half of the nineteenth century, when numerous Muslim revolts flared up throughout China against the Peking Government and its local representatives. The uprisings in the northwest were important factors in helping to undermine the already weakened Ch'ing Dynasty.

When compared with the past, present relations between the Muslims and other Chinese can be described as relatively friendly and peaceful. On a village level, there appears to be little communalism or friction between the two groups. In political affairs, however, the normal (in other regions) relations between the Chinese and minorities is reversed. Instead of the Han Chinese being politically dominant over the minority, the Muslim minority dominates the Chinese—except in Kansu. In Kansu, the Muslims, who constitute less than 9 per cent of the total population, have been relegated, in recent years, to a position in keeping with their numerical importance, and at present, in this economically and strategically important province, a regime under firm national supervision has completely replaced local Muslim minority rule. However, in Chinghai, where the Muslims constitute 40 per cent of the total population of 930,000, and in Ninghsia, where they make up only 25 per cent of a population of 760,000 (not counting the Mongols), political control is firmly in the hands of Hochow Muslims. To be more specific, it is in the hands of two Hochow Muslim leaders: General Ma Pu-fang and General Ma Hung-k'uei. These two men do not maintain very close relations with each other, however, even though they are related and both maintain family ties with Hochow.

Chinghai and Ninghsia are definitely less desirable areas than Kansu, from the point of view of ambitious leaders, but in view of the importance placed upon Kansu by the Central Government, the Ma's do not now have a chance there. The major portions of both Chinghai and Ninghsia are pastoral regions, inhabited by minorities who are neither Han nor Muslim. In Chinghai, the western and southern parts of the province are occupied mainly by Tibetans, with a scattering of other minorities; the Muslims and Chinese, who are agriculturalists, are concentrated in the valleys of the Sining and Yellow rivers in the north and east. In Ninghsia, most of the province, west of the Holan Mountains (sometimes called the Alashan Mountains), is the territory of two autonomous Special Banners of Mongols, controlled directly by the Central Government rather than the provincial administration; the Muslims and Chinese are concentrated in a small area of thirteen *Hsien* in the east and southeast, in the valley of the Yellow River. These two small areas of intensely cultivated, irrigated agricultural land are the centers of power of the Generals Ma.

The regimes in Chinghai and Ninghsia control comparatively small numbers of people, and neither would be of great im-

importance under normal circumstances. However, being authoritarian, militaristic, and autonomous, both are of more importance and of more interest politically than their populations would warrant.

Ma Pu-fang, who rules Chinghai, is a trim, soldierly man with a very Muslim-looking beard, and he is the third member of a local family dynasty that has controlled the province for the past two decades. His father, Ma Ch'i, became provincial chief in 1929, soon after Chinghai was made into a province. Ma Ch'i was succeeded by his brother, Ma Ling, and then, in 1938, Ma Pu-fang inherited the governorship from his uncle.

Ma Pu-fang's regime is one of the most efficient in China, and one of the most energetic. While much of the rest of China is bogged down, almost inevitably, by civil war, Chinghai is attempting to carry out small-scale, but nevertheless ambitious, development and reconstruction schemes on its own initiative.

Three things have almost become trade-marks of the authoritarian Muslim government in Chinghai: worn fly swatters, green tree saplings, and stocky horses.

The streets of Sining, the provincial capital, present a curious spectacle of venerable, bearded, Muslim gentlemen vying with small boys in a never-ending battle against the common house fly. As part of its sanitation program, the Provincial Government periodically announces daily quotas of dead flies that must be handed in to the authorities by everyone, regardless of age, sex, or occupation. As a result, the streets of the city are among the cleanest and most fly-less in China. There is even a black market for dead flies, the current quotation being CNC $50,000 a hundred.

The smooth, crushed-rock highways in Chinghai all are lined with green willow and poplar saplings. An intensive program of tree planting and reforestation has, in fact, made the valleys of east Chinghai among the most verdant in China. Young trees dot the neat farms, cluster around the stream beds, and climb upward on the surrounding hills. Chinghai does not have an Arbor Day; it has an Arbor Fortnight. For two weeks each spring, everyone in the province goes into the countryside and plants trees. During the past ten years, 61 million have been planted, an average of more than six trees per year per man, woman, and child in the province.

Ma, which means "horse" in Chinese, is the most prevalent surname among the Chinese Muslims, and in Chinghai it is appropriate. The Chinghai horses—and cavalrymen—are famous in

China, and, at present, General Ma Pu-fang's troops are among the best soldiers in the country. The bivouacs and camps of these troops are spotless, and the soldiers themselves are well dressed and disciplined. One sees these troops throughout the eastern districts of the province, and they help to create a general atmosphere that is very martial.

There are also other interesting features distinguishing the Chinghai administration. Irrigation projects have been pushed on a scale that is impressive when one considers the relatively small amount of cultivable land available (most of which is used and produces the food needs of the population, plus a small surplus). Within the past year alone, five new canals, irrigating about 7,000 acres, have been completed.

Hospitals and medical facilities are gradually being introduced. Before Ma Pu-fang became Governor, Chinghai did not have a single modern hospital or health center to serve a population badly infected by syphilis, trachoma, and many other diseases. Now, although medical facilities are still pitifully inadequate, the provincial Health Bureau has 10 qualified modern doctors, runs a modern 100-bed hospital, and maintains 7 health stations.

Industrialization is a completely new idea in Chinghai. During the Sino-Japanese War, however, General Ma built small factories for such activities as woolwashing, matchmaking, leather tanning, metalworking, pottery making, and chemical manufacture. These plants did not amount to very much, but they were a start. Some of them have had to close down or reduce the scale of their operations since the end of the war, but General Ma is now soliciting outside technical assistance (he has the capital) to get the ball rolling again. He is also trying to install a sewage system in Sining, and if he is successful, he will have the only sewage system in northwest China.

Perhaps the most impressive development, however, has been in the field of education. The Provincial Government has established many new schools and has greatly reduced illiteracy. The 1,057 primary schools and 13 middle schools now in Chinghai have an enrollment of approximately 94,000 and 4,500 students, respectively, all of whom are provided with free school uniforms as well as books and other needed equipment. In Sining, roughly one-third of the total population goes to school. As yet, there is no institution of higher learning in the province, but 200-300 students are subsidized by the Provincial Government in colleges and universities elsewhere.

The most unique educational project is a special system of

schools called the K'unlun Schools. These include every level from kindergarten through middle school, and their 7,000 students are provided with all needs—including food and clothing —free. Theoretically, it is a private school system, supported financially by the local Muslim Educational Promotion Committee, but actually the schools receive strong moral and financial support from the Governor. The student body is 87 per cent Muslim, and the main objective of the schools, which teach Arabic as a required course for Muslims in the primary classes, is "to raise the standard of Muslim education." In a sense, the K'unlun Schools are producing a new educated Muslim elite under the aegis of a strongly Muslim Governor—who is said to be influenced to a considerable degree by a religiously devout wife.

Ma Pu-fang's entire government has a strong Muslim flavor, and by far the majority of important posts are filled by Hochow Muslims—many of them named Ma, some relatives, some not. The government appears to support itself to a large extent by a commercial and industrial monopoly, rather than by high taxes. During the first half of this year, when provincial expenditures amounted to CNC $600 billion, only $50 billion was received in taxes and $120 billion in Central Government subsidies; the rest came from "loans" extended by the Huang Chung Industrial Company and Chinghai Commercial Bank. The Huang Chung Company, established last year, theoretically is privately owned, but actually it is a semigovernmental organ, controlled by Governor Ma and a key group of supporters. Its profits come from the export of wools, hides, and furs, obtained principally from the Tibetan and Mongol regions of the province, and the import of tea, cloth, and other manufactured articles. Neither land taxes nor other taxes seem to be oppressively heavy in Chinghai, and the farmers—a majority of whom are owner-cultivators who till farms of reasonable size—appear to be quite well-off.

The political price for these constructive policies and developments, however, is a stern authoritarianism that leaves very little room for personal freedom, and the military price is conscription, which imposes a heavy burden on the people. To relieve the burden of conscription on small families, however, a system of "a horse for a man" is sometimes followed, under which small families are allowed to donate a horse instead of a son.

The penalties for disobeying provincial orders or bucking the regime are severe. All important political decisions, furthermore, are made by one man, General Ma Pu-fang himself, and the impetus for change and progress is entirely from above, rather than from below. Nevertheless, General Ma seems to enjoy a considerable amount of popular support, because of the visible improvements that his regime has made. Many of the usual marks of an authoritarian regime—police registration, for example, and the use of travel passes—are present, but they are relatively unobtrusive. It is significant, also, that one does not currently hear accusations in Chinghai of graft or personal corruption leveled against Ma Pu-fang.

The Chinghai Provincial Government, because of its excellent cavalry, is the strongest local regime in northwest China, and in recent years, despite its autonomy, it has been working in close alliance, militarily, with the Central Government. This is partly because of Ma's virulent dislike and fear of Communism, and partly because he is entirely dependent upon the Central Government for military supplies. A large percentage of Ma's estimated 70,000 to 80,000 cavalry and infantry troops have been made available to the Central Government both for use against the Communists and for border defense in Sinkiang. These Chinghai troops are usually conscripted on a lifetime basis, but because they receive excellent treatment, as well as excellent training, their morale is high. Their brilliant commander, twenty-eight-year-old General Ma Chi-yüan, is the Governor's son; he is worshiped with something approaching pure adoration by the Muslims in Chinghai.

Chinghai units stationed in Lungtung, or east Kansu, are the main defense against the Communists for the whole northwest, since Central Government forces in the region are limited. To date, the Communists have not made any major attacks on the area, but Ma Chi-yüan's victory at Pingliang last summer, when the Communists were moving from south to north Shensi, was one of the most important, and one of the few, Nationalist military successes of the year. Chinghai itself is completely free of Communists; it has not been bothered with them since they were given a drubbing in the eastern part of the province on their celebrated Long March from Kiangsi to Shensi over a decade ago.

The Muslim ruler of Ninghsia is Ma Hung-k'uei, a 240-pound, roly-poly man of fifty-six who looks more Chinese than Muslim. He also is the heir to a family tradition of local rule that has dynastic characteristics. His father, Ma Fu-hsiang, was a military leader in the northwest under both the Ch'ing Dynasty and the early Chinese Republic. During part of his career, he was military commander in the area that is now Ninghsia Province—

then part of Kansu. The first two governors of Ninghsia, after it was established as a province, were not members of the family, but the third was an older brother of the present Governor. Ma Hung-k'uei was next in the line of succession.

The Provincial Government in Ninghsia is less thoroughly Muslim than in Chinghai, and Ma Hung-k'uei has the reputation of treating Muslims and Han Chinese without discrimination. Nevertheless, the provincial administration is riddled with relatives of the Governor and other Hochow Ma's. The Secretary-General is a Muslim named Ma (not a close relative); two of the four principal commanders of the Provincial Peace Preservation Corps are relatives of the Governor (Ma Ch'üan-chung and Ma Ni-chung), and the two key military commanders of regular army troops under Ma Hung-k'uei are his sons. His first son, Ma Tung-hou, leads the Governor's cavalry. His second son, Ma Tung-ch'in, heads the Governor's infantry. Other posts of importance are also held by the Ma clan. The Eighty-First Division in south Ninghsia is the only important military organization in the province not directly under the Governor's command, yet it is commanded by one of Ma Hung-k'uei's nephews, Ma Hsün-ch'in. The tentacles of the Hochow Ma's reach throughout the regime, therefore, even though, for various reasons, the regime seems to be less self-consciously Muslim than the one in Chinghai.

Many features of the Ninghsia administration are similar to those in Chinghai, but there are also important differences. The differences might be summed up in an oversimplified way as follows: In Ninghsia, the good is not quite as good and the bad is considerably worse. In both Chinghai and Ninghsia, the regimes are strict and authoritarian, but the emphasis in Chinghai is upon reconstruction, while in Ninghsia it is upon law, order, and control.

In Ninghsia, as in Chinghai, there is efficiency, but it is frequently combined with ruthlessness. There is also a relative absence of corruption, but people slyly intimate that this is because "corruption is monopolized." Ma Hung-k'uei's reputation is, in any case, far from being as spotless in the public mind as Ma Pu-fang's. Ninghsia's extensive tree planting and reforestation are also impressive, but the 40 million trees planted miss the Chinghai mark, and the program is not considered to be quite as good as in Chinghai. The 467 primary schools and 14 middle schools in Ninghsia, with an enrollment of 68,000 and 1,900, respectively, have reduced illiteracy, but the schools do not have a reputation for quality, and the educational enthusiasm evident in Chinghai is lacking. Ma Hung-k'uei has a monopoly commercial and industrial company, the recently established Fu Ning Company—theoretically a joint private-government organization—very similar in its functions to the Huang Chung Company in Chinghai, but taxes, including the land tax, in Ninghsia seem to be much more burdensome upon the population than in Chinghai. The main highways in Ninghsia are reasonably good—an accomplishment of considerable importance, since no roads existed in the region until a few years ago—but they are not as good as the ones in Chinghai. A hospital has been established in Ninghsia City, but it has a bad reputation, and even government officials refuse to use it.

In short, the developmental and reconstruction activities of Ma Hung-k'uei's government follow the same lines as in Chinghai, but without the same degree of success, and the methods Ma Hung-k'uei uses seem to be completely arbitrary. It is obvious to anyone who talks with common people in the cities or in the countryside that these methods are found to be highly objectionable by the population.

Within the past year and a half, every city and large town in Ninghsia has undergone a complete face-lifting—with bricks. A new façade of grey brick—the largest producers of which are reportedly factories owned by relatives of the Governor—has been constructed on the front of every single building in these towns. As a result, the streets of the towns are probably among the most uniform and neat in appearance in China. They are also, however, among the most drab, despite considerable ingenuity in brick designing. This complete surface transformation has been accomplished with relative ease, from the government's point of view. Ma Hung-k'uei simply issued a series of orders stating that, by such-and-such dates, all occupants of buildings in such-and-such districts would complete the construction of new brick fronts to their buildings. The problem of financing this major operation was left up to the individual. Every house occupant had to "figure a way out." If he could think of no way, and construction work could not be financed from personal savings or private loans, he could apply for a special one-year loan from the Provincial Government. But in the final analysis, the burden of financing was shifted entirely to the average citizen, in a most arbitrary way, without any consideration of ability to pay.

The authority backing up provincial orders is so absolute that orders have a magic effect—compared with some parts of China where the relationship between the average citizen and his government is casual, to say the least. One thing people in Ninghsia are instructed to do, for example, is to keep the mud roads in front of their property smooth. This requires constant work, and, consequently, one can see, in any street of the province at almost any time of day, gowned businessmen squatting beside street urchins, smoothing out the ruts with small spades.

Most of the public-works projects undertaken by the government are carried out by unpaid, forced labor. This is true to a certain extent in Chinghai as well, but in Ninghsia the gangs of laborers one sees along the roads, and elsewhere, are particularly dirty, ragged, and bedraggled-looking. Young men are almost completely missing from the civilian gangs; old farmers, many of them with white beards, predominate. One does see uniformed young men working in other labor gangs, however, for the provincial troops are employed as a labor force when they are not involved in training or other military duties.

As mentioned already, the main emphasis in Ma Hung-k'uei's regime is on control, and the Governor boasts that "complete peace and order prevail" and "there are no Communists in the province." Fear and hatred of Communism are fundamental in almost everything the government does, and these feelings appear to be real, not merely rationalizations of Ma's authoritarianism. The proximity of Ninghsia to Communist areas in Shensi may, in fact, be one of the key factors explaining the overall difference between the Ninghsia and Chinghai regimes. An elaborate system of governmental controls, plus military mobilization, affects virtually all facets of people's lives in Ninghsia, making Communist infiltration and desertion to the Communists almost equally impossible.

The techniques of control and mobilization employed in Ninghsia—by a Governor who asserts, feelingly, that what contemporary China needs above all else is "strict law"—are varied and effective. Almost all young men are now drafted into military service on a "lifetime basis"—that is, for the period of their military usefulness. Those best qualified are placed in regular army units—the Eighteenth Division, Tenth Cavalry Brigade, Tenth Provisional Infantry Brigade, and the Independent Artillery Regiment—all of which are nominally a part of the National Army, but are actually provincial troops. The rest are mobilized into Provincial Peace Preservation Corps units. All get rigorous training, including strenuous calisthenics and gymnastics. It is estimated that, at present, perhaps 100,000 men belong to either the regulars or the four main Peace Preservation Corps units; this is roughly

1 out of every 7 persons in the province, and is, of course, an even larger percentage of the male population. All other able-bodied men, old and young, are enlisted in the Self-Defense Corps, the theoretical age limits for which are eighteen to forty-five. The government estimates that these militiamen now number 120,000. They receive a minimum of training, including literacy instruction if they need it, and are used by the government for local guard duty—every road bridge in the province is guarded by them —and as labor gangs, without remuneration. The penalty for military desertion in Ninghsia could hardly be more severe; it is death for the deserter if he is found, and it is said that if he is not found his family must provide three male substitutes to take his place —or pay the established monetary equivalent if the males are not available. Conscription is crude in its methods; often, men are taken from their homes in the middle of the night. Apparently, there is a good deal of passive resistance to this arbitrary and widespread mobilization, or at least reluctance to cooperate fully with the government, but there are not many successful draft dodgers. Almost the only persons who can legally get exemptions are students.

Every citizen in Ninghsia possesses an identity card, which carries either a photograph or a thumbprint. These are constantly checked at key points throughout the province (the visual check on fingerprints is one of the few amusing sights in the province). An official pass is required for any travel or movement, and it is fair to say that there is almost no freedom of movement in the province. There is, in fact, very little movement at all.

The Provincial Government has carried out a thorough census and a complete land survey, which it claims to be the first modern survey in China. These are regularly checked by the Provincial Government. In the offices of the Commission of Civil Affairs, there are detailed maps of every locality in the province, on which every single household is pinpointed. Close track is kept of each family, and it is claimed that anyone can be located at a moment's notice.

At 6:00 A.M. every morning, all able-bodied men in the province, both civilian and military, are mustered at regular meeting places. The muster is followed by an indoctrination and training session, lasting anywhere from twenty minutes to an hour, during which the instruction is devoted primarily to methods of opposing or rooting out Communism.

Every ten to fifteen households are organized into reporting units, and the heads of the households must make regular personnel reports every day, reporting any arrivals or departures, to a designated member of the group. The member receiving the reports changes on a rotation basis. Their reports are passed on to higher authorities.

Administration of justice in Ninghsia is swift, and punishments are severe. Flogging is fairly common and is sometimes even meted out to erring public officials. In Ninghsia City, hardly a day now passes when there is not at least one execution carried out by the Provincial Government.

Price control is absolutely rigid, and it is applied to a long list of commodities covering almost all necessities. This control has kept prices relatively low, but it has also helped to make commodities scarce. Merchants divert goods elsewhere, and farmers often do not sell. However, the authorities are quite proud of the fact that there is no black market.

It is not surprising that a regime of this sort imposes a severe strain on the population, both economically and psychologically. It is not supported with much visible enthusiasm. Solemn, unsmiling faces may not always be a reliable indicator of popular feeling, but it is significant, I think, that I saw more glum expressions in Ninghsia than in any other province except Shansi. After spending a few days in Ninghsia, one hears many whispered grumblings, always made a little furtively.

Ninghsia's Yellow River valley region is a rich agricultural area. The Chinese have a saying, in fact, the gist of which is that, although the Yellow River is China's sorrow in most places, it is the joy of Ninghsia. Extensive irrigation works, hundreds of years old, but well maintained by the present administration, make the farmers independent of the weather. Land is plentiful. According to official figures, in fact, only about one-third of the cultivable land is used at present. Individual holdings are quite large, and most farmers own their own land.

Despite these facts, the farmers in Ninghsia today are poor, and their poverty is very visible. The average farmer now is an old man. He is unassisted by his sons because they are in the armed forces. He often cannot cultivate all the land that he owns because he lacks assistance. Much of his time is spent on forced-labor projects and in Self-Defense Corps duty. A very large percentage of his produce is taxed away by the government to support the many men in uniform. It is true, however, that he lives in an area where there is "peace and order" and where "there are no Communists."

Ma Hung-k'uei's forces have been fairly successful in keeping the Communists out of the province. Despite some reports of their excellence, however, and General Ma's boasts regarding them ("one of my soldiers can handle three Communist soldiers"), the Ninghsia troops are not considered first-rate by many people in the province. Their weakness is attributed to bad morale. They clearly do not constitute as formidable a fighting force as Ma Pu-fang's troops. Generally, they have been kept within the province and used for local defense, and they do not have many successes against the Communists to their credit.

Ma Hung-k'uei's relations with the Central Government are similar to those of Ma Pu-fang. In talking with him, one gets the impression that, although he feels a personal loyalty toward Chiang K'ai-shek, he does not have a very high regard for the other high leaders of the Central Government or for General Chang in Lanchow.

Currently, there are signs revealing more than ordinary stresses and strains in the relations between the Muslims in the northwest and the Central Government. These signs are especially evident in Chinghai. Perhaps partly because it has an abundance (relatively speaking) of both silver and gold bullion, Chinghai has not given the Central Government anything like enthusiastic cooperation, in connection with the recent Chinese monetary reform. Moreover, General Ma Pu-fang has gone into a political shell and has been pouting like a small boy for almost a month and a half. During this period, he has been completely inaccessible even to his own closest officials. It is explained, with a smile, that he has "stomach trouble." But it is universally known that his malady is political. The most credible explanations offered by people in Sining are that he is displeased by the lack of recognition he has received from the Central Government for his military support, and that he is unhappy about the Central Government's failure to grant his requests for military supplies. Both of the Ma's feel that they have been discriminated against in the distribution of military supplies, and this issue rankles. Their freedom of action in relations with the Central Government is severely limited, however—despite their high degree of autonomy —by the fact that the Central Government is their only possible source of military supplies at the present time.

13

CHINESE IN INNER MONGOLIA

Paotow (Suiyuan)
January, 1948

The 510-mile railway between Peiping and Paotow—the end of the line in Inner Mongolia—cuts through four Chinese provinces, and is flanked by some of the most spectacular mountain scenery in north China. Soon after leaving Peiping, the train climbs away from the flat north China plain in Hopeh and winds through the narrow defile of Nankow Pass. From there, it follows a valley toward the mountain-rimmed basin that contains the city of Kalgan. Then it runs westward along the Kalgan plain in Chahar and through the Tatung basin in northern Shansi. To the north of the railway, along this stretch, there is a continuous ridge of mountains, part of the Yin Mountain system, at the base of which twists the outer loop of the Great Wall. From Tatung, the rails turn and go through the eroded Fengchen highlands, where the rolling hills look like tremendous waves about to engulf the thin ribbon of railway. In this region, the line passes beyond the final Great Wall barrier, into the area considered to be the land of barbarians, beyond the pale of civilization, by Chinese of centuries past. In Suiyuan Province, the railway again turns westward and follows the Kweisui plain, at the foot of the Taching Mountains, until it reaches Paotow, the western terminus of the line. When I made this trip recently, the first snow of the year was falling, and both the mountains and plains were white and beautiful.

Although the Peiping-Suiyuan railway crosses four provinces, the territorial zone that it serves has been integrated into a single economic unit; cheap transportation has proved to be of more importance than provincial boundaries. Construction of the railway was started soon after the Russo-Japanese War, when Yüan Shih-k'ai fostered the idea to promote commerce and closer ties between China proper and Mongolia. The initial section of the line, from Peiping to Kalgan, was completed in 1909, and it was the first railway in China to be built entirely with Chinese resources and by Chinese engineers. Thereafter, it was gradually extended until, in the early 1920's, it reached its present terminus at Paotow. The period of its construction coincided with important political and economic changes in the Inner Mongolian territories through which it passed. In January, 1914, special administrative territories known as Chahar and Suiyuan (and Jehol) were formed, and fourteen years later, Chahar, Ninghsia, Jehol, and Suiyuan were given provincial status and administratively assimilated into China Proper.

Surprisingly, the Peiping-Suiyuan Railway today is, in many respects, the most efficient and comfortable railway in China. It has had fewer civil-war interruptions during the past year than any other railway in north China, and its service is unusually good. The line's coaches and sleepers are far superior to those on such important central China routes as the Shanghai-Nanking line, and the "Paotow Special," which runs three times a week, has a dining car and compartment sleepers.

In prewar days, this line was one of the most profitable in China, primarily because it paid less for coal (U.S. $.90 a ton in 1934) and labor (U.S. $.16 average daily wage in 1934) than any other railway in the country. Under present conditions, however, the line is not self-supporting. Labor is more expensive, the Tatung coal mines are not producing at their prewar level, and the paying freight is less than before the war. In addition, the government has kept fares at an almost unbelievably low level. The rate for a lower berth in a first-class compartment is less than three-quarters of a cent (U.S.) a mile.

Cost is obviously not the most important consideration in the line's operation at present. Railways are of primary strategic importance in war-torn China, and ever since General Fu Tso-yi and his men wrested this part of the country from the Communists, control of the Peiping-Suiyuan Railway has enabled Nationalist troops to maintain stable conditions in the area that are unique for Chinese territory north of the Yellow River.

A military atmosphere is apparent along the entire route of the railway. Stone and brick pillboxes surround every station and bridge, and, in many areas, lonely pillbox sentinels dot the ridges of flanking mountain ranges. Trenches and barbed wire are common sights, particularly around cities. There are thousands of soldiers in the railway zone—on trains, at stations, and even in the intervening countryside. Many fully loaded troop trains travel the rails, and every day a thickly armored train smeared with camouflage paint, and carrying machine guns, searchlights,

75mm. guns, and spare tracks and ties, as well as troops, rolls up and down the line.

The number of soldiers I saw on my trip may have been unusual, however, since the trip coincided—accidentally—with the first serious attempt by the Communists to disrupt the line since they were expelled from the region some time ago. On the journey westward, the train was delayed thirteen hours by one Communist attack that had severed the tracks between Kalgan and Tatung and halted all traffic for thirty-six hours. Traffic was again temporarily disrupted, on the return trip, by the destruction of a bridge between Kalgan and Peiping. These, I later discovered, were part of a new general offensive launched by the Communists against all government-held railways in north China. In this instance, however, the damage was repaired, and normal traffic resumed, with impressive speed.

There were thousands of troops on the move in the railway zone. Many were cavalry. All were well dressed in yellow-green padded uniforms, fur hats and coats, and fur-lined boots or shoes. They appeared to be well-equipped with small arms, but artillery and heavy equipment were conspicuously lacking. The men were orderly and disciplined, and apparently their morale was high.

In a nation engulfed by civil war, one tends to be continually preoccupied by the military situation, but there is more to life in Suiyuan—as elsewhere in China—than pillboxes and troops. Suiyuan, together with Chahar, is a part of the general region that is still called Inner Mongolia. It would probably be more literally correct, at present, to call much of this region, including the railway zone areas, Outer China, for the Mongols have gradually been displaced by the Chinese. Even in Paotow, Mongols are so scarce today that they are almost curiosities. The Mayor of that city states that there are only 300–400 Mongols under his jurisdiction, and many of these speak Chinese, wear Chinese clothes, and to all intents and purposes have been assimilated by the Chinese. This does not mean that the Mongols have completely disappeared, but it does evidently mean that they have been largely assimilated or pushed out of the railway zone by the colonization of Chinese agriculturalists and the aggressiveness of Chinese traders and businessmen.

Among some Chinese officials in Suiyuan today, there is actually a feeling that the Mongols are now so small a minority that no Mongol-Chinese problem exists. There is even some resentment over the fact that the Mongols are still given a special status and special privileges—in their autonomous administration, their representation in the Provincial Government, their separate schools, and so on—considered to be unjustified by their numerical strength. Provincial officials hinted, in fact, that if they had their way, the Nationalist Government's policies toward the Mongols would be changed.

According to the Suiyuan Government, there are currently about 80,000 Mongols (this may be a low estimate) in Suiyuan Province, out of a total population of 2–2.5 million. (It estimates the Mongol population in all of Inner Mongolia to be about one-fifth the total population there.) The Suiyuan Mongols fall into four separate groups: the Ulan Chap (Ulan-chab) League in the north, the Ikh Chao (Yeke Juu) League in the Ordos Desert region enclosed by the great bend of the Yellow River, the Tumet (Tümet) Banner in the central part of the province, and the "Four Eastern Banners" (originally the four Western Chahar Banners). The Chinese claim that the last two groups have been almost completely assimilated by the Chinese population.

The "Banners" (into which all Mongol "Leagues" are divided) are the basic Mongol administrative units. It is claimed that the Mongols in them are not taxed or conscripted by the Provincial Government (this is a claim that would require verification), and that the Banners have their own autonomous administrations under hereditary princes, levy their own taxes, and maintain their own garrisons. The Mongols are represented in the Provincial Government, nevertheless, by three members out of thirteen in the top provincial governing body and by several in the elected, representative body in the province.

It seems clear, however, that the Mongols have been completely subordinated politically to the new majority, the Chinese; not a single key post in the provincial administration is occupied by a Mongol. The twentieth-century Chinese policy of Sinicizing Inner Mongolia appears to have successfully de-Mongolized most of the Peiping-Suiyuan Railway zone, and the Mongols' present position is a far cry from the times of the thirteenth–fifteenth-century Khanates, or even, for that matter, from the time of Altan Khan's sixteenth-century Inner Mongolian federation.

A second important minority in Suiyuan Province is the Muslim group. Varying estimates are made of its numerical strength, but it appears that there are now probably about 20,000 Muslims in the province, concentrated mainly in the cities of Paotow and Kweisui. They are intermingled with the Han Chinese majority, however, and even Chinese newcomers to the province often have difficulty identifying Suiyuan Muslims unless they are wearing distinctive skull caps.

Suiyuan Province, interestingly enough, is also one of the strongholds of the Catholic Church in China. A Belgian priest whom I met in Kweisui claimed that Catholics in the province number between 80,000 and 100,000; the village of 300 families where he lives, he said, is entirely Catholic. The Church owns a considerable amount of land, and it carries on an extensive agricultural program made possible, in part at least, by indemnities received from the Chinese Government after the Boxer Rebellion; its strength is primarily in the countryside. The Protestant Church has fewer members than the Catholics in Suiyuan, but it, too, is said to be relatively strong, with its main support in towns and cities.

Suiyuan's economy is a mixed one, by virtue of its intermediate position between the intensive, fixed, agricultural economy of China Proper and the extensive, mobile, pastoral economy of Mongolia. Agriculture has taken possession of the valleys paralleling the railway, and most of the flat land visible from the train is under cultivation, the individual fields being unusually large for China. But much of this land is marginal; some of the soil is very sandy, and erosion is serious in many areas. However, the main agricultural area of the province is located in a region called Hotao, west of Paotow, which is irrigated by canals from the Yellow River. It is reported to be a very rich grain-producing region providing most of the province's food needs, as well as a surplus for export.

Much of the province, however, is still the domain of the pastoral nomad, and livestock of all sorts is raised in large numbers. Flocks of sheep, goats, and other animals can be seen in the regions traversed by the railway, but one has to go outside the railway zone to reach the important pastoral areas. The products of the pastoral economy of Inner Mongolia and western China are seen in abundance everywhere in the province, though, for these are the mainstays of trade, commerce, and business in Suiyuan. Statistics show that most of the animals and animal products not only from Suiyuan, but also from Ninghsia, Kansu, Chinghai, and Sinkiang, are collected and routed via Paotow and Kalgan to Tientsin. And these provinces, together with Chahar and the Manchurian provinces, are the principal animal-producing areas in China. Probably the chief economic significance of the Peiping-Suiyuan Railway is that it provides cheap transportation for these products, and the livelihood of many of the towns and cities along the railway depends on this commerce.

Paotow is the western junction of the Peiping-Suiyuan Railway, and the eastern junction of caravan and trade routes coming from all parts of Inner Mongolia, western China, and beyond. A bustling entrepôt city of between 70,000 and 80,000 people, it is extremely colorful, for it combines old and new in an intriguing mixture. The city lies 3 miles north of the Yellow River, near the foothills of the Taching Mountains. Within its mud city wall, almost all buildings are a dull yellow-brown color; they are made of raw, unplastered mud and straw. Except for two paved thoroughfares, the streets are narrow dirt alleys. Throughout the city, there are open markets and bazaars filled with wool, furs, and skins from the west, and with manufactured articles, including clothes, cloth, and hardware, from eastern industrial cities such as Tientsin and Shanghai. The principal wholesale trading establishments are located in enclosed compounds, which are filled with piles of wool and hides and crowded with camels resting between journeys.

Although it has a quaint atmosphere, the city is not entirely devoid of signs of modern development. Its 2,500-kilowatt electric plant provides better and more dependable lighting than the overloaded plants in Peiping at present, and its dynamo-operated telephone system works reasonably well. It has a daily newspaper (*The Paotow Daily*) and two modern banks. The largest three of the several factories in the city are the electric plant, the flour mill, and a leather factory, all of which are situated south of the city wall, in the direction of the railway station and the river. The leather factory, built by the Japanese in 1938-39, is the most important modern manufacturing establishment in Paotow; it turns out, according to its manager, fifty cowhides and fifty sheepskins a day.

Trade in Paotow is active during most of the year, except during the summer when the majority of the animals upon which trade depends are grazed and rested. In the winter, most trade to and from the west is by camel caravan. There is some trucking, but it carries more traders than trade. At present, three companies operate a fleet of about fifty vehicles, and the main route follows the loop of the Yellow River south to Ninghsia and Lanchow. When it is not frozen, as at present, the Yellow River itself is a major avenue for trade, since it is navigable by rafts and small boats between Ninghsia and Paotow and provides the cheapest transportation between those two points. And, of course, the railway plays a dominant role in the life of the city.

The primary basis of Paotow's trade is the exchange of livestock and animal products—including sheep and camel wool, leather, furs, and skins—for manufactured goods, such as clothing, cloth, tea, sugar, and hardware. The city is currently suffering from a severe trade depression, however, even though considerable activity is observable in the markets and bazaars. One of the leading traders in the city asserts that over-all trade today is only 20 per cent of its prewar (pre-1937) volume, and this figure is confirmed by the local branch manager of the Farmer's Bank of China and others. Several explanations are given for the economic decline. Trade with Outer Mongolia has been entirely cut off. During the past year, a drought is reported to have killed large numbers of livestock in the producing regions of China. And foreign markets for China's animal products have not recovered since the end of the war. Traders in Paotow find it much harder now than in the past to sell to Tientsin, the main foreign-trade outlet for these products. Despite its remoteness, Paotow is very much affected by the general state of world politics and economics.

The trade depression plus inflation—which is serious, even though prices are not as high as in places such as Peiping and Nanking—have greatly reduced the standard of living of much of the population, according to local people. Paotow faces a special problem also, arising from the fact that "several thousand" refugees have arrived in recent months from other areas in China where there is now active fighting or where prices are even higher than in Paotow. Many of these refugees are now beggars in the city's streets.

Although animal products play the dominant role in the economic life of Paotow, and of Suiyuan Province as a whole, other products of some significance are also produced. Coal is mined at several points in the Taching Mountains. Soda comes from the region south of Paotow. Salt is collected in many parts of the province where there are *tsaidam,* or dried marshes. Medicinal herbs and licorice are important products of the Ordos Desert region and other sandy areas. In addition, the province is reported to have some iron, gold, and gypsum. The Mayor of Paotow told me of an intriguing report of recent discoveries made by the National Resources Commission, to the west of Paotow, of "atomic raw materials," but I could not discover exactly what these "materials" are, and the Mayor admitted that they are not yet being mined or exploited.

Paotow is the main trading center of Suiyuan; Kweisui is its political center. With a population of about 160,000, Kweisui is actually two cities: Suiyuan and Kweihua, separated by about a mile. Although somewhat more modernized than Paotow, it is considerably less colorful and, in many respects, less interesting. It is, however, the provincial capital and the seat of the provincial administration.

Although the present Chairman, or Governor, of Suiyuan is a general named Tung Ch'i-wu, the province has been the domain of General Fu Tso-yi ever since Fu moved to Kalgan, soon after the war, to become Pacification Commander. Although Fu is now in Peiping, as Commander of the North China Communist Suppression Headquarters, the imprint of his leadership remains strong in the province. Appointments to the Suiyuan Provincial Commission are made by the National Government, but on the basis of suggestions presented by General Fu, according to a member of the Commission. Tung is one of Fu's men. Every high official whom I met in the province, including even the top local officials in the city of Paotow, has been personally associated with General Fu in the past. With a few exceptions, the top officials are military men. It is also significant, perhaps, that none of these officials claims Suiyuan as his native province. Many come from Fu's own province of Shansi, while others are from Hopeh, Honan, Shantung, and Hunan.

The general political and military situation in Suiyuan Province, since soon after the end of the Sino-Japanese War, apparently has been unique for north China. *T'ai P'ing*, or "Great Peace," is a phrase frequently used by local people to describe it. And General Fu is usually given credit for the present situation. Immediately after the war, the Russians occupied Kalgan, in Chahar, and the Chinese Communists started moving into the railway zone, including the part in Suiyuan. At the same time, however, General Fu moved across the province from his wartime headquarters of Shenpa, in the Hotao district of western Suiyuan, and he was successful in completely clearing the province of Communists. According to local people, until the recent attacks on the railway there had been no major Communist activity in the province for a long time.

General Fu's popularity in Suiyuan apparently is widespread;

support of the regime associated with his name seems to be unusually strong, and the provincial administration in the region
is probably one of the better ones in China.

Some of the military and reform policies in the province were
described to me by Governor Tung and General Ch'en, Mayor
and Garrison Commander of Kweisui. The Provincial Government's land policy, Tung states, is based on the principle of
providing land for the landless without depriving present owners
of their holdings. Land is confiscated from rich owners only in
cases where they fail to register it for tax purposes. Otherwise,
the land distributed comes from territory unused at the present
time. Of course, such a land policy could only be attempted in
China's west, where the population is relatively sparse. It is doubtful, moreover, whether there is more than a limited amount of
good agricultural land still unused, even in Suiyuan. Nevertheless, the policy is an interesting one. It would be useful to know
more, however, about how it works in practice, and how it affects
such nonagricultural groups as the Mongols, who may be interested in some of the "unused" land.

The military tactics attributed to General Fu and his followers
combine a policy of offensive defense—as contrasted with the
static defense of a few points that characterizes so much Nationalist military activity at present—and a policy of actively enlisting the support of the common people in local militia. General Ch'en claims that 210,000 men, out of a total of 240,000
in Suiyuan Province between the ages of eighteen and forty-five,
have been trained as People's Militia. About one out of ten, he
says, has his own rifle; this means that the militia has more than
20,000 rifles. The people buy these rifles themselves, he asserts,
but the government provides ammunition when the situation
requires it.

General Ch'en also declares that in every Suiyuan village there
is an Army and People's Cooperative Station, composed of leading villagers. When the army needs assistance from the people,
he states, it can request help from these stations. And these stations, in turn, can request the officers of nearby military units to
provide soldiers to assist in digging irrigation works, plowing, and
harvesting.

General Fu's soldiers have the reputation of being among the
best in China, and the troops one sees in Suiyuan make a favorable impression. They appear to be healthy, disciplined, well
dressed, and orderly. There is little evidence of friction between

soldiers and civilians. And the lack of ostentation on the part of the officers is remarkable; all officers, including top generals, wear cotton uniforms identical with those of average soldiers.

Over-all, Suiyuan gives one the impression, even today, of still being a frontier area, the potentialities of which are only partially developed. And it is a province where one can observe many of China's frontier problems: the competition between agricultural and pastoral economies, the relations between Chinese and non-Chinese peoples, the infiltration and impact of modern industrial products and the material culture accompanying them, the commercialization of geographically remote areas, and the administration of regions distant from Nanking—to say nothing of the civil war, which today affects virtually all of China.

14

MONGOL AUTONOMY

Alashan (Ninghsia)
September, 1948

Seventy miles west of Ninghsia City, in a small oasis just beyond the Holan (Alashan) Mountains, lies the quaint walled town of Tingyuanying. This town, usually called Wangyehfu by the local inhabitants, rests on a high slope overlooking the steppes, which stretch as far as the eye can see toward Outer Mongolia. To the southwest, huge rolling sand dunes catch the rays of the sun and take on the appearance of a vast yellow sea. The vistas are bleak and treeless, but Tingyuanying itself nestles in the shade of a grove of tall trees. It is a compact, friendly town with a mixed Chinese-Mongol population of about 7,000. This small oasis is the capital of the Alashan Special Banner of Mongols.

There is a romantic legend concerning the founding of Tingyuanying. Originally, the Alashan Mongols are said to have lived in Sinkiang, from whence they moved to the vicinity of Lake Kokonor in Chinghai about 300 years ago. A little over 200 years ago, according to the legend, the Prince of Alashan was returning from Peking to Kokonor with his new bride, a Manchu Princess. The Manchus at that time followed a definite policy of linking peripheral principalities to the throne by marriage, and the Prince of Alashan, so the story goes, had just married a beautiful young girl from the Imperial household. On the return trip, when his entourage reached the present site of Tingyuanying, the Princess became sad and despondent at the sight of the bleak, arid plains of Mongolia. The Prince was so moved that he decided to go no farther. He transferred his whole Banner north and built a Chinese walled town just to please his new bride.

There is also a less romantic explanation of the northward move of the Alashan Mongols. They had been fighting, according to this account, on the side of the Manchus against both the non-Chinese peoples in Sinkiang and the Tibetans in Kokonor, and their move was probably a result of this fighting. It may have been motivated simply by a desire to live in a more peaceful region, or by a desire to be nearer the Manchu Throne, with which the Alashan Banner was closely allied. Whatever the true story, the loyalty of the Alashan Mongols to the Chinese still continues, and the Alashan Special Banner maintains a cordial relationship with the Chinese Central Government that is in marked contrast to the unstable relations between the Central Government and the Mongols in many other areas.

On the map, Tingyuanying is a part of the Chinese province of Ninghsia. According to the Prince of Alashan, this is merely because "Alashan's territory is adjacent to Ninghsia's territory." Actually, the jurisdiction of the Ninghsia Provincial Government does not extend west of the Holan Mountains, and its thirteen *Hsien* all are located in the narrow agricultural region east of the mountains. The major part of the province to the west is divided between two autonomous Mongol units, the Edsengol (Ezen-gol or Etsingol) Special Banner, in the far west, and the Alashan Special Banner, nearby. These two autonomous units are directly under the jurisdiction of the Mongolian and Tibetan Affairs Commission of the Central Government's Executive Yüan.

In all of China, the Mongols are organized into approximately 130 banners, each traditionally ruled by a hereditary Prince, or *Wang*. In normal times, most of these Banners are grouped into thirteen Leagues, each under a chief elected by the Banners themselves, but formally appointed by the Chinese Central Government. Four of the Banners, however, are called "Special Banners" and have a status equal to that of the Leagues. Alashan is one of these.

Although all Leagues and Special Banners theoretically are responsible directly to the Mongolian and Tibetan Affairs Commission, in many areas, particularly where Mongols are intermixed with other racial groups, they have in practice been treated as subprovincial units. In Ninghsia, however, the Holan Mountains form a well-defined ethnic and political boundary, and the Alashan Banner Government, with its seat at Tingyuanying, not only handles the affairs of the 120,000 Mongols within its region, but also has jurisdiction over a very large area. There is a clear boundary between Alashan Territory and Ninghsia proper that follows the crest of the mountains. West of the mountains, Alashan possesses definite territorial jurisdiction. For example, no non-Mongols are allowed to own any land in Tingyuanying, and this includes Han Chinese, who may rent land but cannot own it. Alashan Territory actually covers almost half of Ninghsia Province and is much larger than the territory administered by the

Provincial Government. Similarly, the Edsengol Special Banner has territorial jurisdiction over its area in the west.

Administratively, also, the Alashan Banner has a greater degree of autonomy than many other Mongol groups in China. Some Mongol regions are included in the regular provincial administrative system and are divided into conventional Chinese administrative units, such as *Hsien*. This is not true in Alashan. Although Chinese influence on the Banner Government has been strong, local administration is entirely Mongol in its forms. The Banner's territory is divided into thirty-six *Baga* (*Bag*), each ruled by a so called *Pien Kuan* appointed by the Prince. A number of eastern *Baga* are grouped together into three larger units, each under a *Tsung Kuan* (or *Amban*), also appointed by the Prince. The entire administration is highly centralized. There is no popular assembly, and all orders and instructions come from the Banner Government where power is concentrated in the hands of the Prince, assisted by three *Hsiehli* (*Tusalagci*) and two *Tsangching* (*Janggi*)—the equivalent of counselors and special secretaries—four *Ch'u Chang*, or department heads, and various other functionaries.

The present Prince of Alashan, named Ta, is a genial connoisseur of horses, an amateur photographer, and a hunter. Now forty-four years old, he took over the Prince's duties after his father's death in 1931. During his youth, he spent eight years in Peking, studying with private tutors. Ta Wang appears to be an enlightened and progressive person. He has become so Chinese, though, that he cannot even speak his own native Mongol language—although he understands some. This does not seem to have diminished his popularity among the Alashan Mongols, however, and currently his territory is stable and peaceful.

Because of its autonomous status, the Alashan Special Banner is sometimes called the Kingdom of Alashan, but it is clearly an integral part of China. In political matters, it is faithful in following the instructions of the Mongolian and Tibetan Affairs Commission, which maintains a representative in Tingyuanying. The Prince, also, is a member of both the Executive Yüan of the Central Government and the Central Executive Committee of the Kuomintang. In military matters, Alashan comes under General Chang Chih-chung's Northwest Headquarters in Lanchow, and the Prince, who is a two-star general in the Chinese army, commands about a thousand Mongol soldiers, organized into three battalions of well-trained Peace Preservation Corps troops, all of them cavalrymen mounted on stocky Mongolian ponies. These troops are financially supported by the Central Government. Perhaps because of its strong ties with Nanking, and its pro-Chinese orientation, the Alashan Special Banner maintains no connections with other Mongol groups.

Relations between the Alashan Banner Government and the Ninghsia Provincial Government are more difficult to define, and currently they are rather touchy and delicate. Ta Wang describes the relationship as one of "personal friendship" between himself and the Ninghsia Governor, Ma Hung-k'uei, based upon a friendship formed between their fathers, Ta Wang and Ma Fu-hsiang. There are many factors, however, that make the relationship more complicated than this statement would seem to indicate. Ninghsia's Governor maintains a battalion of about 500 provincial troops on the outskirts of Tingyuanying "as protection against bandits," and this garrison force takes conscriptees from the 5,000 or so Chinese who live in Alashan, almost all of them in the environs of the Tingyuanying city wall. The Prince of Alashan is a member—"as a private citizen"—of the nine-member Ninghsia Provincial Commission, the highest-ranking provincial organ. Alashan Territory, moreover, obtains almost all of its grain from other areas, particularly Ninghsia, and there is resentment in Alashan because "General Ma's tight control of grain makes it difficult to obtain needed supplies." General Ma, on the other hand, claims that China's Mongols are gradually turning Communist or are drifting toward a close allegiance with Outer Mongolia, and he complains that the "Central Government won't allow the situation to be handled properly." There are hints on both sides of the Holan Mountains, in fact, that General Ma Hung-k'uei would like to exercise direct control over the Mongol regions of Ninghsia, and is dissuaded from taking steps to do so only because the Central Government opposes such action and gives moral support to the Alashan Special Banner.

During the Sino-Japanese War, General Ma did establish direct control in the west of Ninghsia, temporarily. At that time, the loyalty of all Mongols in China was suspect because the Japanese had set up a puppet Mongol regime in north China. Further cause for suspicion regarding Alashan in particular was the fact that the notorious Japanese General Doihara had visited Ta Wang. On the basis of this suspicion, Ma Hung-k'uei's troops crossed the mountains in 1938 and took the Alashan capital after a few days of fighting. Ta Wang was sent to Lanchow, where he was kept in honorable detention, under surveillance, until 1944 —even though no evidence of collaboration with the Japanese was uncovered. During that long period, Ma Hung-k'uei's troops exercised local control from their camps outside the walls of Tingyuanying. One incident that took place then is still well remembered by the Alashan Mongols. One day, new street numbers were issued in Tingyuanying, and at the bottom of each there appeared, in small Chinese characters, "Tingyuanying *Hsien*"; systematically and rapidly they were removed by the local Mongols. At present, however, despite this background, relations between the Alashan Banner Government and the Ninghsia Provincial Government appear to be relatively stable and placid—although suspicion continues on both sides.

Within Alashan Territory, life goes on calmly among the Mongol population of 120,000, which is sprinkled thinly throughout the steppes and deserts. The tremendous distances mean that actual governmental functions are minimal, and the average Mongol nomad lives an isolated, independent existence. As a rule, families do not congregate; each family yurt is an independent unit that moves periodically from place to place within its *Baga* to graze the family's sheep, camels, horses, and other animals. The only real town within the entire region is Tingyuanying, and the few other permanent settlements are mainly scattered lamaseries.

Government does not impinge very strongly upon the lives of these nomadic people. Education, for example, is almost non-existent—one reason being that Mongols consider education "bothersome," according to members of the Banner Government. There are no secular schools in the entire territory, in fact, except at Tingyuanying, where the Banner Government maintains one middle and two primary schools. Despite the minimal character of governmental functions, however, order and peace are maintained throughout this tremendous region—by the Banner troops and the few troops attached to each *Baga Pien Kuan* —and banditry and disorder are said to have been completely eliminated.

One reason why the Banner Government cannot even consider expanding its functions and activities, even if it wished to do so, is its financial weakness. The only outside aid it receives is the Central Government's contribution for the support of Banner troops, and fees—also from the Central Government— for the exploitation of the salt lakes in the region. Its local sources of revenue are also limited, consisting mainly of taxes on animals and on the transport of traded commodities.

General economic conditions among the Alashan Mongols are

probably better than in any other Mongol region in China today, for Alashan, unlike most other Banners and Leagues, has not been directly touched by war or civil strife. Consequently, relative prosperity prevails. Even in Alashan Territory, however, economic conditions are poor, compared with better days in past years. There is no starvation, but some people are short of food, and during the past two years, a few beggars have appeared, for the first time within the memory of local people.

The main cause of current economic hardship is drought. The economy of the nomadic population might be called a grass economy, and the livelihood of the people is entirely dependent upon the vagaries of the weather. During the past two years, the weather has not been kind, and, as a result of severe drought, many animals have died.

Another contributing cause has been the decline of trade with the rest of China. Even though Alashan's deserts and steppes are remote, the local economy of the Mongols has become at least partially commercialized. The main Mongol exports are sheep and camel wool, leather, and other animal products. In addition, salt—from the numerous salt lakes—and soda are normally shipped in considerable quantities to places throughout northwest China, and coal and wood from the Holan Mountains are sold to Ninghsia City. These products funnel through Paotow, Lanchow, Tingyuanying, Ninghsia City, and other trading centers —the most important single one being Paotow. Transport is normally by camel caravan or cart. The only motor road currently being maintained in the territory is a dirt trail from Tingyuanying to Ninghsia City, and it is periodically impassable. When I made the trip, I had to go by horseback over the mountains. The former direct Suiyuan-Sinkiang motor road, which skirts the border of Outer Mongolia, has not been used in recent years. Although trade continues, therefore, like almost all domestic trade in China its scale has diminished during the past decade of war and disorder.

The northern border of Alashan Territory touches Outer Mongolia for many miles, and it is completely closed to all intercourse. Despite the ominous claims of Ma Hung-k'uei, however, there does not appear to be any strong attraction exerted from Outer Mongolia in this region. "All Inner Mongolians are afraid of Outer Mongolia," says Ta Wang, and, although developments in some other Mongol areas do not support this statement, in Alashan there apparently is almost no sentiment favorable to Outer Mongolia or the Chinese Communists. Furthermore, while there are a few emigré families from Outer Mongolia living in Alashan, there has not been any recent evidence of underground activity instigated from across the border. The border is carefully patrolled on both sides—reportedly by "many" troops in Outer Mongolia and by one of Ta Wang's three battalions of cavalry on the Chinese side—but for the present, at least, there is no friction.

Alashan's relations with its northern neighbor and its contacts with Communism have not always been so placid and uneventful as at present. In the late 1920's, the Chinese "Christian General," Feng Yü-hsiang—during his period of collaboration with the Soviet Union—used a Ninghsia City–Tingyuanying–Urga route for bringing supplies from the Soviet Union. (Urga, now Ulan Bator, is the Outer Mongolian capital.) Trucks brought the supplies over a steppe and desert route where no real motor road existed. During that period, agents and troops sent by Feng forcibly occupied Tingyuanying and exercised direct control over it for a few months. A few years later, in 1932, according to Ta Wang, a small but well-organized Communist underground carried out a *coup d'état* in Tingyuanying, imprisoned the local officials, and held the city for several days. Mongols throughout the territory rose in indignation, however, and converged upon the city, besieged it, and, after almost a week of fighting, killed or captured the Communist leaders, restoring their own government to power. Two years later, in 1934, a Communist agent from Outer Mongolia was arrested at the border as he was making his way toward Tingyuanying. And in the winter of 1942–43, a small Communist cell was discovered in Tingyuanying plotting against the Banner Government. Because of this background, Ta Wang and his Banner Government are watchful and somewhat uneasy, but Alashan Territory still remains one of the most stable of all Mongol regions.

By contrast, a large percentage of the other Mongols in China have been ravaged by war in recent years and are still involved in confused civil strife and political disorder. This is particularly true in the regions where China's Mongols are most heavily concentrated, namely western Manchuria and the Inner-Mongolian provinces of Jehol and Chahar, and parts of Suiyuan.

In 1937, when the Japanese occupied north China, they established a theoretically independent puppet Mongol state called Meng Chiang, with the cooperation of Teh Wang, the powerful leader of the Silingol (Shilingol) League in north Chahar. Prince Teh was made head of Meng Chiang, and, for the next eight years, many of the proud Mongols of north China experienced a nominal autonomy that the Chinese had not been willing to grant them in that region. One should never forget that many Mongols still remember nostalgically the days of Genghis Khan—whose artifacts, incidentally, are now kept by the Chinese in a repository in non-Mongol territory, in Kansu.

Then, during the late summer of 1945, when Russian troops converged upon Kalgan in their drive against the Japanese, Meng Chiang shared the fate that the end of the war brought to all of Japan's puppet regimes. Prince Teh sought refuge in Peiping. Later, after conferring with Chiang K'ai-shek in Nanking, he managed to avoid collaborationist charges. But today, he is still living in Peiping, in retirement, refusing to cooperate with the Chinese Central Government until he receives pledges of Inner Mongolian autonomy.

With the Russians in 1945 came some Mongol troops drawn from the estimated 1–1.5 million Mongols who live either in the Soviet Union or in its satellite, the Mongolian People's Republic. These Mongol troops were well fed, well trained, and well equipped, and reportedly they made a favorable impression on many of the Mongols in Inner Mongolia.

Soon after V-J Day, some of the former Meng Chiang leaders, under Buyandalai, organized in western Inner Mongolia an Inner Mongolian Autonomous Government, oriented toward Russia and Outer Mongolia. When Russian troops withdrew from the Kalgan region, they took with them perhaps "several thousand" Mongols, including 200–300 educated young men—one of whom was Prince Teh's son—for training in the Soviet Union.

The Chinese Communists moved into Kalgan when the Russians moved out, and they then established an Inner Mongolian Autonomous Association. This was accomplished under the tutelage of a man named Yün Tse, or Ulanfu (Ulanhu), a Moscow-trained Mongol who is the main Chinese Communist agent among north China's Mongols. Mongols who would not cooperate under the new Communist auspices were purged, and gradually the association increased its following among Chahar and Suiyuan Mongols by implementing a program of local autonomy and abolishing the special rights and hereditary privileges of the princes.

These particular developments did not, however, directly affect the region where the majority of Mongols in China are concentrated, namely western Manchuria and the adjacent province of Jehol. Mongol groups in this region of eastern Inner Mongolia—which is estimated to have a Mongol population of almost 2 million—established a Great Mongolian Republic at Wangyehmiao and sent out three feelers at the end of the war: one to the Chinese Central Government, one to the Mongols of Outer Mongolia, and one to the Chinese Communists. The Central Government was not sympathetic to their demands for an autonomous regime and refused to let their delegates come beyond Peiping. The Outer Mongolians treated their delegates well, but promised no help—perhaps because they were afraid of compromising their own newly recognized independence. But the Chinese Communists responded most warmly and indicated that they were willing to help. Subsequently, in the spring of 1946, Yün Tse himself went to Chengteh, capital of Jehol, to negotiate with the Mongol representatives there. And soon thereafter, an Inner Mongolian Autonomous Region Government was set up at Wangyehmiao, about 200 miles west of Harbin in Manchuria; Yün Tse was made chairman. This new government soon began to cooperate actively with Chinese Communist military forces in Manchuria, and its cavalry carried out numerous raids against territory controlled by the Central Government. But some of these raids have harmed other Mongol groups, in north Chahar and Suiyuan, and reportedly certain Mongols in these regions have developed a counterrevolutionary attitude toward the autonomous Mongol regime set up in Manchuria. This government continues to function, however, and it is reported to receive Russian support in the form of arms and ammunition, in return for horses, sheep, and silver—although such reports cannot be verified. Other reports, also unconfirmed, claim that the Wangyehmiao regime is now having a difficult time, and that Yün Tse's popularity has waned considerably. The situation among the Mongols in Manchuria is further complicated by reports that, in the far north, another semi-independent regime has been established; some say that it is under the leadership of a man called Irkimbato. This regime is said to print its own money and to maintain separate relations with both Wangyehmiao and Ulan Bator.

Not all of China's Mongols have been involved in these complicated autonomy movements. The situation of the Ninghsia Mongols has already been described. In Chinghai, the Mongols are an extremely small group, far removed from the major conflict areas in China and under the strict control of General Ma Pufang's Chinghai administration. The Mongols in Sinkiang are also a small group. Although, reportedly, a few of them have been enlisted in the army of the autonomous Ili Government, in northwest Sinkiang, no Mongol autonomy movement exists in the province, and many have remained loyal to the Central Government.

Some of the Mongols in Suiyuan also still support the Central Government. One group of Banners remained loyal throughout the Sino-Japanese War; according to some reports, they set up headquarters at a place called Djassek in the Ordos Desert instead of joining Teh Wang and his puppet government. This group, totaling about 250,000, is now said to be organized under a Mongolian Self-Government Political Committee, with headquarters at Kungmiao, about 40 miles south of Paotow. The Kungmiao Committee reportedly is strongly anti-Communist, but nevertheless favors a united, autonomous Mongol government. The Central Government has not agreed to this, however, since it favors separate autonomous Mongol administrations in various regions. Some friction with the Central Government also results from an unsolved controversy over arms. These Mongols want arms for self-defense purposes, particularly against Communist raids—most of their good weapons were taken away by the Russians in 1945–46—but so far the arms have not been forthcoming from the Central Government. Problems such as these are reported to have discouraged many of the Mongols in this region, and a few, particularly the younger ones, are said to be leaning more and more toward the other Mongol autonomous movements or the Chinese Communists as a result. This discouragement, combined with a severe famine and starvation, has undoubtedly abetted the partially successful Communist efforts among the Ikh Chao Mongols, in the southern Ordos.

These facts add up to a situation that, like the general situation in China, defies generalization. If one generalization is possible, however, it is that the Mongols in China want some form of real cultural and political autonomy. In Alashan Territory— which is still geographically removed from civil-war combat zones, and where a fairly high degree of autonomy exists—peace, stability, and loyalty to the central government continue to prevail. In many other areas, however, where effective autonomy has never been granted, the Mongols—taking advantage of the prevailing chaos, and encouraged by varied groups, including the Chinese Communists, the Russians, and the Outer Mongolians—have merged their own struggle for autonomy with the already complicated military and political conflicts that dominate present-day China.

15

TIBETAN BORDER REGION

Kangting (Sikang)
July, 1948

The borderland between China and Tibet is a remote, little-known region containing some of the highest mountains and most rugged terrain in the world. It is a region of cultural conflict and fusion, and numerous peoples are intermixed in the heterogeneous population. It is also a frontier zone where boundaries are vague. Political authority is often confused, and control shifts with the changing balance of military power. Some areas within this borderland region are wild, inaccessible, and uninhabited. Others are a sort of no man's land, where bandits make their headquarters between raids on communication lines and settled communities. Many areas are the domain of independent tribes that recognize no outside authority, or of semi-independent groups that receive only a minimum of outside control.

The most important boundary in the region is, of course, the one that divides China and Tibet. This is a line that is difficult to define, however. Modern Chinese maps generally color all of Tibet as part of China, but this is wishful thinking on the part of Chinese cartographers, for Outer Tibet, or Tibet Proper, is not under Chinese control, and the previous recognition of Chinese sovereignty—originally in the form of annual tribute—no longer exists.

Chinese influence in Tibet Proper has declined steadily throughout the modern period, especially since the Lhasa Convention of 1904 concluded by Britain's Colonel F. Younghusband. Even before then, the Chinese *Ambans* in Lhasa had become virtually powerless. Consequently, the 1904 convention paid little deference to Chinese claims of sovereignty. It not only established a precedent for direct negotiations between Britain and Tibet, but also set forth British claims to "special interests" in the country. Tibet undertook not to allow any foreign power to intervene in its affairs—a provision that gradually came to include China.

After 1904, British policy toward Tibet—a corollary to its position in India and its concern over Indian security—was based on a desire either to maintain the *status quo* in Tibet or, if that were not possible, at least to prevent competitors from moving in.

In 1906, Britain and China signed an ambiguous convention in Peking that confirmed the validity of the Lhasa Convention; it also, however, contained implicit British recognition of Chinese sovereignty over Tibet. The Anglo-Russian convention in 1907 likewise confirmed the Lhasa Convention, but it, too, contained a reference to, and recognition of, China's "suzerainty" over Tibet. In 1910, however, a period of more active British intervention began after the flight of the thirteenth Dalai Lama to India, as a result of a Chinese punitive expedition against Tibet. Britain also sent troops into Tibet at that time. Then, in 1911, the Chinese garrison in Lhasa revolted; in 1912, the Dalai Lama returned from exile; thereafter, British influence in Tibet was firmly established, while Sino-Tibetan relations were ruptured. In the Simla Convention, signed in 1914, China was asked to recognize the autonomy of Outer Tibet. Even though it was unwilling to sign the Convention, Britain and Tibet thereafter treated China, to all intents and purposes, as a foreign power.

Chinese influence re-entered the picture, although still in only a limited way, in the 1930's. In 1934, China sent a special commission to Lhasa for the inauguration of the fourteenth Dalai Lama, and thereafter a Chinese office in Lhasa, subsequently known as the Tibet Office of the Mongolian and Tibetan Affairs Commission, was set up. This re-established a tenuous link between the Chinese and Tibetans, but it was countered by the establishment of a British Mission in Lhasa—under the Sikkim Political Officer of the Indian Civil Service. Today, Britain's influence still remains predominant in Tibet, even though the British withdrawal from India may well bring about a change.

At present, in any case, the boundary between Tibet Proper and China's southwestern provinces of Sikang and Chinghai, as drawn on most conventional maps, has no real significance. It is an arbitrary line that gives no clue to the actual relationships existing in the borderland. Sikang and Chinghai are relatively new provinces that, less than twenty years ago, were carved out of the region known as Inner Tibet, and their western boundaries are merely an indication of Chinese claims and little more. The real line of division between Tibet and China cuts through Sikang and Chinghai. In fact, there are really two Sino-Tibetan "boundaries" running through these provinces; one is a line defining the extent of Chinese settlement and is, therefore, an ethnic and economic boundary; the other is a line defining the limits of Chinese political authority and military control.

When the province of Sikang was established, it was formed by amalgamating areas formerly belonging to Tibet and Szechwan Province; the Szechwan section was originally known as *Ch'uan Pien,* or "Szechwan Border Region." The first step that led toward the creation of a separate province was taken a few years before the end of the Manchu Dynasty, in 1905, when the Emperor appointed a high-ranking officer to govern the border region overlapping Szechwan and Yunnan. In 1911, during the twilight of the dynasty, it was then proposed that a province of Sikang be established, but no action was taken before the collapse of the dynasty.

Immediately after the founding of the Republic of China, an official named Yin was appointed to rule the border area, much as it had been ruled under the Manchus, and, following Yin, a succession of five other special governors were sent to administer the region. Then, in the late 1920's, General Liu Wen-hui was appointed Commander-in-Chief of the Szechwan-Sikang Frontier Defense Force, and this was, in effect, the beginning of a Sikang provincial regime that still exists today. The establishment of the province is sometimes dated to that period, even though it was not officially organized as a province until some years later.

The formation of Sikang seems to have been due primarily to two factors. One was the accelerated pace of Chinese migration and penetration into the fringes of the region. This process had been going on for a long time, but about forty years ago it speeded up. This, plus a desire to stabilize and regularize administration in China's somewhat amorphous border regions, was one factor. Another, which was at least partially responsible for the timing of the establishment of Sikang, was the chaotic state of political affairs in Szechwan Province. On the Chinese side, and from the Chinese point of view, Sikang is, in many respects, merely a political appendage of Szechwan, and the repercussions of local conflicts and struggles in Szechwan have been, and are, a primary factor in determining the political situation in the adjacent border region.

General Liu Wen-hui, who now dominates Sikang, was once a major warlord in Szechwan. This was between 1911 and 1935, a period in which 400–500 major battles reportedly were fought between local factions in that province. For a brief period, Liu and his private Twenty-fourth Army achieved a position of predominance, and he was Governor of Szechwan. Eventually, however, he was ousted after a military defeat at the hands of his powerful uncle Liu Hsiang, and following this defeat, he moved westward. Sikang then became the center of his power.

In 1935, a commission to establish Sikang as a province was set up at Kangting by the Central Government. Liu Wen-hui was appointed head of the commission. This was similar to many appointments made by the Central Government in regions remote from its centers of power; it was simply a realistic recognition of a *de facto* local regime. Finally, in 1939, the Central Government formally announced the creation of Sikang and redemarcated the boundary between it and Szechwan, giving Sikang two large districts, around the important towns of Yaan and Sichang, which had originally belonged to Szechwan.

Liu Wen-hui's political retreat to Sikang resulted in a regime that was, and is, a purely personal one. Sikang was a poor second choice, from Liu's point of view—it has about one-fifteenth of the population and only a fraction of the arable land and known resources of rich Szechwan—but he had no alternative. In view of his military eclipse, first by Liu Hsiang and later by the Central Government, which extended its effective control westward during the war, he probably was thankful to be left with Sikang. He made the best of the situation, in any case. When he moved to Sikang, he was accompanied by his personal army, a horde of relatives, and the usual host of hangers-on who congregate as satellites and sycophants around a powerful local leader in China. These people took over control of the region, and today they rule in General Liu's name.

There are really three capitals to that part of Sikang which is actually under Liu's control. Liu himself, who now is Governor of Sikang, Pacification Commander of the area, and Commander of the Twenty-fourth Division (his former Twenty-fourth Army), maintains his personal headquarters in a magnificent mansion in Chengtu, capital of Szechwan. He has not given up his aspirations in his old bailiwick. Actually, he spends very little time in his own isolated provincial capital, Kangting, or Tatsienlu, preferring to rule by remote control through trusted deputies and telegraphic instructions sent to them from his Chengtu mansion. Although he appears to be a pleasant, mild-mannered man, Liu rules with an iron will, and when the telegraph lines to Sikang vibrate with his instructions, obedient vibrations take place at the other end.

Within Sikang itself, Liu has two subcapitals. One is the official provincial capital at Kangting, where the organs of civil government are located. Liu's chief deputy there is a man named Chang Wei-ching, who is Acting Governor as well as Provincial Commissioner of Civil Affairs. Chang, who once commanded a brigade in the Twenty-fourth Army, has been Acting Governor since 1939 and, as such, has carried the main load of routine administration. Even though he originally was a military man, he is one of the more able and respected leaders in the regime, and he has a fairly good reputation among the local people, which is somewhat surprising in view of the character of the regime as a whole.

The civil government under Chang is organized along conventional lines, according to national regulations, and routine relations and communications are maintained with the Central Government. This does not obscure the fact, however, that it is really a semi-independent regime, subject to very little central control. In China, the façade of normal relations often veils what, in reality, is a deep chasm of political rivalry. This is the case, at present, in relations between Liu Wen-hui and the Central Government. There is no open struggle between them, but the Central Government clearly disapproves of Liu because of his high-handed exercise of local autonomy. The real relations are more clearly revealed by the personnel in the provincial regime than by the existing forms of organization, or the superficial ties that are maintained between Kangting and Nanking. In both the Kangting administration and the administrative subdivisions of the province, down to and including the *Hsien*, almost every political post is held by a relative, old crony, or friend of Liu's, and the loyalty of these men is a personal loyalty to Liu Wen-hui.

Liu's other subcapital in Sikang is the city of Yaan, close to the Szechwan border, and his three main deputies there are: Liu Yüan-hsüan, Acting Commander of the Twenty-fourth Division and a nephew of Liu; Yang Chia-chen, Chief of Staff of the Twenty-fourth Division, and Wang Ching-yü, Assistant Pacification Commander. All of these men have been loyal subordinates for many years. In many respects, Yaan is more important as a center of Liu's control in Sikang than Kangting, for local rule is primarily military, and Yaan is the center of Liu's military power. The fact that military rule prevails is not too surprising, since the region is still a frontier zone with dissident minorities, "aboriginal" tribes, outlaws, and bandits. An analogy with the early days in the western part of the United States would not be too farfetched. Gun-running, opium trading, and many other forms of illicit activity and lawlessness are common. The authorities participate in some of these activities, but the degree of law, order, and unity that does exist is maintained by Liu's military units.

The core of Liu Wen-hui's military power is his Twenty-fourth Division. Formerly called the Twenty-fourth Army, this was Liu's personal army, even though it was technically a part of the National Army. A few years ago, it was converted into a division, but the same organization continues to exist, and it is still a personal force. Theoretically, a reduction in its size was to have taken place at the time of the change from army to division, but it is doubtful if it ever took place, and probably the army is just as large and as powerful as it ever was.

The Twenty-fourth Division is even more of an organization of family and friends, if possible, than the civil government. Liu Wen-hui is Commander, and his nephew Liu Yüan-hsüan is Acting Commander. According to the military authorities in Yaan, the division has two brigades, each with three regiments, and one independent regiment. The 137th Brigade, with headquarters at Yaan, is commanded by Liu Yüan-tsung, another nephew of Liu. The 136th Brigade, with headquarters at Sichang, is commanded by Wu P'ei-ying, who is married to one of Liu's daughters. The independent regiment, located in the Tibetan areas (called *kuan wai*) is commanded by Fu Teh-ch'uan; although he is not a relative of Liu, he is an old-time cohort. As in the civil government, subordinate positions of importance are filled by other relatives and friends, particularly those from Liu Wen-hui's native *Hsien* in Szechwan. The division has an estimated 200 officers, mostly staff men, sent by the Ministry of National Defense to keep an eye on things, but they do not exercise any basic control.

The troops that are commanded by these various members of Liu's family tree are mainly Szechwanese, with a leavening of native Sikang people. Officially, it is claimed that the division contains roughly 10,000 men, but the actual number may be considerably higher. They constitute a well-armed and formidable fighting force. In contrast to troops one sees in some parts of China, Liu's soldiers all are armed at least with modern bolt-action rifles, and all carry belts full of ammunition. They also appear relatively well disciplined and wear clean, neat uniforms. Liu's supplies are plentiful because he has his own financial resources. According to a responsible officer in the division, every squad of sixteen men has fourteen rifles and an automatic weapon; every company has two mortars; every brigade has a special unit of artillery that includes both mortars and guns; and the division has a battalion of artillery.

In the higher chain of military command in China, Liu Wen-hui and his military forces are theoretically subordinate to the over-all Szechwan-Sikang-Yunnan-Kweichow command of General Chu Shao-liang in Chungking, but relations between Liu and Chu are minimal and, in fact, far from cordial. In the southern part of Sikang Province, a unique and peculiar situation exists, and a delicate balance of power is maintained. This region, with its center at Sichang, is a special area under joint Central Government–Provincial military control. The local Garrison Commander there is General Ho Kuo-kuang, a Central Government man sent directly by General Chu. He controls his own troops, estimated to be approximately equal in strength to those of Liu's subordinates in the area. The result is that Liu's and Ho's forces check and balance each other, and final authority is divided.

In theory, Liu Wen-hui's numerous military and civilian representatives govern all of Sikang Province as it appears on conventional maps. Actually, although their power is complete in the areas effectively under their control, these areas are very limited in a geographical sense. The most secure and unquestioned areas under his control are the regions immediately around Yaan and Kangting, plus the area linking them. These are areas of Chinese colonization that have been assimilated culturally as well as politically. They form a very narrow fringe in the eastern part of the province. Even in this fringe, however, the Chinese population and Chinese control are confined for the most part to the towns along existing communication routes. These towns are compressed into tiny valleys that are almost smothered by the surrounding mountains, and the routes that link them creep along the sides of cliffs in deep gorges where one has to look up to get a glimpse of the sky. Some Chinese farmers, woodcutters, and prospectors have spread into the mountains, away from the more settled regions, but they are a minority. Most of the mountains in this wild region—which contains Minya Konka, about 24,900 feet high, the tallest mountain in China—are inhabited, if at all, by non-Chinese groups that have their own languages and customs. Most of these groups are ruled by their own kings or tribal chiefs. Usually, in areas adjacent to Chinese settlements, these "aborigines" are compelled to submit to some degree of control or supervision, but they do so only reluctantly. And in many areas, the tribes feel a deep hatred of the Chinese that periodically flares into open conflict.

Beyond this eastern fringe, where Chinese and tribal groups are intermixed, there is the vast expanse of the Tibetan plateau, the "top of the world." The Chinese in Sikang have a term that they constantly use to refer to these Tibetan areas—*kuan wai*. It is difficult to translate. The word *wai* means "outside" or "beyond," and the word *kuan* means "frontier gate" or "customs." "Outside the frontier gate" or "outside the customs barrier" might be correct literal translations, therefore, but they fail to convey the full significance of the term. It is true that customs levies on goods coming from Tibet into China are collected just inside of *kuan wai* at Kangting, but when the Chinese use the term, they mean something much broader than "outside the customs barrier"; perhaps it should be translated as "beyond the border," "out in Tibetan country," or "out in the hinterland." No boundary defining *kuan wai* appears on any maps, but all local people know what the term means and where the line for *kuan wai* should be. If drawn on the map, it would indicate a rough, but fairly accurate, geographical, ethnic, and economic boundary dividing China and Tibet in the Sikang region. West of this line, the population is essentially Tibetan. Important centers such as Lihua (Litang), Kantse, Paan (Batang), and Dege contain sizable groups of Chinese; there are Chinese officials and garrison troops in the area; and Chinese traders move through the countryside. But the bulk of the population is Tibetan. The line also marks the beginning of the Tibetan grasslands. The terrain of these grasslands is expansive and rolling. The hills, which rise from valleys well over 10,000 feet to rounded tops 15,000 feet and higher, would be called mountains anywhere else, and most of them, at least in the area just west of Kangting, are rolling and treeless. They are covered with a smooth surface of short grass, which looks as if it has been newly cut, and with a breath-taking profusion of wild flowers. In this region, the Tibetan economy prevails—yaks graze on the hillsides, and barley grows in the valleys.

Not too long ago, this line would also have represented a political boundary of sorts. East of the line, Chinese administration prevailed; west of it, special border administrations were set up. At present, however, the regular forms of Chinese administration have been extended as far west as the Yangtze River, which in Sikang is called the Chinshakiang, or Gold Sand River. However, Chinese administration has undergone modifications in this region to fit the Tibetan situation. Tibetan *Hsiang,* for example, are often composed of *Pao* made up of roving, nomadic herdsmen, and they are very different, naturally, from Chinese *Hsiang* administering settled agriculturalists. In fact, political organization on the lower levels in this region remains pretty much as it always was, despite the fact that old Tibetan forms are now called by new Chinese names.

Economic and social organization in these Tibetan regions is a mixture of agricultural and pastoral elements. A large part of the population is nomadic and raises yaks and other livestock. The grasslands are divided into areas within which each nomad group moves from place to place. There are also some permanent settlements, however. The most important of these are the lamaseries, but there are also widely separated farming villages. Barley is grown in the valleys and provides the staple of the Tibetan diet, *tsamba,* an uninspiring flour made of baked barley. Yaks and sheep provide most other needs: butter, milk, cheese, and meat, as well as clothing, housing in the form of tents, transport, and fuel in the form of dried dung. One staple, tea, must be imported, however.

The farming villages and other permanent settlements, which usually are nothing more than a few flat-roofed stone buildings, are the centers of Chinese-supervised political administration. All *Hsien* magistrates are Chinese, appointed by the Provincial Government, but all *Hsiang* chiefs and other local leaders are Tibetans chosen by their own groups. In both the *Hsien* cities and the *Hsiang,* there are small garrison units of Chinese troops. Organized separately are the local Tibetan self-defense units, composed of mounted militia who patrol the grasslands areas where they are located. The Chinese civil administration does not intrude very deeply into the life of the region, but Chinese military forces are more obtrusive. Frequent friction, and occasionally open trouble, occurs between the Chinese troops and the local people—especially when the Chinese requisition food and other supplies without fair compensation.

Chinese political control between the limits of *kuan wai* and the Yangtze River is rather loose, therefore, and even this ends completely at the Yangtze River. Paan and Dege are the last outposts of Chinese control. Beyond this river boundary, which forms a north-south line bisecting Sikang almost exactly, there is no Chinese control and virtually no Chinese influence. Across the river, the country is Tibetan in every respect. Tibetans can freely cross this line, going westward, but Chinese and other foreigners cannot. The only Chinese regularly allowed to cross are traders with long-established connections in Lhasa or other Tibetan centers; at present, there may be about a hundred who are in this privileged position. The river is also an economic border. Just west of it, at the important Tibetan trading center of Chamdo (Changtu, in Chinese), customs duties are collected by the Tibetans on imports brought in from China. Politically, the region west of the river is entirely Tibetan, and lamaseries, local princes, and envoys from Lhasa all play important roles in the administrative system.

Altogether, these various regions, which are lumped together on maps as the province of Sikang, contain a population that the Provincial Government in Kangting now estimates to be 3.51 million. Of this total, however, 1.65 million is a vague estimate of population in areas not under firm provincial control. Although official statistics list sixteen "racial" groups, the majority of the population is Han Chinese, Tibetan, or Lolo. Fairly reliable estimates of the size of these three groups in areas where there are reasonable statistics indicate that there are perhaps slightly more than a million Chinese, concentrated in the Sichang, Yaan, and Kangting regions; a comparable number of Lolos, concentrated in the mountain regions around Sichang, and slightly fewer than a million Tibetans, spread out west of Kangting. Some people claim that the Tibetan population of Sikang, although not as large as either the Chinese or the Lolos, is greater than the population in Tibet Proper, where the people are very much dispersed except for a few areas, such as that around Lhasa.

The general attitude of the Chinese toward other racial groups in Sikang is highly patronizing and condescending. Ordinary Chinese refer to most of the other peoples indiscriminately as *mantzu* or *yi* people, both of which are derogatory terms. Even the title Lolo is a disparaging term, used only by the Chinese and resented by the tribesmen to whom it is applied. The official attitude of the government is that non-Chinese groups should be civilized, and policy focuses on assimilation, with the main emphasis on education. The Chinese have no doubts about the superiority of the Chinese way of life. Most believe that a little Chinese education will solve all problems. "In fifteen or twenty years, we will have educated them so that people will forget even the names of the minority groups," the Assistant Pacification Commander of the province said to me in a burst of enthusiasm. There is no indication that his enthusiasm is justified, however, for the minorities resent the Chinese intrusion into their lives and have no desire to be Sinicized. What they want is autonomy, which the Chinese are unwilling to grant.

The Provincial Commissioner of Education in Sikang admits that the official policy encounters almost insuperable obstacles. In the case of the Tibetans, for example, there is passive resistance to the government's education policy. All school classes in Tibetan areas, as elsewhere, are conducted in Chinese. Although there are a few Chinese-educated Tibetan teachers, and a few of mixed Chinese-Tibetan blood, by far the majority are Chinese. According to Tibetans with whom I talked, their main objection is not to the language, however, but to the simple fact that they are forced to send their children to Chinese schools. They feel that a formal education is a useless waste of time and of no conceivable use to them. Their attitude toward education is analogous, as one Tibetan pointed out to me, to the attitude of the Chinese themselves toward conscription. Education is looked upon as an onerous obligation to be avoided if possible, and the practice of paying substitutes to go to school in place of one's own children is said to be prevalent.

Interracial relations in Sikang are by no means entirely hostile, however. In Kangting, Chinese and Tibetans get along quite well, and there is a good deal of intermarriage. In the Sichang region, there is intermarriage between Chinese and Lolos. In both these areas, there are groups of non-Chinese who have been Sinicized. Furthermore, Liu Wen-hui currently seems to be pursuing a conciliatory policy toward the Tibetans and Lolos. Outside his own followers, Liu has very few friends or allies, and evidently he wants to keep on as good terms as possible with the major racial groups in the province.

In June of this year, for example, Liu held a conference in Chengtu with a group of ten Lolo tribal chieftains at which an attempt was made to solve outstanding problems; I was fortunate in being able to attend. First, Liu made a speech emphasizing that: there should be close relations between the Han Chinese and the Lolos; the Lolos should be given an education equal to that provided the Chinese; every tribe in Sikang should be equal; the Provincial Government would keep its promise to solve disputes by peaceful means, rather than resorting to arms; the Lolo system of slavery should be abolished; no excessive taxation of the Lolos would be allowed. The Lolo chiefs—with their colorful earrings, pointed turbans, baggy pants, and ornate knives and pistols—listened with respectful silence. Then each rose, in turn, and made a statement, agreeing with much of what the Governor had said, but then proceeding, in a surprisingly frank fashion, to make certain criticisms. Specifically, they complained that not enough attention was being given to their standard of living, and they accused two men—one a Chinese general, the other a tribal leader—of being oppressive.

Despite Liu's seemingly conciliatory attitude, the fact remains that today the Provincial Government in Kangting contains only a dozen or so Tibetans—none in responsible positions—and even fewer Lolos.

Economically, Sikang is backward and undeveloped. There is a considerable amount of trade, nevertheless, since Sikang is the main gateway between China and Tibet. This trade is a spectacular business, for it moves slowly over high mountain passes and through deep gorges, and almost all of it is carried on human backs or pack animals. Yaan, which hugs close to the Szechwan border, is the place where important Chinese trading establishments maintain their headquarters, and it is a bustling Chinese city. The evidence of Liu Wen-hui's personality is omnipresent in the city. There is a Liu Street, a Liu Suspension Bridge over the Ya River, a memorial to Liu's reconstruction of the city, a column erected on Liu's fiftieth birthday, and so on.

The province's most colorful trading city, however, is Kangting, the meeting place of Chinese and Tibetan traders—similar in its position to Kalimpong in India on the other side of Tibet. Chinese goods are brought over the mountains, mostly by human carriers, as far as Kangting, and from there, the Tibetans take over. From the Tibetan caravansaries in Kangting, Chinese goods go by yak caravan up onto the Tibetan grasslands, less than 40 miles away, and then westward.

Kangting is a beautiful, delightful, and amazing little city. It is set in a mere hole in the mountains, and a torrential stream rushes through the center of town. Its architecture is an attractive mixture of Tibetan and Chinese elements, and its population is the same. The temperature is pleasantly cool, even in the middle of summer, for the altitude of the city is over 8,000 feet. Although it takes five days of hard walking to reach Kangting from Yaan, one is flabbergasted upon arriving at the town to discover good electric lights—from a 500-kilowatt hydroelectric plant belonging to a company organized by Liu—a theater with motion pictures, and shops full of gadgets, modern appliances, and manufactured goods of all sorts imported from East and West.

The main item of trade between China and Tibet is tea, an indispensable part of the Tibetan diet, all of which must be imported. A large share comes through Kangting. Most of this is grown in the mountains in the Yaan region and is carried in long, narrow baskets, on human backs, as far as Kangting. There it is repacked in skin containers and is transported by yak to Tibet.

In return for tea, the Tibetans export a diversified line of specialties. The most important, in terms of value, is a high grade of musk—which is shipped from Kangting to Shanghai, and from there to many world markets—for the manufacture of perfume. Tibet is one of the major musk-producing countries in the world. Next in importance are medicinal supplies, mostly herbs, and animal and plant products used for specialized purposes such as dye-making. Exports of less importance include yak and sheep wool, woolen cloth, Tibetan carpets, handicrafts, mica, and some gold and silver. In addition, there is a rather fantastic trade in British manufactured goods—such as cigarettes, serge cloth, and khaki cloth—which the Tibetans carry all the way across Tibet from India to Kangting. British cigarettes, tax-free, are cheaper in Kangting than they are in London!

Apart from the freak prices of these British goods, however, the general price level and cost of living in Kangting, and in other areas in the interior of the province, are extremely high. The average price of food in Kangting, for example, is three times as high as in Chengtu, which is only a little over 200 miles away. The high cost of living is responsible for a good deal of hardship among the common people, and there is considerable poverty. As one goes into Sikang Province, prices mount with the altitude—and the distance—because of the high cost of human transport. It takes ten to twelve days for carriers to take a load of tea from Yaan to Kangting, for example, and the price is doubled in the process.

The most valuable item of trade between Sikang Province and the rest of China comes not from Tibet, however, but from remote Chinese and tribal areas of the province. That item is opium. It is an open secret that opium is the most important export of Sikang Province. It is also an open secret that trade in opium is a monopoly of the Liu Wen-hui's Twenty-fourth Division, the provincial authorities, and the Brothers' Society. Liu and his deputies reap tremendous profits from this opium trade, which is, in fact, the main financial support for Liu's regime.

The trade is not completely open. The actual poppy fields are deep in the mountains away from the roads, so that a casual traveler does not see them along the main lines of communication.

But opium can be bought anywhere along the roads at small inns. The Lolos and some other tribes produce it in great quantities— even though they rarely consume it themselves—and trade it for small arms. It is also grown in considerable quantities by Chinese farmers in the mountains. Collection of the opium is the responsibility of designated agents of Liu, together with troops from the Twenty-fourth Division. A few private operators muscle in, but only at great risk. Once collected, the opium is channeled through Yaan to Chengtu and then into Chinese and world-wide nets of narcotic smugglers.

Much of the banditry and lawlessness in Sikang can be traced to the opium trade. Confused and violent civil strife often breaks out in opium-growing districts after the harvest, and banditry reaches its peak during the periods when opium is being transported from production areas to important trading centers in and out of the province. The prevalence of such lawlessness makes firearms almost a necessity, even for law-abiding citizens. Sikang, in fact, is probably one of the best-armed regions in the world, and it is a rare family, whether Chinese, Tibetan, or Lolo, which does not possess a rifle if it is outside of the largest towns. Most of these rifles, incidentally, even those in Tibetan homes, are bolt-action rifles such as those used by Liu's troops. Thousands are brought into the province by the military authorities every year and are used as a medium of exchange in the trade that they carry on.

The potentialities for future economic development in Sikang Province are difficult to estimate. Now the province is little more than a private domain, used as a military base and source of income by one of the most notorious warlords in China. But even assuming the province had a different administration, it is difficult to know what development could take place. The rugged terrain makes extensive agricultural development impossible. There may be somewhat better prospects for future development of animal industries. The Tibetan grasslands are among the finest pasture and grazing areas in the world, and animal products could be increased considerably, if markets were developed and if the animal industry was commercialized. At present, there is little manufacturing and no immediate prospects for its development. Perhaps the main unexploited natural wealth of the province is in its forests and minerals. Great stands of uncut timber cover mountains in many parts of the province, and although mineral resources are not well known, many people believe them to be large.

For the present, however, Sikang remains what it has been in years past: a wild, undeveloped, confused, and romantic frontier land, far off the beaten track. So far, it has been virtually untouched by the fighting in other parts of China. A few days ago, a small group of soldiers was sent north from Kangting—with speeches, bands, and flag-waving uncommon for China—and several alleged Communists were arrested on the basis of information revealed in the confession of a man in Chungking. But both of these events were unusual. By and large, the civil war is even further from Sikang psychologically than it is geographically—and geographically it is still a long way off.

16

THE PANCHEN LAMA

Kumbum (*Chinghai*)
September, 1948

Yesterday, September 25, I interviewed the Panchen Lama, a lonely eleven-year-old Tibetan boy who lives in a richly furnished hilltop home overlooking Kumbum Lamasery. This small, bright-faced exile from Tibet is, in many respects, a symbol of the present vague state of Sino-Tibetan relations.

Kumbum Lamasery (or Taersze, as it is known by the Chinese) lies in a snug valley in eastern Chinghai in the village of Lushar, one day's cart ride from Sining, the provincial capital. Although it is a long way from the political border of Tibet, Kumbum lies along the fringe of ethnic Tibet in the territory that at one time belonged to the Tibetan province of Amdo. A few miles to the west is Kokonor, the famous blue lake from which Chinghai takes its name. One of the two main caravan routes between Tibet and China winds through Kumbum, and both Tibetan and Chinese influences have left their mark on the place.

Lushar is a small, brown-colored village completely devoid of distinction, but the gold-plated Chinese roofs of the two main Kumbum temples glisten in the sunlight, and the blood-red robes of the lamas and the multicolored ornamentation of the lamasery are accentuated by their drab setting.

A monotonous, droning chant rises from Kumbum, like the sound of a crowded beehive, and the reek of yak-butter lamps fills the air with a nauseating pervasiveness. Within the gloomy interior of the lamasery, more than a thousand lamas—Tibetans, Chinese, and Mongols—perform their rigidly defined routine duties under the direction of a stern hierarchy of religious leaders. The three Living Buddhas, Aja (Akya), Saychr (Sertri), and Minah (Minyag), are the ranking chiefs within the lamasery, but a hierarchy of not-so-exalted personalities handles the routine administration. The *geitsu* (*getsul*), or acolyte lamas, are kept busy with servants' duties, in addition to learning their religious ABC's. The *gerun* (*gelong*), who have learned the basic knowledge required of a lama, spend most of their time chanting services, reciting scriptures, twirling prayer wheels, or performing dutiful prostrations—as many as 2,000 a day—to advance along the road toward the Buddhist conception of perfection.

In front of the main temple building of the lamasery, laymen believers, as well as lamas, prostrate themselves with endless regularity. Devout followers come and go in inchworm fashion, having journeyed tens or hundreds of miles, alternately prostrating themselves and walking three steps, then prostrating again before walking three more steps. The gifts of the many pilgrims—in animals, butter, precious metals, and money, together with the interest from loans issued and rent from the large tracts of land and the many shops in Lushar belonging to the lamasery—make Kumbum an important economic and financial center as well as a religious one. Even more important, however, is its political significance.

Kumbum Lamasery stands on the spot where Tsongkhaba, the great Tibetan religious leader who founded the Yellow Sect of Lamaism, is reputed to have been born. Tsongkhaba, who has been called the "Luther of Lamaism," was a reformer who tried to restore the purity of early Buddhism. The Yellow Sect that he founded is predominant throughout the Tibet–west China–Mongolia homeland of Lamaism, and might be called orthodox Lamaism. The other subdivisions, such as the Black Sect, Red Sect, and Sorcerers' Sect, are of only minor importance.

Leadership of orthodox Lamaism is shared by two persons who jointly occupy the apex of the religious hierarchy. These two leaders are the Dalai Lama, the temporal leader who maintains headquarters at Lhasa, and the Panchen Lama, who is spiritual leader and traditionally has lived at Shigatse, about a seven-day journey south of Lhasa. These two exalted posts are passed from generation to generation, according to the Buddhist theory of reincarnation, in unbroken succession.

During the middle 1920's, relations between the Dalai and Panchen lamas were severely strained by the injection of politics into their relations. The Dalai Lama, by far the more powerful of the two, stood for a pro-British Tibetan orientation and policy. The Panchen Lama came to stand for close Sino-Tibetan relations, an idea not at all popular in central Tibet. When friction became acute, the Panchen Lama left Tibet and began a decade of exile in China. He toured throughout China and not only became a well-known international figure, but gained Chinese sponsorship and support for his cause.

In the middle 1930's, the Panchen Lama started back for Tibet, accompanied by a Chinese military escort, to reassert his rights and reoccupy Shigatse. On the way he died—from a respiratory ailment, according to some reports, although others assert that he was poisoned—and the complicated process of choosing his reincarnated successor began.

Choosing a Panchen Lama involves a good deal of esoteric ritual, the object of which is to identify a child who has been born at the exact moment when the previous Panchen Lama died. Initially, three candidates were chosen, one of whom was to be selected ultimately as the only true reincarnation. Two of these came from the province of Chinghai in China, a region which has always been famous among Tibetans for its religious leaders and its horses. The other came from central Tibet.

Then a chaotic mix-up took place, and political rivalries again entered the picture. The boy first selected as the reincarnate Panchen Lama died. Soon thereafter both of the other two boys were selected, by rival parties, each as the true successor to spiritual leadership of Lamaism. One was set up as the protégé of Lhasa in Tibet. The other became a protégé of the pro-Chinese Tibetan group at Kumbum.

The Panchen Lama now at Kumbum was born at Hsunhua, Chinghai, and was brought to Kumbum in 1944. He lives an isolated, strictly supervised existence. His day begins at 4:00 A.M., and most of his time is spent learning and reciting the Tibetan scriptures. He is allowed no playmates, and his only companions are his pet birds and dogs—especially his favorite black puppy, called "Little Lion." He is surrounded by a rather sinister-looking group of Tibetan teachers and advisers who literally hover over him. Probably the most important and powerful of these are his Regent, a shrewd, bearded old man named Lo Ch'ang Chien Chan, and his Political Adviser, Chi Ch'ing Mei (these are the Chinese forms of their Tibetan names).

The Panchen Lama has an intelligent face, but it is doubtful if he is aware of the aura of intrigue and power politics that surrounds him. When I asked him when he planned to go to Shigatse, he turned a pair of inquiring, boyish eyes toward a trio of elderly advisers encircling him. His Regent replied for him: "He has no plans."

It is almost certain that in his position the eleven-year-old Panchen Lama at Kumbum does not have any plans of his own. It is probable, furthermore, that even his advisers have no definite immediate plans for him. It is highly possible, however, that this small boy may be used in years to come as a pawn in the relations between China and Tibet.

China still claims suzerainty over all of Tibet, even though Chinese control over central Tibet, or Tibet Proper, has been virtually nonexistent for decades. In many respects, the Panchen Lama at Kumbum is the symbol of Chinese claims. He is backed by China's moral support—even though it is largely unofficial. The advisers who cluster around him are completely pro-Chinese, representing only a small minority of Tibetans in this respect. And Kumbum Lamasery is protected by a special Tibetan People's Battalion composed of Chinese-trained and Chinese-equipped Tibetans, who are directly under the command of General Chang Chih-chung's Northwest Headquarters in Lanchow, Kansu.

In China, Tibetan affairs are the responsibility of the Mongolian and Tibetan Affairs Commission of the Executive Yüan. This commission maintains representatives at Lhasa, but has no control over the governing of central Tibet, which is autonomous and has looked to the British in India for moral support during the past few decades. The Mongolian and Tibetan Affairs Commission has seen to it that Tibetan representatives from regions within China Proper have been brought to the National Assembly and other important national meetings, but it does not have a great many direct or close contacts with the Tibetan people, and the Tibetans are one of the most unrepresented and inarticulate sizable minorities in China.

The Tibetan people within the boundaries of China Proper are directly controlled by two semiautonomous, authoritarian, provincial governors, Liu Wen-hui in Sikang and Ma Pu-fang in Chinghai. Both Sikang and Chinghai are recent political creations containing slices of territory once under the control of central Tibet, and both contain important Tibetan minorities (about 160,000 in Chinghai and five to six times that many in Sikang). West of Kangting, the provincial capital of Sikang (*kuan wai*), and west of Kokonor in Chinghai (*kou wai*), the population is Tibetan and the topography and economy belong to the Tibetan plateau, the "grasslands."

Although both Liu and Ma have used a combination of conciliation and force in their dealing with the "unruly" Tibetans, they have had differing degrees of success. In Sikang, Chinese control ends completely at the Yangtze River—or, to be more specific, the Chinsha River, which is a Yangtze tributary—and the rest of the province is Chinese on maps only. Ma Pu-fang, who speaks Tibetan himself, has had more success in establishing and maintaining his control, and almost the whole province of Chinghai, including the Tibetan regions, is under his tight supervision. General Ma first consolidated his rule by a bloody military campaign; he has maintained it by treating the cooperative Tibetans well, but suppressing opposition elements harshly. In neither Chinghai nor Sikang, however, do the Tibetans have either effective representation in the provincial administration or autonomy over their own affairs.

Government throughout Tibet Proper is complicated. The oligarchy at Lhasa controls the region in its immediate environs and exercises control to a lesser extent over all of Tibet. In western Sikang, for example, the Tibetans are said to be oriented completely toward Lhasa and the Dalai Lama, in both spiritual and other matters, and apparently the prestige of the Panchen Lama is at low ebb. In places distant from Lhasa, however, a strong degree of localism still prevails, and local government is a mixture of secular feudal leadership and ecclesiastical rule.

Although Tibet Proper has a small regular army, modeled on British lines and armed with British equipment, it is actually very weak and has only a semblance of political unity. It has been able to maintain its autonomy and to ignore Chinese claims of suzerainty because of a number of factors. One of these is its geographical remoteness and inaccessibility. Another has been the internal strife in China, which has precluded an active policy in remote regions. A third and important factor has been the moral support that the British have given Tibet as a buffer state north of India.

The British have now withdrawn from India, and they are relinquishing their stake in Tibet as well. It is too early to predict what effect, if any, this will have on Sino-Tibetan relations, but the British withdrawal certainly removes one of the most important props supporting Tibetan autonomy. Whether or not India will replace the prop is still a matter for speculation.

China's interest in Tibet is based on a combination of geographic and economic elements, plus the intangible but important factor called national prestige. Probably, Tibet is too distant and inaccessible to be of great importance strategically—it has generally been a barrier rather than a passage region—but, in peaceful times, a profitable China-Tibet trade is possible. Chinese tea, cloth, miscellaneous manufactured goods, and grain are exchanged for Tibetan musk, medicinal plants, animals, wools, hides, and furs. Most of Tibet's natural trade routes, which follow the rivers and the region's natural geographic orientation, flow into

China rather than India. The Brahmaputra and the major Hima-
layan trade routes affect only the southern fringe of Tibet. China's
principal interest in Tibet, however, appears to be based on tradition and prestige. Chinese feel that Tibet "belongs to China,"
and believe that this fact is sufficient reason for re-establishing
control. Factors of national prestige are as important in Chinese
policy as they are in other countries.

Tibet is still remote, however, and China is still torn by civil
war, so it is unlikely that China will attempt to reassert her claims
to Tibet in any effective manner in the immediate future. If, with
the passage of time and changing conditions, any such attempt
is made—by political or other means—the small boy at Kumbum
who "has no plans" undoubtedly will become a focus of attention, for an alliance with the Panchen Lama would give religious,
as well as political, legitimacy in the eyes of many to any Chinese
efforts to reassert control over Tibet.

CHINESE TURKESTAN

Tihwa (*Sinkiang*)
September, 1948

The Manas River lies in northwest Sinkiang—Chinese Turkestan —not far from the Soviet border. At a desolate army outpost overlooking the wrecked spans of the Great West Bridge that crosses the river, sixteen Chinese soldiers keep a watchful eye turned westward. They can see on the opposite bank the silhouetted figures of six Uighur men who form the last military outpost of the unrecognized "East Turkestan Republic." These lonely soldiers are symbols of the "watchful waiting" on both sides of this frontier between Sinkiang Province and the rebel regime in the fertile Ili Valley. On the night of August 5 of this year, six rifle shots rang out from the Ili side. Although no one was hit by these mysterious shots, they have been recorded as the latest incident in the unfinished history of the Ili Revolt.

On the northern crest of the Peitashan Mountains, where China and Outer Mongolia meet, Chinghai Muslims of the Chinese Fourteenth Cavalry Regiment patrol the grassy slopes to prevent enemy infiltration. Through field glasses, these patrols can see Outer Mongolian posts at the foot of the mountains below them. The atmosphere is one of tension, for Mongol and Chinese patrols frequently clash. On July 8 of this year, 120 Chinese met and fought about 80 Mongols. According to Chinese figures, 14 Mongols were killed, and 2 casualties were incurred by the Chinese troops. Approximately a month later, another clash of patrols took place, this time on the highway lifeline leading to Peitashan from the south. These clashes are the latest incidents in the unfinished history of the Peitashan border dispute.

The Manas River and the Peitashan Range are the two key points of military friction, at the present time, in the complex situation existing in Sinkiang and along its international frontiers. These points are extremely unstable and uneasy. They are not the scene of major military activity, however, for, despite mysterious shots, there is no fighting along the Ili border, and the

Peitashan clashes have not developed into all-out fighting. These two uneasy frontiers are symbolic and symptomatic, though, of the many critical and unsolved problems in Sinkiang—problems that combine both internal and external factors. They have been produced by Sinkiang's geographical and economic position, its ethnic diversity, and its political relations, as well as by its turbulent past history. These various factors have produced problems that affect the entire province, including critical border areas adjacent to the Soviet Union and Outer Mongolia.

Sinkiang is China's largest and westernmost province. It is a tremendous area, a part of both northwest China and Central Asia, and is bordered by Tibet, India, Afghanistan, the Mongolian People's Republic (Outer Mongolia), and the Soviet republics of Kazakhstan, Kirghizia, and Tadjikstan, as well as by the Chinese provinces of Kansu and Chinghai. High mountains and vast deserts cover a large portion of the province's 650,000 square miles. Running east and west through the center of it is the towering range of the Tien Shan, or Celestial Mountains, which are said to have over 7,500 glaciers. North of these mountains is Jungaria, a huge expanse of pebble and sand desert bordered by mountain ranges, the most important of which is the Altai Range to the north. South of the Tien Shan is the region sometimes called Kashgaria, the center of which is the Tarim Basin, a low desert fringed by lofty mountains which include the Kunlun, Pamir, and Karakoram ranges.

In this region of mountains and wasteland, human activity is generally confined to areas where the water supply is sufficient to sustain agriculture or animal husbandry. Natural precipitation is exceedingly scarce in the lowland regions, and, in some places, the annual rainfall approaches zero.

Agriculture is concentrated in oases located at the foot of the mountains and along the edge of the deserts. These are fed by glacial streams that flow out of the mountains and are swallowed up by the dry wasteland. The largest oases, which are political as well as economic centers, are linked by dusty motor roads. Almost all agriculture is nourished by man-made irrigation works that divert water into the thirsty fields from the many glacial streams and few small rivers in the province. Dry farming is restricted to a few areas in the northwestern corner of Sinkiang, in the valleys of the Ili, Black Irtysh, and Emil Rivers. Wheat, rice, corn, kaoliang, and barley are the main food staples grown, but other important agricultural products include cotton, silk, melons of all sorts, and a variety of fruits including grapes and apples. Intensive methods of cultivation prevail throughout the oases, but, surprising as it may seem, the pressure on the land is not as great as it is in many other parts of China. The oases are not, as a rule, overcrowded or overpopulated, and they contain a considerable amount of agricultural land that either is not cultivated or could be cultivated even more intensively. Furthermore, if irrigation were developed on a larger scale, the amount of cultivable land could be increased considerably. These facts mean that, although agriculture in Sinkiang is intensive in character, because of its concentration in limited areas and its dependence upon controlled water, food is more than sufficient in most areas, and the pressure of the population upon agricultural land is not excessive. Government officials in Tihwa estimate that, if properly developed by irrigation projects, the agricultural land in Sinkiang could be expanded to support a population of 10 million people, or two and a half times the present population.

Animal husbandry supports fewer people in Sinkiang than agriculture, but it utilizes a larger area (almost 5 per cent of the total area of the province, as compared with just over 1 per cent for agriculture), and the economy of certain groups, including the Kazakhs, Mongols, and Kirghiz, is based almost entirely upon it. Pasture land is distributed throughout the major mountain ranges, but much of the available pasturage in the Kunlun Mountains is not used, and most of the utilized grazing areas are in the Altai Mountains and the Tien Shan. Livestock of all sorts—sheep, goats, cows, horses, donkeys, camels—is raised, but sheep and goats are most numerous and are the primary basis for the livelihood of the nomadic peoples. These nomadic groups live an escalator existence, moving in stages up to the high pastures in warm weather and down to the low pastures in cold weather. Occasionally, they supplement animal husbandry with a small amount of cultivation, of wheat or other grains, in plots at the foot of the mountains; this cultivation is phased so that the harvesting takes place when the animals are moved down to cold weather pastures.

The mineral resources in Sinkiang have long been the subject of unrestrained speculation. From time to time, reports of the "fabulous riches of Sinkiang" have filtered out of the "heart of Asia" to stimulate the imaginations of the credulous optimists who wanted to believe them. The fact is, however, that it is difficult to say definitely whether Sinkiang's resources are fabulous or not. According to Wang Heng-sheng, Chief of the Geological Survey Office in Tihwa, only 3.6 per cent of the province has been systematically surveyed and prospected by the Chinese. (The Russians are said to have sent about 200 geologists into the province during the regime of Sheng Shih-ts'ai, but the results of their findings are not known.) The Chinese surveys have uncovered certain resources that are noteworthy, however. These include reserves of over 2 billion tons of coal, mostly of a noncoking type; about 50 million tons of iron, mainly siderite; considerable oil, wolfram (tungsten) ore, lead, molybdenite, zinc, and gypsum; and some arsenopyrite and copper. The Geological Survey Office has also made guesses which, if correct, mean that Sinkiang, although not "fabulously rich," is definitely valuable to China as a potential raw-material producer. The Survey Office estimates that Sinkiang's total coal reserves amount to 32.9 billion tons, most of which is lignitic bituminous coal, placing Sinkiang in third place among Chinese provinces in coal reserves, behind Shansi and Shensi. It estimates the total iron ore reserves to be 700 million tons, placing Sinkiang second, behind Liaoning in Manchuria. Petroleum reserves are estimated to cover approximately 4,500 square miles, and it is presumed that this area contains the largest petroleum reserves of any area in oil-poor China. The Survey Office also estimates that the province's gold reserves cover an area of 11,000 square miles, but that these reserves are not quite as rich as those in several other areas in China, such as Heilungkiang in Manchuria.

To date, however, there has been very little exploitation even of known resources in the province. A few scattered coal mines are working, but they do not produce much. Only a few operate on a large scale; most are tiny, hand-operated shafts that may produce as little as a ton a day. Actually, the only important utilization of Sinkiang's mineral resources at present is taking place at the mines in the northern and northwestern parts of the province, in the three administrative districts under Ili control. Work is going on there (although production figures are not known by the Chinese) at the Fuwen and Wenchuan wolfram (tungsten) mines, at the Wusu oil wells, and at the Altai gold mines.

Virtually no industrialization has yet taken place in Sinkiang, and the few modern factories are government-owned. At present, according to Provincial Commissioner of Reconstruction Mohammed Imin, the only modern factories in the province are a glass factory, an animal serum plant, and a clothing factory, all in Tihwa (Urumchi), and a small silk factory in Hotien (Khotan). There are plans for a small iron plant and a paper mill in Tihwa, for oil wells and a sugar plant west of Tihwa, and for a textile factory (the provincial government bought 5,000 spindles in Chungking two years ago, but has no funds even to transport them to Sinkiang), but the construction of these units is not under way yet. The Northwest Development Company, a highly publicized organization under Chang Chih-chung's headquarters in Lanchow, has done little in Sinkiang except import clothing and a few other manufactured articles, and export rugs, furs, and wool. Actually, the amount of industry in the province has declined in recent years, for the Russians, when they left in 1943, took out most of the machinery they had brought into the province during Sheng's regime. Handicraft production is carried on fairly widely, and Hotien is famous for its rugs, silk, embroidery, and jade, but even these native handicrafts could be greatly expanded and developed.

In short, Sinkiang is a "backward" and undeveloped area. It retains an atmosphere that in most places bears only faint traces of the twentieth century, and it possesses the romantic feeling of a new frontier in an ancient setting that is partly Oriental and partly Middle Eastern. There are severe limitations on modernization and development, however. Primitive transportation is one. Distances are tremendous, and except for a few crushed-rock motor highways and airlines (Chinese and Sino-Soviet) touching at Hami, Tihwa, and Ining, modern transport is totally lacking. There is not a single railway. The lack of any real economic market is also a limitation. For example, coal and iron resources are probably sufficient (despite the fact that most of the coal is of a noncoking type and is in scattered deposits) to build an iron and steel industry, but there are no consumers near enough to make it economic at present. The nearest potential consumers of importance are the Russians, but they have major iron and steel centers not far away in Kazakhstan, the Urals, and Siberia. Development of a cement industry in Sinkiang would be possible, and probably would be justified because of the demands for road and irrigation canal construction, but it is opposed by cement interests in Kansu. (The Irrigation Bureau is itself producing small amounts of cement in Tihwa, but it would like to produce much more.) In addition to the lack of a market and the opposition of competitive interests, the lack of capital is also an obstacle to development. And besides these economic factors, there are many political and social blocks to economic progress. It would be utopian, therefore, to expect any rapid modernization or extensive development in the province in the near future, and Sinkiang undoubtedly will remain a colorful but economically backward region, with an economy based primarily on oasis agriculture and pastoral livestock breeding, for some time to come.

The population of Sinkiang is spread thinly over the province's vast area. It totals roughly 4 million and is, in fact, one of the smallest among China's provinces. Ethnically, it is the most non-Chinese (excluding Tibet, which is not a province). Between one-half and three-quarters of the population is found in the oases of southern Sinkiang, and the majority is concentrated at the western end of the Tarim Basin, in the Administrative Districts of Aksu, Kashgar, Yarkand, and Khotan.

The ethnic diversity of Sinkiang is a result of its long and complicated history. For centuries, it has been a passage area, swept by waves of invasion and migration. It is believed that originally the area was populated by a group that spoke different types of Indo-European languages, but Scythians, Huns, Uighurs, Mongols, Chinese, and many other peoples have at various times occupied the region as conquerors, settlers, or both, and the present population is extremely heterogeneous.

The Chinese administration in Sinkiang at present lists fourteen different "racial" groups: Uighur, Kazakh, Han Chinese, Tungan, Taranchi, Kirghiz, Mongol, White Russian, Uzbek, Hsipo (Sibo), Tadjik, Tatar, Solon, and Manchu—in order of numerical importance. However, some of these subdivisions can be lumped together in larger groupings.

The Uighurs are a racial group whose name derives from that of a Turkic people, originally inhabiting northern Mongolia, who invaded Sinkiang in the ninth century and sometime thereafter embraced Islam. The present-day Uighurs are probably the result of some racial admixture, but they all speak Turki and are Muslims. Many have a very Caucasian appearance, and they dress in many-colored, embroidered skull caps, trousers, jackets, and leather boots. They are primarily an agricultural people, and the oases of southern Sinkiang are inhabited almost exclusively by them. They are, in fact, the predominant ethnic group in the province and account for roughly 75 per cent of the total population. Their social and economic organization is characterized by extremes of differentiation in the social and economic hierarchy and by strong localism. Traditionally, princes, mullahs (religious leaders), and begs (gentry) have been dominant in the oases, which have been quite self-contained. This pattern of organization is only gradually changing. The Taranchi (roughly 2 per cent of the population) and the Uzbeks (under 1 per cent of the population) can be grouped together with the Uighurs as having the same religion, essentially the same language, and a similar way of life. Taranchi, in fact, is merely a special name given to a group of Uighurs who migrated from the southern part of the province to the north.

The Kazakhs, who make up over 10 per cent of the total population, are the second largest group. They are concentrated in the northern districts of the province. Although they speak a variety of Turki and are Muslims, they live a very different sort of existence from that of the Uighurs. They are a nomadic people who live in yurts and move with their flocks. They are a proud people and, in many respects, the most militant group in the province. Related to the Kazakhs, and similar to them, is another nomadic group, the Kirghiz, who are concentrated in the mountains of southwestern Sinkiang. Although the Kirghiz account for less than 2 per cent of the population of the province, they are numerically the second most important group in southern Sinkiang.

The Han Chinese are the third largest group, but they total less than a quarter of a million, which is slightly under 6 per cent of the province's population. They are concentrated in the northern areas, particularly in the Tihwa, Ili, and Tacheng districts (although they may not be so numerous in the latter two areas now, as a result of the events of the past few years). The Chinese are farmers and merchants, and because they are the ruling group many, quite naturally, are officials and government workers.

The Tungans, Chinese Muslims, are the fifth group in size. Racially, they are a Chinese-Turkic mixture, but they speak the Chinese language. Although making up only about 2 per cent of the population, the group is an important one, for many Tungans hold government positions, or are wealthy landowners or flockowners under whom members of other groups, such as Uighurs and Kazakhs, work as tenants and flock-herders. Their influence is disproportionate to their numbers.

The Mongols, about 1.5 per cent of the province's population, are divided into three groups: one under Ch'ao Ch'ing Wang in the region between Tacheng and Chenghua, one under Min Ch'ing Wang at Wusu, and one under Man Han Wang in the vicinity of Karashar. Like the Kazakhs, they are a nomadic people.

The other minorities, each of which accounts for less than 1 per cent of the population, are mainly in the northern districts. They include the White Russians (who fled Russia at the time of the Bolshevik Revolution), the Hsipo, Solon, and Manchu groups (all three of which are Manchu remnants of garrisons kept in Sinkiang by the Manchu Dynasty), and the Tatars. In the far southwestern corner of the province, there is another small minority, the Tadjiks, a sedentary Iranian people who belong to the Ismaili sect of Islam and speak an Iranian language.

Although the existence of these many groups creates extremely complicated problems of ethnic relationships, there is more uniformity than there might appear to be, for 90 per cent of the population speak the Turki language in one form or another and accept the Muslim faith, and the Uighurs alone constitute 75 per cent of the population.

Many of the basic problems in Sinkiang, however, are caused by the fact that almost 95 per cent of the population are different racially, linguistically, and culturally from the population in the rest of China, to which they belong politically, and many of the complexities of these problems are caused by the existence of diversities and splits within that 95 per cent.

For centuries, Sinkiang has been an arena for local and interregional rivalries. Conflict has been a recurring theme in its history for over 2,000 years, during which time Chinese influence and control have expanded and receded with a sort of tidal motion. In periods when the Chinese Empire was vigorous and aggressive, such as during the Han and T'ang dynasties, Chinese control was pushed westward. In other periods, the limits of effective Chinese control were contracted. Throughout this long period of changing relationships, China was almost continually confronted in the Sinkiang area both by local centers of power and opposition and by outside empires or kingdoms interested in the region. China never lost interest in the region, however, for, before China's reorientation toward the seacoast as a result of the impact and depradations of Western imperialism, Sinkiang was China's principal front door and the pathway to Central Asia and the West. Sinkiang, no longer China's front door, is still an important back door, and it is still a region of conflict.

In the period of modern international relations, Sinkiang suddenly increased in importance about the middle of the nineteenth century. At approximately that time, British imperialism, which was consolidating its position in northern India, and Russian imperialism, which was expanding throughout Central Asia, approached each other geographically in the Sinkiang region and eyed each other suspiciously. In 1851 and 1860, the Russians established consulates in Ili and Kashgar, respectively, and began urging the Chinese to oppose the British actively. The British, even though they were supporting the Manchus in coastal China, responded by supporting a Muslim adventurer named Yakub Beg in a revolt against Chinese rule.

Yakub Beg was a native of Khokand who started his career as a dancing boy and rose to be chief of staff to an ambitious Khoja leader who was expanding his power in southwestern Sinkiang. Soon after the Muslim uprisings that took place throughout northwestern China in the 1860's, Yakub Beg usurped the power of his leader and began a personal conquest of Sinkiang. The Russians thereupon occupied the Ili region in northwestern Sinkiang, in 1871, and played a double game by making a commercial agreement with Yakub Beg and occupying strategic positions at the same time that they were aiding the Chinese troops sent to suppress Yakub Beg. The British, on the other hand, seemed to throw their unqualified support to Yakub Beg when a British envoy named Forsyth signed a treaty with him in 1874. The Chinese forces under Tso Tsung-t'ang, however, were more successful than perhaps either the British or the Russians had expected, for by 1875 the revolt had been successfully suppressed.

Once the Russians had moved into Ili, it was not so easy for the Chinese to oust them from the region. A preliminary Sino-Russian treaty in 1879 gave Russia valuable parts of the region, an indemnity for occupation costs, and commercial privileges, but this treaty was denounced by the Peking Government. Finally, in 1881, a treaty settling the problem was signed, and the Ili region was retained by the Chinese and evacuated by the Russians. The Russians continued to exhibit a lively interest in Sinkiang, however, even though British interest in the region declined after it was discovered in the 1880's that the passes to India from the Sinkiang region were too difficult to permit any real threat from that direction.

In 1882, not long after the suppression of Yakub Beg's revolt, Sinkiang was made into a Chinese province; previously, it had been treated as a special border region. Control of the new provincial regime slipped easily into the hands of the families of the military and civilian officials who had accompanied Tso Tsung-t'ang to Sinkiang.

After the Chinese Revolution in 1911, however, Sinkiang broke away from control by the Central Government authorities in China, and from 1911 until 1944, it was ruled by Chinese but not really by China. There was a succession of local Chinese warlords, each of whom received recognition, as a matter of expediency, by the Chinese government, first in Peking and then in Nanking, but these warlords were really autonomous. They maintained their position by playing along with both China and Russia, without getting too friendly with either and without letting either extract too many concessions from them. The administrations of these local rulers were characterized, in varying degrees, by nepotism, graft, corruption, and misrule.

The first of these warlords was a Yunnanese named Yang Tseng-hsin, who had been a member of the administration under the Manchus and who assumed control in 1911. For a short period during his rule, Sinkiang's relations with Russia were disturbed, first by a Kirghiz revolt in Russia in 1916 and then by the Bolshevik Revolution, but Yang maintained a neutral position and refused to be drawn actively into either the pro-Soviet or anti-Soviet side. When it looked as if the revolution would succeed, Yang established normal relations with the Soviet government. In the early 1920's, he concluded a trade agreement with the Soviets and allowed five Soviet Offices for Commerce and Foreign Affairs to be opened in the province. The Soviet Mission in Ining, headed successively by Limerev, Borchak, and Kolikoff, fomented some trouble and encouraged at least two minor mutinies against the provincial regime, but Yang continued his policy of getting along with Russia. The establishment of formal Sino-Soviet diplomatic relations in 1924 had its effect on Sinkiang, even though the province had been following an independent course, and the first Soviet consulates were opened in the provinces during that year.

In 1928, Yang was assassinated and was succeeded by a subordinate named Chin Shu-jen, a Kansu man. Although relations between China and the Soviet Union were severely strained at the time, because of the 1927 Kuomintang-Communist split and the events that followed—including the 1929 Sino-Soviet railway dispute in Manchuria—Chin continued to follow an independent policy that would not antagonize the Russians. He signed a new agreement with the Soviet Government permitting a number of trade-agency offices to be opened in Sinkiang and reducing customs levies on trade between Sinkiang and the Soviet Union.

Governor Chin, however, was both avaricious and weak, and his attempts to increase taxes created widespread discontent. Following the death of the local prince at Quomul (Hami) in 1930, Chin took the prince's son into custody and tried to abolish the princedom, setting the stage for local revolt. The Hami revolt finally broke out in 1932, set off by an incident in which a Chinese tax collector abducted a Muslim girl. When representatives from Hami requested and obtained aid from Ma Chung-ying, a

Kansu Muslim general who saw a chance for personal aggrandizement, the situation turned against Chin. As the forces of Ma and his lieutenants swept westward through the province, threatening Tihwa, and after a serious rice shortage developed there, the troops and the people placed the blame on the Governor. Chin was forced to flee, and on April 12, 1933, power passed to General Sheng Shih-ts'ai, following a coup launched by White Russian officers.

Sheng Shih-ts'ai was a Manchurian who had been educated at the Hsaokwan Military Academy and in Japan, had participated in the Kuomintang's Northern Expedition, had been appointed to a military post for frontier defense by Chin, and finally had become the active commander of the fighting against Ma. He commanded all the provincial troops, including a group of Manchurian soldiers who had fled from the Japanese via Russia to Sinkiang, but at first he did not make much headway against Ma. Ma advanced farther, and revolt also broke out in the Ili district under a General Chang Pei-yüan. Negotiations between Sheng and Ma were attempted, but were unsuccessful. At this point, Sheng appealed for Russian help, and the Russians responded by coming into Sinkiang more deeply, perhaps, than ever before.

Probably motivated in part by a desire to counter Japanese penetration (the Japanese had set up a puppet Mongol regime and had provided Ma Chung-ying with military advisers), the Russians gave Sheng all-out support, including trucks, armored cars, tanks, and airplanes. Ma was cornered, chased into southwest Sinkiang, and in 1934 was spirited away from Kashgar to Russia, never to be heard of again. The Sinkiang provincial regime established thereafter was really a joint Sheng-Soviet effort. In 1937, the powerful mechanized Soviet Eighth Regiment moved (in Chinese uniforms) to Hami, key to the eastern approach to Sinkiang. Soviet capital and machinery were brought into the province, and the Russians built roads and airports. Several hundred Soviet advisers were attached to the Provincial Government. Oil wells and tungsten mines were developed. Soviet secret police cooperated with Sheng's secret police. And a provincial three-year plan was started with Russian advice. All these developments made the whole province of Sinkiang temporarily a Russian sphere of influence.

Then, in 1942, Sheng made a complete about-face. Perhaps because events were going badly for the Russians in Europe, he reoriented his policy toward China and began arresting Russians and pro-Russians. In the following year, the Soviets withdrew their troops from Hami and took with them, as they left the province, most of the tangible assets that they had brought in.

Sheng's internal policies had been reasonably enlightened during the first part of his regime, and he had been unusually conciliatory toward non-Chinese groups. Gradually, however, he adopted oppressive methods, set up a police state, and antagonized all groups by indiscriminate arrests (it is estimated that he arrested upward of 100,000 persons during his rule). By 1944, he was hated as few men have ever been hated even in Sinkiang.

When Sheng turned away from the Soviet Union and toward the Chinese Government, the latter took advantage of this opportunity and moved in. Sheng was eased out of his ruling position in the fall of 1944 and was shifted to a powerless post in the Central Government as Minister of Agriculture and Forestry. Soon thereafter, Wu Chung-hsin arrived, with two secretaries, as the first Governor of Sinkiang really selected and appointed by the Central Government since 1911. On November 7 of the same year, revolt broke out in the Ili Valley.

The Ili Revolt, initiated on the anniversary of the Bolshevik Revolution in 1944, began as a rebellion against the disorder, misrule, and oppression that had reached a climax at the end of Sheng's regime. It had little relation to the new Governor, Wu, who barely had time to catch his breath before the revolt began.

The Ili forces, backed by Soviet Russia's moral support, and by some Soviet material support (the amount of which has never been accurately determined), soon wiped out two regiments of poorly equipped Chinese troops, about 4,000 men, and by January, 1945, had the whole Ili region in their hands. The leaders of the revolt proclaimed the establishment of an East Turkestan Republic and proceeded to enlarge their area of military control until it included, by the latter part of 1945, the northern administrative districts of Tacheng and Ashan, as well as Ili. Concurrent with the military action, a fairly widespread pogrom against the Han Chinese took place in those regions. Some estimates of the Chinese killed during that period run as high as 25,000.

In the early fall of 1945, the Chinese Government, concerned about the reverses that Chinese forces in Sinkiang had sustained, sent General Chang Chih-chung to Tihwa as the President's personal representative (in 1946, he became Governor). Chang is a conciliatory man and one of the Central Government's most experienced negotiators (he had done much of the negotiating with the Chinese Communists), and it was hoped that he could find some peaceful solution in Sinkiang.

Then the Russians stepped in as mediators. The Soviet Ambassador to China, Apollon Petrov, sent a memorandum to Foreign Minister Wang Shih-chieh reporting that the Ili group had petitioned the Soviet Consul-General in Tihwa, Alexandre Savielieff, to intercede, and that the Soviet Government was willing to mediate. China accepted, and peace negotiations began in October, 1945, between Chang Chih-chung and three representatives of the Ili Group (Rahimjan Sabir Hodjayev, Achmadjan Kasymov, and Abdul Nair Jure).

The events that have followed fall into a pattern duplicated in many other trouble spots in the world since V-J Day. Weeks of haggling finally resulted in a negotiated peace settlement. A short period of cooperation and peace followed. Then, the cooperation disintegrated, both sides claiming that the peace settlement had not been implemented by the other group. The final result was an impasse.

The first step toward what appeared, at the time, to be a solution of the trouble was a general Peace Agreement signed on January 2, 1946, by Chang Chih-chung for the Central Government and the three above-mentioned representatives of the Ili Group. This agreement called for popular election of *Hsien* councils which would then elect *Hsien* magistrates within a period of three months. Administrative District officers (*Chuan Yüan*) and their assistants were to be "recommended by the people." A new Provincial Council was to be elected by the *Hsien* councils. In addition, a general reorganization of the Provincial Government was outlined. According to this reorganization, the Provincial Commission was to be expanded to twenty-five members, ten of whom would be appointed directly by the Central Government and fifteen recommended by elected representative bodies and subsequently appointed by the Central Government. (Normally, all are appointed directly by the Central Government.) The ten direct appointees were to include the Governor (Chairman), Secretary-General, Commissioners of Civil Affairs and Finance, Chief of the Bureau of Social Welfare, Assistant Commissioners of Education and Reconstruction, Assistant Chief of the Health Bureau, and two Commissioners without portfolio. The fifteen members recommended by elected bodies were to include two Vice-Governors, two Deputy Secretaries-General, Commissioners of Education and Reconstruction, Assistant Commissioners of Civil Affairs and Finance, Chief of the Health Bureau, Assistant Chief of the Bureau of Social Welfare, and five Commissioners without portfolio. An annex, signed on the same day, granted even more specific concessions to the Ili group. Of the fifteen above-mentioned members of the Provincial Commission, the Ili Group, although controlling only three of the ten administrative districts in the province, was explicitly granted the right to choose six commissioners, including one Vice-Governor, one Deputy Secretary-General, the Commissioner of Education or of Reconstruction, the Assistant Commissioner of Civil Affairs or of Finance, the Chief of the Health Bureau or the Assistant Chief of the Bureau of Social Welfare, and one Commissioner without portfolio.

The agreement also guaranteed full freedom of religion, publication, assembly, and speech. Further, it promised use of both the Chinese and Turki languages by all administrative and judicial organs and in official documents. It enunciated the right of petition in one's native language and laid down the principle that native languages should be used in primary and middle schools, with both Chinese and Turki being used in higher institutions of learning. Other points included assurances of "free development of racial cultures and arts," taxation based upon "the real productive power of the people" and "their ability to pay," freedom of domestic and foreign trade within the framework of existing treaties, and the release within ten days after the signing of the agreement of all persons arrested for political reasons by both sides.

The agreement also provided for the formation of troop units made up of non-Chinese racial groups, which were to be trained and given orders in their own languages whenever possible. With regard to the Ili troops, they were to be reorganized and integrated into the National Army. The details of these steps were to be outlined in a separate annex.

The question of army reorganization is always a fundamental one in the solution of a dispute involving military conflict. It took almost six months for an agreement to be reached on this question. Finally, however, on June 6, 1946, the second annex to the Peace Agreement was signed. This provided for the reorganization of the Ili troops into three cavalry and three infantry regiments with a total strength not exceeding 12,000 men. One infantry and two cavalry regiments were to be enlisted in the National Army, and the other units incorporated into the Provincial Peace Preservation Corps. The responsibility of these troops was to be exclusively that of maintaining peace and order in the three northwestern administrative districts, and the responsibility for guarding national frontiers was to rest with the Central Government's border defense troops. The commander of the six Ili regiments was to be chosen by the Ili Group and appointed Assistant Commander of the Provincial Peace Preservation Corps, as well as commander of the six regiments of Ili troops. However, he was to fit into the regular chain of command and to follow orders issued by Chang Chih-chung's Northwest Headquarters (recently renamed Northwest Political and Military Authority), the Sinkiang Garrison Commander, and the Peace Preservation Corps Commander. The Ili commander was to be consulted on the reorganization of Peace Preservation units from local Muslims. Military and other equipment for the six Ili regiments was to be supplied by both the Central and Provincial Governments. The commander of the six regiments was required, however, to report his troop dispositions and strength, as well as the equipment of his units.

The signing of the military annex completed the basic Peace Agreement. It was supplemented, however, by an Administrative Program, which was passed at the second meeting of the newly organized Provincial Council on July 18, 1946. This Administrative Program was a utopian document that promised the moon, without specifying means by which the vague promises could be implemented.

Besides reiterating the political pledges of the Peace Agreement, it held forth the vision of fundamental financial reform, extensive agricultural and industrial development, and far-reaching health and educational projects. As a basis for practical policy, it was meaningless.

During the summer of 1946, a coalition government was formed in Sinkiang, and elections were held as promised. Although Chang Chih-chung was Governor, the reorganization filled most of the top-level posts in the Provincial Government with non-Han political figures. The Ili appointees included Achmadjan as Vice-Governor, Abdul Karim Abasov as Deputy Secretary-General, Rahimjan as Assistant Commissioner of Civil Affairs, and Seyfuddin as Commissioner of Education. As the coalition government took shape, many other non-Han individuals were appointed to high posts. These included Uighurs not in the Ili Group, such as Aisabek Aleptekin, Provincial Secretary-General, and Mohammed Imin, Commissioner of Reconstruction. They also included Kazakhs, such as Jarimhan, Commissioner of Finance, and Salis, Deputy Secretary-General; Mongols, such as Erdeni, Assistant Chief of the Bureau of Social Welfare; Tungans, such as Wang

Tseng-shan, Commissioner of Civil Affairs; and one Tatar, Burhan, as Vice-Governor.

The reorganization did not satisfy the Ili Group, however, for the real power remained in the hands of the Chinese: Chang Chih-chung, his Secretary-General, Liu Meng-ch'un, and General Sung Hsi-lien, Commander of the Sinkiang Garrison. Furthermore, no miracle happened to transform the complete administrative and political situation in the province, and discontent spread. Within the government, both sides wanted ultimate control, and obviously both could not have it. So the coalition was doomed to failure.

On February 19, 1947 a "liberty mass meeting," held in the Uighur Club in Tihwa, drew up a petition to the Provincial Government. Two days later, on February 21, a Uighur demonstration of several hundred men took place in the streets of Tihwa. A second long petition was formulated, followed the next day by a third. The three petitions demanded reduction of provincial taxes by half, rapid reorganization of the Aksu and Kashgar Peace Preservation Troops, an increase of native personnel in the administration, cessation of "oppression" by Chinese troops and police, evacuation of the majority of Chinese troops in Sinkiang, prohibition of military purchases of supplies on the open market, and the cessation of political arrests. They also called for re-elections in areas where "oppression" had occurred, complete judicial reorganization, including the removal of "all" chiefs of judicial organs, release of all political prisoners, the end of secret police activities, and organization of a province-wide Uighur police force. In addition, the petitions wrathfully denounced a number of government officials, the most prominent of whom were Jarimhan, Salis, and Hatewan (District Officer of Tihwa). Furthermore, they demanded the arrest and punishment of the Kazakh leader Osman, District Officer of Ashan.

On February 24, Kazakh and Tungan petitions were presented to the Provincial Government. On the next day, the Han Chinese of Tihwa presented a similar document. These petitions (particularly the one drawn up by the Kazakhs) contained lists of minor grievances, but their effect was to counterbalance the Uighur demands, counteract Uighur pressure on the government, and place the Chinese provincial authorities in a better bargaining position.

The climax of this sequence of events was a huge Chinese demonstration in Tihwa on February 25. A riot occurred during which four Chinese and four Uighurs were killed. Achmadjan, the top

Uighur spokesman, was forced to acknowledge many of the demands of other groups and to modify the demands of his own. The tension and fear created by the rioting lasted for over a week, and when calm was finally restored and martial law lifted on March 6, the only real result of the demonstrations and petitions was a general bitterness among all concerned.

The tension, which had spread throughout the province, was temporarily eased by a skillfully worded proclamation drawn up by the Provincial Commission under the direction of Chang Chih-chung. This proclamation, which was published on March 26, humbly admitted that not all of the objectives of the Peace Program and Administrative Program had been achieved, but it reiterated that every effort was being made to achieve them. It was signed by the Ili Group members of the Provincial Commission and gave the strong impression that complete harmony existed among all the groups participating in the administration.

On May 28, 1947, the appointment of Masud Sabri as Governor of Sinkiang was announced. Masud Sabri was a sixty-two-year-old Uighur, born in a wealthy Ili family, and educated in military and medical schools in Turkey. For the previous twelve years, however, he had been in central and southwest China. In Chungking, he had taught in the "CC"-controlled Central Political Institute, and was considered by the Uighur nationalists in Sinkiang to be old, weak, and completely pro-Chinese. His appointment was interpreted as a Chinese attempt to undermine Uighur nationalism by working through a puppet, and demonstrations against the appointment took place at scattered points throughout the province.

On July 7, 1947, Uighur revolt broke out openly, this time in the Turfan, Shanshan, and Toksun oases. In Turfan, it developed into a serious rebellion, but it was suppressed rapidly and efficiently by General Sung Hsi-lien, one of China's ablest young generals. A few of the leaders of the revolt, including agents who had come from Ili, were taken into custody. Shortly thereafter, on August 26, 1947, the Ili Group suddenly left Tihwa for Ining, the coalition collapsed completely, and a state of hostility commenced. The Ili-Sinkiang border was sealed, and open movement between the two areas ceased.

Since August 26, 1947, a number of futile exchanges of notes (the texts of which are available here in Tihwa, but not elsewhere) have taken place between the Ili Group and the Chinese Government, but these negotiations have accomplished nothing. The first note was from Chang Chih-chung to Achmadjan and

Rahimjan on September 1, 1947. It contained a long defense of Chang's "patience and conciliatory attitude." It claimed, on the part of the Provincial Government, "full execution of the Peace Agreement," adherence to the slogan "Peace, unity, democracy, and cooperation," and the achievement of a democratic government. And it contained a long list of grievances against the Ili Group, including: their failure to implement the Peace Agreement, particularly the military terms; their unwillingness to restore normal relations with the Provincial Government and the Central Government; and their efforts to win political control throughout the province. The note also accused the Ili Group of being responsible for the massacres of Chinese at Tacheng and Omin in early 1946, the demonstrations in Tihwa in February, 1947, the revolts in Turfan, Shanshan, and Toksun in July, 1947, and the riots in Kashgar in May, 1947. It further accused the Ili Group of "continuing the secret organization of East Turkestan," opposing unreasonably the governorship of Masud Sabri, sabotaging the sessions of the Provincial Council, and "trying to win party control of the Provincial Government with an attitude of conquering." Despite these accusations, the over-all tone of the letter was conciliatory, and Chang appealed for a common understanding based upon support of the principle of national unity together with "an amicable pro-Soviet and pro-Chinese atmosphere." The note concluded by inquiring if the Ili Group was willing to reopen the negotiations.

The Ili reply from Ining on October 16, 1947, categorically denied the charges made by Chang. For example, it claimed that the Turfan rebellion was "a spontaneous result of overflowing Muslim anguish." In addition, it asserted that the violations of the Peace Agreement were "the work of the Chinese alone." The note contained a long list of counteraccusations against the Chinese, who, it said, had "created a situation that became intolerable." More specifically, it accused the Chinese of quadrupling their military forces in Sinkiang, of failing to reorganize the Peace Preservation Troops at Kashgar and Aksu, and of being unwilling to treat native troops on the basis of equality. The note complained that not only had the Chinese been remiss in not providing ammunition and supplies to the Ili forces, but that the Chinese Army was making "continuous preparations to invade" Ili territory and was supporting "bandits" like Osman in campaigns against Ili. In addition, the note complained that the army and police personnel in Sinkiang made illegal arrests, manipulated local elections, and interfered with local administration. The Provincial Government was accused of instigating the Tihwa riots of February, 1947, fomenting racial friction, expanding its secret police, interfering with the "organization of democratic bodies," disregarding the "opposition of the people of Sinkiang" to the appointment of Masud Sabri and other officials, and using "despotic methods." In the note, it was also claimed that, "since the day the Peace Agreement was signed, the Ili Party at no time proposed, directly or indirectly, secretly or openly, that Sinkiang should secede from China." The note ended by saying that the Ili Group was willing to reopen negotiations if four demands were met. These demands were that: "(1) Oppression and torture of progressive elements in Sinkiang should be stopped immediately. (2) All Muslim prisoners should be freed, and those responsible for their imprisonment should be punished. (3) Masud Sabri should be removed from the governorship of the Provincial Government. (4) All the articles of the June, 1946, Agreement should be fully implemented."

A second exchange of notes took place between December, 1947, and February of this year, in which "the facts" were re-examined, accusations and defense arguments repeated, and new conditions for negotiation defined.

In a note written on December 9, 1947, Chang made a point-by-point refutation of the Ili charges. The number of Chinese troops in Sinkiang, according to this note, had actually been reduced by half since the Peace Agreement, whereas the Ili forces in the same period had been doubled. The note asserted that the reorganization of Peace Preservation Troops had been postponed, and the supply of military equipment to the Ili troops halted, because of the failure of the Ili commanders to reorganize their troops and allow Chinese inspection. Chang also claimed that the Chinese were not giving military assistance to Osman, and that, in fact, Osman had been badly mistreated by the Ili Group. He asserted that the police forces in Sinkiang had been reorganized and were in no way secret, and that persons still detained in prison were there for violation of the law and constituted a "problem of jurisprudence and not one of politics." In defense of Masud Sabri's appointment, he argued that not only was Masud Sabri a competent governor, but that gubernatorial elections would soon be held throughout China, and that there was no reason to make a change in Sinkiang before them. In this note, Chang emphasized another point: "Freedom has a certain limit. No nation on earth could allow rebellion against the mother country to be carried out by its own citizens. People have no freedom to oppose their own country." Finally, the note proposed a renewal of the negotiations if the Ili Group would: (1) eliminate the "irregularities" in their territory, (2) use the Chinese national flag and the Chinese language, as well as Turki, (3) stop military mobilization and preparations, and voluntarily reduce and reorganize their troops, (4) cease the East Turkestan Movement and anti-Chinese propaganda, and (5) restore communications with the rest of the province.

The reply from Achmadjan and Rahimjan on February 17, 1948, accused Chang of producing "words but no deeds" and claimed that there was "no assurance that promises would be kept." However, after repeating some of their major accusations against the Chinese, they professed to be willing to renew negotiations if Masud Sabri was removed from his position, if Osman was punished at a "public trial by the people," and if all the "progressive elements" in jail were released. The note did not even mention the conditions outlined in Chang's note of December 9. As a consequence, Chang's reply on April 1 of this year was curt, stating that the fulfillment of the conditions he had already outlined was the "minimum symbolic proof" of Ili sincerity required before further steps could be taken. Since April 1, there has been a complete stalemate and silence on both sides.

These five notes exchanged between Chang Chih-chung and the Ili Group reveal some of the issues at stake, but both sides mixed truth with exaggeration and falsehood, and the most basic issues were sometimes hidden. In fact, the most fundamental split between the two sides was obscured by the mass of verbiage; it was the split over political power. The Ili Group wanted to achieve a position of predominance in the Provincial Government, while the Chinese were determined to maintain the controlling position they already possessed.

At present, the Ili Group accuses the provincial administration in Sinkiang of being oppressive. Some of their specific accusations are true, others partly true, and others false. Taking all relevant factors into consideration, however, it seems clear that the present Chinese administration is not nearly as black as the Ili spokesmen claim; it is neither completely bad nor completely good.

Tradition and past history confront the Chinese in Sinkiang with a tremendous handicap. When the Central Government moved into the province in 1944 and took control for the first time in over thirty years, it inherited a bad name. Since the Revolution of 1911, Sinkiang had been ruled by corrupt and oppressive warlords who were Chinese even though they were not the Chinese Government. Furthermore, Chinese rule for decades, and even centuries, had not been enlightened. Under the Chinese Empire, Sinkiang was a long way from the capital, and officials were often sent to such faraway posts as punishment for misdemeanors committed elsewhere. It was not uncommon for such officials to accumulate personal fortunes while serving out their terms in the remote and inhospitable borderland. Nepotism, graft, corruption, and even violence were recurring phenomena. Few Chinese officials learned the native languages or concerned themselves with local problems, and the Chinese administration generally maintained its rule by working through dominant native families (particularly the families of Uighur begs) and by promoting group conflicts in a policy of divide-and-rule. The long history of inept Chinese rule, and misrule, reached its climax in the regime of Sheng Shih-ts'ai. Its heritage plagues the Chinese in everything they do in Sinkiang.

Since 1944, however, the Central Government seems to have made a sincere effort to appoint well-qualified men to the top posts in the Sinkiang Provincial Government. As a result, the principal Chinese leaders in Tihwa today appear to be able men who are aware of their special responsibilities, are sympathetic with the aims of minority groups, and are trying to solve Sinkiang's problems by peaceful and conciliatory means. This group of men works under the leadership of Chang Chih-chung, and their approach to Sinkiang's problems seems to be one of conciliation—within limits. They have formulated policies that, if fully implemented, would really mean a new deal for Sinkiang.

Even among top-level Chinese, however, there are a few who advocate force rather than conciliation, and the changes that have been made at the top level have not filtered down very far through the administration. The local police forces and courts, in fact, still retain most of the people who worked under Sheng Shih-ts'ai. The policy of conciliation is completely foreign to many of these men, and they tend to employ traditional high-handed methods in dealing with the people.

The representatives of non-Chinese groups appointed to official positions by the Chinese are of various kinds. A few, such as Yolbas (Yollbars) at Hami, are regarded by many as mere puppets. Others, such as Masud Sabri, are nationalists but now go along completely with the Chinese and probably would never disagree with them on important issues. Still others, such as Aisabek and Mohammed Imin, are strong nationalists who freely criticize the shortcomings of the present regime to which they belong. The men in this category are real representatives of the aspirations of the non-Chinese groups. They are cooperating with the Chinese because they believe that it is impossible to work alone, that a choice must be made between China and the Soviet Union, and that China is the better of the two. In addition, there are a few appointees in the Provincial Government, such as Jarimhan, the illiterate Commissioner of Finance, who are undoubtedly popular figures in the minority groups from which they are drawn, but who are unfortunate choices because they are not qualified for the positions they hold.

Even though there are a good many qualified and competent men among the appointees selected from minority groups, the Chinese are severely criticized for not paying enough attention to popular sentiment in making these appointments. (In a similar way, they are criticized for not selecting a few non-Kuomintang people in making their Chinese appointments.) This is particularly true in regard to Masud Sabri, who for various reasons is far from being a popular leader among the Uighurs. There may be some justification for this criticism, but the most vocal critics seem to forget that in the original coalition government all the major Ili leaders were appointed to responsible positions in the government—which they voluntarily abandoned. These critics also overlook the obvious difficulty, from the Chinese point of view, of finding men who not only are popular leaders among the minorities, but are also unquestionably loyal to China. In undisturbed times, this might not be a problem, but during a period of rebellion and revolt it obviously is.

The persons holding local positions at the lower levels of government in Sinkiang are, for the most part, identical with or similar to those who held such positions in the pre-1944 period. Not even the Chinese claim that the elections held during the reorganization of the government were a real expression of popular sentiment. In a situation where illiteracy is the rule rather than the exception, and where a fairly rigid social structure exists, this was almost inevitable. The elections were manipulated in many ways, and those with power and influence usually came out on top—sometimes with the connivance of local Chinese civil, military, or police officials. Blame for this sort of thing was usually placed on the provincial authorities. In actual fact, however, the Provincial Government was not able to insure honesty in local elections, and the persistence of localism and local rule—under various combinations of begs and mullahs, together with Chinese police, military leaders, and civil officials—presents the top provincial authorities with many serious problems. Masud Sabri said to me: "Perhaps the biggest problem facing the Provincial Government is the fact that the elections held after the government reorganization resulted in the selection of numerous men, particularly in the position of District Officer, who are incompetent and undesirable. These men, who include religious leaders, men of wealth, and others, were elected because of their long-standing hold over the people. The government can't just step in and replace them, for it would then be accused of being undemocratic."

Another problem that plagues the Provincial Government is a shortage of qualified and trained personnel. This shortage has become particularly acute with the attempt, which has been only partially successful, to bring more Uighurs, and other native people who have had little education or experience, into the administration. The goal of this policy is to reduce Chinese personnel to 30 per cent and to raise minority group personnel to 70 per cent of the total number of civil employees in the government, but even minority leaders admit that there are not enough qualified people to accomplish this goal. The Commission of Civil Affairs told me that the minority groups now hold 50 per cent of the jobs, but this may be an exaggeration, and even the changes that have been made to date cause many difficulties. The kind of problem that this policy creates is exemplified by the Commission of Civil Affairs itself. According to the Commission's General-Secretary, formerly fewer than 10 of its 134 members were Uighurs and Kazakhs, whereas now more than half belong to those two groups. Many of the new employees, the Secretary-General states, are poorly qualified, with the result that much of their work has to be shifted to the remaining old employees. The branches of government least affected by this new policy are the police force and the courts, which remain almost entirely Chinese (although in the city of Tihwa, about 30 per cent of the police force are now Uighurs). The men in these two branches of government, however, are far from being among the best Chinese government employees, for many are appointees of Sheng Shih-ts'ai.

Another hindrance to efficient operation on the part of the Provincial Government was the disorganization caused by the breakdown of the coalition. The posts held by the departed members of the Ili Group are still held open, as bait to lure them back. As a result, a number of key posts are vacant, and the responsibilities of these are carried by assistants or other officials.

The result of all these facts is that many of the old and undesirable characteristics persist in the provincial administration, despite efforts to make improvements.

Even when one considers the attitudes prevalent among the top-level Chinese administrators in the province, it is difficult to paint a picture that is all white or all black. Certain attitudes have changed. Both the Chinese and Turki languages are used, for example, and religious and educational discrimination is certainly not a matter of policy, even if it has not been completely eliminated. Some attitudes inherited from the past do persist, however. The policy of divide-and-rule still seems to be, consciously or unconsciously, an important element in Chinese thinking. They appear to encourage fragmentation among non-Han people (perhaps rationalizing it by arguing that "all" groups must be considered), and certain groups are given special consideration and support. At the present time, this applies particularly to the Tungans and to the Kazakhs under Osman. Furthermore, a certain cultural arrogance on the part of the Chinese still hangs on, for the Chinese appear to have few doubts about their cultural superiority. This arrogance tends to antagonize the other groups in the province.

Graft also persists. It is hard to put one's finger on specific cases, but even high members of the Provincial Government admitted to me the existence of graft and deplored it. One form in which it occurs is the use of government funds for business purposes and speculation. There is graft in the collection of the land tax, only part of the tax being passed on to the Provincial Government by local authorities.

Although arrests have not been nearly so widespread as the claims of the Ili Group might indicate, there still are political arrestees who have not been released. A Uighur member of the government with whom I talked estimates that they probably total a hundred (some of whom were arrested legitimately for seditious agitation), and the same man claims that political arrests are still being made in Kashgar and Turfan. Personal freedom, and freedom of the press and of assembly, are partially protected in Sinkiang, but they are not complete by any means.

Financial reform has not yet been accomplished, and the Commission of Finance and the Sinkiang Commercial Bank (which issues local currency) are still the cause of considerable scandal. Moreover, not much progress has been made toward accomplishment of the utopian economic and social reform program outlined by the Provincial Government, and Sinkiang is still woefully backward in education and medicine. There are only about

20 hospitals in the province, not one of which is really modern and up to date (the Russian hospital in Tihwa is the best), and in the provincial capital, there are only 500 hospital beds (150 of which are in the military hospital). The number of primary schools has been increased during the past two years, but there are still only 15 middle schools in the whole province, and the one institution of higher learning, the Sinkiang College, is rather a joke.

A few reforms and accomplishments can be listed in the government's favor. These include the institution of training courses for administrative personnel, and the development of irrigation. Last year, the principal taxes were halved to lessen the economic burden on the people. It should always be remembered, furthermore, that the Sinkiang Provincial Government, like government organs in the rest of China, is handicapped by the chaotic conditions caused by the civil war.

It is also handicapped by its financial position. Last year, the provincial budget amounted to $49 billion. Only $18 billion was received in tax income, and the rest was made up by Central Government subsidies and by the printing of unbacked currency. This currency added to local inflation and, consequently, to general discontent. The price inflation in Sinkiang (which is not as bad in food products as in the rest of China, but is worse in manufactured goods) is also aggravated by the virtual cessation of external trade. The main trade routes to Russia via Ining and Tacheng are completely closed at the Ili border, although there is a very small amount of smuggling. The route to Russia west of Kashgar is also completely closed. The China trade via Kansu is just a trickle, most of the commodities being military supplies. The only trade that approaches prewar volume is that over the mountains to India, and even those routes are occasionally disrupted by banditry and political troubles.

The subsidies to Sinkiang from the Central Government have been much less than requested, and even the small amounts allocated must be obtained through the Chinese military authorities in the province. All provincial requests for aid from the Central Government are channeled through the army, and if the money is granted, it is doled out sparingly. The problem of relations between the civil and military authorities, and the economic burden of the military on the province, are fundamental factors in the present situation.

Apart from the involvement of military personnel in local politics, which has already been mentioned, the garrisoning of large numbers of troops in Sinkiang gives rise to two problems that are sore points among the local people. One is the problem of inter-marriage; the other is the economic burden. The Muslims are ex-tremely sensitive about marriage of their daughters to infidels. There seem to be very few cases of rape on the part of Chinese soldiers, but even respectable marriage frequently enrages the sensitive Muslims, particularly the Uighurs. The economic burden of the Chinese military forces in Sinkiang is almost unavoidable in many respects. The garrison troops there are so far away from the rest of China that they are forced to rely principally on local food. The natural result is the decrease in food supplies available to the local population, and an increase in food prices. In the past, furthermore, the problem has been aggravated by certain malpractices on the part of the military. Individual soldiers and, in some cases, responsible officers have used their position and power to buy food on the open market at specially reduced prices.

The Chinese authorities are aware of the friction between mili-tary personnel and the civilian population in Sinkiang, and they are attempting to lessen it, with some success. The irrigation proj-ects in the province, which are probably the most constructive projects presently being pushed by the government, are motivated to a large degree by a desire to lessen the economic burden of the Chinese garrison troops. The main project is in the vicinity of Tihwa (a food-deficient area which formerly depended upon imports from the Ili Valley and more recently has imported food from Kansu and southern Sinkiang). The Tihwa irrigation project is being constructed by military labor, and the agricultural area it irrigates is being cultivated by troops to feed the local garrison. The project includes a large reservoir, which stores water diverted from the Urumchi River during the winter months, and a 22-mile canal, which carries this water to the area under cultivation. Lack of funds has delayed completion of the project, so that to date only 15,000 mou of land are irrigated, but when existing plans have been completed, the canal will irrigate 200,000 mou of fer-tile land, through three branch canals and six distribution canals totaling over 60 miles in length. (Other irrigation projects in the province include: a completed flood prevention dam at Aksu, plans for a 100-mile canal to irrigate a half million mou in the old river bed of the Tarim River, a water-control scheme in the vicinity of Kuche where there have been repeated quarrels over water rights, and a canal in the Turfan area to supplement that region's unusual system of horizontal wells.) The Chinese au-thorities have also tried to curb irregular purchasing by military personnel, and the Provincial Government has formulated a plan that it hopes to put into effect whereby the government will make all purchases of food, fuel, and other local supplies for the garrison troops.

These measures, if successfully carried out, will mitigate the economic burden of the troops in Sinkiang, but they cannot eliminate it. As long as there are large numbers of Chinese soldiers in the province, there will be a strain on the local economy and resentment on the part of the local population, and undoubtedly the Chinese Government will not find it possible to reduce the number of troops in Sinkiang to any great extent as long as the present military situation continues.

The military situation today is an extremely complicated one. In the northwestern part of the province, there is now a military truce, but that is all it is. In the northeastern region, next to the Outer Mongolian border, there is intermittent, undeclared warfare. In the rest of the province, garrison forces occupy key positions throughout a huge territory that is still uneasy and unstable.

The Chinese have a total of not more than 100,000 regular troops in Sinkiang. When they moved in after Sheng's political about-face, they sent into the province the Fifth and Forty-Second Cavalry Armies and the New Second Army. Since then, a complete military reorganization has taken place, and all the divisions have been converted into brigades and their troop strength readjusted. The total table-of-organization strength of units now in Sinkiang totals about 100,000, but actually many units are down to one-third or two-thirds theoretical strength. During the past three years, the Chinese have replaced old troops and reinforced their total military strength in the province, but they do not seem to be bringing in new troops at present, contrary to some reports.

The military chief in Sinkiang is the Commander of the Garrison Forces, General T'ao Chih-yüeh, who recently succeeded Sung Hsi-lien. The soldiers he commands are often called "crack troops," and, on the basis of my observation in a limited number of places, they appear to be superior in organization, discipline, and morale. The high quality of these troops leads one to suspect that some of the complaints leveled against the Chinese Army in Sinkiang are probably due as much to natural resentment, which would be felt toward any garrison forces, good or bad, as to specific abuses on the part of the army.

The majority of troops are stationed in the northern part of the province, but some are spread throughout other areas as well.

Military headquarters are located at key points, but there are a few troops in every major oasis and town. In southern Sinkiang are the Forty-Second Army, composed of two cavalry brigades, with headquarters at Kashgar, and two infantry brigades, with headquarters at Aksu and Yenki (Karashar) respectively. The over-all command headquarters, however, is located in Tihwa to the north. Major military responsibility in northern Sinkiang falls upon the Seventy-Eighth Division, the Seventh Cavalry Brigade, and the Sixth Cavalry Brigade (but they are backed up by other forces, which include the 231st Brigade at Turfan, the 179th Brigade at Tihwa, and the 178th Brigade at Hami). The Seventy-Eighth Division, which maintains headquarters at Khotubi, guards the Ili border, and its 227th Brigade, at Suilai, is in almost direct contact with the enemy forces across the Manas River. The Seventh Cavalry Brigade of Chinghai troops guards the Outer Mongolian border and the Peitashan Range from its headquarters in Chitai. The Sixth Cavalry Brigade, also composed of Chinghai troops, blocks the northwestern road approach to Tihwa.

The garrison troops in Sinkiang, composed almost exclusively of Han Chinese and Chinese Muslims (only about 5 per cent are Uighurs and Kazakhs), depend entirely for military supplies upon a long and dangerous supply line stretching over a thousand miles from Tihwa to Lanchow. All munitions and arms must be transported over this vulnerable route by a fleet of fewer than a thousand trucks, at least half of which are always out of commission. All oil and gasoline must be brought from the Yumen oil wells in western Kansu.

In addition to the difficulties resulting from dependence on a vulnerable supply line, problems are often caused because the troops are so scattered that it is estimated the maximum effective striking force that could be mustered to fight in northern Sinkiang would not exceed 30,000. Despite these facts, however, the Chinese military commanders in Sinkiang are confident of their relative strength and are contemptuous of the Ili troops. They claim that they could easily defeat the Ili army if the Russians stayed out of the picture, but they add that they prefer to support the present policy of peaceful conciliation. Neutral military observers seem to back them up on their claims.

The Ili army is estimated to contain between 15,000 and 20,000 regular troops. Chinese intelligence officers believe that it is made up of between eight and thirteen regiments, seven of which have been definitely identified. The First Infantry Regiment at Anchihai and the Second Cavalry Regiment at Ulan Usu (both under over-all headquarters at Wusu) protect the road entrance from Sinkiang proper into the Ili Valley. Fortifications are said to have been constructed in this region along a north-south axis between the marshes at Shawan and the Tien Shan foothills in the south. Shawan is considered to be a key point, from which any Ili offensive against Sinkiang would be launched. The Second Infantry Regiment protects the Wusu oil wells at Tushantzu. The southern Ili flank is guarded by the First Cavalry Regiment at Tekeszu. In addition, there are three other known regiments: the Third Infantry Regiment at Tacheng, the Fifth Cavalry Regiment at Chenghua, and a training regiment at the Ili capital, Ining. Behind these units, however, looms the power of the Soviet army; some Chinese believe the powerful, motorized Soviet Eighth Regiment stayed in the region just west of Ili after it evacuated Hami in 1943 (although this seems improbable in many respects).

The Ili armed forces, which they themselves sometimes call the Sinkiang Democratic Army, are reported to be conscripting and training men on a short, two-to-three-month basis—which is one reason the Chinese do not have a very high regard for their fighting ability. The Chinese say that they are doing this because they cannot support a large army on their economic resources and because they are short of arms, despite Russian assistance.

The chief military commander in Ili is reported to be Isakjan, a Soviet-educated Kirghiz (conflicting reports claim he is a Taranchi) from southern Sinkiang. Isakjan commanded one of the Soviet army units that were sent to aid Sheng Shih-ts'ai. He is reported to hold dual Chinese-Russian citizenship papers and is said to be one of the most completely pro-Russian men in the Ili Group. The majority of his subordinate officers are Uighurs. It is claimed that a few of his officers are Soviet Slavs, that many of his officers hold dual citizenship papers, and that Soviet advisers (most of them Asians from Kazakhstan and Uzbekistan) are attached to every major Ili military unit. It would be difficult to obtain absolute verification of these assertions even if one could visit Ili territory (because of the difficulty of racial identification), but it seems probable that the Ili army is definitely oriented toward the Soviet Union, and it is possible that it contains many Soviet advisers.

Although leadership in the Ili army, as in the Ili civil regime, is monopolized by Uighurs, the majority of its troops at the time of the revolt in 1944–45 were Kazakh cavalrymen. The Chinese front-line officers in Sinkiang assert, however, (and there is some evidence to support them) that this situation has been changed by a widespread disaffection on the part of the Kazakhs. The first large-scale desertion of the Ili cause was made by Osman and his followers, but it is reported that more recently, in November, 1947, 10,000 more Kazakhs who refused to fight against Osman and the Chinese fled from Ili territory to the Chinese side. Chinese intelligence officers at Suilai now claim that only 30 per cent of the Ili troops are Kazakhs, while 60 per cent are Uighurs and 10 per cent are Mongols and representatives of other minorities. If this is true, it probably means that the Ili army has been greatly weakened, for the Kazakhs were the backbone of their fighting strength.

Military supply on the Ili side is somewhat of a mystery, even to Chinese intelligence officers with whom I talked in Suilai. There is not enough industrialization in Ili territory to support sizable numbers of troops. Although some of their arms (including German-made ones) were captured from the Chinese in the initial campaign, they undoubtedly have received aid from the Russians. Top Chinese military authorities believe that Soviet military supplies are still being received in Ili, and they cite as evidence reports from refugees, as well as captured arms. But, for some reason, the Chinese play down these assertions and discredit reports of Soviet tanks, artillery, and antiaircraft guns on the Ili side. It seems probable, however, that the Ili army is dependent upon Russia for some military supplies, and it is definitely known that the Ili troops wear a Russian-type uniform.

Whatever the characteristics of the Ili armed forces, they maintain complete military control of the territory in Sinkiang west of the Manas River and in the three administrative districts under the Ili regime. All movement between Ili territory and the rest of Sinkiang is completely cut off (except for underground agents and smugglers), and the Chinese, although confident of their military superiority over the Ili army, are keeping hands off—probably because of a fear of military involvement with Russia, as well as a preference for peaceful negotiations.

Elsewhere in Sinkiang, there have been military clashes in two other border regions within the past three years. The incidents in these two regions, Sarakol in the southwest and Peitashan in the northeast, were not directly related to the Ili Revolt, but they may have been indirectly connected.

Very little is known about the Sarakol Revolt, which took place in the region of southwestern Sinkiang around Tashkurgan, near the borders of India, Afghanistan, and the Soviet Union. It started about August, 1945, and lasted for roughly a year, during which time the "revolting" forces threatened Kargalik, Yarkand, and, to a lesser extent, Kashgar. Beyond these bare facts, information about what took place is difficult to obtain. However, one foreign observer, who lives in southwestern Sinkiang, told me that he believes it was more of an invasion than a revolt. In his opinion, the fighting was done almost entirely by troops from the Soviet republics across the border, and he believes that these troops actually antagonized the Tadjiks and Kirghiz in southwestern Sinkiang by destroying their crops and flocks. He further states that the region is now completely stabilized and peaceful under the Chinese regime, and that the local people tend to be pro-Chinese. The timing of the trouble in the Sarakol region suggests that it might have been a diversionary incident, designed to distract the Chinese authorities from the more important problems related to the Ili Revolt. In a similar way, the periodic attacks by Outer Mongolia, a satellite of the Soviet Union, upon Peitashan may have been attempts to give indirect assistance to the Ili Group.

Peitashan is a small range of mountains, about 20 miles long and 10 miles wide, on the border of Sinkiang and the Mongolian People's Republic. The range runs in a southeast-northwest direction and, at its highest point, rises to 10,000 feet. It is an extremely important point, for it lies in the midst of a large gobi and sand desert region and dominates the entire Sinkiang-Outer Mongolian border, from a strategic point of view, not only because of its height, but also because it possesses adequate water supplies. In addition, it flanks the Hami-Chitai-Turfan area and the Sinkiang supply line from Kansu; in non-Chinese hands, it could be a stronghold capable of severing Sinkiang from the rest of China.

Although, in 1915, a tripartite agreement was signed among China, Russia, and Outer Mongolia that stipulated that the China-Outer Mongolia border should be demarcated by mutual agreement, the borderline has never been formally decided, and the dispute over its location has become more critical since the formal recognition by China of Outer Mongolian independence in 1945. Both Outer Mongolia and China claim the Peitashan range. The Chinese insist that their claim is the valid one because they have garrisoned the region for many years, and the Chinese front-line commander in that area, Major General Han Yu-wen, told me that he believes the border should be about 40 miles north of the mountains. The Chinese military authorities in Sinkiang are adamant about not relinquishing the Peitashan range, because it protects their supply line. They do not fear any immediate attempt by the Mongols to cut the supply line to Sinkiang because, they claim, the Outer Mongolians do not have more than a regiment or so that they could effectively use in that area, owing to communications difficulties. But the Chinese do not want to take any chances.

The Peitashan Incident began on June 5 of last year when, according to the Chinese story, the Outer Mongolians began an attack on Peitashan, with 500 men and 5 aircraft, which lasted for 2 days and nights and resulted in 3 Chinese and more than 30 Mongolian deaths. Between June 5, 1947, and July of this year, there has been a total of 13 clashes. At present, the Mongols hold several positions at the foot of the northern slope of the mountains; they also maintain two companies of troops just north of these positions and one company at Tapusun to the northwest. In addition, they have an airfield a few miles away, which is used for observation aircraft. These Mongol positions face the Chinese Fourteenth Cavalry Regiment, which holds the mountain tops and the difficult supply line that cuts through the desert between Chitai and Ulun Bulak. A state of suspended hostilities prevails continuously; it is only interrupted by occasional open clashes.

Although there is no evidence of close cooperation between the Ili Group and the Outer Mongolians, there is some evidence of local collusion between their troops. Chinese intelligence officers at Chitai told me that the Mongols at Tapusun maintain friendly relations with the Ili troops at Ertai, 42 miles to the West, and Osman claimed that while he was still on the Ili side the Outer Mongolians were cooperating with the Ili Group in the Ashan District.

Although information about the government established by the Ili Group in Ining is fragmentary and incomplete, one thing is clear: Although in their official dealings with the Chinese they have consistently disavowed any separatist intentions, they have proceeded, in fact, to set up an autonomous regime, which they call the East Turkestan Republic. They have established a completely new administration with their own leaders in top posts. They use their own flag, which bears a white star and crescent on a green background. In short, they have achieved temporary independence from China.

The three administrative districts of Ili, Tacheng, and Ashan, which are controlled by the Ining Government, together form the most valuable part of Sinkiang Province. They include one-fifth of the total population, as well as the only two work-ing tungsten mines, the only working oil wells, and some of the best gold mines in the province. The Ili River Valley is often called the granary of Sinkiang because it is the most fertile agricultural region in the province, and the belt of pastureland stretching from Ashan District to Ili District contains some of the best grazing regions in Sinkiang.

The population controlled by the Ili regime is extremely heter-ogeneous, and although the leadership in the Ili Group is predominantly Uighur, the population in the region is pre-dominantly non-Uighur. The majority group, the Kazakhs, com-prise 53 per cent of the total population. The Uighurs and Ta-ranchis (second and third largest groups, respectively) together make up only 23 per cent of the population. In addition, the three Ili-controlled districts contain members of every other mi-nority in the province. As a matter of fact, in terms of the percent-age of each group in the whole province, these three districts con-tain not only a majority of the Kazakhs, but also of the Taranchis, Mongols, White Russians, Manchus, Uzbeks, and Tatars. The principal Uighur concentration in Sinkiang is in the south, and in terms of racial and cultural groups, therefore, the Uighur-led Ili Government is a minority government within the region that it controls. The Ili Group has obtained the cooperation of some non-Uighur groups, but it has antagonized others. In particular it seems to have antagonized many Kazakhs. Although at the start it made a strong bid for Kazakh support by appointing a few Kazakhs—including Osman, Talilihan, and Halibek—to po-litical posts of relative importance (District Officer of Ashan, Assistant District Officer of Ashan, and Magistrate of Shawan, re-spectively), many Kazakhs, including Osman and Halibek and their followers, have deserted the Ili side.

The top posts in the Ili hierarchy are held by men who are not only Uighurs, but are Russian-educated or pro-Russian. The pres-ent Ili chief is Achmadjan Kasymov, thirty-three-year-old son of an Ining carpenter, who was both a student and a teacher in the Soviet Union and who was imprisoned by Sheng Shih-ts'ai after the latter's break with Russia. Around Achmadjan is a small core of trusted men, including Rahimjan Sabir Hodjayev, pro-Russian nephew and son-in-law of Masud Sabri; Seyfuddin, who originally came from Kashgar but was educated in Russia; and Abdul Karim, a revolutionary who was educated in the Sinkiang College. There are fairly reliable reports that not only most of the top leaders, but also many others in Ili territory (some estimates place the figure as high as 20,000), have become Soviet citizens. There are other reports that top leaders such as Achmadjan and Rahimjan are members of the Russian Communist Party. The Chinese in Sinkiang also assert that the Ili regime, like the Ili army, has Russian advisers attached to it at all levels. None of these claims is verifiable, but many of them are specific enough in details to lend considerable credence to them.

The broad base of the Ili Group's power seems to be a youth group, called the Yashlar Tashkilati, led by a man named Seyfullaev, whose birthplace was Turfan but who later lived in Ili and was educated in the Soviet Union.

Regarding the degree to which the Ili Group is oriented toward Russia, it is significant, perhaps, that the original leader of the Group, a man named Alihan Toere, who had the reputation of being primarily a religious and nationalist leader and was not particularly pro-Russian, has disappeared from the scene and is believed to be under arrest in the Soviet Union. There are some reports, which may or may not be true, that significant splits exist within the Ili Group on the question of how closely the Group should work with the Soviet Union. It seems almost certain, however, that the least one can say is that the Ili regime is subject to strong Russian influence. It is probable that this influence is exerted not only indirectly, but also directly, through advisers and through the three Soviet consulates in the region—in the cities of Ining, Tacheng, and Chenghua.

The available evidence indicates that, even though it is probably subject to strong Russian influence, the Ili regime is following policies that are primarily nationalistic rather than ideological. To date, it has neither sovietized nor socialized the region it controls. It has maintained the Chinese forms of organization, including the *Hsien* and the Administrative District, and apparently no comprehensive economic reform policies have been formulated as yet. In regard to religion, the regime has followed a completely non-Marxist policy, and the District Officer of Ili is a venerable Muslim religious leader named Hakimbeg Khoja.

Although socialism seems to play only a minor role in the thinking of the Ili leaders, the economic orientation of the Ili region toward the Soviet Union inevitably must have been strengthened since the closing of the Ili-Sinkiang border. Before the Ili Revolt, part of the surplus production of the three zones under Ili control was exported to other parts of Sinkiang; the only outlet for this surplus at present is the Soviet Union. Furthermore, the most natural and strongest economic ties have been with Russia for many years, because of proximity, convenience of transport, and the existence of complementary economies. Ili agricultural and animal products and raw materials are exchanged for Russian manufactured goods.

At present, it is reported that Russians are supervising the operation of the gold mines under Ili control, as well as the Fuwen and Wenchuan tungsten mines, which are among the best sources of tungsten in Central Asia. In addition, the Russians are said to be obtaining large amounts of wheat, wool, and animal products, as well as gold and tungsten, from Ili territory. Reports of this sort are probably true, since there are no other markets for these products of the rich Ili-Tacheng-Ashan region. (Wusu oil is said to be barely sufficient for local needs, so the Russians probably are not making use of it. Maximum production at the Wusu wells in the pre-revolt period was only 600 tons a month, and two of the six wells were reported to have been destroyed by fire in 1947.) Some Chinese claim that the Russians are milking the Ili region in a systematic way and that, as a result, price inflation in basic necessities is worse there than in the rest of Sinkiang, even though it is the most productive region in the province, but it is difficult to know whether or not there is any truth in these claims.

Whether there is a link between the Ili Group and the Chinese Communists is even more of a mystery than most aspects of the Ili regime. One might expect such a link, but there has been no concrete evidence to reveal it, and recent editorial discussion in the leading Ining paper, the *Democratic Daily*, of whether or not such a link should be established would seem to indicate that none has existed in the past.

Although the facts and the surmises already cited give some hints concerning the character of the Ili regime, it is difficult to know whether, on balance, the regime is an enlightened or an oppressive one. Its bitterest enemies and critics (a category that does not include all Chinese leaders in Sinkiang by any means) state flatly that it is an oppressive, Russian-dominated police regime. There is not enough evidence to prove or disprove such an assertion. Whatever its character, however, it still evokes the approval and sympathy of many (but not all) Uighurs and some other non-Han Chinese throughout Sinkiang. To these people, it represents an embodiment of nationalistic aspirations.

Stripped to essentials, the major problems in the present situation in Sinkiang are caused by two basic factors which overshadow all others. One is Sinkiang's geographical position, and the consequent importance of the area to two great nations, China and Russia. The other is the growth of nationalism among the people native to the province.

There are many factors responsible for the growth of nationalism among the native groups in Sinkiang. One is a natural desire for greater self-rule. Another is a desire to maintain cultural unity and racial homogeneity, about which the Muslim groups are extremely jealous and defensive. Still another is a resentment against the superiority complex of the Chinese rulers and the past policy of Sinicization, involving conscious neglect of native education and native languages. (No Chinese-Turki dictionary has ever been compiled, for example.) Reaction against Chinese misrule, which finally became intolerable under Sheng Shih-ts'ai, made all of these issues explosive. And the spark in the tinder box was instigation and moral support by the Soviet Union and by pro-Soviet agents, and, perhaps equally as important, what has been called the Soviet "politics of attraction"—i.e., exploitation of the attraction created by the alleged cultural autonomy granted to similar racial and cultural groups within the Soviet Union.

The last factor has been an important element in the situation in Sinkiang, for it has provided much-needed moral support to the minority groups in Sinkiang. The Soviet Union, since the early days of the Comintern, has been extremely sympathetic toward Asian nationalist movements. In the case of most Sinkiang minority groups, moreover, there has been the pull of racial affinity with people in Soviet Central Asia, geographical proximity, and economic ties. Further ties with the Soviet Union have been created since many Uighurs and other representatives of Sinkiang's minorities have been educated in Soviet institutions—principally because of the lack of educational facilities for them elsewhere.

Despite the attraction of the Soviet Union to some groups in Sinkiang, however, there is by no means unanimous sentiment among minority groups on the question of relations with Russia. Native nationalism in Sinkiang is, in fact, an indecisive force because of many splits along racial, economic, and other lines, which deprive the movement of unity and cohesion. Even within the majority Uighur group, there is fragmentation. When a dance performed in the Uighur Club in Tihwa depicts a heroic scene from Uighur history, everyone will cheer enthusiastically, but differences appear when decisions must be made on political action.

One split among the Uighurs is along economic and traditional lines. The conservative and wealthy begs and mullahs generally line up behind the Chinese, who have supported them in the past and continue to do so in many ways; they oppose the nationalist movement. The leaders of the nationalist movement are for the most part representatives from the middle class, and from iconoclastic youth, many of whom have been educated in the Soviet Union or strongly influenced by Soviet propaganda. The Uighurs who oppose the nationalist movement are numerically a small (but influential) group, and a large majority seems to go along with the nationalists. The educated and articulate supporters (men from middle-class groups and men who have divorced themselves from an upper-class background) are vocal, while the mass of Uighur farmers go along with the movement more passively.

Even among the nationalist Uighurs, there are splits, however. All agree in a vague way that they want more cultural and political autonomy, but there are two issues that are particularly controversial: what the immediate goal of their nationalism should be, and whether they should work through China or rely upon the Soviet Union for assistance. Liu Meng-ch'un, who is Chang Chih-chung's Secretary-General and probably the most influential Chinese official in Tihwa, said to me that in his view the Uighur nationalists fall into three groups: those who are working for independence, those who are working for a high degree of autonomy within the framework of the existing Chinese administration and Chinese sovereignty, and those who feel they must choose sides and be either strongly pro-Chinese or pro-Soviet. His analysis seems to be essentially correct. The number of adherents to each of these three groups varies considerably, however. Masud Sabri says that "no responsible persons have considered how real independence could be maintained if achieved," and apparently this is true. Actually, only a very few Uighurs, I believe, think complete independence is a practical possibility now. (Although it is difficult to know for certain what the ultimate objectives of the Ili Group may be, it is possible that some of that group fit into this category.) A fairly large number of persons can be placed in the third category. These include the most strongly pro-Chinese Uighurs working in the provincial administration in Sinkiang, and the pro-Soviet members of the Ili Group. It seems probable, however, that the majority of Uighurs outside of Ili territory still fall into the middle group, which is adamant in its demands for more self-rule and autonomy, but is working to achieve its nationalistic objectives within the framework of Chinese sovereignty. This group includes a number of important leaders such as Aisabek, who is amazingly candid in criticizing the regime he has joined, but who said to me, "I believe the Chinese side, despite faults, is better than the Russian, and I will continue to work for autonomy under Chinese rule."

The situation in Sinkiang is further complicated by cleavages between various cultural and racial groups. One of these splits involves the Tungans, or Chinese Muslims. There is a considerable amount of ill-feeling between the Tungans on the one hand and the Uighurs and Kazakhs on the other. The most important cause of this ill-feeling is an economic one. A great many Tungans own land and flocks of sheep, and act as landlords and "flock-lords" over groups of Uighurs and Kazakhs. The bad feelings between the Tungans and the Uighurs, furthermore, was inflamed by the looting and killing done on a large scale by Ma Chung-ying's Kansu troops over a decade ago; the resentments aroused at that time have not died out. As a result of this racial friction, the Chinese Muslims tend to line up with the Provincial Government rather than with the nationalist movement, and some of the most reliable Chinese troops in the province are the Muslim cavalrymen from Chinghai. The Chinese Muslims themselves have rebelled against Chinese rule many times in the past, but now they are numbered among the strongest supporters of the Chinese administration in Sinkiang.

Another confusing and uncertain element in the over-all picture in Sinkiang is the position of the Kazakhs, who are the most militant, the most colorful, and numerically the second most important group in the province.

As has been mentioned already, the Kazakhs are Turki-speaking Muslim nomads who live by constantly migrating with their flocks, herds, yurts, and families. Each Kazakh family owns its animals independently, but pasture land is used communally. An average family among the Kazakhs who live in the Tien Shan owns about twenty to thirty sheep and goats, twenty horses, two or three camels, and one or two cows, but the wealthier families own much larger numbers of animals, and the poorer ones may tend flocks that do not belong to them. Animals provide almost their entire livelihood—transportation, felt for their yurts and rugs, wool for clothing, dung for fuel, and milk, cheese, and mutton for food. Their traditional pattern of life has not been changed to any great extent in recent years, although a few minor changes have taken place. As a rule, they now sell some of their animals to buy tea, sugar, and manufactured cloth. A few of them cultivate small plots of grain at the foot of their mountain pasture lands to supplement their animal foodstuffs. And their leaders are now given Chinese titles, such as *Pao* Chief and *Hsien* Magistrate, in addition to their own Kazakh titles. But these changes have not altered their way of life, for they live in remote mountain regions isolated from urban, modern influences.

The Kazakhs are organized tribally. There are, according to Osman Bator, three main tribes in Sinkiang: the Naiman, concentrated in Ili District; the Kirei, formerly concentrated in Ashan District but now spread over several regions, including the Tien Shan; and the Auwak, scattered in small, unimportant groups throughout northern Sinkiang. These three tribes are supposed to be related through close blood ties. Each has a chief called the Wang (a Chinese title, meaning Prince, bestowed on the chiefs during the Manchu period).

The main Kazakh tribes are broken down into subtribes. In Sinkiang, there are twelve in the Kirei, nine in the Naiman, and three in the Auwak. Each subtribe has a leader called the Taiji, who controls 1,000 to 3,000 yurts, the Kazakhs' round, collapsible, felt tents. The hierarchy below each Taiji consists of Okurday, who control 300–600 yurts; Zaleng, who control 100–200 yurts; Zangen, who control 50–100 yurts; and Kunde, who control 10–30 yurts. The positions of Taiji, Okurday, and Zaleng are always inherited, but the lower two positions are held by persons who are sometimes chosen by the people. In addition to these leaders, each subtribe has one or two Bi, elders who administer the law (a combination of Muslim precepts and local customs) in cooperation with the Taiji. Each subtribe also has an assembly called the Majlis, to which all leaders from Taiji to Kunde belong, and which meets every year during the Muslim New Year period and irregularly (three or four times) during the rest of the year, when called into session by the Taiji.

In addition to the regular tribal hierarchy, however, the Kazakhs have a number of popular leaders called Bator (Hero) who have achieved a position of prominence and leadership through their heroism and military prowess. These popular leaders are often more important and powerful than the regular tribal leaders. At present, for example, the real leader of the Kirei tribe is the Bator named Osman. The regular tribal chief, Ailin Wang, is an ineffective, hen-pecked little man who is overshadowed even by his wife, the 250-pound Hatewan, who is District Officer of Tihwa. By contrast, Osman is a huge man with a tremendous frame, ham-like hands, and a terrific ego. He is forty-nine years old, but has tremendous vigor. His cool grey eyes, set lips, and black beard make him look the part of a heroic warrior, and he reminds one of the Hunnish conquerors who terrorized a major part of the Eurasian continent centuries ago.

The Kazakhs are a proud people. The women, who look medieval in their long skirts and Muslim headgear, which cover them completely except for their oval faces, do most of the routine work. The men, who dress in high black boots and wear colorful fur-lined, silk-covered bonnets, appear to spend most of their time riding through the mountains in a dashing, martial fashion, sitting together in their yurts drinking kumis, an intoxicating elixir of fermented mare's milk, or fighting.

The Kazakhs admit that they like to fight, and at the beginning of the Ili Revolt, they joined the Ili side and did most of the fighting for the Ili Group. Since that time, however, they have split, and some of the Kazakhs in Sinkiang are now in Ili and some on the Chinese side. The majority of the Naiman stayed in Ili, under the leadership of Kazakhs such as Mustafa Achlachjik, Bashbai, and Talilihan. The Naiman are the largest of the three tribes that have members in Sinkiang, but many of the Naiman are in the Soviet Union, and they are outnumbered in Sinkiang itself by the Kirei. Many of the Kirei have deserted the Ili side and have migrated under leaders such as Osman, from their Ashan homeland to pasture areas outside of Ili territory. They are now, temporarily at least, supporters of the Chinese regime in Sinkiang. It is difficult to assess the importance of the split among the Kazakhs, and to determine its real causes. Undoubtedly, the geographical distribution of the two major tribes helps explain the cleavage, but other factors are involved too. Osman claims, for example, that the Naiman have been "infected by Russian propaganda."

Osman, whom I visited in his yurt headquarters high in the Tien Shan, is an extraordinarily colorful figure, and he has had a career that almost sounds fantastic. During the past decade, he has fought on the side of every important faction involved in the complicated struggles in Sinkiang.

Osman really began his fighting career during the regime of Sheng Shih-ts'ai. Between 1937 and 1940, Sheng antagonized the Kazakhs by arresting a large number of their leaders. This led Osman to organize widespread resistance, and on February, 1940, a long struggle against Sheng was started. Osman was not strong enough to achieve any signal success, however, and he was driven out of Chenghua in Ashan. As a result, he began, in January, 1942, cooperating with the Outer Mongolians and received their aid. At that time, he set up headquarters in Tayingkul—which is just inside the border of Outer Mongolia, north of Ashan—and carried on a rather ineffective sort of resistance against Sheng. Then, on September 6, 1945, when the Ili army arrived in Chenghua with 6,000 men, he formed an alliance with the Ili Group. He split with the Outer Mongolians, in November, 1945, but he continued cooperating with the Ili Group until April 1, 1946. On that date, he denounced the Ili Group and began a trek southward to Peitashan. He soon came to terms with the Chinese and fought with them against the Outer Mongolians at Peitashan. Then, on August 26, he launched a large-scale raid on the Ili forces in Ashan. He captured Chenghua in the middle of September, but was forced to evacuate it soon thereafter, when, according to the story as he recounted it during my visit, 160 Russian trucks arrived with Ili troops. Osman alleges that in December last year he received an emissary sent from Outer Mongolia who was a nephew of his and who brought a Mongol offer to supply him with military aid if he would again cooperate with them. He turned the offer down, however, and handed his nephew over to the Chinese authorities (because, he says, "he was my enemy"), despite the tearful pleas of his sister.

Osman rationalizes all of his past decisions and moves in terms of anti-Communist objectives, and if one believes all he says, he is a rabid Russophobe. Actually, however, his past moves seem to have been based primarily on expediency and a desire to maintain his own power and the autonomy of his own group. He cites a long list of grievances that he had against the Ili Group, asserting that they were completely Russian-dominated and Russian-controlled, but his real reason for splitting with them seems to have been that they tried to bring him under control and ensure his obedience to their orders.

At present, Osman lives with some of his followers (he says he has about 4,000 yurts and 15,000 Kazakhs with him) in the Tien Shan, just south of Chitai. Like a potentate, he is surrounded by a group of loyal lieutenants, including Hanatbai, his political chief-of-staff; Habas Bator, his military chief-of-staff; and Nurga, Lias, Lasihan, and Arumkan, his principal subordinate military leaders. He is not engaged in active fighting at present, but in addition to his loyal old guard of supporters, he controls three battalions of Peace Preservation Troops (all cavalry) assigned to him by the Chinese, and he is a force to be reckoned with not only for his own military power, but also for the influence he exerts upon large numbers of Kazakhs—including some of those still in Ili territory.

All of these facts make the Kazakhs one of the most uncertain factors in the situation in Sinkiang, and the position of the Kazakhs complicates the confused racial and group interrelations in the region.

Burhan, a prominent Tatar who appears to be playing the subtle game of keeping in the good graces of all sides in the hope of becoming governor as a compromise candidate, summed up Sinkiang very aptly during a conversation I had with him. "Sinkiang," he said, "is like a guitar. All the strings must be in tune for it to play." The strings certainly are not all in tune at present.

International rivalries and conflicts are equally as fundamental in the present situation as the growing nationalism in the province. Primarily because of its geographical position, Sinkiang is a focal point where international boundaries meet and where national interests often conflict.

During the last century, the strategic and other interests of three powers clashed in the region. These three powers were China, Russia, and Great Britain. The British began to lose interest in Sinkiang by the 1880's, however, and now that they have withdrawn from India, they are turning over their last listening post in Sinkiang, their consulate at Kashgar, to the Indian Government. The major parties now interested in the province have been reduced to two: China and the Soviet Union.

China's interest and objective in Sinkiang is simple and clearcut. The Chinese Government is determined to maintain its sovereignty over the province, and considers its claims morally unquestionable and legally unassailable. The motives for China's determination on this issue seem to be based more on history, tradition, and prestige than on tangible interests. The Sinkiang region is an important one strategically, but it would be virtually impossible for China to defend against a serious Soviet attack, because of the supply problem, and a frontier defense could probably be established more successfully at points farther east. Economically, Sinkiang is a financial drain rather than an asset to the Chinese Government at the present time. It is probable, however, that the economic potentialities of the province (particularly as a source of supply for oil, tungsten, and gold) influence Chinese thinking. The most important concern of the Chinese, however, seems to be the defense of traditional rights and the maintenance of China's prestige.

Russia's interest in Sinkiang is based upon a number of factors. Economically, the Ili Valley in particular and the whole province to a lesser extent are oriented toward the Soviet Union. This is natural because of proximity, and it has been particularly true since the completion of the main line of the Turk-Sib Railway in 1930. Russian trade with Sinkiang has expanded rapidly in recent decades, with a few ups and downs. Between 1923–24 and 1930, for example, the total trade between Sinkiang and the Soviet Union rose from less than 3.5 million rubles to about 32 million rubles annually, and it consisted of a profitable exchange of Russian manufactured goods for Sinkiang's agricultural and animal products. Even though this trade is profitable, however, it certainly is not vital to the Soviet Union, and from a commercial point of view, the Soviet interest in Sinkiang would seem to be simply the maintenance of a peaceful and orderly regime willing to trade freely with the Soviet Union.

As a source of raw materials, Sinkiang is potentially of some importance, but actually, the only materials in Sinkiang that would seem to be of real interest to the Soviet Union are tungsten, oil, and gold (with tungsten particularly important, since the tungsten mines in northern Sinkiang are among the best in Central Asia). If this is a major interest affecting Soviet policy, a friendly regime in northern Sinkiang, such as the present Ili regime, probably satisfies the Soviet Union's objectives at least temporarily, for the only working tungsten mines and oil wells, as well as some of the best gold mines in Sinkiang, are in Ili territory.

Most probably, however, the Soviet Union's main interests in Sinkiang are not economic, but are related to power and national security. One aspect of the Soviet Union's security problem is an ethnic one. The people in Sinkiang are closely related, and in many cases racially identical to the people inhabiting Kazakhstan and the Soviet Central Asian republics of Kirghizia, Tadjikstan, Uzbekistan, and Turkmenia. Ethnic groups overlapping national boundaries often create an unstable situation, in which both nations involved fear instigation of trouble across the border line. In time of war, a border of this sort is particularly unreliable and undesirable.

The geography of the Ili district also makes it especially important to the Soviet Union from a strategic point of view. The three important rivers in northwestern Sinkiang all flow into lakes within the Soviet borders, and their valleys provide an easy land approach to Soviet territory. This undoubtedly is a matter of concern, even though the possibility of land attack from that quarter is fairly remote.

Perhaps the main Soviet strategic concern in Sinkiang, however, is the potential importance of the province in terms of a future air war. Some observers have speculated upon the possibility, if a third world war were to occur, of United States air attacks upon western Siberia and Soviet Central Asia from a major air base on Okinawa. These observers have concluded, probably correctly, that the Russians have considered this prospect and are interested, first, in preventing any possibility of the establishment of supplementary American air bases in Sinkiang, and, second, in being able, in time of war, to establish Soviet air bases in Sinkiang for interceptor aircraft. Air attacks on Soviet Central Asia would strike at the vulnerable underbelly of the U.S.S.R., a region that has become vitally important with the development of industrialization during the past twenty years and the eastward migration of Russia's industries during World War II.

It seems likely, therefore, that in Soviet eyes Sinkiang is an area of considerable security importance and slight economic importance, and the policy the Russians have pursued in the region for the past eighty years appears to confirm this. It is difficult, however, to determine accurately just how important Sinkiang is in the minds of the Soviet leaders at the present time, or what the specific objectives of current Soviet policy in Sinkiang are.

In recent years some aspects of the Soviet Union's policy have been puzzling. The available evidence indicates that the U.S.S.R. is giving the Ili regime at least strong moral support and possibly a good deal of material support, yet it was the Russians who intervened and sponsored mediation at a time when the Ili forces were at the peak of their military success. Furthermore, instead of intensifying their policies of penetration into the rest of Sinkiang, outside the Ili regime's territory, the Russians since 1943 seem to have been following a policy of gradual withdrawal.

During the regime of Sheng Shih-ts'ai, all of Sinkiang was a Soviet sphere of influence. Today, although Soviet activities in Sinkiang are on a scale much larger than those of any other foreign nation, they are being gradually cut down. There are still five Soviet consulates in Sinkiang (a consulate-general in Tihwa and a consulate in Kashgar, as well as the three consulates in Ili territory), but they are much less active than they have been at certain periods in the past. During the initial and critical stages of the Ili Revolt, the Russians followed an ominous policy of enlisting Soviet citizens within Sinkiang by granting citizenship papers to large numbers of native people, many of whom had never even been in the Soviet Union. (In 1946 alone, according to the Foreign Affairs Section of the Tihwa Police Bureau, the Soviet Consulate-General in Tihwa issued citizenship papers to an estimated 1,000 persons in Tihwa, only 123 of whom registered their new citizenship with the Chinese authorities, and the Chinese were worried about the creation of a large group with dual citizenship and divided allegiance.) But this policy now seems to have been stopped almost completely. In Tihwa, there are active Soviet propaganda organizations, such as the Information Bureau, the Sino-Soviet Cultural Association (which has the leading Chinese officials as titular heads), and the International Bookstore, and there is still a Russian Trade Mission (inactive) in the city, but the total personnel of all these organizations, together with the Consulate-General and the Russian hospital, has been reduced from roughly 130 to 103 in the last six months.

Almost the only tangible asset now belonging to the Soviet Union in Sinkiang is the Sino-Soviet Airline, which operates biweekly flights between Alma Ata and Hami. This corporation was set up under a special ten-year Sino-Soviet agreement signed in 1939. The initial capital (U.S. $1 million, divided into 1,000 shares, according to the Chairman of the Board of Directors) was contributed by China and the Soviet Union on a 50-50 basis, and the corporation was to have been operated as a joint enterprise. Actually, however, the Soviet General-Manager has run it with very little reference to the Chinese. The key positions are held by Soviet citizens, and the Board of Directors (three Chinese and three Russians), which is supposed to meet annually, has not met for the last four years. The Chairman of the Board, Liu Tse-yung, has no voice in the management of the corporation. Even this last remaining Soviet asset in Sinkiang appears to be scheduled for liquidation, however, for the Chinese Government has recently announced that it does not intend to renew the airline agreement.

The Soviet Union's simultaneous support of the Ili regime and gradual withdrawal from the rest of Sinkiang, during the past few years, makes it difficult to understand what Soviet policy objectives are. One can interpret those objectives in several ways, all of which may contain an element of truth. Perhaps the Soviet Union feels that the *de facto* independence of a friendly regime in northern Sinkiang achieves its major short-run aims and that, therefore, to avoid further friction in the region, it should reduce its activities elsewhere in the province. It is possible that the

Russians believe an active policy is unnecessary in Sinkiang and that the whole province will ultimately fall into the Soviet sphere of influence, either as a result of success on the part of the native nationalists in Sinkiang or as a consequence of a Communist victory in the Chinese civil war. Or perhaps the Soviet Union fears that other serious international complications might develop from a more active policy in Sinkiang and is unwilling to risk such an eventuality when it has so many problems and commitments elsewhere.

It also is possible, however, that the Soviet Union contemplates the possibility of ultimately adding the entire province of Sinkiang to the galaxy of satellites that it has established or supported along its borders, but does not consider the present time opportune. It would be an easy matter, militarily speaking, for the Soviet Union to take Sinkiang, if it made a decision to do so.

Whatever the specific objectives of current Soviet policy toward Sinkiang may be, Soviet attitudes and actions will continue to be vital factors in the situation in the province. The Chinese recognize this, and their present policy is to avoid antagonizing the Russians at all costs.

The fact that international complications loom large in Sinkiang should not, however, obscure the equally important fact that many of the province's problems are indigenous and would exist even if no international rivalries were involved. "The crucial question in the Sinkiang problem," Liu Tse-yung, the scholarly Commissioner of the Ministry of Foreign Affairs in Tihwa, said to me, "is a Chinese one, and the solution of the problem depends upon our performance during the next two or three years. If we have a good administration, the people of Sinkiang will support us; if we do not, the people will oppose us."

18

DISUNITY IN THE SOUTHWEST

On October 15, Marshal Yen Hsi-shan—the Shansi warlord who was recently appointed Premier of Nationalist China—stated at a press conference in Chungking that the Central Government is "studying the possibility" of making Kunming its future "wartime capital." Now that Canton has fallen, the Nationalists' headquarters are divided between Chungking and Taiwan. Chungking is the official seat of "Acting President" Li Tsung-jen's regime, but the greatest concentration of military and financial power still left in non-Communist hands is in Taiwan, under "Retired President" Chiang K'ai-shek's direct control. Taiwan, however, appears to be Chiang's personal last-stand stronghold. It is cut off from the shrinking areas still under Nationalist control in China's southwestern provinces—Szechwan, Sikang, Kweichow, Kwangsi, Kwangtung and Yunnan—and there is no indication that Chiang is willing to commit his hoarded Taiwan resources to the losing battle on the mainland.

Southwest China, therefore, is largely on its own, militarily and economically, and Chungking, the largest city in the region, is the most logical location for the Nationalists' headquarters. If they move their capital once again, from Chungking to Kunming, it will probably not be before they are forced to do so. But Nationalist military strength in Szechwan is not impressive, and once the Communists are ready, there is a strong possibility that they can carry out a pincers movement, from north and east, that could make Szechwan untenable, despite its natural geographic barriers. If that takes place, the Nationalists may, as General Yen suggests, move to Kunming, and they would in that event have "gone about as far as they can go" on the mainland. What would their chances be for fighting back, or even holding out, in Yunnan? Although part of the answer to this question must be sought in the over-all national situation in China, and in the international factors affecting it, the local situation in Yunnan is certainly not irrelevant to the question.

Yunnan is a high, mountainous plateau, with an area estimated to be more than 150,000 square miles, and a population of about 12 million. Its international boundaries touch Burma and Indochina, and its provincial borders touch Kweichow, Sikang, Szechwan, and Kwangsi. Like many peripheral Chinese provinces, which are geographical as well as political entities, it has long had a somewhat tenuous relationship to the Chinese body politic. Prior to its consolidation into China Proper by the Mongol Dynasty in the thirteenth century, Yunnan was the seat of two important independent kingdoms: the Nanchao, with its capital in Tali, and the Nashi, with its capital in Likiang. Since the thirteenth century, Yunnan has had a continuing tradition of autonomy, under the direction of China's central authorities.

Roughly half—estimates are rather vague—of the province's population is made up of tribesmen. These include the Miao, Yao, Lolo, Shan (T'ai, or Thai), Tibetan, Hsifan, Min-Chia, Wa-Palaung, Burmese, and Kachin groups, to name some of the major ones. Since most of these people are hill-dwellers, the greater part of the territory of the province is inhabited by non-Chinese tribesmen, many of whom have not been assimilated into Chinese culture. The relationship between the Han Chinese and the tribesmen is not subject to easy description or generalization, but there are some areas within the province that have a large degree of local autonomy under local leaders; in the south, for example, there are areas that are divided into self-administering "Shan states."

The most important agricultural areas in Yunnan are inhabited by Chinese, most of whom are the descendents of colonists, garrison troops, and exiles, who entered the province during the rule of past Chinese dynasties. The areas that they, together with some Sinicized tribesmen, inhabit and control are the best developed areas of the province, consisting principally of scattered agricultural valleys tied together by imperfect lines of communication.

Yunnan's geographical remoteness and isolation, and the longstanding localism on the part of the Chinese as well as the tribesmen, were factors that led to the development of warlordism and provincial autonomy in the province when the Manchu Dynasty disintegrated in 1911. A leader named T'ang Chi-yao took over the provincial government at that time and ruled with little outside interference, even though he, like other local warlords, recognized the theoretical overlordship of the Central Government. He died in the late 1920's, and after a brief struggle for power, he was succeeded by General Lung Yün, who stayed in power until 1945.

Lung Yün is a Sinicized Lolo from the Chaotung district of northern Yunnan. A military man, he ruled in the classic warlord manner: He maintained his own armed forces, issued his own currency, and ran the province as he wished, with little reference to either the Central Government or the people under his rule. When war broke out in 1937, however, Lung formed a close alliance with the Central Government to resist Japanese aggression. Aroused to a considerable extent from their political indifference to national affairs, the Yunnanese supported the fight against foreign invasion, and their province became an important base for the war effort, both Chinese and Allied. It was also an important link with the outside world, being the China terminal not only for the Hump airlift, but also for the Burma and Stilwell roads. Lung Yün continued to maintain his grip on the local political situation, however, until, at the end of the war, Chiang K'ai-shek saw a chance to break his power and consolidate the province more fully into a unified postwar China.

For many years prior to 1945, Lung's principal protégé and military subordinate had been General Lu Han, also a Lolo from Chaotung, and a relative of Lung. (Descriptions of the relationship of Lu and Lung are so varied that one can only conclude that the exact relationship is obscure.) Once, in the early 1930's, Lu had helped to organize an abortive minor revolt against Lung, but his loyalty to his patron thereafter had seemingly been exemplary, and during the Sino-Japanese war, he led the major Yunnanese forces against the Japanese and participated in engagements such as the famous battle of Taierhchuang. When Japan was defeated, Chiang sent Lu and his Yunnanese troops to occupy Indochina, and Lung was left without strong military forces in Kunming. In a quick coup, Chiang's own troops then surrounded and disarmed Lung's retainers, and Lung himself was packed off to Nanking, where he could be kept under surveillance. Lu Han was appointed to be his successor as Governor of Yunnan, but the Yunnanese armies under him were later sent to Manchuria. This complicated maneuver destroyed Lung Yün's power and put in his place a man who was Yunnanese—and therefore more acceptable to the province than an outsider—and who not only owed his job to Chiang, but was also deprived of at least part of his military power. It was a maneuver that prevented the resurgence of warlordism and political autonomy—for a while.

Lu Han, who still remains Governor of Yunnan, played along with the Central Government until the beginning of this year. Although a Yunnanese, he was not popular in the province. The Yunnanese resented Chiang's bold interference in their affairs, and, in the minds of many people, Lu Han was a Central Government stooge. As a governor, he was probably no worse, and probably not much better, than Lung Yün, but the national as well as the provincial authorities contributed little to the welfare of the Yunnanese people, while demanding much from them, particularly in the form of taxes and conscriptees. (In addition to the taxes it levied, the Central Government "borrowed" 7.5 million piculs of rice, worth about Yunnan Silver $100 million, between 1943 and 1948, and it has never repaid it.) Many policies, particularly those toward educational institutions, were repressive. Lu's personal popularity probably reached its nadir on February 12 of this year. On that date, a riot took place at the Kunming branch of the Central Bank of China, as a result of the bank's failure to redeem some counterfeit banknotes found to be in circulation in Yunnan, and Lu in a fit of anger personally supervised the execution of twenty-one participants without any legal proceedings.

However, when the Central Government's power and authority started to disintegrate early this year, under the impact of Communist military advances, the forces of localism began to re-emerge in Yunnan. Lu Han started to re-examine his position, and gradually a trend toward Yunnanese autonomy reappeared. Step by step, in a slow and often subtle way, Yunnan severed its ties with the Central Government. By the end of August of this year, it looked to many people as if Lu Han was flirting with the idea of complete autonomy. Then, in the first week of September, Chiang K'ai-shek moved into the picture again and in a heavy-handed way brought the situation to a climax. Instead of carrying out a "coup" and "declaring independence," as was prematurely reported to the world from Hong Kong, Lu Han was forced reluctantly to resubmit to direct Central Government control.

The sequence of events during the first eight months of this year, from January through August, when Yunnan traveled steadily along the road toward autonomy, gives a revealing picture of some of the disintegrating forces that have been at work recently in Nationalist China. What has taken place in Yunnan cannot be generalized, without qualifications, but a similar process—involving the breakdown of the Central Government's power and control—has taken place in different forms in many Nationalist areas during the same period. This is why there has been no basis, on a political level, for a unified or effective war effort against the Communists.

Well-informed observers in Kunming, who have talked with Governor Lu at regular intervals during the past year, generally agree that he has never believed that Yunnanese independence, on any sort of complete or permanent basis, was a real possibility, because of the intrinsic military and economic weakness of his position. He has, however, seemed to aim toward a degree of local autonomy that would enable him to sit on the fence, refrain from active participation in the civil war, and negotiate some sort of settlement with the final winner—which he believed would probably be the Communists. This policy seemed to be based on an almost total loss of confidence in the Nationalists' cause.

The first moves toward reasserting local autonomy in Yunnan began in January this year. In mid-January, Lu, after returning from a quick trip to Nanking, abolished the Yunnan Garrison and took over command of the military forces in the province. On January 20, he removed a man named Yang Wen-ch'ing from the key post of Commissioner of Civil Affairs and replaced him with An En-fu; An, a local Yunnanese general, was a relative of Lu, and a long-time subordinate, who stood for local autonomy. At the same time, Lu appointed a new Commissioner of Finance, Lin Nan-yüan. Lin, a young Yunnanese banker who was founder and head of the Overseas Banking Corporation, was closely allied to native banking circles; his appointment strengthened local control over the province's finances. At about the same time, Lu began to take steps to keep Yunnanese conscriptees within the province, and the Provincial Council recommended that he keep in Yunnan all the income from taxes levied within the province, including those collected by Central Government agencies.

In February, the Yunnan provincial government "requested" the Kunming branch of the Central Bank to suspend all shipments out of the province of gold and silver that had been received during the currency conversion of August, 1948; the local manager of the bank complied. In early March, Lu achieved the dismissal of the manager, charging him with responsibility for the February 12 incident, and arranged for the appointment of one of his own Yunnanese followers, Chao Kang-chieh, to replace him. Chao, a nonentity, merely carried out Lu's wishes, and with his appointment, Yunnan achieved greater financial autonomy in banking than it had had since 1941, when the Kunming branch of the Central Bank was first established. On March 4, the provincial government went a step further and legalized the circulation of *Pan K'ai*, the local Yunnanese silver currency (which rural districts had continued to use, even when it was banned). On March 11, Yunnan took an even more drastic step and abolished the land tax in kind, substituting a levy in silver currency, in contravention of national laws. A decision was also made to keep the receipts of this tax within the province, to replace the national subsidy which had been discontinued.

In the political field, similar trends took place. In March, Lu Han became head of the provincial Kuomintang organization, replacing Chang Pang. From March to May, moreover, almost no military defense preparations were made to strengthen defenses against attack from the outside. When, in fact, it was revealed that the national Eighth Army, and some of Hu Tsung-nan's troops, would be moved into Yunnan, there was a great outcry in the local press, and protests were made by the Provincial Council on the grounds that Yunnan was not in a position to support any more troops. As a result, the planned move of these troops into Yunnan was indefinitely postponed. Local conscription in Yunnan was abolished and a system of voluntary enlistment instituted at about the same time.

Throughout this period, and until last September, the Provincial Government permitted free criticism of the Central Government, and praise of the Communists, to an extent unheard of previously. Leftist student agitation became widespread, and large crowds led by students danced and sang Communist songs at public meetings in Kunming. A pro-Communist press flourished briefly alongside the pro-Kuomintang press; one Leftist paper was run by Finance Commissioner Lin, another by supporters of former Governor Lung Yün, who had escaped from Nanking to Hong Kong and, after establishing contacts with Communist and pro-Communist groups there, had begun actively instigating anti-Kuomintang activities in Yunnan. In Kunming, a man named Yang Chieh, a former Chinese ambassador to Moscow who had connections with Lung and possibly with other antigovernment groups as well, reportedly worked to organize pro-Communist sentiment. A man, believed to be a Communist leader, with the pseudonym of Tseng also was active. The Provincial Council, normally conservative, openly condemned the Central Government, and several of its members became vocally pro-Communist. All of this activity, which reached its peak in August, received, if not the support, at least the tacit approval, of Lu Han.

In May, a provincial Financial and Economic Reform Planning Commission was established, and Y. T. Miao, the leading local industrialist, was asked to draw up plans for a local currency and financial autonomy (a plan was formulated but never implemented). And in June, the provincial government took over the revenues of the Central Government's Customs, Salt Administration, and National Tax Bureau in Yunnan. These steps cut the last important financial ties with the Central Government. At the same time, steps were taken to reform and rationalize the tax structure in Yunnan.

Because Central Government subsidies on which Yunnan had previously depended were not forthcoming, the province had been encountering considerable financial difficulties. Expenditures exceeded receipts, and the deficits were met by loans, totaling Yunnan Silver $10 million, extended by the New Fu Tien Bank—a subsidiary of the semigovernmental Yunnan People's Development Corporation headed by Y. T. Miao and L. C. King. In May, the budget was altered to provide for the use of receipts from the Central Government's tax agencies to meet the deficits, and this was put into effect in June. Budgetary difficulties continued, however, because of the heavy costs of "bandit suppression" within the province; military expenditures made up 80 per cent of total expenditures.

The Central Government found it difficult to block the trends toward autonomy in Yunnan during this period, since it was absorbed with its own more immediate problems and was having difficulty functioning at all as a government. In July and August, however, the national authorities finally started to increase their pressure on Lu Han to cooperate. They demanded, among other things, that he clamp down on local Communists and pro-Communists, institute censorship, curtail student agitation, limit Yunnanese financial independence, accept the national paper currency, resume conscription and the land tax in kind, and reorganize the provincial military forces. Lu Han at first resisted doing any of these things, and he seemed to be backed by local public opinion—or at least by the small group that was politically conscious in any positive sense. The national authorities then started negotiating with Lu, and a few compromises were agreed upon on paper. After a Central Government mission to Kunming in July, Lu agreed, in theory, to the institution of censorship, the acceptance of national currency notes (if they were backed up by silver bullion reserves kept in Kunming), the acceptance of more national troops in the province, and a reconsideration of conscription and the collection of land taxes in kind. However, none of these compromises was ever put into effect. Censorship was announced in July, but it was never enforced.

Then, during July and August, the Central Government started to send large numbers of its secret-service men into Yunnan, where they quietly canvassed the situation. But at the same time, pro-Communist activities and propaganda reached a peak. In August, Lung Yün sent a letter to the Provincial Council urging an open pro-Communist declaration. Lung undoubtedly wanted to get credit for a pro-Communist coup in Yunnan, thereby to earn a place in the new government that was expected to be established soon in Peking. Eighteen Council members responded by making such a declaration.

Tension between the national and provincial authorities increased, and finally reached a climax at the end of August. On August 29, General Yü Chi-shih, sent as an emissary by the Central Government, arrived in Kunming to confer with Lu Han for three days. Through Yü, Chiang K'ai-shek issued an "invitation" for Lu Han to come to Chungking for consultations, and Chang Ch'ün urged Lu to agree. Lu at first refused, but sent his General Secretary, Chu Li-tung, to Chungking with General Yü. Then Chiang and the Central Government really put the heat on. A quiet political battle developed between two groups of Lu's advisers in Kunming. One, which included anti-Chiang men, Lung supporters, Yunnanese autonomists, supporters of the Kuomintang Revolutionary Committee and varied pro-Communists, urged Lu Han not to go to the capital, but to make an open break with the Central Government. The other argued that it was necessary to go and impossible to hold out. From September 1 to September 3, Lu vacillated. Wild rumors spread through Kunming. There were reports that national troops were fighting the Peace Preservation Corps, that Chiang had threatened to bomb Kunming, that Lu would declare his independence. Barricades appeared in Kunming's streets. On September 4, the Nationalist commercial airlines withdrew from Kunming, on orders from Chiang.

Finally, Lu Han decided he had no alternative but to accept the "invitation," and on September 6, after declaring martial law in Kunming, he flew to Chungking with P'ei Ts'ung-fan, one of his advisers who is pro-Chiang. It is impossible to know exactly what took place at the conferences in Chungking, but when Lu Han returned to Kunming on September 8, his position had radically changed. He could no longer sit on the fence. He was committed to the Nationalist side, and the days of his autonomy had been cut short. Chiang had won a diplomatic victory, however short-lived it might prove to be, in a domestic situation that was rapidly falling apart.

After Lu Han's capitulation, the expected reaction began, on September 9. All publications in Kunming, except two pro-government papers, were closed, and all public meetings without official approval were forbidden. On September 10, the Provincial Council was dissolved. The next day, secret-service men began widespread arrests of students, Council members, and others; Yang Chieh and Tseng escaped, however. (Yang was assassinated in Hong Kong not long thereafter.) The arrests included some who were really pro-Communist and some who were simply critical of the Kuomintang. On September 13, Kunming's two universities and all its middle schools were closed for "readjustment," a polite name for a purge. Reregistration is now taking place, but hundreds of students have not yet reappeared. Many have undoubtedly joined guerrillas in rural areas. The result of all these measures was a very thorough suppression of civil liberties. It was all done by Kuomintang secret-service men; Lu Han had very little control over the situation.

As these events were taking place, "reinforcements" sent by the Central Government started moving into the province. Previously, the Twenty-Sixth Army had been the only important Central Government unit in Yunnan, but in September, the Eighty-ninth and Eighth armies began moving in from Kweichow. This, more than any other single thing, altered Lu Han's position and eliminated, for the time being at least, the possibility of independent action on his part.

Since those hectic days of early September, gradual changes have taken place in the financial and economic, as well as in the military and political, relationships between Yunnan and the Central Government. It is interesting, and perhaps significant, however, that on the detailed questions that were under dispute between Lu Han and the national authorities, Lu has not given in completely. For one thing, An and Lin, the two commissioners who clearly have leanings toward autonomy, remain in the government, despite predictions that they would be removed.

A compromise solution has been reached, in principle, on Yunnan's financial position. It restores over-all national financial control of Yunnan, but some concessions have been made to Lu Han. Provincial tax receipts, including the province's share of the land tax, now provide about 20 per cent of the amount required to balance Yunnan's budget, just enough to pay for administration and other civil purposes. The funds for "bandit suppression" will continue to be met, during an interim period, by the use of tax receipts from Central Government taxes in the province. According to the plan worked out, however, the Peace Preservation Corps will be reorganized into two armies under national control. When this is done, the support of these troops will be taken over by the Central Government, and the province will then turn back to the Central Government the tax receipts that legally belong to it. The land tax will be levied in silver currency instead of in kind, but two-thirds of the receipts will be paid to the Central Government. Finance Commissioner Lin has formulated a detailed plan for making the land tax more equitable, but it is doubtful if he will have much success implementing it under a financial situation in which increased Central Government pressure can be expected, since the Central Government's sources of revenue are constantly shrinking. Lin has been successful, however, in keeping the national paper currency out of the province. He insists that he will accept it in Yunnan only on two conditions: that it has adequate backing in silver bullion deposited in Kunming, and that the notes be surcharged "Yunnan" to differentiate them from unbacked notes that might flow in from outside the province. It is not likely that these conditions will be met, but Lin may find it hard to resist further pressure to accept the notes. When the Central Government assumes the burden of paying large numbers of troops in Yunnan, it may insist on using paper currency rather than silver.

In the military sphere, the plan for reorganizing Yunnan's Peace Preservation Corps (currently in the process of expansion from 12 to 18 regiments and from 30,000 to more than 40,000 men) into 2 armies under Central Government control is scheduled to be carried out "soon." The provincial authorities still oppose conscription, however, and all expansion to date has been on the basis of voluntary enlistments.

The present military situation in the province is uncertain. In addition to the Peace Preservation troops, which are poorly equipped and not well trained, there are now three national armies. The Twenty-Sixth Army under General Yü Ch'eng-wan has roughly 28,000 men, and its headquarters are at Kaiyuan in the southeast part of the province. Its troops are above average, and its commander, a graduate of the first class at the Whampoa Academy, is cocky. "I can beat the Communists," he said to me when I visited Kaiyuan, but "I'll retreat into Indochina rather than give up if the Communists take Yunnan." Yü has been fairly successful in pacifying the Communists and "bandits" in the areas where he has operated in the past, but even though he claims to have fought 213 "battles" since last March, it is not known how much fighting has actually gone on; fairly reliable sources report, in fact, that some of his junior officers have maintained cordial relations with officers under Chu Chia-pi, the chief Communist commander in his present area. The Eighty-Ninth Army under General Liu Po-lung, which has recently moved into Yunnan from Kweichow, has about 25,000 men, and its headquarters are at Suanwei. The Eighth Army under General Li Mi is still moving its 25,000 men into Yunnan; its headquarters will be at Chani. The Eighth and Eighty-Ninth armies are both relatively inexperienced units. General Yü of the Twenty-Sixth, in fact, sums up his opinion of them, and of the Peace Preservation Corps, with the word "useless."

Most of the troops in Yunnan have not received any pay for almost two months. They lack first-class equipment, especially heavy weapons. Yü told me that the Twenty-Sixth does not even have winter uniforms. Although they are all under the theoretical command of Lu Han, who is Yunnan Pacification Commander, the prime loyalty of these commanders is to Chiang K'ai-shek. Lu Han's chief of staff, General Hsieh Ts'ung-wen told me, furthermore, that no comprehensive plan of defense, to say nothing of offense, has yet been drawn up; it awaits action by higher authorities, he says. Hsieh also says that no direct liaison is maintained with military forces in adjacent Kweichow and Kwangsi, because they are "battle areas," whereas Yunnan is a "rear area."

The military forces in Yunnan are far from formidable, therefore, in view of what they may have to face before long. General Hsieh states, moreover, that "Yunnan cannot support any more troops than it has now." The plain fact is that great difficulties are being encountered in supporting the forces already in the province, and local feeling seems to be strongly opposed to any more troops. To understand this feeling, one must realize that the prevalent attitude toward Nationalist troops is that they are simply mouths to feed; the performance of Nationalist troops elsewhere in China makes most people feel that it is not worth the cost of feeding them. If the Nationalist troops now being pushed back by Communist advances in Kwangsi and Kweichow eventually retreat into Yunnan, they may be received not as potential defenders, but as unwanted mouths. A concentration of refugee troops in Yunnan might actually multiply Yunnan's economic and political problems, without increasing the province's ability to defend itself to any significant degree.

The troops now within Yunnan are more than adequate to pacify internal opposition from local Communists and bandits, if concerted efforts were made in that direction, but pacification has been only partially successful to date. It is true that many areas have been cleared of guerrillas in the past six months, but large areas are still not under the government's control. The known antigovernment forces include local Communist regulars, numbering perhaps 20,000 or more, Communist irregulars, supporters of Lung Yün (often led by opportunist members of the gentry), and old-type bandits. Even if they all worked together, which they do not, they could not directly challenge the provincial regime. But they have caused it a lot of trouble by hit-and-run tactics. For example, they have temporarily occupied a number of large cities, such as Paoshan, and they still hold a few cities, such as Likiang in the northwest part of the province. Probably no one can say with any accuracy how much of Yunnan is occupied by antigovernment forces, but the most common estimate is that only one-third to one-half of the province is actually under effective government control.

The most important antigovernment forces in the province, of course, are Communist regulars. Their head is said to be Chuang T'ien, former Vice-Commander of the Communist Hainan Island Column, who is reputed to have the title of Yunnan-Szechwan-Kwangsi Regional Area Commander. But Chuang's whereabouts and activities are unknown. The most active field commanders are: Chu Chia-pi, formerly a Colonel under Lu Han and reputedly Yenan-educated; Yü Wei-min, a local Yunnanese leader; and Yang Shou-tu, a Yunnan University graduate. These men and their troops cannot directly threaten the government in Kunming, but they can be expected to intensify disruptive attacks when Yunnan is threatened by external attack from Communist forces.

The French Consul in Kunming, incidentally, asserts that on July 17 of last year Chu Chia-pi's forces retreated into French Indochina and spent five months there, cooperating with Ho Chi-minh and studying in Vietminh training centers, before returning to Yunnan. He also claims that informal liaison is still maintained between Ho in Indochina and the Chinese Communist guerrilla leaders across the border in Yunnan. The French expect the Chinese Communists eventually to give moral support and indirect assistance to the Vietminh, he says, although they do not expect direct attacks or intervention. An even more immediate problem for the French, however, may be presented by retreating Nationalist troops. If Nationalist troops do retreat into Indochina, the French will attempt to disarm them and deal with them according to accepted international law, according to their Consul in Kunming.

These are some of the political, military, and economic factors in the local situation in Yunnan at present. How about popular support? And the will to fight? As in most of China, the large mass of people in Yunnan are playing a passive role in the situation. Throughout the province, there are, as already indicated, large numbers of people of various sorts who are in revolt. But most other people are trying to mind their own business. There is certainly no indication of any positive will to fight, and the future is accepted, whatever it may be, with fatalism—as it now seems to be in virtually all of the remaining areas of Nationalist China. The official attitude of provincial officials is that "the Communists will never be able to get into Yunnan." But they are vague on what will stop them, and one cannot help but remember that their present attitude is very different from their opinions of two months ago. One cannot forget, either, that their present stand is maintained, in a sense, under duress. There is no mobilization, either materially or spiritually, comparable to what took place during the Sino-Japanese War, and comparisons between the present and the wartime period have no validity. The threat this time is not from a foreign invader but from Chinese countrymen, and the fact that the Chinese Communists have close affiliations with a Soviet-dominated world movement does not seem to affect the opinions of many people. I have asked people of many sorts: "Do you expect the Communists to take over control of Yunnan?" The almost universal answer, except from those directly connected with the government, has been simple: "Yes." In response to "When?", few people have a definite answer, but most seem to be thinking in terms of a few months.

These are the conditions and attitudes that the Central Government would meet if it were forced to move its capital from Chungking to Kunming. If Yunnan were to become a final bastion of Nationalist resistance, it is doubtful whether the situation in the province would change materially. If anything, the problems that already exist would be increased as a result of the influx of Central Government troops and personnel. There is little reason to believe that the Central Government could hold out for any length of time, if the Communists were to concentrate on taking the province after cleaning up areas to the north and east. If the Communists stop or bog down, if completely unforeseen factors enter the picture, if the entire China situation changes, or if a third world war starts, the Nationalists may have a future in Yunnan. None of these things seems likely at the present time.

19

END OF THE LINE

Haikow (Hainan)
November, 1949

Haikow, capital of Hainan Island, which lies off the coast of southern China, is normally a quiet city of a quarter-million inhabitants who feel remote from the mainstream of events on the Asian mainland. Today, Haikow is a chaotic refugee center whose streets and sidewalks are teeming with tens of thousands of disorganized Nationalist soldiers who have fled from the Chinese mainland.

During the past few weeks, hordes of hungry, demoralized Nationalists have swarmed across the narrow Hainan Strait from Liuchow Peninsula, which juts out into the ocean from Kwangtung Province. Others have made a longer voyage, from islands near the Portuguese colony of Macao, which lies just west of Hong Kong. These refugees have come in ships and boats of every conceivable description—freighters, LST's, small coastal craft, fishing boats, motor boats, junks. At the moment, Haikow's harbor—one of the world's worst—contains more than twenty freighters and large ships and numerous junks and small boats, many of them still filled to overflowing with soldiers who have been waiting for days to debark.

Reliable estimates place the number of soldier-refugees now in the city of Haikow alone at over 100,000. The number of troops who have funneled through the city in recent weeks is even larger, because some have spread into the Hainan countryside, and a few have stopped only briefly in Hainan before moving on to southern Kwangtung. Most of the refugee soldiers now on Hainan are Kwangtung troops who have retreated in front of advancing Communist armies since the fall of Canton, but some are men who have been pushed all the way from north China to this southernmost outpost of Nationalist control.

Yesterday I was talking with a tall, good-looking soldier in a Haikow hospital. As the doctor examined his crooked arm, stiffened into an unbending angle by lack of treatment for an elbow shattered many months before, I asked, "When were you wounded?" "Hsuchow"—the battle that decided the struggle for central China—he answered in a Peiping accent. "How long have you been in the army?" "Twelve years," he replied in a flat voice. Twelve years! He still looked young, but for twelve years—his whole youth—he had been tramping through the mud and dust of China, from the Burma border to the north China plains, fighting Japanese and Communists periodically, and continually fighting for existence. He started to describe the battle at Hsuchow. "After we were surrounded," he said, "we held out as long as we could, but we ran out of ammunition. Food, too. We ate horsemeat and leather until that was all gone. Then there was nothing else we could do but try to escape south." His voice was bitter. Suddenly he exclaimed, "The army general staff is full of traitors! It's their fault, not ours. They care nothing for the country; they care only for themselves." He looked at the doctor with sad eyes and repeated, "The general staff is full of traitors." The doctor could not do anything for his arm; too many months and too many miles had gone by since the battle of Hsuchow.

The refugee troops in Haikow are completely demoralized. The faces of the soldiers wading ashore through the surf, or climbing onto the dilapidated concrete pier at the landing point outside of Haikow, have a bleak look of hopelessness. There is almost no organization or order in the evacuation. On the pier where the troops land, there is a weird assortment of equipment—telephone wire, tarpaper, tent pegs—much of it useless and most of it in bad condition. The majority of the evacuees are coming as individuals or in small groups who must fend for themselves and find their own shelter and food. They are wet, tired, and dirty. Some have rifles and small arms, but they are rusty and in bad shape. Many soldiers have brought wives, children, and bundles containing all their worldly possessions.

The 7-mile road to Haikow from the pier outside the city is lined with straggling soldiers and civilian camp followers streaming into town. Along the roadside, one sees occasional groups that have stopped to rest, while here and there are sick men who are lying helpless and alone, unnoticed by the tired men trudging past. A majority of the soldiers have malaria. A few have advanced cases of beriberi.

Within Haikow itself, there is almost no place that is not jammed with soldiers and their families. They have set up housekeeping in churches, public buildings, schools, private homes, and on the sidewalks. On all the main streets, one has to thread through open-air "homes" to go anywhere. People and belongings are piled together in an incredible, filthy mess. Only the fortunate ones are able to keep dry; the others are exposed to the steady drizzle of fall rain.

During daylight hours, when it is not raining heavily, thousands of soldiers spread their loot and belongings—clothing, bedding, hardware, and junk of all sorts—on the streets and sell them to local inhabitants or to other soldiers. Most of them have to sell something in order to buy food. As a result, the whole city looks like a "soldiers' market." Almost every night, there is an incident of some sort. Considering their condition, the soldiers are fairly well-behaved, but a few always create trouble. There are quarrels, shootings, and occasional casualties. Disputes arise between soldiers and civilians, soldiers and police, soldiers and gendarmes, soldiers and soldiers. During the past three nights, six persons are reported to have been killed in street shootings.

This disorganized influx of troops has created tremendous problems for General Ch'en Chi-t'ang who heads the Hainan Island Special District. Ch'en did not ask for the Kwangtung troops to come. He did not want them to come. But there has been no way to stop them. The chaos created by the refugees may defeat the Nationalists on Hainan, even before the Communists get around to dealing with the island.

Ch'en Chi-t'ang is an old-time political figure in China who, until early this year, had been in eclipse for over a decade. In the 1930's, he was the leading military figure in his native province. In that period, he exercised a good deal of local autonomy and was associated with the Kwangtung-Kwangsi clique and many other still-prominent figures; they included men such as Li Tsung-jen (now Acting President of the Nationalist Government), Pai Ch'ung-hsi (now the Nationalist Commander in Kwangsi, whose troops, numbering about 200,000, are the only relatively strong force the Nationalists still have on the mainland), Hsüeh Yüeh (now Governor of Kwangtung), and Li Chi-shen (now a Vice-President of the Communist Government established last month in Peking).

In 1936, General Ch'en was forced into retirement by Chiang K'ai-shek, and soon thereafter left to travel in Europe. According to Ch'en's own account, he split with Chiang because of the latter's "appeasement of Japan," but the issue was undoubtedly one of local rule versus Central Government control. When the Sino-Japanese War broke out, Ch'en returned and filled two politically unimportant posts in the Central Government: Minister of Agriculture and member of the Kuomintang's Supreme Council. After the war, he went into retirement again. In April of this year, however, Hainan Island was made into a Special District, containing sixteen *Hsien* that previously had been an integral part of Kwangtung, and Ch'en emerged once again to become head of the Special District, as well as local military commander and chief of the committee set up to make Hainan into a province.

Hainan Island is one of the least developed and most neglected areas in China. Its population is only 2.5 million, despite the fact that, according to local leaders, it could probably support 10 million people. Its resources are almost entirely unexploited, and there are large tracts of cultivable land on the island that are unused.

What little development has occurred on Hainan took place under Japanese rule. Before the Japanese came, most Chinese did not even know the potentialities of the island, but the Japanese landed on February 10, 1939, with a comprehensive blueprint for imperialistic exploitation. During the years they occupied Hainan, they ruthlessly disregarded the local population's welfare, but they proceeded to develop the resources of the island and to make Hainan an important source of raw materials and a military staging base. Several large airfields were built. Yulin, on the southern coast, was made into a major naval base with first-class port facilities. Mining of iron ore and other minerals was started, and a railway was built, skirting the entire southern and western coast line, to connect the iron mines with port outlets. Agricultural production and fishing were encouraged and a few small industries were established. The Japanese accomplished a great deal in developing the island for their own purposes, while the local population suffered from malnutrition and mistreatment.

At the end of the war, the Chinese inherited the mining, industrial, and transportation facilities that the Japanese had built, but today, four years later, that inheritance has been almost completely squandered. The mismanagement, corruption, and inefficiency that have been so tragically prevalent in Nationalist China in the postwar years have almost entirely erased the positive assets that the Japanese created and left on Hainan. Most of the roads, and all but two of the airfields, have fallen into disrepair. Only one small section of the railway, at Yulin, is still in use. The docks and port facilities at Yulin have deteriorated badly. A fleet of almost seventy modern fishing boats has disappeared. No trace remains of the large amounts of Japanese road-building and other equipment that filled several acres of parking space near Yulin on V-J Day. The fish cannery, cement factory, leather tannery, sugar refinery, and cotton weaving plant built by the Japanese all stopped operating soon after the war. The Japanese naval hospital at Yulin, containing about 700 beds, has disappeared into thin air. In short, construction and development stopped soon after the Chinese administration took over.

The postwar decline on Hainan has been all the more tragic because a few of the potentialities of the island are now widely known for the first time. The island is rich in resources, in terms of its area and population. It has some of the best iron ore deposits in China, and the only important deposits in south China. At Yaihsien and Tientu, on the southern coast, there are rich deposits, well developed by the Japanese, of several million tons of ore, which has an iron content of 63 to 68 per cent. At Paishahsien, Shihlu, and nearby places on the west coast there are deposits—only partly developed by the Japanese and now unexploited—that are equally as rich, which are estimated by some to total 200 million tons. There are also less important resources of tin, copper, manganese, lead, gold, silver, coal, graphite, antimony, tungsten, and mercury. Agricultural export products could also be developed on a significant scale in Hainan's mild tropical climate. Sugar, pineapples, coconut (copra), rubber, and betel nuts are produced in small quantities now, and these and other agricultural products could be expanded greatly. The salt produced in Hainan is of excellent quality, and the cattle and hogs raised on the island are in great demand in Hong Kong and elsewhere. Despite these potentialities for development, however, Hainan has fewer industries and is worse off economically now than four years ago. Instead of a postwar development boom, Hainan has experienced a severe economic slump, intensified by inflation and a steadily rising cost of living.

When General Ch'en Chi-t'ang arrived at Haikow in April of this year, he set to work energetically to halt the process of deterioration on Hainan. Ch'en is a competent man, and, reportedly, much of the modern industry in Canton and elsewhere in Kwangtung dates to the period of his leadership and can be traced to his sponsorship. On Hainan, he has used his own money to finance the local administration, because funds have not been forthcoming from the Central Government or other sources. He has pushed a number of reconstruction projects, and in six months he has restored one small factory (the Japanese-built cotton weaving plant), increased monthly iron ore production from 30,000 to 40,000 tons, built two new hospitals, set up a broadcasting station, organized adult education institutions in every *Hsien*, repaired a few miles of roads, and established an experimental farm. He has also defeated a few local Communists and has paid his own troops, something few other Nationalist leaders in China have been able to do in recent months.

Despite his accomplishments, however, the situation on Hainan is becoming more and more hopeless. "In two years time," he said to me, "I could have really done something." But time is running out. The internal situation on the island is becoming increasingly chaotic every day. The island's military refugees make problems more and more insoluble. And the external military threat to the island is sowing seeds of panic.

The troops directly under Ch'en's command on Hainan include two armies, the Thirty-Second at Tingan and the Sixty-Fourth at Chengmai. Together with special units, such as the salt guards, and air force and naval personnel, Ch'en's forces total about 80,000 reasonably well-trained, well-equipped men. These men might have constituted an effective defense force under favorable conditions, but 100,000 demoralized soldiers who have come as refugees have thrown the island into confusion, and have detracted from, rather than added to, the strength of Hainan's defenses. The morale of all the island's troops has been affected; some of them are known to have sold arms recently to local Communist units.

The two most critical problems facing the Hainan administration now are money and rice. General Ch'en has almost exhausted his personal financial resources, and this week, he flew to Taiwan to try to obtain money from Chiang K'ai-shek's hoarded treasury funds. The success of his mission is doubtful, however, because Ch'en is not one of Chiang's own clique. Neither Ch'en nor any of his advisers knows any way to meet the island's food deficiency either. Even in normal times, Hainan is a rice importing area, but usually it is able to buy rice from the mainland and foreign sources and to pay for it with exports of pigs, cattle, iron, and other products. Hainan still exports 10,000 pigs and 2,000 head of cattle a month to Hong Kong and all of its iron production to Japan, but rice is harder to get, and the island's rice requirements have jumped with the flood of refugees. At present, Hainan needs to import 3,000 to 4,000 tons of rice a month. Attempts are being made to buy part of it from Indochina, Siam, and other Southeast Asian countries, but without much success. A severe rice shortage is expected, and in less than a month, the food situation may become critical. If it does, the hungry refugee soldiers on Hainan may get out of hand.

The Central Government has neglected Hainan, as it has many other areas, by ignoring its problems, military as well as economic. The Nationalist Navy to date has not sent adequate units from Taiwan to defend the Hainan Strait, separating the island from the mainland. At present, only four small patrol boats guard the Strait. Air force units on Hainan are also below the strength needed for an adequate defense. There are now twenty-four bombers and six fighters on the island, but only a few of these are operational. Chiang K'ai-shek has hoarded the Nationalist regime's navy and air force, as well as its money, on Taiwan.

At present, the Chinese Communists' main military drives seem to be directed toward Szechwan and Kweichow, rather than to the south, but Communist guerrillas have already reached the Liuchow Peninsula, and regulars are not far away. From Liuchow Peninsula's main port of Kwangchowan, still precariously in Nationalist hands, it is only an overnight trip by junk to Hainan. The Communists, therefore, are almost on Hainan's doorstep.

The Communists are also well-entrenched on Hainan Island itself. One-third to one-half of the island, including most rural districts, is held by local Communists under a leader named Feng Po-chün. These Hainan Communists have a continuous history of twenty-two years of guerrilla activity, and neither the Japanese nor the Nationalists have been able to root them out. Although a relatively small force, they are one of the most celebrated of Communist guerrilla units. They possess their own government, and their own troops, with headquarters at Five Finger Mountain, the highest peak in the range that forms the backbone of Hainan Island. These Communist troops are organized into five "divisions," with a strength of about 10,000 to 12,000 men. They are not well-armed, and consequently cannot directly challenge the Nationalists, but by harassing attacks on communications, they constantly threaten the Nationalists' rear.

According to an adviser on General Ch'en Chi-t'ang's staff, furthermore, it is "almost certain" that the Communists have infiltrated the troops coming to Hainan from the mainland. They can be expected, therefore, to foment trouble and disorder among the refugee Nationalist soldiers and to undermine further the morale that is already near rock bottom.

Despite the poor prospects for improving the situation on Hainan, however, General Ch'en is still trying to solve some of the island's critical problems and to bolster its defenses. He is almost helpless in many respects, though, and at a recent meeting with some of his junior officers, there were tears in his eyes as he chided the officers for eating in good restaurants while so many troops were hungry on the streets.

A number of south China leaders, all suffering from the same neglect and seeming abandonment on the part of Chiang K'ai-shek, who controls most of the remaining real assets of the Nationalist Government, have recently made attempts to coordinate their plans and give each other mutual assistance to the best of their ability. These include, besides Ch'en Chi-t'ang, Hsüeh Yüeh, and Pai Ch'ung-hsi. Hsüeh, who is Governor of Kwangtung, has had temporary headquarters on Hainan for the past several weeks, but is now moving to Pakhoi on the Kwangtung coast just south of the Liuchow Peninsula. Pai, the Kwangsi commander, who now has his headquarters at Nanning and Poseh, is reported to have agreed, at a recent conference that he attended in Haikow, to send two divisions toward Pakhoi in order to improve the defenses of the Liuchow Peninsula region. Although Ch'en, Hsüeh, and Pai are all able men, even Ch'en himself does not seem to have much real confidence that they can accomplish their defensive aims.

The general atmosphere in Haikow at present is one of near-complete discouragement and disillusionment. Most ordinary people seem to believe that the local situation is already so chaotic that increasing disorder and, possibly, troop defections are all that can be expected. The prevailing lack of confidence in the future is indicated by the fact that many high officials' families have already left for Hong Kong and other safer places. Ch'en Chi-t'ang's family is no exception.

A highly placed source in Haikow, who prefers to remain anonymous, told me a few days ago that informal discussions regarding the possible evacuation of Nationalist troops to French Indochina have already been initiated. It is even possible, this man said, that the incorporation of some Nationalist troops into Bao Dai's Indochinese forces is being seriously considered. There is no doubt, however, that, come what may, Hainan is the end of the line for most of the soldiers on the island.

This morning, I overheard a conversation carried on by five soldiers milling around in a crowd on the main wharf in Haikow. One impatient soldier said, "Let's get going." Another turned to him and snapped, "All right, but where are we going?" No one seemed to have an answer to that one.

20

ISLAND REFUGE

Taipeh (Taiwan)
November, 1949

Fifteen miles from Taipeh, capital of Taiwan (Formosa), there is a small, Japanese-built resort town called Tsaoshan, perched on a mountainside amid semi-tropical flora. Tsaoshan is the seat of the Generalissimo's Headquarters, an unofficial government within a government, where the diehards of the Nationalist regime advise their "retired" leader in his attempts to reassert control over a situation that is almost entirely out of control.

When Chiang K'ai-shek went into "retirement" in January of this year, nominal leadership of Nationalist China passed to General Li Tsung-jen, who had been elected Vice-President in April, 1948—despite the vigorous opposition of Chiang and the Kuomintang party machine. Chiang's "retirement" has never been more than a fiction, however, and the power of Li Tsung-jen, and his Kwangsi clique and other supporters, has remained purely nominal. As party chief of the Kuomintang, Chiang has continued to pull strings, give orders, and direct his personal followers from behind the scenes.

For over twenty years, Chiang K'ai-shek and the Kuomintang regime have been so tightly wedded that the split since January has been merely a separation, not a divorce. During the past year, Li and his supporters have never had a chance to determine policies with any degree of independence, because they have been undercut by Chiang's constant interference and obstruction. Many observers believe that Chiang has deliberately undermined the position of Li and the Central Government on the mainland, to insure that Chiang himself would have no strong political competitors among the non-Communists in China. There is considerable evidence to support this view.

In the spring of this year, Li wanted to fight the Communists along the Yangtze River, which is one of the best natural defense barriers in the country, but it is reliably reported that Chiang, although holding no official government post, withdrew most of the navy and air force to Taiwan and gave personal orders to General T'ang En-po, commander of the lower Yangtze Valley, to withdraw toward Shanghai; as a result, the Communists' crossing of the river was virtually unopposed. Li then wanted to reorganize the government and army, and to purge incompetent men, but there is abundant evidence that Chiang blocked almost every move in this direction. To cite a specific example, Li is reported to have vetoed the appointment of T'ang En-po as commander in Fukien, but Chiang's influence placed T'ang in the job nevertheless. Subsequently, T'ang, who is a fellow Chekiang provincial of Chiang's, lost the battle for Fukien, as he has lost almost every other important battle during his long career. Li controlled none of the financial resources of the National Government, and while his capital was in Canton, expenditures (about fifty million silver dollars a month) exceeded revenues (about twenty million silver dollars a month) to such an extent that the troops could not be paid, and the financial strain on the government became intolerable. Despite Li's suppliant requests for financial assistance, Chiang, who had shipped the monetary reserves of the Central Government to Taiwan and kept them under his own control, refused to bail Li's government out of its predicament and doled out money, as well as air force and navy units, in pitifully inadequate amounts. Discouraged but not defeated, Li wanted to attempt the defense of south China by maintaining a defense line on the Kwangtung-Hunan border. Chiang, however, went over Li's head and, according to reliable sources, in late September ordered a general withdrawal to the environs of Canton. This move predetermined the loss of Canton, which was given up without a fight, and Pai Ch'ung-hsi's soldiers, the only important Nationalist troops left on the mainland, barely missed Communist encirclement and were forced to withdraw precipitously to Kwangsi.

For over ten months, Chiang K'ai-shek's intervention in government affairs on the mainland, in direct opposition to Li Tsung-jen's plans and policies, has destroyed the last vestiges of unity in the Nationalist camp. Cleavages of all sorts have widened, and the basic rivalry between Li and Chiang has reached an explosive point. Chiang's apologists explain that he has been trying to conserve the Nationalists' dwindling military strength, but if that has been his objective, his efforts have been remarkably misguided; his policies have doubtless aided the Communists in destroying the remaining Nationalist strength on the mainland.

As long ago as July, Chiang, in an interview with a foreign correspondent, said: "Regardless of whether I hold any political office, I cannot give up my revolutionary leadership." He has shown that these were not idle words. Last week, Acting President Li Tsung-jen apparently gave up his attempts to govern without power, and ignoring Chiang's requests that he meet him in Chungking, he flew to the British colony of Hong Kong for medical treatment. He hopes to proceed to the United States.

It is too early to predict whether Li Tsung-jen will be persuaded to return to the mainland to assume once more his post as nominal chief of the Nationalist Government. Although this seems unlikely at present, it is still possible. It is also possible, however, that Chiang will abandon the fiction of "retirement," now that he has defeated his major political opponent within the Kuomintang, and will openly reassert his rule over the remnants of Nationalist China. Or some lesser figure may rise to become a powerless chief of state in a shadow-government controlled by Chiang. But the possibility of any new and vital leadership asserting its control over the Kuomintang on the mainland is now difficult to conceive. Chiang K'ai-shek has completely undercut his party rivals. His political victory certainly seems to be a Pyrrhic one, however, because the Nationalists are now so weak and divided that a complete Communist military victory on the mainland is undoubtedly only a matter of time.

Chiang K'ai-shek's actions during the past year seem, on the surface, to have been suicidal. They make sense only in terms of the following surmises and facts. Chiang seems to have an unshakable belief in his own destiny, and he has therefore obstinately refused to relinquish power to anyone else, Communist or non-Communist. He has openly proclaimed his belief that a third world war not only will come, but has, in effect, already started. He seems confident that he will ride the crest of Western military advances in an eventual Soviet-American struggle and will be reinstated as ruler of a non-Communist China. And he controls the island of Taiwan as a military base and final personal stronghold. It is reliably reported that Chiang now wants the official Nationalist capital to be set up on Taiwan. Taiwan is the center of Chiang's power and hopes, therefore, and the small resort town of Tsaoshan is the nerve center of his operations.

What little positive popular support the Kuomintang has continued to evoke on the mainland during recent months has generally been based on the hope that Li and other leaders would be able to change the character of the Party after Chiang's "retirement." These hopes have not materialized. Chiang has not retired, and the tight group of men in the Kuomintang who still accept the Generalissimo's leadership is composed, for the most part, of the oldest Party and army workhorses, men who still feel a personal loyalty to Chiang, or who have such strong vested interests in the old regime that they hope it will continue unchanged. A majority of these men are now concentrated on Taiwan.

The Generalissimo's Headquarters, organized on Taiwan after the fall of Nanking and Shanghai, is made up of a group of Party elders who form an unofficial cabinet for an unofficial ruler. Officially, it is called the Kuomintang Director-General's Office, and its personnel totals about a hundred men, organized into six major sections. In addition, there are many untitled advisers. This group is the Generalissimo's organized brain trust. The job of its members is to advise the chief as a cabinet would, and many of the brain trusters are former cabinet members. They spend their time drawing up plans, policies, and reforms. But it is the Generalissimo's prerogative to make the decisions and, when the spirit moves him, to take action by issuing orders and instructions to loyal subordinates, often forcing or persuading these subordinates to disregard the Central Government to which they theoretically now owe allegiance.

A few of the well-known younger men in the Generalissimo's Headquarters are competent and qualified for responsible positions. One notable example is K. C. Wu, who probably administered the complicated city of Shanghai as efficiently as any other man in China could have. But men of this sort are in a minority. It is by no means certain, furthermore, that this minority is satisfied with the system under which they work, even though they have followed the Generalissimo to Taiwan. There are recurring rumors in Taipeh that there is a group within the top inner circle that would like to end Chiang's arbitrary control, but not many people believe them capable of doing it.

The organized brain trust is only a small part of the entourage that makes up Chiang's unofficial government on Taiwan. The island is crowded with old Party hands, including the most diehard, unchangeable, uncompromising ones, as well as numerous old commanders and generals, who are a dime a dozen. Many of these men are advisers of one sort or another—to Chiang, to the Director-General's Office, and to the Provincial Government. Even T'ang En-po is still around as adviser to something or other. The same men who have brought Nationalist China to its present state of political and military bankruptcy still hang on, and on

Taiwan there are more of them concentrated in less space, and with less to do, than ever before. Figuratively speaking, advisers lean over the shoulders of almost all legitimate officials on Taiwan, including those in the Provincial Government, and the influence of their dubious advice reaches far into the remaining Nationalist-held areas in west and south China and interferes with the functioning of many officials there.

The influence of the Generalissimo and his unofficial government on the mainland situation is sometimes exercised by remote control, but sometimes it is applied directly through what has been called Chiang's "mobile cabinet." A small group of key members of the Generalissimo's Headquarters, plus some of the high-ranking advisers attached to it, travel with Chiang wherever he goes. When Chiang flies to Chungking, for example, these men hop into the plane with him, and on arrival, they act as a general staff to assist the Generalissimo in his political maneuvers—all unofficially, of course.

The territorial base from which Chiang's pocket-size, but potent, government operates is confined to Taiwan, however, despite the peregrinations of the "mobile cabinet." It is the relative strategic position and invulnerability of this base, together with the financial, naval, air, and military strength that Chiang controls on the island, which give the Generalissimo the material basis for power, regardless of what titles he may or may not possess. Before the fall of Nanking and Shanghai, Chiang managed to bring virtually the entire treasury of the Central Government, including its gold bullion reserves, to Taiwan. Not even the most astute outside observers seem to know where these funds are guarded or how they are disbursed, but everyone agrees that Chiang himself holds the purse strings and has refused to allow the Central Government authorities on the mainland, who should be the custodians of the treasury, to draw freely on the reserves. These funds, which generally were valued at about U.S. $300 million when brought to Taiwan, have been used only when and where Chiang has permitted. Employment of the navy and air force is also subject to direct orders from the Generalissimo, and since the loss of the Yangtze Valley, he has concentrated the forces of both these services at Taiwan, to the detriment of Nationalist efforts on the mainland. A sizable military organization is also being created on Taiwan, and Chiang has concentrated his efforts on building this island defense force. He has shown far less concern about remedying the equipment deficiencies and lack of pay plaguing the remaining Nationalist troops who actually face the Communists on the mainland than he has about strengthening the military potential of Taiwan, his own final stronghold.

Chiang has entrusted the administration of Taiwan to one of his closest personal followers, General Ch'en Ch'eng, who was sent to the island at the end of 1948 to prepare a base to which Chiang could retire. Reportedly, Wei Tao-ming, the Governor of Taiwan, was not even informed that Ch'en was coming, but in January this year, Ch'en took over Wei's job. Ch'en, like Chiang himself, is a native of Chekiang and a graduate of Paoting Military Academy. He has held a succession of important jobs under the Generalissimo. At present, in addition to being Governor of Taiwan, he is Southeast China Commander—a post created on September 1 of this year to include Taiwan, Kiangsu, Chekiang, and Fukien provinces, the last three of which are largely in Communist hands. As Southeast China Commander, Ch'en is military deputy to Chiang K'ai-shek—who officially holds no military post, but is still "the Generalissimo" and therefore the highest-ranking officer in the Chinese Nationalist Army.

Today, Taiwan in theory is simply a province, one part of Nationalist China, without special status. Actually, it is Chiang K'ai-shek's personal reserve, governed by the "retired" Generalissimo himself with the help of loyal supporters. The Nationalists' disintegrating Central Government on the mainland does not control Taiwan; instead, Chiang's unofficial government on Taiwan exercises a considerable degree of control over the few remnant Nationalist elements on the mainland. Chiang undoubtedly chose Taiwan as his final stronghold because strategically it is the most defensible area still left in Nationalist hands. Any invasion force from the mainland must cross the Taiwan Strait, over a hundred miles of choppy water. And from late autumn until spring, the northeast monsoon adds to the difficulty of the crossing.

The military forces still under Nationalist control, and under General Ch'en's command, total about 600,000 men, roughly half of whom are infantry effectives. These are divided into four subordinate command areas: Tinghai and the whole Chusan Island group near Shanghai (Tinghai is the base from which Nationalist destroyer-escorts and smaller craft are blockading the river entrance to Shanghai); Quemoy (Kinmen) Island, off the coast near Amoy; the Pescadores, southwest of Taiwan; and the island of Taiwan itself.

The difficulty of amphibious operations against the offshore islands, if the defending troops fight, was indicated a month ago by two Communist invasion attacks that were decisively smashed by the Nationalists. On October 25, 17,000 Communists with supporting artillery made a night attack on Quemoy. By October 27, the three Nationalist armies there, sparked by regiments trained under General Sun Li-jen, had annihilated the attackers; 8,000 were captured and 9,000 killed or drowned. On November 3, a somewhat smaller Communist force attacked Tengpu Island (near Tinghai), and by November 6, they were destroyed. These two battles resulted in the only significant Nationalist victories in recent months. The morale of the Nationalist troops participating was good, and as a result of the battles, they captured artillery and small arms that strengthened their position. (It should be noted, however, that the equipment captured undoubtedly had once belonged to other Nationalist units on the mainland.)

On Taiwan itself, General Sun Li-jen commands a defense force of about 130,000 men, one-third of whom, however, lack small arms. General Sun is a distinguished and accomplished soldier, a graduate of Tsinghua University, Purdue, and the Virginia Military Institute, but he is non-political and belongs to no clique. This fact has constantly undermined his position throughout his career, and has repeatedly prevented his assignment to key command posts his talents have deserved. During the past two years, Sun has not seen combat. The Fengshan training base which he established on south Taiwan in 1947 has produced four armies of qualified soldiers, however, and those still left on Taiwan form the nucleus of his present command, to which he was assigned this fall.

Even though Sun Li-jen's troops are of relatively high caliber, and are comparatively well paid and fed by Chinese standards, a number of factors make their position weaker than it might appear. Arms, ammunition, and other supplies are lacking. The bulk of the Nationalists' military supplies have already been lost to the Communists on the mainland. Taiwan produces only a few of the items needed by an army; a few small arms and mortars are manufactured, but the numbers are negligible. Sun, furthermore, does not control the allocation of supplies or finances to various units on the island. Since August of this year, he has been given an increasing amount of authority, but this has been done grudgingly, and Sun still feels he does not have a free enough hand to organize an effective coordinated defense. There are some commanders on Taiwan completely out of his control, and this split command permits political jockeying and creates friction. The Nationalists still seem incapable of setting up a completely unified command. "If you are familiar with any part of China," Sun said to me when I interviewed him recently, "then you will see the same old political situation here."

The command situation is not as bad as it might have been, however, considering the confusion that reigned on Taiwan immediately after the Nationalist refugee troops arrived from the Shanghai-Nanking area. The reorganization of these troops is, in fact, one of Ch'en Ch'eng's major accomplishments. Within a relatively short period after their arrival, Ch'en abolished twenty army designations (!), accounting for almost two-thirds of the paper strength of the refugee units, and reorganized the soldiers into units placed under Sun for retraining. As a result, unemployed generals were, and are, a drug on the market. This reorganization process, Ch'en told me, when I met him not long ago, was "harder than forming new units" because all the vested interests involved naturally opposed it, but it brought some order out of chaos.

If the fate of Taiwan is ultimately decided by military rather than political means, the brunt of defense will probably fall on General Sun Li-jen, and Sun himself says, "We have the determination to defend Taiwan, but we need both financial and military support from the outside to do it." It is doubtful if all the Nationalist leaders on Taiwan have the same soldier's determination as Sun, but it is certain, as Sun says, that outside aid is a prerequisite for a long-term defense of the island.

PART IV

COMMUNIST TAKEOVER

21

SIEGE AND TURNOVER

Peiping
February, 1949

On the morning of December 17, I left Nanking aboard a C-47 bound for Peiping. None of the thirteen persons aboard the plane knew whether we would be able to land at our destination. Four days previously, the Communists had opened an attack on the city. Its western airfield was known to be out of commission. The southern field was reported to be under fire from Communist artillery, and Red troops were said to be closing in everywhere. We crossed our fingers and hoped it would be possible to land; fortunately, it was.

We landed on a deserted concrete strip of no man's land. The Nationalists had already evacuated South Field, leaving it littered with old equipment, abandoned personal possessions, and relics of the Chinese Air Force, but the Communists had not yet moved in to take over the shambles. The soft thud of exploding mortar shells sounded nearby as we stepped out of the plane, so we hastily climbed into vehicles sent from the city to meet us, and wound our way through retreating troops and defense barricades into the surrounded city of Peiping.

In the month and a half since I landed on South Field, many changes have taken place in Peiping. Yesterday, January 31, the first troops of the Chinese Red Army marched into the city, and Peiping changed from Nationalist to Communist hands. This is a report of some of the things that have happened during this eventful period. It is a report of a siege, a surrender, and a political turnover as they have affected one of China's most important cities during a critical period in the Chinese civil war.

The siege of Peiping began on December 13 and lasted forty days. At the start, there was intense fighting on the perimeter of the city, particularly in the west where the Communists concentrated their initial attack. Both the Communists and Nationalists used mortars and artillery, and the sound of heavy gunfire made the 2 million inhabitants of Peiping realize that the civil war was finally closing in on them.

For about a year before the Communist attack began, Peiping had been a Nationalist island in north China, but it had maintained fairly continuous connections with other islands, such as Tientsin and Kalgan, and normal life in the city had continued without interruption. Now all the railway lifelines out of the city were rapidly and completely blocked by Red troops. Suburban towns within sight of the city walls were occupied by the Communists, and audible sounds of fighting made the war real to people in Peiping for the first time.

In a military sense, however, the warfare around Peiping was never completely real. By the second day of Communist attack, the Nationalist defenders of the city began retreating from their outlying positions and hurried to the sanctuary behind the city walls. The area around Yenching and Tsinghua universities, 6 miles north of Peiping, was in a vacuum by December 14 and was peacefully occupied by Communist soldiers two days later. West Field nearby was taken over about the same time. The Shihchingshan power plant, 15 miles southwest of Peiping, which supplies the city's power and light, was captured by the Communists on December 15. South Field, 5 miles from the city wall, was deserted on December 17 and in Communist hands the next day.

Everywhere, Nationalist troops faded away after the first brief flurry of fighting and moved orderly but rapidly through the massive gates leading into the heart of China's most beautiful city, while the Communists closed in behind them outside the city walls. The Nationalists literally crawled into their shell. Within a week, the fighting had turned into a sitting war, and for many days, only occasional shell explosions or machine-gun bursts disturbed the strange silence.

The so-called front lines stabilized about a mile outside Peiping's walls. Within the defense cordon adjacent to the walls, the Nationalists dug in. Beyond the front lines was a fluid no man's land that varied from a few hundred yards to several miles in width. Beyond that was Communist "liberated territory."

Neither the Nationalists nor the Communists attempted any large-scale attacks once the front lines were drawn. The "battle of Peiping" thereafter consisted simply of local sorties by both sides. A few men were killed, a larger number were injured, and thousands stood their watches cursing the bitterly cold wind that swept down from the north, but once the battle turned into a siege, the most important fighting was carried on with political weapons.

The Nationalist commander at Peiping was General Fu Tso-yi, head of the North China Bandit Suppression Headquarters, who was charged with the defense of all north China against the Communists. General Fu was one of the best military commanders of the Nationalists' side. Starting as a protégé of Shansi warlord Yen Hsi-shan, he later acquired a first-class reputation for his local regime in Suiyuan Province, as well as for his military resistance against the Japanese and his victory over the Communists at Kalgan after the Sino-Japanese War. Politically, Fu was considered progressive, at least by comparison with other local military leaders. Militarily, he enjoyed an outstanding reputation for his tactics of attack and mobility and for his long record of success. Fu's troops were once among the best in China, and even Communist officers are reported to have said, "We know we could beat Fu in battle, but we'd rather not have to try."

By December 13, however, General Fu had already lost the war in north China, and his military position was hopeless. His minimum requirements for any success against the Communists were adequate military supplies and effective employment of "his own" loyal, well-trained Suiyuan troops. For several months prior to December, however, adequate supplies had not been forthcoming from the Central Government, which acted as if it had already abandoned north China, and at the beginning of December, Fu received a fatal blow. The Communists in a decisive battle at the top of the Nankow Pass cut Fu off from his crack troops in Inner Mongolia. Militarily, everything that happened to Fu after that defeat was simply a *coup de grâce*. It was then that he began to withdraw to a militarily hopeless, but politically advantageous, position around Peiping.

From early December on, General Fu was only hypothetically in command of the situation, even in the territory nominally under his control. The bulk of his own troops were in isolated pockets around Kalgan and Kweisui, in the Inner Mongolian provinces of Chahar and Suiyuan, and could not come to his assistance. The troops under his command in Tientsin were largely Central Government soldiers from the south commanded by generals whose loyalty to Fu was doubtful. These forces in Tientsin, furthermore, were also cut off from Fu when the Peiping-Tientsin railway line was severed at the start of fighting around Peiping. Thereafter, Fu was left with a motley collection of units, totaling about 150,000 regular troops, around Peiping.

The morale of the forces directly under General Fu in the Peiping area was dangerously low. The units included elements of at least seven Nationalist armies, together with the equivalent of three cavalry divisions and one tank regiment. There were deep-rooted rivalries between unit commanders, and some of the units were little more than shattered remnants of outfits recently mauled by the Communists. Most important of all, only a small percentage of the troops—estimated from 20 to 30 per cent —were "Fu's own." The rest were southern troops with divided allegiance. Their officers felt no particular loyalty to General Fu, and he was never certain that his orders would be obeyed. Some of his orders, in fact, were not obeyed. In short, the 150,000 Nationalist troops crowded into Peiping were a disorganized, ineffective mass of soldiery, not a strong fighting force.

With this material, Fu Tso-yi knew he could not defeat the Communists. The Communists had grown stronger rather than weaker in recent months. Not only were Nieh Jung-chen's forces in the northwest intact, but Lin Piao's northeastern "Liberation Army" was already pouring south through the Shanhaikuan corridor onto the north China plain after their victories in Manchuria. They brought with them first-class American equipment captured at Mukden and Chinchow. They moved fast and spread like a red flood over north China.

In an age when military technology is characterized by rockets and atom bombs, it may be difficult to realize the defense value of a mud and brick city wall, even when, like the Peiping wall, it is 40 feet high and broader than Fifth Avenue. In China, however, a city wall is still a formidable defense against infantry attack, and retiring behind the Peiping wall gave Fu and his troops temporary sanctuary.

In adopting snail tactics, moreover, General Fu had more than a mere wall protecting him. He made the whole city of Peiping his hostage. As one Chinese observer expressed it, "General Fu Tso-yi holds a beautifully delicate and priceless vase in his fingers. If anyone tries to take it, it will be destroyed." It was generally believed that the Communists not only respected the popular sentiment attached to Peiping, but also had an even more practical reason for wanting to capture the city intact. Political observers predicted that the Communists would establish their national capital in Peiping.

With a knowledge of these facts, and a confidence that no one would dare desecrate their city, the people in Peiping settled down for a long siege, once the first noises of battle had died away. They shrugged their shoulders and went back to the normal business of buying, selling, eating, procreating, and dying. "Peiping has seen many conquerors over the centuries and doesn't pay a great deal of attention to most of them," one philosophical citizen said to me. "People try to carry on as usual."

During the siege, people did carry on as usual, to the best of their ability. At times they showed nervousness ("No one has ever shelled Peiping before!"), annoyance ("We can't even buy pork for New Year!"), or disgust ("Why tear down the archway of Eternal Peace Avenue? They'll never finish building the airfield there anyway!"), but there was never any mass fear or hysteria, even during the most tense moments. The prevailing attitude was resignation, although conditions of siege and martial law temporarily destroyed much of the city's usual charming placidity and saddled ordinary people with a heavy economic burden.

Food and soldiers were the two major problems that complicated and disorganized life in Peiping. There was a shortage of the former and a plethora of the latter.

The economic blockade of Peiping was never 100 per cent complete even though the city was completely surrounded. There were gaps in the line, and a constant trickle of persons and goods slipped in and out the city gates. Persons visiting the front lines or crossing no man's land for the first time (as a correspondent friend and I did on one occasion) were inevitably amazed to see farmers and merchants wandering casually through fields and country lanes, or Nationalist soldiers gathering cabbages to cart into the city. These peculiarities sometimes gave the siege a phony, comic-opera atmosphere. In actual fact, however, the supplies that slipped through the lines were infinitesimal in terms of the needs of the 2 million inhabitants of the city, and the blockade was effective in forcing Peiping to rely upon its own reserves.

The military authorities held stocks of basic grains (wheat, millet, sorghum, etc.) to last out a long siege, but civilian supplies, even including stocks in homes as well as in shops and public warehouses, were definitely limited. Poor people were the ones who suffered. Food experts estimated that perhaps 70 per cent of the population was quite well off, with about two months supply of flour or grain in their homes. Most of the poorest 30 per cent, however, had only two to four days personal reserve. They felt the squeeze. As commercial and public stocks decreased, prices jumped with alarming regularity every day. The price inflation affecting meat, eggs, vegetables, and all foodstuffs other than basic grains was even worse and affected everyone.

For a while, meat and eggs almost disappeared from the market. The civil authorities were concerned about their ever-diminishing supplies of food, and after repeated requests, were able to arrange a few flights to transport food from Tsingtao, but the attempted airlift was completely unsuccessful. Most of the flour bags dropped exploded when they hit the ground, and ironically one of them struck and killed a casual bystander. If the siege had continued for several months, Peiping would have been starved out—or at least many people would have starved. Fortunately, the war ended and trade was resumed before the starvation stage was reached, but the economic blockade caused considerable suffering and hardship before it was over.

Certain groups in the city were particularly hard hit. Thousands of refugees, many of them homeless, received only the barest subsistence, while an increasing number of civil servants failed to get paid because of a shortage of paper money in the hands of government organizations.

The burden of supporting 150,000 soldiers was added to the effects of the blockade to make things worse. Peiping does not normally have billets for a large number of troops, and when the soldiers started moving in, they had to be absorbed by nonmilitary establishments. The billeting process was not well-organized or systematic. It was a sort of human osmosis. At first, the troops took over unessential public buildings, such as schools, and occupied every major temple, palace, and historic site in the city, including the Forbidden City and Temple of Heaven. The men who jammed into these places lacked such essentials as construction materials and fuel, and many of Peiping's beautiful buildings began to suffer a process of slow attrition.

Then, because public places accommodated only a small percentage of the troops, the rest moved into already crowded private homes. Soldiers roamed the streets knocking on doors. "How many rooms and how many people do you have?" they would ask, and if they then said, "we're moving in," there was no appeal to higher authority. Military commanders made only a few efforts to care for their troops, so the men had to fend for themselves, and both civilian and military morale suffered as a result.

The Nationalist troops never got out of hand, and generally speaking, they were well-behaved considering the lack of care given them, but discipline and morale were low, and many small unpleasant incidents occurred between civilians and soldiers. "Hungry soldiers shot my children's pet dog today," a professor said bitterly to me one day. That relatively unimportant fact seemed to symbolize for him the unpleasantness of military occupation.

Every minor need of the troops had to be supplied, in the final analysis, by the civilian population, because there were no regular sources of supply, and requisitioning of all kinds of supplies took place. In addition, civilian manpower was mobilized. The military draft was intensified, and a system of forced labor put into effect; the latter drew thousands of men from their normal work to labor under military direction on defense works. Civilians received no monetary or other remuneration for either their goods or their labor, and the heaviest load fell on the poorest, who could not bluff or buy their way out.

The normal administrative system in the city—the *Pao-Chia* system—was converted into a quasi-military organization to requisition supplies and mobilize labor. The main city districts were given new titles as Military and Civilian Cooperation Stations, and requests, or rather orders, went from the military authorities to *Ch'ü*, or District, Chiefs to be passed on down the line to *Chia* chiefs, who had the unpleasant task of being intermediaries between the army and the civilian population.

One *Chia* of about sixty households was affected as follows during a single two-week period of the siege. In five of the households, soldiers moved in to stay. Three men in the *Chia* were called up in the draft, but all three managed to buy their way out, by hiring substitutes at the prevailing price. Every day the *Chia* had to provide a number of able-bodied men for work in civilian labor gangs. The lowest daily quota during the period was five; the highest was about twenty. During the two weeks, the following things were requisitioned from every household: hay for fodder, lumber, rope, gunny sacks for sandbags, and money. The money levies varied roughly with ability to pay, but the other orders were arbitrary, and any household lacking the specific things requested had to buy them. In addition, certain things such as carpentry tools and extra furniture were "borrowed" by soldiers from households that possessed them. In short, there was no sanctity of either home or pocketbook. What happened in this one *Chia* was duplicated in the rest of approximately 7,000 *Chia* in Peiping.

The psychological strain on ordinary people was almost as great as the economic pressure, even though most people maintained a calm exterior. Martial law was complete. A strict curfew was imposed, starting first at 10, then at 9, and finally at 8 P.M. The streets were ink-black and dead after curfew, and even those with special passes avoided going out at night if they could. Those who had business after dark that could not be postponed until morning walked through the black streets slowly and listened carefully for clicking rifle bolts and the bellowed cries of "Halt," which always came unexpectedly from the unseen, nervous sentries.

A special Discipline Supervisory Corps was established to combat speculation, rumor-mongering, and anything else that might create social disorder. Truck-mounted teams of gendarmes, policemen, and soldiers, carrying submachine guns and huge broad swords, careened through the streets and were ever-present reminders of military rule. These teams had the power of on-the-spot trial and execution. The total number of people actually executed was relatively small, but the appearance of these trucks and their hatchet men was always rather terrifying. Arrests were more numerous than executions, and people had to be careful of what they said and to whom they said it. Spreading rumors was an offense punishable by death, and even facts were considered rumors until they were officially revealed. During the last stages of the siege, "peace-mongering" was also a criminal offense, but those punished were always small fry.

Control of the press, radio, and other media of public opinion was complete. Few facts of either military or political significance were reported until they were outdated or had become general knowledge via the rumor markets, which could never be effectively controlled. News sent abroad was not controlled until January 1, but on that date, strict censorship was imposed on foreign cables also. Peiping became the only place in China with complete censorship of everything.

Under this sort of martial law and military control, civil government took a back seat. It still functioned and carried out ordinary responsibilities, but the military authorities made all important decisions. Civilian leaders were inconspicuous, even though Peiping was overcrowded with them since there were not only the normal municipal officials in the city, but refugee officials from seven north China provinces and municipalities as well.

In addition to the heavy economic and psychological strain endured by the people, there were innumerable minor inconveniences that were extremely irritating. The electric supply was cut off, at first completely and later partially, and people had to relearn ways of groping through darkness and reading by kerosene lamps. The city water supply, dependent upon electric pumps, also failed periodically. People gave up baths for a while, and queued up at the 7,000 private wells in the city to obtain drinking water. Sewage piled up until a working arrangement was made at the front lines for the "honey cart" drivers to move their pungent loads of manure out of the city to the farmers in the countryside.

Although it was the civilian population that was most affected by the siege of Peiping, the troops were not entirely inactive, even though fighting was limited to local skirmishes. Soldiers, together with civilian labor gangs working for them, made feverish defense preparations both inside the city and within the defense perimeter around the walls. The military value of their preparations was questionable, but there was a certain symbolic importance attached to this military activity. The preparations made it clear that Fu Tso-yi was making it even harder to take his delicate, priceless vase, and increased the bargaining power of the defenders—or at least that must have been the theory. The practical effect of the defense preparations, however, was to increase the hardships and burden imposed on ordinary people and to mar permanently some of the beauty of Peiping.

At first, the military authorities concentrated their attention on the job of building airfields within the city wall. This was done with amazing speed. Hordes of forced laborers converted the former glacis and polo field east of Legation Quarter into an airstrip in three or four days, and on December 18, the first transport plane landed there. Within a few days, a second field was completed next to the Temple of Heaven, and a third (which was never completed) was begun on the glacis north of Legation Quarter. The first plane took off from Peiping, re-establishing connection with the outside world, on December 21, and even after the Communists started lobbing mortar shells onto the fields on January 12, some air traffic continued until the day the Communists marched into Peiping. The new airfields never assumed much military importance, however, even though some planes of the Chinese Air Force (which paid almost no attention to Fu's orders and had evacuated from Peiping in utter confusion) started returning. The fields were not important economically either, because the arriving planes brought in almost no supplies (some medicine being a notable exception). The main use to which the fields were put was the evacuation of Very Important Persons and the two-way exchange of political envoys and some mail between Peiping and central China. Although some people had evacuated from Peiping before the siege began, most had stayed on, and a small-scale evacuation of VIP's resumed after the new airfields were opened.

After the first two airfields were completed, the effort to construct military installations was diverted into new channels. Within the city, foxholes and blockhouses were prepared against the improbable eventuality of street fighting. Outside the walls, the countryside was denuded, and the dusty, brown, north China plain was made browner and dustier. A weird honeycomb of ditches was dug, and the pillboxes of all shapes and sizes that were constructed made a crazy-quilt pattern. Everywhere, valuable trees were chopped down to make roadblocks and fence-like traps. In human terms, the most distressing thing was the needless leveling of thousands of poor people's homes around the city walls, ostensibly to provide a good field of fire for the defending troops. Of the thousands made homeless in the process, some received nominal compensation, but only a few were allowed to enter the city. Cynics in Peiping, watching the military vandalism of the defense work, characterized the whole process as one in which "the troops, when in doubt, chop down the trees, demolish everything in sight, and then dig in."

The net effect of all that happened in Peiping during the siege was slow, but definite, social disintegration. No effort was made by the authorities to explain, to either soldiers or civilians, what was being done and why. On top of the past accumulation of dissatisfaction with the ineffective Nationalist regime, the deterioration caused by the siege resulted in the complete undermining of whatever popular support the Nationalist regime had previously enjoyed. No will to resist existed among the rank and file of soldiers or civilians. With few exceptions, people wanted one thing: peace at any price. They hoped that the Communists would take the city soon and finish the siege. Only a small minority looked forward to Communist rule with enthusiasm, but the majority, although skeptical of what Communist rule might mean, no longer had any reservations about accepting it as an alternative superior to existing conditions. Everyone began talking about peace. Those who did anything about it, however, were few.

In a theoretical sense, conditions in Peiping reached the point where the city was ripe for revolution; that is, for some sort of mass action springing from the universal dissatisfaction existing among soldiers and civilians and directed against the authorities. It is significant that not only did no revolution occur, but there were not even any moves to exert mass pressure or influence on the government or army. A few individuals and small groups did exert some pressure on the authorities, but actually the decisions that finally turned the city over to the Communists were made by a handful of men. Ordinary people knew almost nothing of what was going on, and there were no indications that if the top leaders had decided upon a different course—for example, a suicidal defense resulting in widespread destruction and loss of life—the masses of people would have done anything but accept their fate. Political apathy and inertia were stronger even than the universal dissatisfaction. The Chinese Communist revolution finally engulfed Peiping, but it was born full-grown and did not grow gradually within the city itself. The revolution arrived in the form of a powerful peasant army which, after being handed the keys to the city by the Nationalists, marched in, with the political workers following close behind, to take over. This did not happen, however, until a few key individuals had completed the devious maneuvers and negotiations that finally resulted in a face-saving peace settlement.

Despite the lack of mass participation in the decisions that settled the future of Peiping, there were a few people who spoke out in favor of peace. These men, who acted on their own initiative and for a variety of motives, reflected the prevailing public mood, but could not claim to represent the public.

One of the first spokesmen for peace was a man named Liang Shu-ming. Liang, an old scholar and politician whose career dates back to the early days of the Chinese republic, had been a leader of the Democratic League. In an attempt to develop a peace movement, he advocated making Peiping an open city and founded the Peiping Society for the Protection of Public Monuments. Liang was one of the few who could speak openly in favor of peace during the early days of the siege, before General Fu had decided his future course, because his age and reputation as a scholar guaranteed him protection. A number of other persons worked more quietly, without fanfare, trying to influence people in high places. The most important of these was a Yenching University professor of philosophy named Chang Tung-sun, also a leader of the Democratic League.

As time went on, an increasing number of peace advocates came into the open, but this was more an indication of the swing in the attitudes of Fu and other top officials than a sign of increasing intrepidity on the part of the peace advocates themselves. Members of the Peiping City Council and Chamber of Commerce, representatives in Peiping of the Legislative Yüan, Control

Yüan, and National Assembly, and the chairmen of seven north China Provincial and Municipal Councils all added their voices to the general clamor for peace, which became increasingly loud not only in Peiping, but all over the country after Chiang K'ai-shek's New Year's message last month.

Student and faculty groups, composing one of the most anti-government elements in the population, became more active as the end approached. So did the Communist underground. From the first week of January on, mimeographed propaganda sheets appeared in folded newspapers, were received by prominent citizens through the mails, and popped up unexpectedly on shop windows and walls. Actually, however, even the Communist underground played almost no role in preparing the way for a Communist takeover, although it did make preparations to assist in the takeover process once it began.

The final decision as to whether Peiping should make peace—or less euphemistically, surrender—rested with Fu Tso-yi. For a long time after he had pulled in his horns militarily, Fu sat in his Winter Palace headquarters trying to decide what he should do. A man close to Fu says that he changed his mind at least nine times. He knew he could not fight, and yet he felt he could not give up. In spite of the stepchild treatment he had been given by the Central Government, he felt a soldier's loyalty to Chiang. He also knew that the loyalty of some of his subordinates was attached more strongly to Nanking than to himself. Furthermore, if he was going to make peace on his own, some formula had to be found by which he could save face. He kept hoping that Nanking would give up soon, for then he could reach some sort of local settlement with no qualms of conscience. He kept waiting, but in the meantime, he sent out the first quiet peace feelers. From the moment the first feelers were made to the Communists, secret negotiations continued until the final settlement was announced. Fu never made a single public statement of his plans and intentions during this period, however, and public preparations for war continued until the peace agreement was finally revealed.

One of the factors that gradually forced Fu to adopt the course he ultimately chose was that, as Peiping sat out its siege, the remaining Nationalist outposts under his command in north China fell to the Communists, one by one. The first to go was Kalgan, capital of Chahar Province. The Communists captured Kalgan on December 24, after decimating the last important units of Fu's own troops in that area. The Nationalist announcement of

Kalgan's loss significantly pointed out that all the industry in the city had been left intact. "Since these properties belong to the country and the people," the statement said, "government troops have appointed definite persons to protect them with clear hand-over lists on hand." This statement sounded as if someone was trying to butter up the Communists and perhaps prepare the way for dealing with them later on.

On January 15, Tientsin, the largest industrial and commercial metropolis in north China, was captured by the Communists. Even before the 15th, Fu's secret peace negotiators had tentatively agreed to a settlement with the Communists, but the local commanders at Tientsin were not peacefully inclined, and the Communists fought their way into Tientsin before any definite agreement came into effect. The capture of that city finished off all high-priority Communist objectives in north China with the exception of Peiping, and it left the Red Army free to concentrate all its attention here.

The Communists really started putting the pressure on Fu, with political as well as military weapons, as early as December 25. Fu was branded a "major war criminal," along with most other leading Nationalists, but the Communists offered him a pardon if he agreed to give up. Simultaneously, Lin Piao, Commander of the Peiping-Tientsin front "People's Liberation Army," and Lo Jung-huan, his political commissar, broadcast an eight-point program outlining promises "to the people" under Fu.

These eight points, which formed the basis of much subsequent Communist propaganda, were as follows:

1) People's lives and property will be protected. Keep order and don't listen to rumors. Looting and killing are strictly forbidden.

2) Chinese individual commercial and industrial property will be protected. Private factories, banks, godowns, etc., will not be touched and can continue operating.

3) Bureaucratic capital, including factories, shops, banks, godowns, railways, post offices, telephone and telegraph installations, power plants, etc., will be taken over by the Liberation Army, although private shares will be respected. Those working in these organizations should work peacefully and wait for the takeover. Rewards will be given to those who protect property and documents; those who strike or who destroy will be punished. Those wishing to continue serving will be employed.

4) Schools, hospitals, and public institutions will be protected.

Students, teachers and all workers should protect their records. Anyone with ability to work will be employed.

5) Except for a few major war criminals and notorious reactionaries, all Kuomintang officials, police and *Pao-Chia* workers of the Provincial, Municipal, and *Hsien* Governments will be pardoned, if they do not offer armed resistance. They should protect their records. Anyone with ability to work will be employed.

6) As soon as a city is liberated, displaced soldiers should report immediately to the new garrison headquarters, the police bureau, or army authorities. Anyone surrendering his weapons will not be questioned. Those who hide will be punished.

7) The lives and property of all foreigners will be protected. They must obey the laws of the Liberation Army and Democratic Government. No espionage or illegal actions will be allowed. No war criminals should be sheltered. They will be subject to military or civilian trial for violations.

8) People in general should protect all public property and keep order.

These eight points formed the basis of the "city policy" which Lin Piao promised to follow during the takeover period.

On January 5, the north Shensi radio fired another shot at Peiping from the Communists' political arsenal. Lin Piao and Lo Jung-huan issued an "open letter to the Kuomintang officers" in Peiping and Tientsin. In effect, it was an ultimatum that called for surrender or else.

With Peiping, Tientsin, and Tangku completely surrounded, your way of retreat has been completely cut off. Although a few may escape by air or sea, the majority have no hope of escape. Chiang K'ai-shek is powerless to look after himself, and the United States cannot help you either. There is no outside help. If you intend to break through, think of the lessons of Kalgan and Hsuchow. There is only one course for you: Follow the example of Cheng Tung-kuo in Changchun—that is, surrender en bloc. If you do not kill POW's or murder people, and hand over all your weapons, materials, godowns, and local industrial and communications installations intact, we will treat you generously, as we did General Cheng Tung-kuo. The lives of you and your families will be completely protected. As for Fu Tso-yi, although he has been listed as a war criminal, we will give him another chance to repent. If he leads all of you to surrender en masse, we promise protection of his life and property. If you agree, send negotiators to see us. General officers of any rank will be welcomed. Our offensive will soon be launched, so you must make a decision immediately—otherwise, don't say we didn't warn you.

While the Communists' propaganda weapons were laying down this barrage on Peiping, Communists in the city's suburbs were making both military and political preparations for the takeover. Political workers, including some high-ranking persons, began moving in soon after the troops. The people in the suburbs were treated deferentially, with kid gloves. Yenching and Tsinghua universities were encouraged to continue normal activities. The Mentoukou coal mines, Shihchingshan power plant, and other industrial installations resumed operations under new management. Every effort was made to minimize resistance to a Communist takeover and to obtain local support. These efforts paid dividends, because reports favorable to the Communists were carried across the lines into Peiping. In addition, however, the Communists began to construct long scaling ladders to be used to mount Peiping's walls if this became necessary.

With political astuteness, the Communists also played a game of "power politics" with electricity. Peiping had been literally in the dark since the capture of its power plant on December 15 and the cutting of the Tientsin power lines five days thereafter. The Communists over their radio then made a public offer to supply Peiping with electricity across the front lines, stating that they did not want to inconvenience the people. The Nationalist authorities finally accepted the offer in part, and allowed a certain amount of electric current for essential needs to flow into the city, but there was never any official revelation of where the electricity was coming from. People in Peiping soon knew, however, that it was coming from the Communists.

On January 1, the Communists formally established a Military Control Commission for the takeover of Peiping. The commission set up shop in the village of Lianghsiang, southwest of Peiping, and began making preparations to move into the city. It set up its organizations and gathered together personnel. It also started to work in the suburbs of the municipality. Educational cadres established sub-headquarters in the village of Chinglungchiao and began discussing future plans and policies with both students and faculty at Tsinghua. Indoctrination courses and entertainment programs were arranged for the workers at Shihchingshan and elsewhere. Investigations of rural conditions were started. Before the Communists came into Peiping, therefore, they had made considerable preparations for taking over the city.

The chairman of the Military Control Commission from the start was Yeh Chien-ying, forty-five-year-old high-ranking Communist military and political veteran. Born in Kwangtung and educated in a Yunnan military and political school, Yeh joined Sun Yat-sen in 1923, taught in the Kuomintang's Whampoa Military Academy, and fought on the Northern Expedition. He broke with the Kuomintang in 1927, went to study in France and Germany, and then returned to China to become Chief-of-Staff of the Chinese Red Army in Kiangsi, a participant on the Long March, and finally, in 1945, a member of the Communist Central Committee. His experience as one of the negotiators during the 1936 Sian incident, and as Communist representative in the Peiping Executive Headquarters during General Marshall's mediation attempt in 1946, had established him as a top Communist political as well as military leader.

Yeh Chien-ying, in addition to being head of the Military Control Commission, was slated to become Mayor of Peiping once a "People's Government" was set up there. The choice for Vice-Mayor was Hsü Ping, a fifty-year-old German-trained Communist leader who originally came from one of the wealthiest families in Peiping, a family named Hsing.

The complicated developments at Peiping had an even more complicated backdrop on the national scene. Conclusion of a separate peace in Peiping was delayed because Fu Tso-yi kept hoping that Nanking would make some decision that would solve all his problems, or at least leave him in a position to solve his own problems with a clear conscience. The whole country was excited and agitated by a flood of peace rumors. Innumerable conferences, discussions, and meetings took place between important political leaders. Through the haze of confused and confusing rumors, however, it gradually became clear that the "peace movement" was not accomplishing very much and that the road to national peace might be a rocky, and perhaps long, one. The Communists, on the crest of a winning military tide, were in no mood to make important concessions, while the Central Government, crumbling in front of everyone's eyes, hung on and refused to give up or collapse completely.

Concrete steps toward national peace progressed no further than a number of public peace statements by both sides. Nationalist Premier Sun Fo talked about an "honorable peace," while Chiang in his New Year's speeches expressed readiness to negotiate "if the Communists are sincerely desirous of peace," but warned that if they "are not sincerely desirous of peace the government, with no other alternative, will fight to the finish." Chiang added that "the Shanghai-Nanking area, as the political nerve center of the country, will be defended at all costs"; he did not mention north China or Peiping.

The Communists were suspicious of these somewhat ambiguous Nationalist peace feelers, suspecting that all Nanking wanted was a breathing period in the war, and on January 14, Mao Tsetung set forth eight terms on the basis of which he would be willing to negotiate:

(1) Severe punishment of war criminals. (2) Repeal of the bogus constitution. (3) Abolition of the bogus government structure. (4) Reorganization of all reactionary armies in accordance with democratic principles. (5) Confiscation of bureaucratic capital. (6) Implementation of agrarian reforms. (7) Abrogation of all treaties of national betrayal. (8) Convocation of a Political Consultative Conference, without participation by reactionary elements, in order to form a Democratic Coalition Government to take over the authority of the reactionary Kuomintang Government in Nanking and of its affiliated organizations in the provinces.

These were not the sort of terms Nanking would jump to accept, and national peace began to look remote again.

On January 12, the Communists began lobbing random artillery and mortar shells into Peiping, just to show that they could make things pretty nasty if they wanted to. Although almost every shell killed one or two people, the over-all damage was not great, but the shells had the desired psychological effect on Peiping, as did the bombardment of Tientsin which started immediately thereafter.

All of these military and political developments influenced General Fu and gradually forced him to conclude that he would probably have to make a separate peace with the Communists. It is uncertain when Fu actually made up his mind, but he sent out his first secret negotiators on January 6. Possibly, he did not finally make up his mind until Chiang decided to leave Nanking on January 21, but the negotiations initiated on January 6 paved the way for the final peace agreement.

The man sent out by Fu to see the Communists was Chang Tung-sun, the Yenching professor and Democratic Leaguer. He went to Chihsien, about 60 miles north of Peiping, accompanied by Chou Pei-feng. Chou, a former adviser of Fu in Suiyuan, had been captured by the Communists in 1947 and then later released. In Peiping, he was head of Fu's land reform bureau. Both Chang and Chou had friends on the Communist side. They met with General Lin Piao and spent three days discussing peace terms, finally reaching a kind of tentative agreement. These first steps failed to crystallize into anything definite, however, one reason being that some of Fu's most powerful subordinate generals in Peiping, including Cheng Ting-feng, Shih Chüeh, and Teng Wen-chao, opposed independent peace moves.

On January 13 Fu sent a second negotiator, General Teng Pao-shan. Teng, an old-time Kuomintang commander, had at one time, while at Yulin in north Shensi during the Sino-Japanese war, concluded a local truce with the Communists, and he too had Communist friends. Chou Pei-feng again went along. These two men talked with Lin Piao, Lo Jung-huan, and Nieh Jung-chen near Tungchow, east of Peiping. Peace terms were once again discussed and a tentative settlement agreed upon. There are two different accounts of when this tentative agreement was reached. According to one story, the agreement was made on January 16, the day following the Communists' capture of Tientsin. According to another account, however, it was made on January 14, and had a proviso that both Peiping and Tientsin would be included if the latter was not captured by the Communists within twelve hours. The fall of Tientsin on January 15 limited the problem to Peiping, in any case, and two days later, Teng and Chou returned to Peiping with a Communist named T'ao, who was Lin Piao's Chief-of-Staff, to work out the final details.

The general public in Peiping knew nothing of the progress of these negotiations, or even of their existence, for they were shrouded in complete secrecy. Communist shells continued to fall into the city, making all peace rumors sound rather absurd. The public's hope for peace and its undivided attention were focused upon the activities of a newly formed organization called the North China People's Peace Promotion Committee, under ex-Mayor Ho Szu-yüan. This self-appointed group of prominent citizens, who claimed to represent the "people's organizations" in Peiping—and actually did, in regard to their views about peace —obtained clearance from General Fu to make a trip across the lines as a peace mission. Their trip was delayed when two freak shells landed on Ho's home, killing a daughter and wounding most of the family, but the committee finally started out in a rattling bus on January 18. In the western suburbs, they talked with a Communist political officer named Mu Wen-hua and then returned the following day, "hopeful" about peace prospects, but without anything definite to tell the public.

The window dressing that the Peace Promotion Committee's mission provided prepared the public only partially for the immi-

nent peace, and the end came suddenly and somewhat unexpectedly. On January 21, Chiang K'ai-shek announced his temporary
"retirement" from the Nanking Government. This act released
both Fu Tso-yi himself and his subordinate Central Government
generals from loyalty to Chiang's government. Things happened
rapidly after that. Everyone agreed to a separate peace.

A cease-fire went into effect at ten o'clock on the morning of
January 22, and that night, Fu Tso-yi's headquarters announced
to the public that a peace agreement had been signed. Forty days
after it began, the siege was formally ended. The city breathed a
tremendous sigh of relief.

The thirteen-point peace agreement concluded between General Fu and the Communists was basically nothing more than a
surrender, but it was in the classic tradition of Chinese compromise and saved face for everyone involved. The preamble stated
that both sides had agreed upon the necessity of peace because of
the "public desire for peace" and asserted that the agreement
aimed to "bring forth the early realization of a nationwide and
thorough peace." The agreement provided for the establishment,
for the "transitional period," of a Joint Administrative Office
with representatives of both sides to handle "all military and political problems."

All Nationalist troops within Peiping belonging to army groups
—i.e., combat troops—were to be moved out of the city, starting
on January 22, with their original unit designations (a face-saving
proposition that Fu had insisted upon), to be "reorganized about
a month after arrival at designated areas" (i.e., incorporated into
the Red Army). Construction of military fortifications was to
be stopped immediately. A few troops were to remain in the city
to help maintain order.

According to the agreement, all public organizations and government bodies were to maintain the *status quo* and carry on
pending "over-all settlement by the Joint Administrative Office."
The personnel of these organizations were guaranteed safety. The
agreement also stated that Gold Yüan currency would circulate
until further notice, that newspapers could carry on as usual until
reregistration and examination later on, and that postal and
telegraphic connections with outside places would be maintained.
It specifically promised protection of foreigners' lives and property. Furthermore, it guaranteed freedom of religion and protection of cultural monuments and relics. Finally, it exhorted all the
people to "carry on life as usual."

The turnover, in short, was to be made painlessly, and the sur-

render was made to look like the establishment of a coalition—
for the "transitional period." The Nationalists remaining in Peiping lost a minimum of face, and the Communists obtained
peaceful entry into the city and the promise that everyone would
cooperate in turning over power to them.

Peiping became the first major city in the Chinese civil war to
come under Communist control by peaceful agreement between
Communist and Nationalist leaders, rather than by capture or outright military surrender. The local agreement for Peiping established a new pattern, at a critical juncture in the Chinese civil
war, which might be copied elsewhere by local Nationalist commanders in a militarily hopeless position. Peiping also became
one of the most logical places in China for an over-all national
peace to be negotiated. Before the Communists moved into the
city, two unofficial representatives flew up from the south, apparently with the intention of being in Peiping when the Communists took over. These men were unofficial representatives of Li
Tsung-jen, Acting President of the Nationalist Government, and
Pai Ch'ung-hsi, Nationalist commander in central China. It began
to look as if Peiping might be the stage for national peace negotiations—as well as for the Communist-sponsored Political Consultative Conference and the establishment of a Communist government for the whole country.

The peace agreement for Peiping went into effect on January
22, but the first Communist troops did not enter the city until
yesterday, January 31. During the interim eight-day period, Peiping was in a strange vacuum.

Throughout the eight days, airplanes continued to arrive from
Nationalist territory, and to depart for Nationalist cities with last-
minute evacuees. Fu Tso-yi had insisted that those who wanted
to leave should be allowed to go. The last stragglers of the Kuomintang secret service and of Fu's recalcitrant subordinate generals boarded C-47's and left Peiping—even though the city was
theoretically in Communist hands.

Pictures of Chiang K'ai-shek disappeared from the walls, but
no substitute faces replaced them immediately. Occasionally, an
artillery shell burst inside the city, although no one was supposed to be fighting. A few of the shells came from the guns of
obstinate Nationalist units, particularly those belonging to the
Thirteenth Army, who did not want to surrender even after they
were ordered to do so. Others may have been fired by isolated
Communist gunners who were not sure what was going on. There
were reports that 1,000–2,000 gendarmes had disbanded without

giving up their weapons. This worried the public, which feared there might be incidents when the Communists marched in. Prices zoomed. People did not know how much Nationalist money would be worth when the Communists issued their own. General nervousness, plus the fact that Peiping's prices were gradually rising to the level of those in other cities under Communist control, increased inflationary pressures even though the gates of Peiping were opened and trade began to resume.

The public did not know what was going on. Neither did many people whose business it was to try to know. The entire corps of foreign and Chinese newspaper correspondents could not locate a single representative, either military or political, of the city's new Communist rulers. The few who were in the city, and had been there for several days, were elusive; in fact they were invisible.

Nationalist troops, many still armed, wandered freely through the streets. Their numbers thinned out as the evacuation proceeded, but the process was very gradual. Everyone in Peiping, however, including government employees, ordinary civilians, and the soldiers who stayed on, continued about their normal business, slightly mystified but patiently waiting for something to happen.

A few things did happen gradually. Communist propaganda in larger quantities appeared on walls throughout the city, and anti-Communist slogans were blotched out. Political prisoners were rapidly released from the jails. Chiang K'ai-shek's residence and other places were prepared by the Nationalists for expected Communist leaders. Student groups and others worked hard to print propaganda, plan parades, learn songs and dances, and generally prepare for the Communists' entrance. The Communist underground began slowly to emerge from the shadows, and some of its representatives made unofficial visits to heads of many organizations and institutions. These representatives often popped out of unexpected places. In one hospital, for example, a humble dresser began having serious talks with the director. At a higher level, General Fu and other officials held endless conferences and tried to carry out the peace agreement as smoothly as possible.

The main delay in the turnover was caused by the slowness of evacuating Nationalist troops. Some of the troops caused trouble, and it took time to evacuate even those who left without arguing.

Finally, however, the vanguard of Communist troops, together with a few propaganda trucks, began entering the west gates of the city yesterday. They marched in solemnly, to billets previously arranged for them, and they looked a little tense and worried. Their arrival caused no particular stir among the general population. There were no huge crowds to greet them, and the ordinary civilians watching from the curbs along their route seemed to express no emotion more intense than curiosity. This was true even of the scattered Nationalist troops, who also stood on the curbs and watched silently.

The lack of any sort of excitement when the first troops marched in was striking. "The Communists have arrived," one man said. "And prices have gone up," said his companion. The word was passed around that a big parade would be held soon. A pedicab driver was unimpressed. "Anyone can put on a parade," he remarked; "even the Japanese did." A philosophical cook observed that "the Chinese people are like blades of grass. They lean the way the wind is blowing." The people of Peiping leaned toward the Communists, but the first reception given to the entering troops indicated that the Communists would be working in an environment characterized by skeptical pragmatism. People would wait and see what happened before they got emotional —if, indeed, they ever did. Communist political workers, with their decorated trucks, lively folk dances, songs, and propaganda, toured the streets and put on a good show, however. They attracted interested crowds wherever they went, and children followed the propaganda trucks as if they were Pied Pipers.

Today, the first of February, ten days since the cease-fire, the Communists have made their first moves toward actually taking over the city. They began with organizations whose business is influencing public opinion. The Kuomintang Central News Agency and North China *Daily News* were converted into the New China News Agency and the *People's Daily*, respectively, and the radio station was also taken over. Other organizations await their turn.

The first session of the Joint Administrative Office also took place today, in the Summer Palace outside Peiping. This office, functioning under Lin Piao's Peiping-Tientsin Front Command, has the responsibility of turning the city over as rapidly as possible to the Communist Military Control Commission, which will then turn it over, ultimately, to the Communists' Peiping People's Government and Garrison Command. The Chairman of the Administrative Office, as well as of the Control Commission and the People's Government, is Yeh Chien-ying. Altogether, there are seven members in the Joint Administrative Office—four Communist and three Kuomintang. The six besides

Yeh have been placed in three committees, each of which has one Communist and one Kuomintang member. On the military committee are T'ao Chu and Kuo Tsung-fen, the former a ranking Communist general and the latter one of Fu Tso-yi's Vice-Commanders who is closely associated with Yen Hsi-shan. On the political and cultural committee are Hsü Ping and Chiao Shih-tsai, the latter Fu's Secretary-General and the former a university professor in the Peiping Normal College. The economic and financial committee is composed of Jung Tsu-ho, finance chief of the Communists' North China People's Government, and Chou Pei-feng.

Fu Tso-yi has slipped into temporary oblivion and is alternately reported to be in Suiyuan or the western suburbs of Peiping. The Communists have come to stay.

The political "turnover" of Peiping has been completed today, in a formal sense. The political "takeover," however, has just begun. A big victory parade scheduled for day after tomorrow will probably mark the beginning of many changes. So far, the question marks concerning what the Communists are like, and what they will do, remain question marks. Two million people in Peiping, including myself, are waiting for answers.

22

TAKEOVER AND CONSOLIDATION

Peiping
February, 1949

Yesterday, February 27, I achieved the dubious distinction of appearing in print on the front page of the official Communist newspaper in Peiping. In the *People's Daily*, I was listed along with sixteen others of various nationalities who are correspondents or contributors to foreign news agencies and newspapers. The list of our names was appended to an order issued by the Peiping Military Control Commission that said: "during the present military period [which was not defined], all foreign news agencies and newspapermen are forbidden to carry on any of their activities in this city." Apparently, thinking that this was not sufficiently clear, the Commission added that both "sending news dispatches" and "gathering news" are forbidden.

This official act lowering the "bamboo curtain" on news sent out from Peiping has not been entirely unexpected. It became clear soon after the Communist entry into the city that non-Communist foreign observers were *persona non grata*. It was unclear until yesterday whether this was in accord with a definite policy, and it is still not clear whether the policy is a short- or long-term one. But the Communists have effectively prevented foreigners from fully reporting current developments, in any case. No foreigners (except, perhaps, for a handful in the Communists' own ranks), whether consuls, newspapermen, businessmen, students, or what have you, have talked with a single ranking Communist leader in the month since the city was taken. Nor have any been allowed to enter the inner sanctum of a single important Communist office. Even mass demonstrations and meetings have been out of bounds for curious foreigners, since a week or so after the Communists' arrival. In innumerable ways, the Communists have gradually isolated foreigners from the Chinese community as a whole, as well as from the Communists themselves.

Because of this fact, no "inside story" of the Communist takeover of Peiping can be told by an outsider such as myself. Along with the other foreigners here, I have had to endure the frustration of being on the spot, yet knowing precious little of the story of what has taken place. Nevertheless, certain aspects of the takeover have been clear, even to a person on the fringe of events, and this is a report on some of my impressions during the takeover period.

"The takeover of Peiping is almost complete," according to an article printed this morning in the *People's Daily*. In roughly a month, Peiping has been "liberated" and consolidated into the rapidly expanding territory controlled by the Chinese Communist Party. From now on, cartographers the world over will color it red.

The Communist takeover of Peiping has been systematic, undramatic, and bloodless, without any of the violence and terror that often mark the accession to power of a revolutionary army. No violence was called for, because the city was plucked like a piece of ripe fruit. Furthermore, to the Chinese Red Army, Peiping was neither the beginning nor the end of their military struggle; it was merely one further step on their way.

The first solemn Communist troops entered the city walls on January 31, after a ten-day interregnum following Fu Tso-yi's "peace agreement," and they marched past curbs lined with silent civilians who were, for the most part, unemotional and undemonstrative and seemed to show neither antipathy nor enthusiasm, but rather a simple curiosity about their "liberators," their new rulers. The Communist troops that came in on January 31 and February 1 were the new garrison forces, and when they were finally settled in prearranged barracks, the Communists had "secured" Peiping in a military sense.

The garrison troops were the advance guard, and after their arrival, it was considered safe for the political and administrative bodies to move in and start functioning. On February 1, the Joint Administrative Office, composed of both Nationalist and Communist members, held its first session and mapped out plans for facilitating the transfer of power. On the same day, the Military Control Commission, which had been formed some time previously in the suburbs, and the People's Government, destined to be the new municipal authority, were officially and formally organized. The new Peiping Garrison Headquarters began to function at the same time.

The Communists went about the takeover in a businesslike way, and the process was not unlike the reorganization of a bankrupt corporation. The old regime in Peiping had been placed in receivership by Fu Tso-yi's surrender, and the Nationalist representatives in the Joint Administrative Office were assigned the job of revealing all remaining assets. (This Office quickly slipped into the background.) The Military Control Commission acted as receiver and was the supreme local authority during bankruptcy proceedings. Its job was to take possession of the Nationalists' assets, and then to pass them on to the Peiping People's Government and other Communist administrative and governmental organs. The People's Government, in the meantime, took over the most important assets, as well as most of the personnel, of the previous municipal government and began to function in a modest way.

The period of receivership has not yet ended, but the Military Control Commission has already completed the takeover of most of the important Nationalist assets in Peiping, and in due time, the Commission will probably complete its tasks and either pass out of existence or take a back seat.

The Communists' takeover of Peiping was obviously preceded by considerable thought and preparation. The process seemed slow at times, but it followed a definite and logical pattern. Probably because they did not have enough trained political workers to take over all Nationalist organizations and institutions simultaneously, the Communists proceeded gradually, step by step, and took control of various bodies according to their priority rating.

The first organizations affected were the obvious instruments of power, thought control, and propaganda. On February 1, the *North China Daily News*, Central News Agency, and Central Broadcasting Station were transformed into the *People's Daily*, New China News Agency, and New China Broadcasting Station. With as little fuss as a chameleon changing color, these organizations abruptly changed their propaganda line and continued operations. On February 2, a new police commissioner installed himself in office, and the Bureau of Police became the Bureau of Public Security. The new commissioner brought a few assistants along with him, but no policemen. The protectors of law and order simply continued on their old beats. Within a relatively short period of time, however, the police force was disarmed and its personnel reduced. Its members became little more than traffic cops, and real responsibility for law and order passed to the garrison troops, who had arms and ammunition.

The government printing plant was also taken over on February 2 and immediately began printing People's Bank notes to replace the Nationalist Gold Yüan. Preliminary steps were taken to transform the Central Bank of China into the People's Bank soon thereafter. The way in which the takeover of the printing plant was accomplished illustrates some of the Communists' methods of working. It was described to me by a former official of the Central Bank who assisted the Communist political worker in charge of financial matters for Peiping and Tientsin. "This man asked me to take him to the printing office," the Central Bank official said. "There, we had a twenty-minute interview with the man in charge, the former deputy manager. After this conversation the Communist said 'Let's visit the plant.' There he gave the place a quick once-over, asked a number of questions about organization, production, methods, and wages and then turned to the deputy manager. 'You seem to know what you're doing. You're in charge,' he said. He handed over the new plates for People's Bank notes and ordered the plant to continue normal operations." If later developments followed the same procedure as in some other organizations, the Communists probably installed their own people in top posts, but continued operations without any great changes. The Central Bank official was greatly impressed, however, by the initial takeover, and by the Communist political worker who carried it out: by his frankness and directness, his knowledge and apparent competence, his lack of old-style ceremony, his willingness and authority to make on-the-spot decisions, and his energy. "He sleeps on the floor next to the desk in his office!" the Central Bank official exclaimed with a note of awe in his voice.

During their first days in Peiping, the Communists not only began a takeover of key organizations, but also carried out an intensive sales promotion campaign. Once the garrison and police force were theirs, they had a monopoly of the instruments of force in the city, but in dealing with the population as a whole, they relied primarily on persuasion. They organized parades and mass meetings and used all the propaganda techniques at their disposal to sell themselves to the people.

The first big demonstration was held on February 3. The occasion was a monster victory parade, and it was a spectacular show. Thousands of people assembled in the square south of Chien Men, the front gate of the Tatar city. Hundreds waved colored paper pennants scrawled with slogans. Brass bands blared. Propaganda trucks crawled slowly through the crowd, distributing leaflets to everyone. Professional dancers wearing opera costumes and heavy make-up performed the Communist theme-dance, the Yangko, or Rice Transplanting Dance (a folk dance that combines elements of the Big Apple, the Charleston, and the Shag). Many non-professionals tried it too. Huge cloth banners with Communist slogans written in large black characters were hoisted above the crowd. Portraits of Mao Tse-tung and other Chinese Communist leaders, some pasted against large red-paper stars, were prominently displayed. And the most brilliant touches of color, standing out against the drab grey mass of people, were several crimson Communist flags, each with the hammer and sickle emblem forming a yellow patch in the upper left-hand corner.

The assembled thousands came not as individuals but as groups, and therefore represented the most effectively organized sections of the population. Student groups, government employees, guild and labor union members, and others were turned out en masse. They watched, and some joined, an extremely impressive parade of Communist military might. For roughly six hours, the Red Army put on a show of force that made it quite clear to everyone present that they had not captured Peiping by bluff. Infantrymen, motorized troops, armored cars, tanks, artillery, and cavalry (part of the equipment was American and part Japanese) poured in one city gate, through several main streets, and out another gate, in a steady stream. The troops were well-equipped and tightly disciplined. They marched through the city unsmilingly, with eyes front, or rode through sitting on their vehicles, with backs almost as stiff and erect as the bayoneted rifles between their knees. This army looked very different from the demoralized Nationalists. It looked like a powerful fighting force. By the time the parade was over, the onlookers were tired and impressed.

However, except for the organized groups that turned out or were turned out to provide this official welcome to the Communists, not many ordinary citizens bothered to watch. Even among the organized spectators, there was no wild spontaneous outburst of emotion. A sort of happy-go-lucky carnival atmosphere prevailed throughout the crowd, and the students were excitedly enthusiastic, but the parade did not noticeably disturb the apathy of a large part of Peiping's populace. When this fact was reported by certain foreign correspondents, it aroused the righteous indignation of both the Communists and their strongest supporters, and for almost three weeks thereafter, the local press reverberated with bitter recrimination against the calumny of "foreign imperialist newspapermen" and rapturous praise for the "joyous welcome" given to the Communist "liberators" on February 3.

More mass demonstrations followed. On February 7, a Workers' Mass Meeting of sizable proportions was held on the glacis east of the former Legation Quarter, the field that Fu Tso-yi had made into an airstrip. On February 12, there was a tremendous Liberation Parade and Meeting in front of the Forbidden City, where top Communist leaders addressed the people. For the latter meeting, every *Pao* in the city was ordered to turn out some of its citizens to participate.

These were the big shows, but in addition, there were innumerable smaller ones. Student teams and army propaganda groups toured the streets, gave lectures, passed out leaflets. The press and radio got into the groove and repeated innumerable proclamations, official orders, and editorials praising the Communists. Two large Communist information centers were set up, and in them, eager political workers from the Red Army Political Department answered questions about the Communists and their policies. Communist slogans were painted all over the place. Posters by the thousands were pasted on walls, store windows, telephone poles. The red star and Mao's portrait replaced the Kuomintang's twelve-pointed white star and Chiang's portrait. Even the apathetic sections of the population gradually got the idea that something new had been added to Peiping.

The theme of the Communist takeover was "liberation"—from "Kuomintang reactionaries and American imperialists"—and the beginning of an era of "New Democracy." Many people who had been bitterly anti-Kuomintang did experience a sensation of political liberation. A larger number of people felt liberated during the first few days in a more prosaic way—from the stringent blockade of the siege, from the curfew, and from the thousands of Nationalist soldiers who had been billeted in their homes. (Some Communist troops were also billeted in homes, but they were fewer in number, and were usually put in large homes of wealthy people, so the average citizen was much less affected than under the Nationalists.)

The parades and all the ballyhoo did not interrupt the less dramatic but more important tasks of taking over the city, however, and on February 4, General Yeh Chien-ying, the appointed Communist chief of both the Military Control Commission and the People's Government, walked casually into the municipal government building, made an informal speech, and assumed his job as new mayor. In his speech, Yeh said, "We've been living in the hills right along, and we know much less than you gentlemen about municipal government. Henceforth, we must learn from you." This sort of humility was characteristic of the Communists' line in taking over many organizations, but the Communists did not hesitate to start issuing orders, and soon began teaching as well as learning. The mildness of these first official contacts with the Communists, however, surprised and pleased many persons who had been apprehensive of the takeover, and in many respects Peiping reacted like a small puppy which, when told to roll over, turns over meekly. During the first weeks of the takeover, there was almost no resistence on the part of non-Communists and almost no violence on the part of the Communists.

A catalogue of dates on which specific organizations were taken over by the Communists would be of no great interest or significance. Suffice it to say that the list included all military, political, economic, and cultural organizations that had previously been a part of, or under the control of, the Kuomintang and the Central Government, and all of their administrative, provincial, and local subdivisions. In addition, it included organizations and enterprises formerly the personal property of prominent Kuomintang leaders, property the Communists label "bureaucratic capital." Government offices, communications, transport, utilities, banks, hospitals, museums, schools, factories, and mines in the above categories have all been placed, or are scheduled to be placed, under Communist management. Private institutions and enterprises, except for so-called "bureaucratic capital," were not included in the initial takeover. In short, the takeover, in addition to being a transfer of power, has been a transfer of ownership, in which the new government has taken possession of what had belonged to the old regime. In human terms, it has been somewhat like a game of musical chairs. The top personnel of key organizations, together with certain titles and names, have been reshuffled and changed overnight, but the organizations continue to function much as they did before. There are new stamps at the post office, new money at the banks, and new name plates on the doors, but the same offices and administrative organizations continue. The Communists may plan to carry out a more drastic housecleaning and reorganization in the future, but they have begun slowly and cautiously.

No steps have been taken so far to sovietize the government. This still lies in the future, according to current party doctrine. The major administrative districts have been retained, and they are now headed by Communist appointees, put in as "elected" representatives. The *Pao-Chia* system has already fallen into disrepute, however, and although it still carries out some functions, nobody calls a *Pao* a *Pao* or a *Chia* a *Chia*. The system may get a new name, or it may be abolished and replaced by something else, after the present transitional period is over.

As these facts indicate, the first stage of the Communist revolution in Peiping has been mild, and in a sense, no revolutionary changes have occurred, although the way is now clear for the Communists to introduce revolutionary changes when they decide to do so. For most people in Peiping, who do not even try to look very far into the future, the change of regime has been a sugar-coated pill that has been easy to swallow. It is difficult to predict, however, what the popular reaction will be in the future, if the medicine becomes stronger and the sugar coating is dispensed with.

It is difficult, in fact, even to analyze exactly what the reaction of various persons and groups has been to date. It is safe to say, however, that, apart from a few diehards with strong vested interests in the old regime, and a few Kuomintang troops and secret-service men who have gone underground, there has been no real opposition to the Communists. Almost everyone has accepted the Communists as the wave of the future in China. Their acceptance takes various forms, though, ranging from enthusiastic optimism or moderate hopefulness to passive acquiescence or cynical resignation. On the basis of my limited observation, I would say that a large part, if not the majority, of professors, students, professional workers, intellectuals, and the like, together with certain labor leaders, fall into the first category and are enthusiastic about what they believe the Communists will do for China. In my opinion, most other people, the numerical majority of the population, are either moderately hopeful, passively acquiescent, or cynically resigned.

Student groups have been invaluable allies of the Communists in the takeover period and have worked energetically to help transform Peiping into a Communist-controlled city. It probably is not going too far to say that the Communists would have had a difficult time getting along without them. Although only a few students are members of the Communist Party, almost all of them in Peiping now accept its credo of "New Democracy" and have worked tirelessly and idealistically to assist the Communists. In addition to carrying out widespread propaganda activities, which has been their most important service to the Communists, they have provided a reservoir of manpower for minor political tasks that has been particularly useful because of the Communists' shortage of political workers. Almost 500 students went to work for the Military Control Commission soon after it was set up. They have been kept busy doing such things as making surveys, giving indoctrination lectures in schools, *Pao*, and *Chia*, and helping to "re-educate" teachers in primary and high schools (whose textbooks, incidentally, are to be re-edited and whose students are to have their outside reading "supervised"). They have done various sorts of leg work as well.

At times, the exuberant students have wanted to move faster than the Communists themselves. For example, although the Communists have taken over the major public universities in Peiping, they have not yet introduced any startling innovations, but in many institutions, both public and private, pressure for immediate changes has come from the students themselves. The students have also reorganized their self-governing bodies and formed an enlarged and strengthened Peiping Student Union, which will take part in the All-China Student Congress scheduled to convene in Peiping tomorrow, March 1. The students, in fact, have been almost too exuberant to suit the Communists at times. The authorities flatly forbade them to hold one demonstration they had planned.

During the takeover period, the students have been on vacation, but classes are scheduled to reopen shortly. When studying resumes, however, the traditional three R's of education will have been increased to four: reading, 'riting, 'rithmetic, and revolution. The students are now much more interested in revolution than in normal study, and the Communists, who are well aware of this fact, have set in motion a tremendous scheme to mobilize students for revolutionary activities. The Communists' North China University and Political and Military University are attracting many students from established institutions in Peiping. In addition, the Communists have specially appealed to students to join two other newly organized bodies. One is the North China People's Revolutionary University, which will give a four-month training course for political workers. The other is the Southgoing Corps (Southgoing Working Group), which is organizing political workers to send along with the Red Army in the near future as it moves south, to help take over new areas. The Communists have appealed for 10,000 persons to join each of these groups! Students have already responded to these appeals in hundreds, perhaps thousands, and are flocking to take the necessary examinations. It is not yet clear what effect this will have on older established educational institutions in Peiping, but if the figures already published are correct, the existing student bodies of some of these institutions will be virtually wiped out.

The relationship between the Communists and the students is one of mutual support. News of student activities is given more front-page space in the local Communist newspaper than any other single subject, and the "people's opinions," which take up most of the back page of the official daily, come largely from student groups. Mao Tse-tung and Chu Teh have recently made personal statements arousing student enthusiasm, and the forthcoming, officially sponsored All-China Student Congress will doubtless spur further student activity. Recently, also, the Communists have given a lot of publicity to their Youth Corps (Youth League). The Communists, in other words, have placed a great deal of emphasis upon the importance of harnessing and directing the energy and idealism of student groups. It is a policy that seems to be paying dividends. It may become increasingly important, furthermore, as the Communists take over more urban areas, for although the students are not competent to do many of the things that they, in their enthusiasm, think they can do, they certainly can be put to work by the Communists doing many important minor jobs.

The reaction to the Communists on the part of other groups is harder to judge, because no other group is as active or articulate as the students. In Communist propaganda, however, organized labor is given considerable attention—although in Peiping it has been given less attention than the students. Peiping is not an industrial city, but certain lines of labor policy have been vaguely discernible, nevertheless, in the actions taken in the few plants operating here. The Communists have started to organize their own unions, to replace former Kuomintang unions (in private plants, as well as the ones "taken over"), and have exhorted workers to adopt a "learning attitude" and to study Marxism and "New Democracy." The workers have been encouraged and urged above all to increase production for the revolutionary cause. To date, however, there has been little talk of such basic union issues as collective bargaining rights and increased wages, and in the short period during which Communist labor policy has been implemented here, it seems to have followed a line similar to that of Kuomintang policy, in the sense that the approach to unionism and labor generally seems to be primarily political rather than economic. I do not know how laborers in Peiping have reacted to the new regime, but undoubtedly some have responded favorably to the Communists' effort to raise the level of their political self-consciousness. The Communists repeat ad infinitum, in their policy statements and propaganda, that they are a workers' and peasants' party, and they attempt in many ways to increase the feeling of importance and sense of dignity among laborers. My guess is that, as a result, many workers in Peiping feel that the new government is more interested in their welfare than the previous one. It is also possible, however, that some workers have been disappointed because no spectacular change has yet taken place in their earnings. If any of them expected the millennium immediately after the "liberation," they have been disappointed, because the scanty available reports indicate that wages are being kept at approximately their "pre-liberation" level, for the present at least.

Compared with conditions during the siege, however, economic conditions in Peiping have improved greatly during the past month. Railway connections to all parts of Communist territory were restored speedily after the Communists took over, and trade began to reopen. With the economic blockade ended, prices soon began to follow a downward curve.

The exchange of Nationalist GY currency for the Communist JMP (Jen Min, or People's, Currency) started on February 4 and continued until February 22. Sixty-five exchange points were designated, and two different exchange rates established. One was a general rate of ten GY to one JMP, while the other was a special "complimentary" rate of three to one for all workers and special groups such as students, up to a maximum of $500 per person. When the exchange was completed, over one-half of the GY turned in had been exchanged at the special rate, according to official figures.

The first public reaction to JMP, like the reaction to many other things, was skeptical, one reason being that the notes were poorly printed on low-grade paper. Many merchants began quoting prices in silver dollars, and a large open curb-market for silver and American dollars grew and festered on the corner of a major thoroughfare. People wondered whether or not JMP had any better backing than GY. The value of JMP in terms of silver dollars and American currency began to depreciate rapidly (and is still depreciating). This did not affect ordinary people very much, however, because in terms of basic commodities such as grain, JMP managed to maintain a constant value, and then gradually increased in purchasing power as trade grew and commodities became more plentiful. Finally, this morning, the circulation of silver dollars was banned, although people were not forced to surrender them immediately, but could do so as they wished at an official rate. No regulations have yet appeared regarding foreign currencies, but it is reported that an official exchange rate for American dollars is being discussed.

In general, the Communists' approach so far to the economic situation in Peiping seems to have been based on a desire to avoid disrupting normal production and trade as much as possible, and to introduce only a few changes during this transitional period. Even the cumbersome, inefficient tax structure that the Nationalists had used has been restored. In the economic field, however, a few innovations have been introduced, although it is too early to say what effects they will have. A municipal cooperative system is now in the process of organization, with the announced purpose of eliminating the "skinning" of people by middlemen. (These are not, of course, the first cooperatives in Peiping, but they appear to have stronger official backing than previous ones.) And a state-owned commercial company has been set up. The latter, the Peiping Trade Company, has several purchasing branches and fifty-five sales agents or outlets for selling daily necessities, such as flour, coal, vegetable oil, and salt, at fixed prices slightly below the prevailing open market quotations, to stabilize the price level.

The payment of wages and salaries in kind has already become even more firmly established, in the short time the Communists have been in Peiping, than it was under the Nationalists, who also used the system extensively. But whereas the Nationalists usually gave out wheat flour in wage payments, the Communists are now paying wages with coarse grains such as millet. There has been no enthusiasm about this change, and there is grumbling about what has already been labeled the "Communist millet economy." A few civil servants who have not received any pay since the "liberation" have an added reason for grumbling—under their breath.

In the long run, whether or not the Communists can win and ensure firm popular support in a city such as Peiping will depend to a large extent on their ability to solve basic economic problems, because the average Chinese is a pragmatic person who will judge the Communists on the results of their policies. Most people in Peiping are still reserving judgment. Land-reform slogans do not interest them very much, and they are waiting to see what happens regarding inflation, taxes, and wages.

Peiping people have a certain smug feeling of superiority as sophisticated, cosmopolitan urbanites that, in addition to all other factors, influences their attitude toward the Communists. The city is full of yokel stories about the hicks from the country who are trying to run their city, about how Communist soldiers use latrines for wash basins, and how they would rather sleep on wooden boards than on soft beds. Whether or not the jokes circulated are true is unimportant, because true or not they indicate a widespread attitude that will probably induce the Communists to move slowly in making changes. Any Communist failures will provide the raw material for more jokes, and ridicule is a potent social weapon.

Despite the yokel stories, however, the Communist troops, which people see every day in the streets, have made a favorable impression. They are well-behaved, dignified, and obviously take pride in being "warriors of the liberation," as they are called in the press. And they have a strong political consciousness. When asked by a student whether or not he belonged to General Lin Piao's army (which he did), one soldier replied, "I belong to the people's army."

Soldiers are less in evidence in Peiping now than they were a month ago, because the present garrison is small compared with the mass of troops crowded into the city during the siege, but a military atmosphere persists. The Communists, in fact, guard themselves more closely, and are physically more isolated from the general population, than former Kuomintang leaders in Peiping. Sentries keep strict watch at every Communist office, including many, such as newspaper offices, where there were no guards under the old regime. No one is allowed to take photographs without a permit, and photographs of soldiers, parades, and demonstrations are banned. A military sort of discipline appears to be characteristic of all the Communists—including political workers, who wear uniforms similar to those worn by the troops.

One reason for the Communists' strict security is undoubtedly a feeling of nervousness about underground opposition by Kuomintang troops and secret-service men. There is no indication that the underground is sizable, but apparently the Communists are slightly worried about it, nevertheless. During the past two weeks, a number of Kuomintang secret-service men (or at least persons given that label) have been arrested. There have been a few political arrests, also, since the initial honeymoon period immediately after the takeover, when everyone was left alone, but the number has not been large. They have included "bad" *Pao* chiefs and former "reactionary" officials.

The Nationalist Nineteenth Military Police Regiment, which dispersed in the city with its arms just before the Communists came in, has also been the source of some trouble. On February 5, a military proclamation ordered the surrender of all illegal arms. On February 12, the Garrison Commander specifically ordered all members of the Nineteenth Regiment to turn in their arms and register with the authorities by February 20. On February 19, this order was repeated, but the deadline was moved up to February 25. Apparently, some of those who went underground were not giving themselves up. There has been no evidence, however, that the Communists have had any trouble with the bulk of the 150,-000 Nationalist troops who had been moved to concentration points outside of the city. On February 16, the Communists took over responsibility for these troops and began to supply them; at present, the final plans for incorporating them into the Red Army are being completed.

Although the *People's Daily* can say with some justification that "the takeover of Peiping is almost complete," many aspects of Communist policy have not yet crystallized in any definite form. The Communists' press policy in Peiping, however, is an exception and is already fairly definite. To American observers, it looks disturbingly like the pattern already established in the Soviet Union and its satellites elsewhere. It is a policy that ends freedom of the press as it is understood in the United States.

When the Communists first entered Peiping, they took over only one newspaper. The official Kuomintang North China *Daily News* was converted into the official Communist *People's Daily*, under the editorship of Fan Ch'ang-chiang (Yangtze River Fan), a well-known Communist journalist who is often given credit for starting feature writing in China in his pre-Communist days. This newspaper is a pure propaganda organ, which takes its national and international news from the releases of the official Communist New China News Agency (which merely quotes *Pravda* and Tass in much of its foreign news). The New China News Agency releases are fairly accurate on certain things, such as war casualty figures for example, but are entirely one-sided and heavily slanted in general content. Actually, only a small portion of the *People's Daily* is devoted to news of any sort. Editorials, proclamations, and policy statements take up a large part of the space. No clear distinction is made between news stories and editorials, however, because no clear-cut distinction between the two is made by Communist journalists. The press in their eyes is clearly and admittedly an "instrument of revolution."

At first, other newspapers were allowed to continue publishing, and even more surprising, all censorship was lifted as a result of "liberation." The non-Communist papers copied the *People's Daily*, took most of their material from the official news agency, and became redder than the rose (although they continued to have more national and international news than the official daily, because they printed some news stories telegraphed from Nanking and Shanghai!). An article in one non-Communist paper stated that some Chinese writers who have the "habits of European and American bourgeois newspapermen," often "only ask for news value, but sometimes don't pay attention to revolutionary aims and the people's interests." The article went on to say that "from now on, however, this should be corrected." This was the Communist line, but even though the non-Communist papers adhered to it strictly, the squeeze was gradually put on them. One by one, they were closed down for being "reactionary" or for "spreading pro-Kuomintang propaganda" or, in some cases, for no reason at all. At present, besides the official paper, there is only one single-sheet newspaper left in business in Peiping, out of twenty-odd papers that were operating a month ago. The life expectancy of the remaining sheet is doubtful.

Foreign correspondents were handled in a different way. First, they were subjected to a bitter smear campaign, which was started by an official Communist release, followed up by the official paper, and then echoed by the rest of the Chinese press. The press attacks concentrated on two "American imperialist newspapermen," neither of whom, ironically, is an American citizen, although both work for American news agencies. The dispatches of these two correspondents were called "an insult to the people of Peiping." The denunciations became more vehement and the epithets more colorful as the campaign developed, and the papers printed a flood of written protests, many of which demanded that these correspondents be "driven out" of Communist territory. The reporting of foreign correspondents was called "a plot of Americans purposely to destroy the Chinese people's democratic revolution."

This smear technique—which has also been used against certain Chinese, including the former chairman of the Peiping City Council—affected all foreign correspondents. It made them pariahs. Many of the correspondents' Chinese friends stopped contacting them, and the correspondents themselves were reluctant to risk the possibility of embarrassing Chinese friends by calling on them. In addition, correspondents were not permitted to see or interview any Communists, and even written communications went unanswered. It was not even possible to interview a private in the Red Army, because the troops had been instructed to avoid talking with foreigners. Foreign correspondents were effectively isolated, therefore, and it became impossible to do a good reporting job. The Military Control Commission's ban today on all activities by foreign correspondents merely completes the process begun by the smear campaign.

Today, it is impossible for a person in Peiping to keep abreast of world events unless he has a short-wave radio—and equally impossible for the world to keep abreast of developments in Peiping. The picture of the world that the Communist propaganda machine is feeding to the people here is one in which a dangerously predatory United States is spreading its octopus tentacles over the globe and is meeting desperate resistance from the countries following the leadership of the Soviet Union. Every scrap of propaganda issued in Peiping indicates that at present the Chinese Communists have close and strong psychological ties with the Soviet Union and follow the Soviet and Cominform line completely on international questions. Every mention of the Soviet Union is laudatory. No mention is ever made of Dairen or Port Arthur, and the current Russian negotiations with the Nationalist Central Government over rights in Sinkiang have not been mentioned once. Conversely, all United States action is portrayed as motivated by sinister imperialism, and every indication of United States weakness (as, for example, a slight drop in employment) is seized upon and played up as proof of America's impending disaster. The Communists do not try to hide the fact that they believe in Marxism-Leninism and are close friends of the Soviet Union (as some writers have done on their behalf); they are obviously proud of it. It is very difficult, however, on the basis of publicly known facts, and without any inside information, to know what the real relations between the Chinese Communists and the Soviet Union are. In Peiping, though, there has been no visible evidence of Russian manipulation or interference. Unless evidence to the contrary is uncovered, there is no reason to believe that the Chinese Communists are puppets of Moscow. Their strength seems to be their own. Their degree of dependence upon, or independence from, the Soviet Union should become clearer, however, in the months to come.

The anti-American propaganda line is used very effectively by the Communists. Strong nationalism, perhaps mixed with a general sort of xenophobia, is one of the strongest and most widespread sentiments in China today, and when the Communists point an accusing finger at the United States and say, "there is the culprit who is interfering in China's affairs, robbing us of our sovereignty, and prolonging the civil war," many Chinese agree and become indignant.

Much of the Chinese Communists' current propaganda seems to be based on a belief in the overriding importance of the present American-Soviet antagonism and split, and the dangers of a third world war. The propaganda makes quite clear that if a war comes while the Chinese Communists are in their present frame of mind they will be supporters of the Soviet side.

Incredible as some of the distortions of Communist propaganda appear to an American observer (Nehru's support of the Indonesian nationalists, rather than of the Indonesian Communists, is somehow blamed on the United States, for example), most of the propaganda seems to be credible to a large number of Chinese. Another fact that should be noted is that few Chinese seem to be disturbed about what has happened to their local press during the past month. Freedom of the press, of course, was subject to severe limitations under the Kuomintang, but in recent weeks, there has not even been a murmur of protest against the disappearance of that degree of freedom which did exist previously.

Even though the Communists, in their propaganda, have been vituperously anti-American, they have not molested individual Americans or other foreigners in Peiping and have lived up to their promise that foreign lives and property would be protected. For the most part, the Communists have politely ignored foreigners, refusing to see them or answer communications from them. Until recently, foreigners were given the runaround even on such things as requests for automobile registration certificates and passes to go in and out of the city walls, and have felt very much like "the little man who wasn't there." The establishment of a foreign affairs office on February 17 changed the situation slightly, but it has not changed the basic fact that the Communists still politely ignore foreigners.

Foreign consular establishments, as well as individuals, have been ignored and have had no contacts with the Communists, who make a point of classifying consular personnel as "private citizens." Apparently, the Communists believe that any contact with the consulates would imply recognition of governments that do not recognize them, although, in international law, consular activities are generally divorced from the issue of recognition. For some unknown reason, however, the Communists have placed armed guards at the gates to all consulates, to watch the people coming and going. The Communists seem to regard all foreigners as spies and are extremely wary of them. They have specifically warned the populace, through the newspapers, that all American newspapermen can be considered potential spies.

The American Consulate, like the rest of the consular establishments in Peiping, has been ignored. The United States Information Service has been ordered to stop distributing its news releases, and on February 17, the Communists removed 6,666 bags of flour from the Peiping office of the Economic Cooperation Administration. This ECA flour was removed by armed guards who showed no credentials and gave no receipts, and the protest against the "unlawful seizure," made by the American Director of ECA in Peiping, has never even been answered by the Communists.

Also on February 17, the Russian Consulate took a step that was curious and difficult to interpret. It officially went out of existence, and the consul became what the Chinese Communists now insist all the consuls are: a private citizen. This step was apparently ordered by the Russian Embassy in Canton. And the consul in Peiping, who has scrupulously avoided anything that might even hint of Russian involvement in China, has now taken up the study of Chinese history!

Some foreign observers predicted that when the Communists took Peiping and Tientsin, they would begin modifying their present attitude toward the United States and Western countries, and would begin looking forward to the day when they would want to bargain for foreign recognition and international relations. Their actions in Peiping to date have given no clue that such an adjustment in attitude is imminent. In the future, it is possible, of course, that their attitudes and policies can change, and if such a change comes, the motivation undoubtedly will be economic, because the Communists will need materials for reconstruction and industrial development which will be difficult to obtain solely from the Soviet Union. In the past month, there has been one outstanding instance where economic realities have dictated Communist policy. On February 13, it was announced that Mao Tse-tung had approved negotiations for reopening navinorth China. In short, he officially sanctioned "open trading with the enemy," primarily because of a need for flour imports. Negotiations have now been completed between the Communists and gation between Kuomintang-held Shanghai and Communist-held representatives of Shanghai shipping interests who came north, and limited trade is about to commence. The main basis of this trade will be an exchange of flour from Shanghai, to be used principally for distribution at the Kailan coal mines, for coal, which is needed in Shanghai. Even though the Kailan Mining Administration is a Sino-British concern, it has been given every encouragement by the Communists, because it is the main coal producer in north China, and the Communists cannot afford to have their coal supply interrupted. On February 19, also, an American President Liner was allowed to discharge a previously contracted-for cargo at Tientsin. Whether or not economic considerations of this sort will force a major change in the Communists' attitude toward foreign countries still remains to be seen, however.

The prediction that Peiping would become the Communists' national political headquarters, and probably their capital, seems to have been borne out by events of the past month. For one thing, Peiping has been the center for informal peace negotiations between the Communists and two groups unofficially representing Li Tsung-jen and that part of the Central Government which remains at Nanking. The first group consisted of several relatively unknown and unimportant professors from Nanking, and they apparently accomplished little, but the second was more important. Headed by Shao Li-tzu and W. W. Yen, it negotiated from February 14 to February 27 and made a three-day trip to Shihchiachuang to talk with Mao Tse-tung. Their talk with Mao, and the fact that they participated in several important Communist meetings in Peiping, made it look as if Li Tsung-jen and the Communists might be making progress toward a peace settlement—which, if it followed the pattern set by Fu Tso-yi, would mean Nationalist surrender (called by another name) on the basis of Mao's eight points, and pardon for Li and those of his cohorts now on the Communists' list of war criminals. Fu, incidentally, is still in Peiping and is now participating in many Communist-sponsored meetings.

On February 20, the Communist North China People's Government, under Tung Pi-wu, moved to Peiping. Five days later, the leaders of all the small "democratic groups" slated to participate in the Communists' coalition—groups that I described earlier in a report from Hong Kong—arrived in Peiping and were greeted with great fanfare. Included were Li Chi-shen, Shen Chün-ju, Chang Po-chün, Ma Hsü-lun, and many others. At about the same time, Communist leaders began to converge on Peiping in larger numbers. Included among them was Li Li-san, one-time leader of the Chinese Communist Party before Mao, who is now Vice-Chairman of the Communists' All-China Labor Union and is preparing to set up union headquarters in Peiping. Delegates for the All-China Student Congress also flocked to Peiping.

These developments look like the overture to big events, and all that is now needed to transform "Peiping" to "Peking," i.e., to make it the capital of Communist China, is for Mao Tse-tung and Chu Teh to transfer their headquarters from Shihchiachuang. Now that the takeover of Peiping is almost complete, this may happen soon.

With the stage set for major developments in Peiping, the Communist ban on foreign writers may be explained by a desire on their part to veil these developments from the probing eyes of foreign observers. It is also possible, however, that the ban is merely part of a general tightening-up of their control, now that the city has been taken over. Reports from other cities have indicated that a tightening-up process generally has begun only after the transitional takeover period. There already are a few indications that an over-all tightening-up may take place here. There have been several reports, for example, of *Pao-Chia* and student meetings called for the purpose of denouncing "reactionaries" and rooting out "enemies of the people." It is too early, however, to say whether or not this sort of thing already presages a general witch hunt against "enemies."

23

FAN SHEN

Peiping
August, 1949

I know several young Chinese in Peiping who are now trying to enter the Chinese Communist Party. A year ago, probably not a single one of them would have considered this step, but now that the Communists have "liberated" Peiping, they not only think it is logical and necessary, but they are highly enthusiastic about the prospect. Recently, I had a long talk with one of them, a bright young student who, despite a case of tuberculosis, has just graduated from Peking National University with one of the highest academic records in his class.

"Do you plan to join the Communist Party?" I asked him.

A somewhat startled look appeared on his face, as if he thought: "What a strange question." He answered, "Of course!" Then, becoming thoughtful for a moment, he added, "But I don't know if I can qualify or not. I still have so much to learn."

"Have you read much about Marxism—Marx and Engels, Lenin, and Stalin?" I asked. "Yes." "And the works of Mao Tse-tung?" "Yes." "And you accept the doctrines in all of them?" "Yes." "Then what is it you have to learn before you can join the Party?"

Humility seemed to creep into his voice when he started to talk about the Chinese Communist Party. "Well," he said, "before I can join the Party, one thing I must learn is to subordinate my own personal ideas and myself. I don't think I know yet how to sacrifice myself, to carry out Party decisions. I'm afraid, too, that I'm still somewhat of an individualist. I must completely rid myself of individualism before I'm qualified to join the Party."

"Individualism?" I interrupted. "Why do you have to rid yourself of individualism? Isn't it a good thing for a person to stand firmly for the ideas he personally believes? Must not a person individually make up his mind on important political issues?"

"You don't understand what I mean," he answered. "The Communist Party represents the people. An individual cannot maintain his selfish ideas against the good of the people. One must subordinate himself to the Party and observe discipline." As he went on, it became clear that "individualism" and "selfishness" meant the same thing to him, so I stopped him and asked if the two words were interchangeable as he used them. Yes, they were. In short, in his mind, it was self-sacrifice versus selfishness. The alternative to subordinating oneself to the Party, to observing Party discipline, was individualism, selfishness. "If one is individualistic, one acts contrary to the interests of the people."

After hearing him talk for a while, a flood of questions came to my mind. Many concerned the meaning of words, because it was obvious that to understand what he was saying it was necessary to have him define a great many terms. I postponed many of my questions, however, and continued along the line we had started.

"You speak of Party discipline," I began. "How about democracy? The Communist Party also says that it is democratic. In what formula are discipline and democracy combined, and what do you mean when you say the Party is democratic?"

"Certainly the Party is democratic. It represents the broad masses of the people, and every Party member can contribute his ideas and participate in choosing the leaders."

"But how about the recent article on 'The People's Democratic Dictatorship' written by Mao Tse-tung?" I asked. "It lays down the Party line on many important policy matters. How did the average Party member have a part in that?" As an afterthought I added, "And as I understand it, almost half the Party's membership has joined since the last Party Congress and therefore had no part at all in choosing Mao Tse-tung or, for that matter, any of the other members of the Central Committee who make important policy decisions."

"Again I'm afraid that you don't understand," he answered. "Where do you think Mao Tse-tung gets his ideas? On what basis do you think he makes decisions on policies? The answer is that he considers the welfare of the masses. Furthermore, he weighs the ideas and suggestions that are passed along by all the Party's members. Those that really express the feelings of the majority and are really desirable for the masses are the basis of policy. That's democracy. As for the Party members who had no part in electing Mao, they accepted his leadership when they joined the Party. No one questions his leadership, so what you say is purely academic."

"What if you were already a Party member," I interrupted, "and disagreed with a policy after it was defined; could you dissent?

Could you openly disagree with the policy and decline to follow it while you worked toward changing it?" "Of course not," he said. "Once a policy is adopted, everyone must follow it. An individual must accept the will of the majority. It's the period before a policy is decided upon that is the period for discussion and suggestions, but after adoption, a policy is democratically carried out. Everyone can make suggestions on how to carry it out, however. There is continual criticism and, even more important, self-criticism."

The term "self-criticism" interrupted my train of thought, and I conjured up scenes of earnest young men and women, like the one in front of me, who were spending hours every day in soul-searching. "Self-criticism" and "learning"—these are two of the most universal slogans of the times. They appear in the newspapers every day; they pop up in almost every conversation. For the young men and women trying to enter the Chinese Communist Party, they are practically a way of life.

Self-criticizing myself for letting my mind wander, I jerked my attention back to the main line of our conversation. "What do you mean by democracy?" I asked. "How about everyone outside of the Communist Party? There are only 3 million Party members, but there are somewhere between 400 and 500 million people [the current estimate in 1949] in the country. How do they fit into the picture? Does your democracy include them?"

"Very definitely," the student answered. "Everyone except reactionaries will take part in the political life of the country. The people will elect representatives in the government, and the government will be a coalition under the leadership of the Communist Party."

"In Peiping," I interrupted, "the members of the government are appointed by the Party and not elected." "They will be elected," he answered. There was no trace of doubt in his voice.

"What do you mean by 'reactionaries'?" I asked. I had an idea of what this word might mean in his mind, because I had been reading much Communist literature in Peiping. Landlords, "old-style" rich peasants, "bureaucratic capitalists," unreconstructed Kuomintang leaders, Kuomintang "secret-service men"—the Communists continually spoke of these as reactionaries. Anyone else? "Well," he said, "even I could become a reactionary, although I hope I won't." I must have looked surprised, because he smiled. "Certainly I could. If I began to doubt that 'New Democracy' was the road China must follow, if I insisted on asserting my individualism, if I obstructed the leadership of the

Communist Party, I could become a reactionary." The term began to take on new dimensions.

"How about 'the people'? Who is included?" "The people," he answered, "include mainly workers and farmers, but also others such as progressive intellectuals, the petty-bourgeoisie, and so on. The workers and farmers are most important, though. Altogether these main classes include about 90 per cent of the whole population of the country, the 90 per cent that has been exploited and oppressed by the other 10 per cent." In short, "the people" are 90 per cent of the people.

I kept on asking about words, but I do not think he minded it. In fact, I felt that he enjoyed it. It was a chance for him to do a little extracurricular work on an unbeliever.

I took my next cue from his last sentence. I was interested in knowing what he meant by the word "exploited." I myself have seen much exploitation in China, in the high rents and interest charges from which so many farmers suffer, for example, but I wanted to know exactly what he was talking about when he used the word. "That involves a fundamental concept," he answered. "The elimination of exploitation is one of the main objectives of the revolution. You ask what exploitation means. It means getting something that you yourself don't produce. If you hire people to work for you, for example, the income that you derive from them is exploitation, because they earn it, but you take it away from them. Of course we can't completely eliminate exploitation until we arrive at Socialism and Communism. That means that in the period of 'New Democracy' we have to put up with a good deal of it. But eventually it will disappear." It was an answer straight out of the textbooks.

At the risk of being tedious, I asked for a definition of one more word. "You used the word 'leadership' a few moments ago," I said. "That's a word I see constantly in Communist publications. Everyone is to accept Communist leadership. What does that mean?" "It means just what it says," he answered. "The Communists will be the leaders in all important organizations, in the government, and in the general development of the country. That's natural and inevitable. They speak for the masses, and furthermore they are"—I prepared myself for words I had seen in Communist propaganda hundreds of times—"the most progressive, advanced, revolutionary, and politically conscious people in the country." Although he was speaking with obvious sincerity, it sounded a little too much like a catechism, so I broke in and asked, "But how exclusive is their leadership? Who else can take part?" "Look at the coming Political Consultative Conference [an assembly appointed by the Communists to establish a new national government in the fall of 1949]," he said. "There are about a dozen other parties, participating and representing all sorts of people." "Parties?" I asked. "There are only two real political parties in China, and one of them, the Kuomintang, is excluded. The others may hope to become real parties, but now they are merely groups or cliques." He granted my point, but maintained that they certainly would become real parties in time. "But," I said, "at present none of them has an independent platform. They all accept 'New Democracy' entirely, and that is why they've been invited to participate." "You're quite right," he said. "But except for the reactionaries, everyone in the country accepts 'New Democracy.' That's the point. Everyone recognizes that the Communists have determined the correct road for the future, so naturally all accept their leadership." "Let me ask you another question then. I will make it hypothetical. Suppose some group in the future disagrees with 'New Democracy,' will they be allowed to oppose it openly, to write books and make speeches about it, and to propose a counter-program of their own? What if some group didn't think China should travel the road toward Communism? Or, to take a different sort of example, suppose some group was even more revolutionary than the current Communist line and proposed skipping over 'New Democracy' and going directly to Communism? Would either be tolerated?" His answer was emphatic: "Absolutely not. 'New Democracy' and the general program of the Communist Party is the correct line and everybody accepts it." "But if somebody in the future wants to change the general line?" I asked. "Then," he answered, "that will be decided by discussion within the Party and not by open attack from the outside."

I wondered whether he approved of everything the Communists had done since taking over Peiping. I decided to test him on one issue. "What do you think of the way freedom of the press has been limited," I asked. "But we have complete freedom of the press!" he said. I passed over the fact that almost all "pre-liberation" publications had disappeared in Peiping. I did not cite the regulations on publications. Nor did I say that previously I had written for an American newspaper, but for the past five months had not been allowed to write a single word for publication, because of an official order telling all foreign correspondents to cease and desist. I confined myself to a single question, "How is it, then, that no criticism of policies ever appears in print?"

"Because everyone agrees with the general policies," was his quick answer. I watched him closely and saw that he appeared to believe what he said was true. I could not quite let the matter rest there, however, so I continued. "My impression is that many people, including non-Marxists, now accept 'New Democracy' as a general program. But I think that at least on specific policies there undoubtedly is disagreement." He answered, "Any criticism can be made in the form of suggestions to the Party. Anyone can make criticisms. For example, many businessmen opposed the export tax, so the Party abolished it." I immediately thought of a dozen other controversial questions, but decided to pass over them. "What if the Party had disagreed in that case?" I asked. "Could there have been any appeal to public opinion outside the Party?" His answer was definite. "If a suggestion is reasonable, the Party will accept it." I tried another tack. "If a person wrote a letter to the newspapers attacking 'New Democracy,' should it be published?" "No. Such a person would be a reactionary." "If he wrote disagreeing with some specific policy?" "Perhaps. But it would be better to take it up with a Party member. Printing all sorts of wild criticism would be a waste of paper which China cannot afford." A waste of paper? Well, I doubted if anyone had tried. I mulled over in my mind what we had been talking about. Freedom of the press—he believed it existed, I believed it did not. Obviously, we were talking about different things, because he was as sincere as I.

At this point, I recalled how our conversation had started. Would the student I was talking with be qualified to join the Chinese Communist Party? I silently decided that he would make the grade, but aloud I said, "Besides conquering individualism, what else do you think you must do before you'll be qualified to join the Party?" He smiled. "I'm afraid I still have a petty-bourgeois outlook," he answered. "I've got to become more proletarian in my thinking." "How can you become one of the proletariat in your thinking?" I asked. "You've had a college education. Do you think you can ever think like a farmer or worker without having had their experiences? If you could, would you want to? You want to be a revolutionary, and you're a lot more revolutionary already than most workers I've had contact with. Have you talked much with workers? They're interested in their daily millet, not in abstract principles. They have a lot less concern for other workers than you do. No, I don't think you really want to or can become proletarian in your thinking." "You don't really understand the proletarian viewpoint," he said. "The proletariat is actually much more revolutionary than members of the petty-bourgeoisie such as myself. Especially factory workers. Farmers have a somewhat petty-bourgeois outlook, but the workers are by far the most advanced class in their thinking."

He continued, "In a revolution, people have to change their whole outlook. It's not always easy to do. I find it difficult in many respects. But I'm working on it." "You mean you must *fan shen?*" I asked. "Yes, I must *fan shen.*" That was it. The Chinese Communist phrase *fan shen* summed up much of what he was talking about—literally to "turn over the body," to change completely, to turn a new leaf, to start a new life. To be a Communist, he would have to *fan shen.* To be a Communist country, all China would have to *fan shen.* Is it possible? What sort of person will he be, and what sort of country will China be, if it is possible?

We talked for a long time and about many things. He wanted to know why "the people" in America did not do something about the country's "imperialistic" foreign policy. There was no question in his mind about American policy being "imperialistic," and he assumed that it was a policy made by "a few capitalists" without any popular support. He talked about what a great country he believed China would be after a period of Communist rule—a modern industrial country in which, he was convinced, the common man would get a break. He could see no fault with the Communists. He dismissed the difficulties that the regime would face. He had unlimited confidence in the future.

When the hour was getting late, and he was on the verge of leaving, I decided to ask one final question. He was a Christian, or at least had been, and several months previously he had been uncertain, on philosophic grounds, whether he could accept Communism. "It's clear to me that you have accepted Communism politically," I said, "but how about philosophically? Do you accept materialism too?" My question was followed by a long pause. Finally in a quiet voice he answered, "Yes." I waited for him to elaborate, but he did not. Simply "yes." But this meant that his *fan shen* was complete. He had a new faith.

He had to leave then, and I saw him to the door. "I haven't much doubt that you'll be able to join the Communist Party," I said, but I added, "After you do, don't forget your old reactionary, imperialist friends." He laughed. "Of course not." He meant it, but I thought to myself that there might be some things he still had to learn. I had not had a single long conversation with any important Communist Party member during six months in Communist Peiping.

INDEX